AMERICAN EXODUS

AMERICAN EXODUS

The Dust Bowl Migration and Okie Culture in California

James N. Gregory

OXFORD UNIVERSITY PRESS
New York   Oxford

Oxford University Press

Oxford   New York   Toronto
Delhi   Bombay   Calcutta   Madras   Karachi
Petaling Jaya   Singapore   Hong Kong   Tokyo
Nairobi   Dar es Salaam   Cape Town
Melbourne   Auckland

and associated companies in
Berlin   Ibadan

First published in 1989 by Oxford University Press, Inc.,
198 Madison Avenue, New York, New York 10016-4314

First issued as an Oxford University Press paperback, 1991

Oxford is a registered trademark of Oxford University Press

Library of Congress Cataloging-in-Publication Data

Gregory, James Noble.
American exodus.
Includes index.
1. Includes index.
1. Migration, Internal—California—History—20th
century.   2. Migration, Internal—Oklahoma—History—
20th century.   3. Agricultural laborers—California—
Economic conditions.   4. Agricultural laborers—
California—Social conditions.   5. Depressions—1929—
United States—History.   I. Title.
HB1985.C2G74   1989   034.8'794'0766   88-36230
ISBN-13 978-0-19-507136-8 (PBK.)

Printed in the United States of America

For Susan and Rachel

Contents

Acknowledgments

THIS BOOK IS ABOUT MIGRATION AND ITS CONSEQUENCES. IT IS ABOUT PEOPLE remaking their lives and remaking society in new locations. In many ways, the process of writing the book has echoed its subject. It has been a long journey—lonely in some stretches. But the experience has not really been as solitary as it seemed. Many kind and generous people have assisted along the way, and if this book proves valuable, it is in no small measure because of them.

My thanks begin with those who made the research possible. Among the many librarians who helped, the staff at Bancroft Library, Christy Gavin at California State College, Bakersfield, and Nina Caspari at Bakersfield Public Library deserve special mention. My deepest gratitude goes to Walter Goldschmidt for sharing his personal files with me, including the field notes from his 1941 San Joaquin Valley research. Gerald Haslam graciously allowed me to examine the materials he has compiled, and Margo McBane and Tom Norris were equally generous with their collections of taped interviews. Sharon and Jack Goldsmith and Tod Moquist not only made it possible for me to use the California Odyssey oral history collection but also followed my suggestions for some of the interview questions. Most generous of all were the two dozen individuals who shared their personal stories and often their living rooms with me. Their names appear in the notes. Here, I want to add my sincere thanks.

Chris Day, Ilona Einowski, and Ann Gerken of the State Data Project, University of California, Berkeley, helped me obtain the Census
Public Use Microdata Samples and provided encouragement as I wrestled inexpertly with two of the samples. Ron Yanosky deserves equal
thanks for relieving me of those labors on the third. Jill Schlessinger, Larry
Glickman, Nancy Quam-Wickham, Victor Silverman, and John Gerring
helped with other research tasks. I am grateful as well for some important
editorial advice.

The University of California, Berkeley, has been generous with research
money, including a career development grant that provided a year's leave.
Thanks are also due the Mabelle McLeod Lewis Memorial Fund.

Quite a number of friends and colleagues have read some or all of
this manuscript. At a critical stage, Donald Worster and John Womack,
Jr., helped me see some important lines of inquiry. Roger Daniels and
Gunther Barth each read the manuscript closely and saved me from a
number of errors. Archie Green guided me through some of the mys-
teries of country music. I am grateful for other advice and encouragement from Leon Litwack, Dan Carter, Richard Abrams, Jon Gjerde,
Jack Potter, Sheldon Rothblatt, Neil Basen, Michael Kazin, Robert
Middlekauff, Randolph Starn, and Erich Gruen and for the opportunity
to discuss parts of the work with members of the Berkeley American
Studies Group.

Sheldon Meyer has been a most patient and supportive editor, and Ste-
phanie Sakson-Ford a careful copy editor. Cherie Semans drew the maps,
and Therese Heyman and Kate Ware of the Oakland Museum helped with
the photographs.

This project began in graduate school and it was my very good fortune
to share those years with Steve Bray, Liz Cohen, Lynn Dumenil, Jim
Grossman, Barbara Loomis, Jan Palumbo, and Bob Weyeneth. Separately
and collectively they have contributed much to this book. It was with them
that I first learned the meaning of intellectual comradeship.

A different kind of thanks is due two friends who have also been my
teachers and more recently my colleagues. Paula Fass has helped this
project mature from seminar paper to dissertation to book. Her tough-
minded criticism and unflinching support through the many stages and
many readings have often kept me on track. My debt to Lawrence Levine
has no parallel. Anyone familiar with his scholarship will understand part
of what I mean. You would have to know his warmth and generosity to
realize the rest.

A final acknowledgment. In an off-beat moment I once promised Susan
Glenn that this book would bear her name followed by the inscription,
"without whom none of this would have been necessary." That I have kept
my word will only remind her again that it was perilous to marry a fellow

historian. The truth is that she has made this book possible. My toughest critic, my best editor, my staunchest supporter, my partner, my friend, and my love—this is also yours.

Berkeley   J. N. G.
1989

Introduction

THE RAIN FELL STEADILY THAT DREARY MARCH MORNING AS PHOTOGRAPHER Dorothea Lange drove north towards San Francisco on California's Highway 101. In a hurry to get home, she initially ignored the crudely lettered sign leading to the pea-pickers' camp, deciding only after she had driven past to return and investigate. It was a decision that would make her famous. For on that wet day in 1936 Dorothea Lange would take her most memorable photograph. She had stumbled upon a scene of appalling proportions. More than a thousand people—men, women, and children—huddled against the rain in ragged tents and makeshift lean-tos, starving. They had come to San Luis Obispo County to pick peas, but a late frost had delayed the harvest. So they camped and waited. First their money had run out, and then the food. Ignored by local relief authorities, with nowhere to turn, many were now desperate.

America learned about the pea-pickers' camp through Lange's photographs, especially the one she called "Migrant Mother." The full-faced portrait of a gaunt, sunburnt woman, an infant cradled in her lap and two other children clinging close, touched the heart of a nation. Her face lined with worry and despair, this migrant madonna helped to awaken Americans to the plight of these particular families and thousands of others facing similar difficulties in Depression-torn California.[1]

The press called them Dust Bowl refugees, although actually they came from a broad area encompassing four southern plains states: Oklahoma, Texas, Arkansas, and Missouri. Victims of drought and depression, they had headed west by the tens of thousands, hoping for a brighter future in California, only to find, it seemed, more misery. No wonder reporters rushed to tell their story. It was a spectacle rich in drama and pathos. Here were themes dear to the nation's heritage—westward migration, the search for opportunity, the dignity of the American farmer—presenting themselves in ironic and disturbing ways. The struggles of the Dust Bowl migrants seemed to suggest a pathetic failure of the American Dream, a failure of all the promises of opportunity that formed its vital core, a failure which if true confirmed Americans' worst fears about the meaning of their Depression-era experience.

That is why the Dust Bowl migration became such an important focus of public concern during the last years of the 1930s. Even before John Steinbeck translated the experience into one of the classic American novels of the twentieth century, the migration had become a media event. America looked at the Dust Bowl migrants and saw itself: first finding a symbol of Depression-era failure, later an affirmation of success and deliverance. As the decades passed, journalists went back to learn what had become of the Okies, usually reporting that America's losers had become modest winners; that poverty lay behind them now; that the Dust Bowl migrants had made comfortable homes for themselves in California; that the fears had been for naught; that the promise had eventually been met; that America was America after all.[2]

Such has been the lens through which the Dust Bowl migration has been and continues to be viewed. The story it reveals is an important one, and if at points the scenario has been exaggerated, the outline remains essentially true. But there is a deeper story to be told about the same people. It has to do not just with economic trials but also with social confrontations and cultural transformations, with the way California received these newcomers and their impact on the state. It has to do with regional cultures and the role of internal migration in twentieth-century American society.

This is an account of the experiences of a particular group of Americans: the more than one million Oklahomans, Texans, Arkansans, and Missourians who settled in California during the 1930s and 1940s. Called "Dust Bowl migrants" sometimes, "Okies" and "Arkies" more frequently, and "Southwesterners" in more respectful moments, they have since the 1930s occupied a unique place in California society. Unlike most of the other white native-born Americans who have settled in that state, Southwesterners were slow to be absorbed into the social fabric of California. For reasons that had to do partly with their social and cultural background and partly with the configurations of politics and economic opportunity in Depression-era California, many Southwesterners developed something of an inde-

Figure 1. Mother of six and recently widowed, Florence Thompson was thirty-two years old when this photograph was taken. She later settled in Modesto where "I worked in hospitals, tended bar, I cooked and worked in the fields." Never far from poverty, she died in 1983. (*Dorothea Lange,* © *1982, The Oakland Museum, The City of Oakland*)

Figure 2. "Migrant Mother" from another perspective. The pose lacks the classic references, but the setting and meager possessions tell an equally profound story. (*Dorothea Lange, © 1982, The Oakland Museum, The City of Oakland*)

pendent socio-cultural community life. Settling in separate neighborhoods called Little Oklahomas, socializing primarily with newcomers like themselves, they created a distinct subculture based on values and institutions brought from their region of birth.

This Okie subculture survives today. It is most apparent in the San Joaquin Valley, where so many of the Dust Bowl migrants made their homes. Visit Bakersfield or one of the surrounding towns in the southern portion of the valley near where Steinbeck's Joad family was supposed to have settled. These days a large Hispanic population shares these communities. But talk to the Anglos, especially in the working-class neighborhoods. The accents are Oklahoman and Texan, and they come not just from aging expatriates of the Dust Bowl states but also from their California-born children and grandchildren, indeed from Anglos of all sorts of backgrounds. Notice the churches. Bakersfield, a city of about 280,000 people, claims more than four hundred of them, mostly Pentecostal, Southern Baptist, or other evangelical Protestant denominations. The commercial establishments give forth other cultural clues, especially the coffee shops with their Dr. Pepper signs out front, their jukeboxes filled with country-western hits, and their menus featuring chicken-fried steak, chili, biscuits and gravy. The political climate is also revealing. Experts consider this one of the state's critical swing districts. Strongly Democratic in registration, the area votes for conservatives of either party who talk tough on defense, crime, and moral issues and who stay away from minority causes like school busing or Cesar Chavez's United Farm Workers.[3]

Here is the real legacy of the Dust Bowl migration. Fifty years later, parts of California show signs of significant cultural change. Institutions and outlooks imported from the Southwest have taken root; people who were once viewed as despised outsiders now help to set community standards. "We won—we took over," says one former Oklahoman who has watched the San Joaquin Valley change over the years. "When I go there . . . I feel I am in Oklahoma, Arkansas and Texas."[4]

These developments are tied to one of the most important and least understood demographic events of the recent past. The Dust Bowl migration was the western variant of a much larger sequence of internal migration that has profoundly reshuffled American society in the twentieth century. Between World War I and the start of Southern sunbelt migration in the 1970s, at least fifteen million people left the American heartland for the job-rich regions of the North and Far West. A giant crescent of mostly rural and mostly Protestant states bending down the Great Plains and stretching all the way across the South sent its sons and daughters to the nation's more industrialized, more cosmopolitan perimeter. The implications of this heartland exodus have never been adequately calculated. The three million blacks who joined the outflow have attracted the most notice, and for good reason. Their redistribution ultimately transformed the nation's pattern of racial relations and with it key aspects of the political system.[5]

One stream of the white exodus has been studied. Whites from the upper South and Appalachian highlands moved into Northern cities during the same decades that large numbers of Southwesterners were heading west. The two experiences appear to have much in common. Called "hillbillies" instead of "Okies," white Southerners in cities like Chicago and Detroit acquired the same kind of socio-cultural definition as Southwesterners in California. Distinctive subcultures, shaped somewhat like those belonging to immigrant ethnic groups, emerged in both settings.[6]

The explanation for these developments turns chiefly but not exclusively on issues of regional culture. Frequently ignored in an age that likes to contemplate the homogenizing effects of mass society, meaningful regional differences have persisted through the twentieth century. And they can become highly salient under certain circumstances. But context is critical. As we will see, the Southwestern experience in California has depended on various historical conditions. Questions of class, political climate, and the changing configurations of institutions and values among broad groups of Americans have affected the opportunities and orientations of California's Okie population.

The study is also concerned with the ways this group in turn affected California. Historians of migration and ethnicity have generally looked at only one side of cultural adjustment experiences, analysing the implications for the subject group, missing the implications for the host society. This book concentrates on the experiences of Southwesterners, but it is also about California, and beyond that about American culture and how it is remade through the interaction of the nation's diverse peoples.

The book is presented in two parts. The first four chapters examine the process of migration and resettlement in the 1930s. Although Southwesterners had been coming to California before the Depression and many more would come during the 1940s and 1950s, the Depression was the defining moment in California's Okie experience. Put into play then were the conditions that marked Southwesterners as a separate and unique group. Two factors were especially critical: the hostile response of the established population and the very limited economic opportunities which consigned many Southwesterners to low-paid agricultural labor.

Part II looks at the dynamics of the Okie subculture and the group experience since the 1930s. Here the analysis turns to the regional heritage of the Southwest and the ways it figured in the newcomers' evolving relationship with California. Several institutions and outlooks were critical: their allegiance to evangelical Protestantism, their grounding in the social and political perspectives of what can best be described as "plain-folk Americanism," and their proprietorial claim to an entertainment medium of expanding popularity that we now know as country music. These were the building blocks that gave the Okie group integrity and ultimately also its expanding cultural authority.

Some of the quotations that appear in this book contain misspellings or grammatical inconsistencies, and others are marred by unfortunate attempts by the original recorder to capture the phonetic patterns of the speaker. Only when comprehension is at issue have I edited or called attention to these inconsistencies. I do want to call attention to the fact that some contemporary reports used pseudonyms to protect the anonymity of informants. When a pseudonym appears in this volume, it is indicated with an asterisk, as in Jesse Carter*.

I

MIGRATION AND RESETTLEMENT

1

Out of the Heartland

"NOT QUITE THE TWANG OF THE MIDWEST NOR THE DRAWL OF THE DEEP SOUTH, but a composite of both," an observer once said of the Oklahoma and Texas accents she heard in California.[1] Something similar might be said of the culture and identity of the people the Dust Bowl migration brought to California. Their states of origin—Oklahoma, Texas, Arkansas, and Missouri—are best understood as border states marking the limits of the South as it shades into the West and Midwest. This is where the great regions of the American heartland come together.

Actually, the four-state area lacks a clearly defined regional identity. Residents profess a variety of loyalties. Arkansans generally agree on their ties to the South, but Missourians cannot decide whether their state belongs to the Midwest or the South, Oklahomans alternately consider themselves Southwesterners or Midwesterners, while Texans will accept either the Southwest or the South.[2]

Much of the difficulty of regional identification is traceable to the settlement history of the area. Southerners were the leading population element in all four states, but strong representations of Northerners and European immigrants along with particular economic structures helped to limit Southern influences in certain places. A combined force of lowland Southerners moving up the Mississippi Valley and uplanders pushing west from Kentucky and Tennessee began the settlement of

Arkansas, Texas, and Missouri during the first half of the nineteenth century. German immigrants and Northerners from the Ohio Valley made their presence felt in central Texas and still more in northern Missouri, where their efforts helped to keep that slaveholding state out of the Confederacy during the Civil War. Oklahoma, set aside as Indian territory until the very end of the nineteenth century, in time became another meeting ground for North and South. The eastern half of the state was brought firmly into the orbit of Southern civilization, first by its Indian proprietors—the Cherokee, Creek, Choctaw, Chickasaw, and Seminole, all tribes that had been forcibly removed from Southeastern states—and second by a steady stream of illegal white settlers from neighboring Arkansas, Missouri, and Texas. In contrast, western Oklahoma, largely empty until the famous land rushes began in 1889, enjoyed a mixed pattern of settlement, with Kansans and other Midwesterners dominating the northwestern quadrant and sharing the remainder with former Texans and other Southerners.[3]

Throughout the four states, initial occupancy patterns were reinforced in some cases and modified in others by later migrations and by the character of the rural economy emerging in different sectors of the region. By the early twentieth century several distinct cultural-economic zones revealed the considerable diversity of the four-state area. West Texas was mostly ranching country, home to cattle, horses, and cowboys. The two panhandles and much of northern Oklahoma belonged to the wheat belt, the way of life there learned from Kansas and the northern plains states. Northern Missouri was pure corn belt, prosperous, efficient, hardly distinguishable from nearby Iowa and Illinois. If on the perimeter, then, one encountered the West and Midwest, the rest of the four-state region seemed part of the cotton South, not the old South of the eastern cotton belt but a distinctly Western South.[4]

Cotton had come late to much of the region, and thus except in eastern parts of Arkansas and Texas the area did not develop the caste-like social structure of the Old South. Settled by yeoman farmers during an era dominated by the family farm logic of the Homestead Act, most of this western cotton belt lacked both the plantation system and the large black population common to the rest of the South. Two other factors gave Oklahoma and Texas in particular a social system atypical of Southern society. One was the attachment to their Western heritage. With "no leisure class to romanticize cotton farming," observed anthropologist Oscar Lewis in his study of a central Texas county, cotton, despite its preeminence, "could at no time compete with ranching in capturing the imagination of the people as an ideal way of life."[5] The other was oil, the zone's footloose second industry. Complementing in many ways the folklore of the cattle West, the boom and bust oil economy kept the pioneer mythology of the second

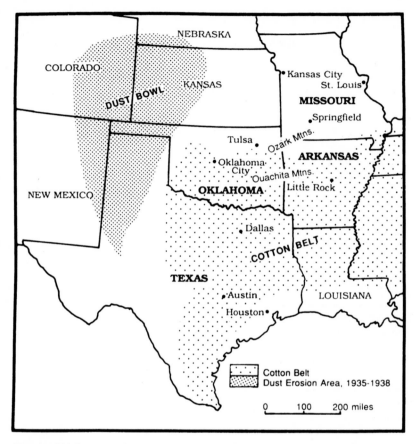

Map 1. Oklahoma, Arkansas, Texas, and Missouri, with major cities, cotton region, and Dust Bowl

chance and the quick strike alive long after the agricultural system had lost its resilience.[6]

This, then, was the geographic region which gave birth to the Dust Bowl migration. Settled primarily by Southerners, its initial heritage had been modified in some areas dramatically, in others hardly at all. To call it either the "Western South" or the "Southwest" is to take liberties with the identity of some residents. Both terms will be used here—interchangeably—

Table 1.1. Western South Natives Living Outside the Region, 1910–1970

	Living Outside region	Living in California	Net Calif. Increase	Percent of Calif. pop.
1910	661,094	103,241	—	4.3%
1920	1,419,046	187,471	84,230	5.5%
1930	2,027,139	430,810	243,339	7.6%
1940	2,580,940	745,934	315,124	10.8%
1950	3,887,370	1,367,720	621,786	12.9%
1960	4,966,781	1,734,271	366,551	11.0%
1970	5,309,287	1,747,632	13,361	8.8%

Sources: U.S. Bureau of the Census, Census of the United States, Population: 1910, Vol. I, 732–33; 1920, Vol. II, 628–29; 1930, Vol. II, 155–56; 1940, State of Birth, 17–18; 1950, State of Birth, 20–24; 1960, State of Birth, 22–23; 1970, State of Birth, 28–29.

to call attention to the dynamic, border-zone character of the four-state area.

Outmigration

The Southwesterners who relocated to California between 1910 and 1950 represented one large stream of a more general exodus from the region. By mid-century nearly four million people, 23 percent of all persons born in Oklahoma, Texas, Arkansas, or Missouri, resided outside that region. More than a third of them—1,367,720 people—made their homes in California (Table 1.1). Other Western states—Arizona, New Mexico, Oregon, and Washington—along with Kansas and Illinois, also claimed substantial numbers of the outmigrants. The rest had scattered widely.

Much has been written about the causes of this outflow, most arguments centering on the process of agricultural modernization. The twentieth century drained rural Americans from the land as surely as it improved the technology and efficiency of farming. With each passing decade, mechanization and rationalized land-use practices took a steady toll on farm populations throughout the nation. Nowhere was the process more abrupt than the Western South.[7]

One of the last farming frontiers, these plains states had filled in and then overfilled in the late nineteenth century as farmers fought for one more chance at the independent, agricultural way of life the nation had always revered. They had had it for a time. But after World War I, conditions caught up with them. Declining international markets for wheat, corn, and cotton, mineral depletion and erosion of marginal soils, pests, drought, and the introduction of tractors and new farm machinery combined to usher in a massive reorganization of agriculture as acreage was consolidated into more efficient farming units and machines replaced mules and family labor. Census figures tell the story. Between 1910 and 1930 the number of farmers and agricultural workers in the Southwest declined by 341,000. That was followed by the loss of at least 800,000 more in the next two decades. By 1950, Oklahoma had lost 55 percent of its agricultural labor force, Arkansas 52 percent, Texas 51 percent, and Missouri 47 percent. At mid-century, rural farm areas in the Western South supported two million fewer people than just twenty years earlier.[8]

But if agricultural modernization was broadly responsible for the massive population dispersion from the region, the process unfolded in ways that defy neat summary. Not all of those who left were farmers. Furthermore, the exodus spanned three distinct eras, each with fundamentally different imperatives. The 1910s and 1920s initiated the outmigration, but under circumstances that seemed calm and orderly by later standards. The 1930s, the Depression era, saw the region's economic problems turn nightmarish, and marked the most publicized period of outmigration. The 1940s then climaxed the process as war industries, hungry for labor, provided powerful external attractions. Migration continued after mid-century, but at a more modest pace as Southwestern cities finally began to absorb their full share of rural surplus population.

We know a great deal less about the particulars of outmigration in the early period than about the middle, Dust Bowl, phase. In excess of 1,300,000 people left the Southwest between 1910 and 1930, roughly 24 percent of them resettling in California (Table 1.1). Just who they were or what parts of the region they came from is difficult to determine. Census reports show that rural counties in eastern Oklahoma and the Ozark Mountains of northern Arkansas and southern Missouri lost population during the 1920s, but it does not follow that individuals from these counties left the region. Southwesterners had a number of options prior to the Great Depression. Many looked for land in western Oklahoma where commercial cotton growing was still expanding; others found work in the oil industry or moved to one of the Southwest's growing cities.[9]

Migration to California before the 1930s seems to have followed the standard logic of American westward movement. Historically, people usually moved west not out of desperation but in response to the perceived attractions of opportunity-filled new settings. Symbolically, the West had always been the land of new beginnings, and for that reason the business of moving west had been dominated by the middling classes: neither the rich nor the very poor, but men and women imbued with the desire and possessing the wherewithal for an ambitious new start.[10] California, especially, had long attracted settlers on those terms. Born amidst the frenzy of the Gold Rush, the state had ever since sustained a reputation as a place where fortunes were made, where opportunities abounded. And blessed with a remarkable climate and a wondrous array of natural resources, California's pecuniary attractions had been fused with equally compelling images of exceptional beauty. The development of southern California and its promotion as a sun-drenched paradise beginning in the 1880s had refined and extended these original sources of attraction. Middle-class Americans, just discovering the joys of uninhibited leisure, found the perfect setting in the Mediterranean-like environment of rapidly growing Los Angeles. "In California . . . you live life, elsewhere you merely spend it," advertisements produced by the state's innovative tourist industry announced.[11]

Come to California to find the "good life," Americans were told. And come they did, from every state, doubling the population every two decades. The wave crested between 1920 and 1930 as more than two and a half million newcomers poured into the state, proportionately the largest peace-time migration in American history. Southern California absorbed most of the flood. Within a few decades Los Angeles was transformed from a sleepy village into a raging metropolis; its 1930 population of 1.2 million was twelve times what it had been at the turn of the century.[12]

Southwesterners had participated in this migration from the beginning. Missourians, their state strategically located at the head of the Oregon-California trail, had played a prominent role in California settlement since the Gold Rush days. In smaller numbers, Texans and Arkansans (and later Oklahomans) had also made their way west. By 1910, 103,241 Southwesterners, two-thirds of them Missourians, were already living in California. More than 300,000 others joined them during the big surge of the 1910s and 1920s (Table 1.1).

Socially and economically, there was little to distinguish these Southwestern migrants from the several million other Americans, the largest number of them Midwesterners, crossing into the state during the pre-Depression period. Comprehensive data on backgrounds are not available, but other evidence suggests that, unlike those who followed during the 1930s, few Southwestern newcomers were poor. Most were opportunity seekers, often modestly prosperous farmers or townsfolk looking for something new, or young people starting their work careers.

The Southwest's economic problems were just beginning in the 1920s and only a select and probably ambitious minority responded to the tightening of opportunities by leaving the area. Feeling the pressure of low crop prices and declining fertility on his 120-acre Oklahoma farm, Elbert Garretson's father decided to try working in a southern California steel mill for a time. The plan was to "resuscitate financially" and then go back to the farm, his son recalls. The family moved back and forth between Los Angeles and Oklahoma several times before finally giving up on the profitless farm.[13]

In Oklahoma, the Woodall farm was prospering when the family decided to sell it and move to California in 1922. Father "just wanted a change and wanted to see what California was like," Ruth Woodall Criswell explains.[14] Walter and Audie Moffitt had similar reasons for leaving their Arkansas home and moving to southern California in 1928. A postman like his father and grandfather before him, Walter Moffitt had been out west briefly once before, had liked what he had seen, and felt sure that good things awaited them in California. Taking a job initially in a Goodrich tire plant, he applied for a post office position and before long was delivering mail near the family's new home in Long Beach.[15]

Cities, particularly the communities of greater Los Angeles, were the destinations of the large majority of Southwesterners entering California during the first third of the twentieth century. But a significant minority headed into the state's southern agricultural valleys where since 1900 cotton cultivation had become a steadily expanding enterprise. With their knowledge of that crop, Southwesterners were more or less assured work opportunities. Growers in the Imperial Valley began advertising in Oklahoma and Texas for cotton pickers as early as 1917, and their competitors in the San Joaquin Valley would often pay railroad fares for families willing to work in the fields. "[We came] because we could see the promise of the cotton future here, and we were cotton ranchers," recalls Velma Davis, who, along with her husband, arrived in the valley in 1925.[16] It was "a fine place to work then," another Oklahoma woman reported from the vantage point of the 1940s. "The farmers would meet you at the trains. Naturally people came out."[17] And not everyone came just to work in the fields. Land companies were looking for experienced cotton farmers to whom they might rent the newly opened lands. "They were advertising for Eastern people," another Southwesterner told anthropologist Walter Goldschmidt.

> I had a couple of cousins here already, and they sent me the Wasco News with large articles in it about opening up new land. That was in the fall of 1925. In '26 I started work at the [cotton] gin, and the gin company wanted me to farm—almost anyone could get a farm at that time.[18]

Thus, by the mid-twenties, the San Joaquin Valley, later to be the most publicized destination of the Dust Bowl migrants, was already attracting significant numbers of Southwesterners. Oklahoma farmers "in their second-hand flivvers, piled high with furniture and family . . . have been pouring through the divides by the hundreds," a journalist reported in 1926, introducing images that would become standard a decade later.[19]

If the initial migration to California can be understood as a conventional westward trek by moderately well-off opportunity seekers, what followed during the Depression decade seemed quite different—indeed different enough to attract international attention. The volume was not the critical distinction. At least 315,000 and perhaps as many as 400,000 Southwesterners moved west during the 1930s, compared with the 250,000 to 300,000 who had slipped unnoticed into California during the 1920s.[20] What distinguished the later group and brought them to public attention was their social composition and purpose. Unlike most westward movements of earlier eras, this one seemed to be comprised mostly of poor people and dominated not by the pull of California attractions but by the push of desperate conditions back home. Contemporaries decided that they were witnessing something unprecedented in the history of white Americans: a large-scale refugee migration, a flight from privation of the sort Americans read about elsewhere but hoped never to see in their own land.

That was the way photographer Dorothea Lange and her husband, economist Paul Taylor, interpreted matters as they drove through Oklahoma, Arkansas, and Texas in the summer of 1938. It seemed as if part of the American heartland was dying. With camera and pen they recorded the scene. Their book, *An American Exodus: A Record of Human Erosion*, is one of the classic contemporary statements on the Dust Bowl migration. Taylor's eloquent descriptions tell of the destruction of a once fertile land and the displacement of a proud people. His narrative details the awesome ravages of drought and the destructive ways of man. Lange's photographs say even more. Grim-faced with worry yet armed with some inner strength, her men and women of the plains stand at the edge of despair. Driven from their homes by forces beyond their ken or control, their only option is California.[21]

Poignant, dramatic, and still the prevailing image of the Dust Bowl migrants, the portrait is nonetheless extreme. The refugee notion misleads on two counts. It elevates the tragic connotations of the migration, inviting inaccurate comparisons with the refugee experiences of Europe after the two world wars or the even more devastating sagas of human misery which have so often plagued the Third World. The Dust Bowl migration was a tragedy in the rather privileged white American sense of the term. The refugee image also exaggerates the distinctions between this and other westward migrations. As we will see, many of the 1930s migrants were neither destitute nor the dirt farmers of popular paradigm, and even those who fit that image responded to many of the same kinds of attractions and dreams—"pulls"—which had traditionally been the chief basis for migration to California.

Still the kernel of the distinction was valid. Economic problems were driving this experience in ways at least more noticeable than previous mass internal migrations of white Americans. Not a refugee situation, the 1930s flow was nevertheless distinguished by its poverty and the strength of the expulsive forces at its rear.[22]

The economic conditions which provided that push have been extensively explored. In the context of the business depression which followed the

1929 stock market crash, the already troubled regional economy of the Western South dissolved in ruins; the few sectors that had remained strong in the twenties, notably oil, transportation, and construction, now declined even faster than agriculture. It would be hard to establish that one part of the country suffered more than all others during the Depression decade, but certainly few would disagree that the Southwest was among the hardest hit. Distress descended upon the region from several directions at once. Urban unemployment reached levels uncommon in other predominately rural states, while farmers staggered under a merciless combination punch: first the blow of collapsing crop prices, then a deadly follow-up series of environmental disasters.

Farmers everywhere suffered through the early years of the 1930s as prices fell and the markets for agricultural commodities disappeared, but on the Great Plains the problems were compounded by the worst drought of the century, a dry spell which scorched much of the region from Texas to South Dakota. For several years rain refused to fall in normal amounts, and it disappeared altogether in some areas in 1934 and again in 1936. Farmers could do nothing but watch their crops wither and die. The chief victims were wheat farmers, but the drought also hindered cotton production in western Oklahoma and northwestern Texas and burned crops in Arkansas and Missouri during certain years.[23]

The most spectacular feature of the drought, the awesome dust storms which blackened the sky over much of the central United States on numerous occasions between 1933 and 1935, actually affected relatively few farms in the Southwestern states. The area of severe wind erosion, soon known as the Dust Bowl, comprised a section of the wheat belt near the intersection of Kansas, Colorado, and the Oklahoma and Texas panhandles (see Map 1). Farms in that immediate area were devastated and many families packed up and left. But despite the popular perceptions, less than 16,000 people from the Dust Bowl proper ended up in California, barely 6 percent of the total from the Southwestern states. Journalists are to blame for the misunderstanding. Confusing drought with dust, and assuming that the dramatic dust storms must have had something to do with the large number of cars from Oklahoma and Texas seen crossing the California border in the mid-1930s, the press created the dramatic but misleading association between the Dust Bowl and the Southwestern migration.[24]

Prices, drought, floods in certain areas, even the boll weevil, accelerated the distress of farmers in the Western South and in some cases drove them from the land. Mortgaged farms were especially vulnerable. In Oklahoma, 10 percent of the state's farms changed hands in bankruptcy sales between 1931 and 1933.[25] More serious rural demographic disruption came with the implementation of the federal government's Agricultural Adjustment Act. Introduced in 1933 as a New Deal relief measure, the AAA offered cash

Figure 3. A small cotton farm in eastern Oklahoma, 1938. This, rather than the parched and dust-blown high plains, was the area of greatest rural outmigration. (*Dorothea Lange, © 1982, The Oakland Museum, The City of Oakland*)

subsidies to farmers who agreed to take land out of production. In the cotton belt where prices had fallen from an already low 16 cents per pound in 1929 to below 7 cents in 1932, desperate land owners eagerly signed up. As they did, the once mighty cotton empire began to shrink. By 1939, 12.5 million cotton acres had been turned to other uses; the Southwestern cotton belt had been reduced to half its former size.[26]

Crop subsidies soon helped to trigger a major social reorganization of the rural Southwest. Since the turn of the century the area had experienced a steady increase in the number and proportion of tenant farmers. Share-cropping, the most debilitating form of tenancy, remained rare except in the plantation areas near the Mississippi River, but cash renters and share renters (who furnished their own implements and team and turned over one-quarter to one-third of their crop) in time became the majority of farmers in the region. By 1930, more than 60 percent of Oklahoma, Arkansas, and Texas farms and 35 percent of farms in Missouri were operated by tenants.[27] Tenants found themselves the unwitting victims of the AAA subsidies. Required to reduce cotton acreage, landlords evicted many of their renters. Some also took the opportunity to consolidate their holdings

Table 1.2. Unemployment Rates for Selected States, 1933, 1937, 1940

	1933[a]	1937[b]	1940[c]
Oklahoma	29%	22%	18%
Arkansas	39	22	14
Texas	32	22	13
Missouri	32	—	15
California	29	19	14
Kansas	27	17	13
Nebraska	30	17	14
Mississippi	25	19	10
Tennessee	23	19	12
N. Carolina	18	17	9
Georgia	3	17	10
All states	33	20	14

[a] Estimates for nonagricultural unemployed only.
[b] All unemployed and emergency workers. Data available for census divisions not by states.
[c] All unemployed and emergency workers.
Sources: Tolan Committee, Report, 526–27; U.S. Bureau of the Census, Final Report on Total and Partial Unemployment (Washington, D.C., 1938), Vol. 4, 83–87; Donald J. Bogue, Henry S. Shryock, and Siegfried A. Hoermann, Subregional Migration in the United States 1935–1940, Vol. 1, table 3, cxcii–ccxi.

and operate them themselves using tractors and hired labor, thereby displacing additional tenant families. "I bought tractors on the money the government give me and got shet o' my renters," one landlord announced dispassionately. "They got their choice—California or WPA."[28] By 1940, the region's tenant population had been reduced by 24 percent, headed towards an even bigger reduction in the following decade. The era of tenant farming in the Southwest was drawing to a close.[29]

As evictions and lowered crop prices squeezed tens of thousands of farmers from the land after 1934, they ran headlong into the pattern of economic distress that had dominated the nonagricultural economy since the start of the decade. If anything, the cities and towns had suffered more than rural areas as the Depression tightened its grip on the commercial life of the region in the first half of the thirties. Depression-era unemployment data are sketchy and not always reliable, but the available estimates indicate that the Southwest contended with higher percentages of unemployed than other predominantly rural sections of the country. The federal government's Committee on Economic Security estimated Arkansas's rate of nonagricultural unemployment to be the third highest in the nation (39.2 percent) during the nadir year of 1933. Oklahoma, Texas, and Missouri, with rates varying between 29 and 32 percent, exceeded nearly all other states in the South or on the northern plains (Table 1.2). We have no data on the four recovery years which followed, but the 1937 federal unemployment census, taken just as the nation's economy entered another decline, found 22 percent of all available Southwestern workers either unemployed or engaged on work relief projects. Another 10 percent were considered partly unemployed. Conditions improved somewhat during the last two and a half years of the decade. When census takers visited homes in 1940, the unemployment rate in the Western South was down to 14.3 percent, but the level still remained higher than most rural states.[30]

With the partial exception of Missouri, the Southwestern states had few resources with which to assist the jobless and needy. Local and state relief funds were quickly exhausted as unemployment soared and tax revenues fell in the first years of the Depression, and usually offered little more than emergency groceries to those in need. Private charities like the Red Cross also helped, but in general the level of assistance available prior to 1933 was minimal. The establishment of the Federal Emergency Relief Administration shortly after Franklin Roosevelt assumed the presidency improved matters considerably. Through 1934 and 1935, federal relief funds sustained more than two and a half million Southwesterners, almost 20 percent of the region's population, on a continuing basis. In some areas the relief burden was much larger. During certain drought months in 1934, up to 90 percent of the population of particular eastern Oklahoma counties collected relief payments.[31]

Still, relief programs never proved capable of meeting the enormous need. Mismanagement and lack of cooperation at the state level caused federal officials to suspend aid to Arkansas and Oklahoma at several points during the decade, leaving hundreds of thousands without assistance. And even when federal funds were available, without the supplemental contributions that most other states were able to make, relief grants in Arkansas, Oklahoma, and Texas were routinely among the smallest in the nation. With federal assistance at a maximum in 1934 and 1935, grants averaged about $10 to $12 a month for a family of four, half the national average. After 1935, Works Projects Administration (WPA) jobs became available for some of the unemployed at an average wage of $30 to $50 a month. But families forced to continue on general relief found their monthly grants reduced by half as federal funds for that program were cut back. This was at a time when welfare analysts considered $60 a month the minimal subsistence income for an urban family of four.[32]

Thus at any given point during the 1930s somewhere between a fifth and a third of the Southwest's population suffered the effects of unemployment and severe poverty. Many in this tragic subpopulation found it difficult to obtain adequate food and shelter. Rural and urban unemployed alike drifted into the appalling squatter encampments found on the outskirts of many of the region's cities. A huge complex of camps and shack towns spread out next to Oklahoma City's stockyards, home to up to 2000 people, most of whom subsisted on a combination of odd jobs, relief, private charity, and ingenuity.[33]

Roy Turner and his family spent two years amidst the squalor and hunger of that camp before deciding to try their luck in California. Their house "was made of old automobiles, old lard cases, buckets, paste board, just anything that we could get to build one out of. . . . The people that lived around me . . . lots of times all they would have to eat was milk from those stock pen cows, cows that people would haul for market. They would go and milk those cattle." Finally, the Turners had had enough. Looking for something, anything, that offered hope, the family packed its few belongings and headed west on U.S. 66, "walking, me and my wife and two babies," on the first leg of a hitch-hiking journey that would take them to California, 1200 miles away.[34]

The Turners were representative of just one segment of the population moving to California in the 1930s. Dispossessed and sometimes desperately poor farm families like the Turners or like Steinbeck's Joad family were indeed an important element of the migration, but there were also many other participants who defied the popular image of the rural Dust Bowl migrant. In 1939, the Bureau of Agricultural Economics collected information from some 116,000 families who had settled in California during the 1930s. The backgrounds of Southwesterners in the sample come as a surprise. Most were not farmers, but rather had come from the region's cities and towns. Only 43 percent had engaged in agricultural pursuits immediately prior to migration.[35] This is confirmed by census data. In 1940, the Census Bureau asked a special set of questions intended to illuminate interstate migration patterns during the second half of the 1930s. Each person enumerated in 1940 was asked where he or she had lived as of April 1, 1935. Of the Southwesterners who migrated to California between 1935 and 1940, only 36 percent had resided on farms as of that earlier date. On the other hand, more than 50 percent had lived in areas classified as urban, with the remainder coming from small towns.[36]

The large number of migrants from the region's cities and towns needs to be emphasized. By concentrating solely on the farmers, until now students of the Dust Bowl migration have missed its diversity. Without an awareness of the different backgrounds from which the migrants came, it is impossible to understand the varied resettlement strategies they would follow in California.[37]

In terms of occupation, the migrants came quite close to matching the range of statuses found in the region they were leaving (Table 1.3). Middle-class occupations were under-represented, but not severely. The fact that nearly one migrant in six was a professional, a proprietor, or a white collar employee should qualify the destitute dirt-farmer image of the migration. Lillie Grose May's family certainly did not resemble the Joad stereotype.

Table 1.3. Pre-Migration Occupations of California Migrants from West South Central States,* 1930–1939, Compared With All Male Residents of That Region, 1930

Occupation	West South Migrants	West South Residents
Professionals	2%	3%
Proprietors	6	8
Clerical/sales	7	10
Skilled laborers	14	10
Semi-skilled/service	13	8
Unskilled laborers	12	15
Domestic and personal service	2	2
Farmers	26	28
Farm laborers	17	16
	99%	100%
	(N = 21,238)	

*Oklahoma, Texas, Arkansas, and Louisiana.

Source: Calculated from U.S. Department of Agriculture, Bureau of Agricultural Economics, Seymour J. Janow, "Volume and Characteristics of Recent Migration to the Far West," Tolan Committee, *Hearings*, Part 6, table 16–A, p. 2307.

Her father had been a prominent merchant in Quinton, Oklahoma, before the Depression, owning a well-provisioned grocery store. But 1931 found the store without customers and forced to close. That is when a neighbor suggested California. The friend had a brother in Bakersfield who supervised the Safeway stores in that area and could probably provide a job. Mr. Grose sought him out and was soon managing one of the grocery chain's Kern County outlets.[38]

Robert Kessler and his family were also among the usually overlooked middle-class migrants. A tractor salesman in western Oklahoma, he too had prospered in the decade before the Depression. "We were living in a very large house and making good money," his son recalls, until "POW—Dad didn't have a job anymore." Three tough years of hard-to-find work followed before the Kesslers decided to head for southern California.[39]

Like Kessler, many of these white-collar migrants were out of work. But not all of them. California continued to lure a trickle of the Southwest's more fortunate citizens: businessmen whose firms transferred them, professionals who applied for new positions, students sent to California universities, investors with money to put into real estate or businesses out west, and retirees, not as many as before, but the lucky ones with fortunes intact who could still look forward to spending their waning years in the southern California sun. Hollywood, a big lure in the 1920s, remained seductive, attracting both dreamers and established performers like "Oklahoma's singing cowboy," Gene Autry.[40]

For this segment of the migrant group, little had changed since 1929. The reasons for going to California were the same as always. Oklahoma's governor, Leon Phillips, stung by the image of his state as a wasteland of poverty, took pains to point out to Congressman John Tolan's investigating committee that not everyone heading for California was indigent or in need of a job. The land-of-sunshine advertising images were still drawing well-heeled Oklahomans, he observed, including both his former stenographer and a banker friend. "The man that ran the bank at Okemah when I went there to practice law twenty-five years ago is one of the group that wants to go to California," Phillips explained, "and he has money."[41]

If white-collar migrants were somewhat underrepresented, Southwesterners with blue-collar experience made their way to California in numbers that exceeded their representation in the region, and which again defied the stereotype. Some 39 percent of all Southwestern male household heads settling in the California during the 1930s came from that occupational group. Of course, it is legitimate to wonder how many of these men were former farmers who after losing land tried for a time to find work in the Southwest's cities before heading west. Indeed, the number may have been large. As we will see, fluidity between agricultural and nonagricultural job sectors was common in the Southwest even before the Depression.

In any event, the identifiable farm people were not the majority. Comprising 43 percent of the migrant group, farmers seem to have left the Southwest in numbers quite close to their representation in the general population. However, they were drawn excessively from certain parts of the rural sector. Tenants, quite naturally, predominated; farm owners generally had less reason to leave.[42] Migrants also came from particular areas, chiefly the Oklahoma–north Texas cotton belt. As Map 2 indicates, that broad band of counties contributed more rural newcomers to California than any other part of the nation during the Depression decade. Secondarily, farm families left the Ozark Mountain area of northern Arkansas and southern Missouri, a chronically poor and partially isolated region dependent on timber, mining, and low-yield general agriculture. Neither the wheat-belt (Dust Bowl) parts of Oklahoma, nor corn-belt Missouri, nor southern and western Texas contributed many farm families to California.

What else do we know about those who left? Ninety-five percent were white. Blacks had been leaving the Western South since World War I but mostly following networks that led north. Not until the next war did blacks join the westward flow in substantial numbers.[43]

Most of the migrants were young. As is usual among people who undertake a dramatic relocation, those who set out for California tended to

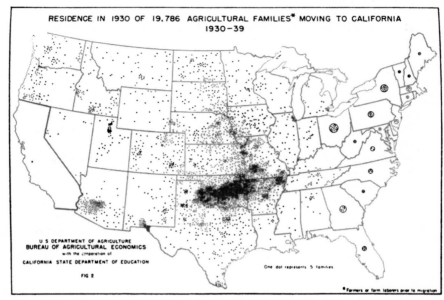

RESIDENCE IN 1930 OF 19,786 AGRICULTURAL FAMILIES* MOVING TO CALIFORNIA
1930–39

U S DEPARTMENT OF AGRICULTURE
BUREAU OF AGRICULTURAL ECONOMICS
with the cooperation of
CALIFORNIA STATE DEPARTMENT OF EDUCATION

FIG 2

One dot represents 5 families

*Farmers or farm laborers prior to migration

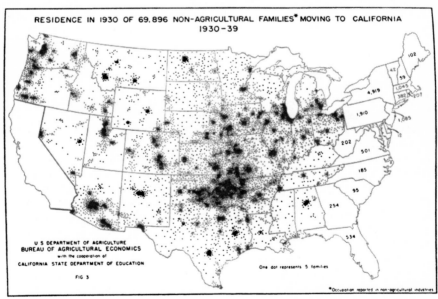

RESIDENCE IN 1930 OF 69,896 NON-AGRICULTURAL FAMILIES* MOVING TO CALIFORNIA
1930–39

U S DEPARTMENT OF AGRICULTURE
BUREAU OF AGRICULTURAL ECONOMICS
with the cooperation of
CALIFORNIA STATE DEPARTMENT OF EDUCATION

FIG 3

One dot represents 5 families

*Occupation reported in non-agricultural industries

Map 2 (*top*) and Map 3. *Source*: *Land Policy Review* (July–Aug. 1940), 29, 31.

be in their twenties and early thirties. More precisely, some 60 percent of adults were under thirty-five years old.[44] Schooling was also a distinguishing variable. Migrants on the whole were slightly better educated than those of the same age group who stayed behind in the Southwest. This held true for both rural and urban departees[45]

Finally we know something about the gender and family structure of the group. Fifty-three percent were males, a rather small proportion for a migrating population since young males are the prime candidates for re-location in most cultures and situations. Although single men frequently went to California on their own, what stood out about the Dust Bowl migration was the preponderance of families on the move. But despite the image created by Steinbeck's fictional Joad family, extended-family house-holds were atypical. Husband, wife, and children was the usual arrange-ment; only one household in five included different sorts of relations. Still, families tended to be a bit larger than California standards. Households of Southwestern newcomers averaged 4.4 members, compared with 3.9 for all California households and 3.6 for newcomers from other regions of the country.[46]

California

That many Southwesterners had economic incentives for leaving the region only begins to explain the migration of the 1930s. Why did they choose California and what gave them the confidence to relocate at a time when most Americans found it prudent to remain close to home? These were questions asked frequently fifty years ago, but rarely answered in much detail. Investigators often found the newcomers tight-lipped about their reasons for coming to California. Sensitive to the controversy surrounding their Depression-era relocation, they typically responded with no-nonsense references to troubles back home and jobs up ahead. "It just got so hard, a hard get-by" back in Oklahoma, fifty-seven-year-old Marvin Montgomery told the congressional committee looking into the causes of the migration. "I just drug along as long as I wanted to. I wanted to change countries to see if I could find something better."[47] Inspecting a newly opened govern-ment camp for migrant workers, Vice President Henry Wallace asked another newcomer what he was doing in California. "Well, Mister, I was farmin' back ther in Oklyhomy and it jist kep a gittin' droughthier and droughthier, and droughthier so . . . Here I be."[48]

But behind these matter-of-fact pronouncements—the cautious words of a people given to stoic understatement—lurked a complex of expecta-tions that is revealed in the songs and poems that some newcomers com-posed during their early years in California. A number of these compositions survive, many in the mimeographed newspapers published

by the Farm Security Administration camps which temporarily housed
thousands of migrants during the late thirties and early forties.[49] Others
were collected by a pair of folklorists, Charles Todd and Robert Sonkin,
who spent two summers among the migrant families in the state's Central
Valley.[50] No source reveals more about the range of concerns and attractions which brought people to California.

Many of these compositions told of great initial hopes for economic
deliverance:

> When I first came to California,
> Was in the year of thirty-seven,
> From what I read in papers,
> I thought it was poor man's heaven.[51]

Or:

> They said in California
> that money grew on trees,
> That everyone was going there,
> Just like a swarm of bees.[52]

Others looked beyond strictly economic promises to evoke California's
reputation for beauty. Referring to the "shining of your sun/ The beauty
of your orange groves," or using stock phrases like "California where the
sun always shines," the migrant poets told of their hopes for a different
kind of life—a more comfortable and perhaps more aesthetic existence
than what they had previously known.[53]

Several suggest a blend of economic and aesthetic concerns as reasons
for the migration. Jack Bryant's song "Sunny Cal," recorded in a migratory
labor camp near Firebaugh, is one example.

> You've all heard the story
> Of old Sunny Cal
> The place where it never rains
> They say it don't know how.
> They say, "Come on, you Okies,
> Work is easy found
> Bring along your cotton pack
> You can pick the whole year round."[54]

Similar images are forthcoming from the old folk song that was widely
touted as the theme song of the migration. "Goin' Down the Road Feelin'
Bad," took its title and dominant mood from a powerful chorus which tells
of the pain of leaving home and yet at the same time of the determination
to do so:

> I'm goin' down the road feelin' bad,
> I'm goin' down the road feelin' bad,

> I'm goin' down the road feelin' bad,
> Lawd, Lawd,
> And I ain't gonna be treated this-a-way.

Most of the other verses then provide the reason for going down the road, using lines like, "They fed me on corn bread and beans." But the song also includes a passage whose subtle imagery conveys a longing for a new and different style of existence:

> I'm goin' where the climate suits my clothes,
> I'm goin' where the climate suits my clothes,
> I'm goin' where the climate suits my clothes,
> Lawd, Lawd,
> And I ain't gonna be treated this-a-way.[55]

Like the dreams which drew many towards California, the promise of the verse is vague, intangible. It never specifies how things will be better, and yet it is clear that life in California will be an improvement, somehow more appropriate, more comfortable.

Flora Robertson's "Why We Come to California" provides another look at expectations of California. An unschooled mother, new to California, Robertson evokes the much-used image of a California cornucopia to explain the migration of a hungry people.

> California, California,
> Here I come too.
> With a coffee pot and skillet,
> And I'm coming to you.
> Nothing's left in Oklahoma,
> For us to eat or do.
> And if apples, nuts, and oranges,
> And Santy Claus is real,
> Come on to California,
> Eat and eat till your full.[56]

The poem's reference to "Santy Claus" complicates the meaning, suggesting wonderful dreams of what California will be and at the same time introducing the possibility that all will prove to be a fantasy, a false and empty illusion.

The impressive balance of Robertson's poem probably captures the mix of hopes and doubts with which most people set out for California. In the context of the time, pragmatic concerns, the search for work and ways to make a living, predominated. Yet interlacing those practical economic goals were more aesthetic, expansive dreams. California, they hoped, would mean a new and fulfilling way of life, combining exciting opportunity and gentle beauty. Still most kept these yearnings firmly under control, as they had been taught by both culture and experience.

Where did these expectations come from? Certainly in large part they were based on the images that California had carefully propounded during earlier, more prosperous eras. But it would be a mistake to conclude that the 1930s newcomers were the victims of out-of-date promotional schemes. On the contrary, their understandings of California's prospects were about as accurate as might be expected under the circumstances. Even now, with all the tools available to the historian, it is not easy to decipher the outlines of opportunity in 1930s California. For contemporaries the task was made all the more complicated by the conflicting messages of various information media, some of which portrayed the state in rosy, others in somber hues.

Had they believed what many journalists and public officials said about California, few would have come. From the start of the Depression, state officials tried to discourage newcomers from heading west. Anxious to head off the migration of job seekers, authorities spread the word that economic conditions in California were deplorable. At the end of the decade a billboard on Highway 66, just outside of Tulsa, Oklahoma, carried the message that the state tried to promote:

NO JOBS in California
If YOU are looking for work—KEEP OUT
6 Men for Every Job
No State Relief Available for Non-Residents[57]

The official line, however, was no match for the commercial media that in various ways continued to show a more positive side of California. The tourist industry tried to cooperate with state migration policy but succeeded only in confusing the issue. Ads for sunny California vacation spots appeared all through the 1930s, each carrying the fine-print warning, "Come to California for a glorious vacation. Advise anyone not to come seeking employment, lest he be disappointed; but for tourists, the attractions are unlimited."[58]

Hollywood's role was more subversive still, and doubtless much more important. The film industry suffered little damage in the 1930s; whatever else they did, most Americans kept going to the movies. And quite often they found there confirming images of California's appeal. Sound stage cinematography gave films the impression of geographic variety, which film makers generally used to confirm ready stereotypes. Films with any sort of social message rarely suggested California settings. Most of the projects of King Vidor, Charlie Chaplin, and Frank Capra, not to mention the popular gangster films that conveyed the dark and dangerous side of urban life, seemed to be set in the East, while the escapist musicals, good-time comedies, and western horse operas were more likely to have references to California. The film industry itself remained a favorite topic for both screen and print treatment. In films such as *What Price Hollywood* (1932),

A Star Is Born (1937), and *Hollywood Hotel* (1938), as well as the prolific gossip columns and fan magazines, the feast of lush images of sunny and prosperous southern California continued virtually uninterrupted.[59]

One film, W.C. Fields's 1934 comedy, *It's a Gift*, dealt directly if not resolutely with the question of California opportunity. Fields plays a bumbling New Jersey storekeeper who buys, sight unseen, a southern California orange grove, packs up the family, and heads across the country. The Los Angeles that greets them is a mix of wealth and poverty, of posh estates and hungry hobos. The family seems destined to join the dispossessed, because of course they have bought a worthless piece of real estate. But no! In a classic reaffirmation of California's promise to fulfill dreams, at the last minute a land developer needs the property and pays a fortune for it. The film ends with Fields settling into a life of orange-squeezing luxury on a newly purchased southern California estate.

With its up and down tale of bold dreams, wrenching failure, and sudden success, *It's a Gift* was not a bad guide to Depression-era California. In point of fact, California's economic profile was varied and confusing; the economy claimed enough strong points to sustain the dreamers, but also showed the kind of weaknesses that scared pessimists.

The downturn of the early 1930s had hit the state hard, and many Californians had learned to know deprivation and fear along with other Americans. Business failure and unemployment had soared, leaving more than 700,000 Californians, 29 percent of the work force, jobless by early 1933 (Table 1.2). However, as New Deal programs began to take effect later in that year, the state's diversified economy helped California to reclaim its status as one of the nation's more prosperous states. By 1937, after four years of recovery, California manufacturing enterprises employed 106 percent of their 1929 work force. Nevertheless, unemployment remained a serious problem until the very end of the decade, with rates usually just below national averages. Critics blamed the million and a quarter newcomers who moved to California during those troubled years.[60]

Even with its increasing population, California enjoyed a higher per capita income than most states, roughly 40 percent above the national average. During the worst years of the Depression, between 1930 and 1934, per capita income in California averaged $635 a year, down dramatically from the 1920s, but much above Texas, to take a Southwestern example, where the average was $298. By the end of the decade the difference had diminished somewhat, but Texans on the average earned only 53 percent of Californians' income.[61]

Some of the state's per capita edge was due to the disproportionate numbers of wealthy individuals making their homes there, but wage rate data indicate that average Californians also enjoyed advantages over residents of many other states. Most manufacturing jobs in California paid

Table 1.4. Average wages per Hour for Industries Employing 1,000 or More Persons in California and the Southwest, 1935

Industry	California	Okla-Texas	Missouri
Meat packing	$ 0.68	$ 0.46	$ 0.56
Petroleum refining	0.84	0.72	0.71
Cement	0.64	0.45–0.53	0.66
Clay Products	0.46	0.33	0.44
Machinery	0.67	0.60	0.54
Machine shops	0.63	0.56	0.64
Steam railroad	0.66	0.60	0.59
Ice manufacture	0.55	0.33	0.46

Source: U.S. Bureau of the Census, *Census of Manufacture: 1935, Man-Hour Statistics for 59 Selected Industries* (Wash., D.C., 1938), 6–42.

Table 1.5. Average Wage Rate for Picking 100 Pounds of Cotton in Selected States

	1932	1934	1936	1938
California	$ .45	$ .90	$1.00	$ .75
Arkansas	.44	.60	.75	.60
Texas	.45	.60	.65	.55
Oklahoma	.48	.75	.75	.70
Missouri	.52	.80	.95	.75

Source: California State Chamber of Commerce, *Migrants: A National Problem and Its Impact on California* (San Francisco, 1940), reprinted in Tolan Committee *Hearings*, Part 6, p. 2785.

between 10 and 40 percent more than in the four Southwestern states (Table 1.4). In the petroleum industry workers earned an average wage of 72 cents per hour in the Southwest and nearly 84 cents per hour in California, while in meat packing the spread was 10 to 20 cents an hour in favor of California workers.[62]

Of course, finding work was often difficult. But after the first three awful years and with the exception of the 1937–38 recession, the California economy grew steadily, creating new jobs each year. The easiest work prospects were in agriculture, which was one of the few job sectors to experience anything like a labor shortage during the 1930s. Between 1934 and 1937, California growers needed thousands of new farm workers to harvest their crops, both because agriculture was expanding and because part of the traditional labor force had been repatriated to Mexico. For farm families in the Southwest it was a perfect opportunity, especially since the California crop where labor was most needed was cotton, the crop they knew best.

Cut back drastically when the price fell to six cents a pound in 1932, cotton made a dramatic resurgence in California in the following years, even as cotton farmers elsewhere faced ongoing difficulties. Able to produce three to four times as much high-quality cotton to the acre as farms in the Southwest, growers in the San Joaquin Valley quadrupled their acreage from 123,000 acres in 1932 to 620,000 four years later.[63] With the acreage increase, the demand for cotton pickers soared, and wages rose accordingly. Whereas in 1932, growers had paid an average of 45 cents for a hundred pounds of picked cotton, two years later the rate had doubled, and by 1936 $1.00 per hundredweight was standard (see Table 1.5).[64]

By the middle of the decade, California cotton growers were paying 20 to 50 percent more for picking than was customary in the southern plains states. To the families of tenant farmers and agricultural laborers facing the prospect of another year of struggling to make a living in the Southwest, it was an invitation to travel. Asked why he had come to California, Thomas Derryberry, a former Oklahoma cotton farmer, put it succinctly: "I started looking this way and when I found cotton, that's where I stopped."[65] Others who had grown up working in the cotton fields made the same calculations. Says Tom Palmer, who brought his family west in 1936, "I knew if there was cotton to pick I wouldn't starve to death."[66]

California enjoyed another important economic advantage over the Southwestern states: it was prosperous enough to support a comparatively generous system of unemployment relief. After 1933 the California State Relief Administration saw to it that eligible unemployed residents received relief checks averaging about $40 a month for a family of four. That was at least double what most Southwestern states paid in unemployment relief.[67]

To people living in a region where conditions were much worse, all this looked promising. When Southwesterners heard that unskilled laborers usually earned $3 to $4 a day in California or that farm workers could expect to make $2.50 to $3 a day, it seemed to them like a lot of money. As one Arkansan put it, "People . . . think they are just a-flyin' if they git $3.00 a day."[68] Similarly, the thought of receiving $40 a month in relief benefits could be quite attractive. "California is best on relief in the world," an Oklahoman explained. "I don't bar none, the best I've seen in several states."[69] Not that prospective migrants were primarily interested in living on welfare, especially if they realized that a full year's residency was required to qualify. Most insisted that it was work they wanted. But years of Depression had taught many that relief was a necessity: "just a matter of have-to," said one. Thus some looked with interest at California's relief programs. A young Texan summarized the standard view of the economic prospects that California seemed to offer: "Well, if they have lots of work out there and if relief is good, then if I don't find work I'll still be all right."[70]

Figure 4. In newly painted English and faded Spanish, this road sign recognizes the changing contours of California's agricultural labor force in the mid-1930s. Note that the ranch had recently expanded cotton production from 3,000 to 10,000 acres. (*Dorothea Lange,* © *1982, The Oakland Museum, The City of Oakland*)

Migration Chains

Work opportunities, the relief system, the climate, the glamour—despite the state's problems, for outsiders there were real enough reasons to contemplate a move to California. But the vagaries of the Depression era made these reasons insufficient. An additional factor—personal ties to relatives already in California—played a critical role in the decision to migrate. Most Americans stayed close to home during the 1930s, knowing that high unemployment rates made any move risky. Compared with the 1920s, the frequency of moves across state lines declined by half. In most parts of the country not even destitution readily dislodged families. In the Eastern South, for example, farmers and tenants suffered many of the same difficulties as their trans-Mississippi counterparts without taking to the highways. The net migration of whites out of the East South Central states (outflow minus inflow) was less than 30,000 during the decade of the 1930s, compared with a net outflow of nearly 500,000 West South Central residents.[71]

The different migration responses had much to do with the configurations of extra-regional personal relationships available to residents of the two areas. Southeasterners had been leaving home in large numbers in the decades before the 1930s, but most had moved to areas (Northern cities and the Western South) where opportunities disappeared once the Depression struck. California on the other hand was distant and new. Few in the Southeast had the kind of personal ties that might have directed them there. That was the critical difference for Southwesterners. A fully developed migration system invited them to California. Former Southwesterners—some 400,000 of them by 1930—provided the framework of information and assistance that made it feasible to think seriously about a long-distance move.[72]

Those earlier migrants who were doing well in California sent back the hopeful news that set the migration in motion. From Los Angeles, families who had settled there in the 1920s wrote to relatives in the Southwest telling them about their circumstances and the opportunities that might be available to others if they should come west. From the Central Valley, others told of the wages being paid for field work. People struggling to earn a living in the southern plains states could not help but be impressed. "Everyone writes back he's heeled. He's got him a job," an Arkansan explained.[73] Even more impressive were the return visits of people who had settled in California. The signs of their prosperity were often boldly apparent. "It leaves a good impression on the home folks that they are doin' well," said one migrant, when "they left in an old wreck and come back in a good car."[74] Jesse Carter*, who had come to California from Oklahoma in 1936, analyzed the process. All "this kinsfolks business," this writing back and forth between relatives, he explained, "gits the folks back home to talkin' that work is pretty good in California, so they decide to pull up stakes and come."[75] Another newcomer confirmed the pattern. "We come to Wasco because times were bad in Arkansas, and my cousin wrote us that things were pretty good out here."[76]

The experience of the Shahan family illustrates the importance of such ties in the decision to head west. Despite the economic difficulties which impelled them to leave Oklahoma, the Shahans would not have considered the "drastic move" were it not for the fact that they had relatives living near Los Angeles. "It was not like coming to a land where you didn't know anybody," Melvin Shahan recalls. Indeed not, for their kinfolk not only urged them to come west but also offered them a place to stay and help in finding jobs.[77]

The Shahan's move west bore little resemblance to the migration scenario depicted in *The Grapes of Wrath*. Unlike Steinbeck's Joad family, which set out all alone for an unknown California only to wander helplessly from one difficulty to the next, the majority of migrants followed a directed course. "I knew exactly where I was going," Marvin Montgomery ex-

plained, "I had a son and married daughter here."[78] Data from several
locales confirms that at least half of the 1930s migrants followed and depended upon already settled relatives in California. Almost two-thirds of
the migrants interviewed in a study conducted in the Salinas Valley had
relatives living in the state when they decided to come west. Forty-seven
percent of the newcomers living in a Sacramento Valley town told another
investigator they had come to California in part because of relatives or
friends already there, and others who declined to give that as a reason for
migration nevertheless said they had kinfolk living in the state. Similar
findings were reported among migrants living in two Kern County communities, with the majority of respondents in both towns admitting that
the presence of relatives or friends had been instrumental in the decision
to relocate.[79]

All this suggests that the Dust Bowl migration was not an atomistic
dispersion of solitary families but a guided chain migration of the sort very
typical for both trans-Atlantic immigrants and rural-to-urban migrants. Of
course not everyone participated in such networks. Unconnected families
did come west in substantial numbers, especially as the migration "fever"
spread through the Southwest late in the decade. Many of these, however,
created their own migration chains, waiting until a teenage son or young
male relative had explored California and then joining him there. John
Blake rode the freights to Los Angeles in 1936 at age sixteen or seventeen,
picked oranges in the area for a few months, and then returned home to
convince his father and uncle that California was the place to be.[80] James
Lackey spearheaded the migration of a much larger group of relatives to
the Arvin area of Kern County, but it took him two exploratory trips west.
Leaving his eastern Oklahoma home in 1932 at age eighteen, he rode the
rails to California with a friend on a fruitless search for work. Four years
later, after some college and a stint with the Civilian Conservation Corps,
he and his brother tried again, found jobs, and encouraged other members
of the family to join them. Cousins, aunts, and uncles soon settled nearby.
"I'd get them all jobs," he explains, "I was kind of like a politician . . . I
knew all the bosses."[81]

The chains of relation which marked the route to California appear to
have been more restrictive than the connections which often guide mass
migrations. Reflecting the strong emphasis on family and the relatively
unstable community ties found in the Southwest, most migrants followed
relatives to California rather than participate in the broad community migration sequences which students of European immigration often uncover.
Nevertheless some examples of community migration have turned up. One
of Paul Taylor's graduate students discovered a sizable colony of migrants
from Carroll County, Arkansas, living in and around the Salinas Valley
town of Greenfield. In all, there were nearly 200 people in the Greenfield

area who had come from that sparsely populated section of the Arkansas Ozarks.[82]

Sociologist Carl Withers found a similar pattern of community migration linking a small town in the Missouri Ozarks with a community in the Sacramento Valley. By 1940, so many townsfolk had settled in that California locale that each new arrival found "a complete replica of his social situation (kin, neighbors, intimacies, security system) back home." Moreover, migration or at least a trip to California had become more or less expected of the Missouri town's young people. As one old timer noted playfully, "A boy's education ain't finished around here till he's been to Californy."[83] Another community network was evident in the Yuba City Farm Security Administration camp. The facilities seemed just like home, one resident cheerfully declared, since "about half" of his Arkansas home town was living there.[84]

If these were somewhat exceptional situations, communities did facilitate the migration process in less directed ways. By 1936 and 1937, when the exodus from the region reached its prewar peak, letters and return visits sometimes contributed to a gold-rush mentality: the idea of going west became contagious, spreading from neighbor to neighbor. "All you could hear was 'Go to California,' " a newcomer said of the migration fever in his town.[85] Dorothea Lange and Paul Taylor saw the same contagion at work in a couple of Oklahoma communities, and not everyone was happy about it. "Ain't it a fright—how they're a goin'," they heard one Oklahoman say. "My neighbor over yonder to the south has got two boys and a girl out there, and my neighbor over thataway on the north section, he's got a son gone out there." In another community so many had gone west that it seemed to one resident that "half the people of this town and around here have gone out there."[86] A newly arrived migrant in California told another investigator that the migration spirit was running so high in his Oklahoma hometown that you "could take a truck down there and damn near load it full of folks in a day and hit out fer this way."[87]

If social factors, either personal ties to relatives already in California or contagious community talk, contributed to the decision to migrate, so did a particular orientation and habit common to the Southwest. As several scholars have noted, the Western South enjoyed a history and tradition of mobility, of geographic and occupational fluidity, which may have left residents in some measure predisposed to leave home in search of opportunity.

Rural communities have rarely been the stagnant, tradition-bound worlds that so many urbanites of that generation liked to assume. Farmers moved into and especially out of even the most hidebound areas, selling old farms, buying new ones, moving on when the opportunities were right. But if a certain amount of fluidity has always been common to American rural life, the volume of movement in the Southwest was exceptional. Asked by 1930 census enumerators how long they had inhabited their current farms, 47 percent of farm operators in Arkansas, 44 percent in Oklahoma, and 40 percent in Texas said less than two years, while nationwide 28 percent answered similarly. The prevalence of tenant farming accounted for much of this mobility, for without a permanent tenure renters were free to move about in search of better land or nonagricultural opportunities. But especially in Oklahoma, where frontier memories remained fresh, the pattern of mobility seems also to have been informed by a spirit of restlessness.[88]

"Tumbleweeds" was what the regional director of the Farm Security Administration called Oklahoma's tenant farmers, saying they "break loose like the tumbleweed every year, and go rolling across the prairie until they lodge for a year against a barbwire fence, only to break loose next year and go tumbling again."[89] Paul Taylor used similar metaphors. "The roots of Oklahomans in the land are shallow," he argued. "By a curiously symbolic coincidence Oklahoma is the most wind-blown state in the country, its newly broken red plains are among the worst eroded, and its farm people are among the least rooted to the soil."[90] The data to back up these observations came from a study conducted by sociologist Robert McMillan. Compiling the life histories of 1,032 Oklahoma farm families from four different counties in 1937, he found that over the course of their work careers the average Oklahoma farmer moved four times, five if he was a tenant. Most of these moves were made before the age of thirty-five, during the youthful "floundering period" when the quest for opportunity was keenest, and were often confined to a localized area. Forty percent of Oklahoma farmers had spent their working lives within a twenty-five mile radius of their first farm. Localized movements of this sort were typical of farmers in other states. What was unusual about the Oklahomans were the large number who had moved considerably greater distances. Just under half, 46 percent, had accomplished moves of at least one hundred miles in the course of their work lives, compared with less than 20 percent of farmers surveyed in Ohio, New York, and North Carolina. Equally atypical, a substantial minority, 36 percent, had nonagricultural work experience, having left farming for a time and then returned.[91]

The fluidity of this rural population had various implications. Community life in the western cotton belt seems to have been less integrated and stable than comparable wheat- and corn-belt communities where mobility rates were lower. Large numbers of tenant families remained beyond the reach of local churches and social institutions, dependent all the more on family and kin networks for their social life, a habit which would shape their community interactions in California.[92] Beyond that, historian Sheila Manes has suggested that "migratoriness" contributed significantly to the willingness to contemplate migration to that state. The trip west was just one more in the long tradition of opportunity-seeking moves that these individuals and perhaps their parents and grandparents had become accustomed to making.[93]

Consider the personal history of Lonnie Nelson*, as recorded by sociology graduate student James Wilson. Nelson's decision to go to California in 1940 is easy to understand; in the previous twenty years he had tried just about everything else.

> I've lived in Oklahoma since I was eight years old, stayed on the farm till I was sixteen. I went to railroadin' when I was 22. Come out durin' the big strike. I really believe in the Union. I got married in 1922, 12th of July—six o'clock in the evening. Then me and the bride went back to the farm, and stayed on the farm till '24. From that I taken up ginnin' and concrete work 'cause the drought hit and wasn't makin' nothin' . . .
>
> I went back to the railroads in '26, with a different outfit and worked there till '32. . . . The second day of January '32 I got cut off from the railroad, laid off fer good. . . . The only thing to do was to go back to the farm and stayed there one year. About this time, in '33, my wife was operated on fer thyroid goiter. Then I worked on C.W.A for one year, buildin' and such like as that.
>
> In '34 I got a job with the Government killin' cattle. It lasted seven weeks and I killed from 26 to 135 head a day. . . . After that was over I picked up odd jobs till January of '35 and went back to farmin'. The drought struck again in '35, and high waters come on in the late fall. In other words, what the drought didn't git the high waters did. I was overflowed five times in two months. A farmer can't stand the like of that. So there was nothin' to do but to throw up my tail and go back on relief. We all got hit and hit hard. That was from '36 to '39, by gosh. . . . So the 15th of January, 1940 we loaded up and come out here, leavin a snow storm to our back, sunny California to our belly and here we are. The good Lord is just lettin' me sit around to see what the hell will happen next.[94]

Nelson's career was exceptional, but it illustrates in exaggerated form the fluid habits of many. Neither occupational categories nor communities of residence enjoyed much constancy. Today's oil worker was yesterday's farmer and tomorrow's farm laborer. Similarly, residence in Arkansas one year might lead to Oklahoma the next and then back to Arkansas the following. Everything depended on the winds of opportunity—winds that shifted erratically throughout the 1920s and 1930s.[95]

Despite the fact that it lay more than a thousand miles away, California became part of this tumbleweed circuit. The reason was its perceived accessibility. Both because of the presence of relatives in that state and because of the miracles of modern transportation, the distance meant relatively little. This is one of the most misunderstood aspects of the Dust Bowl migration. In their desire to dramatize the migrant experience, novelists, journalists, and even historians have exaggerated the hardships of the journey to California. In tones more justly reserved for the era of covered wagons, they too often portray an arduous trip, forgetting that since the 1920s California had been linked to the Southwest by a well-traveled highway. Scenic and already legendary, U.S. Route 66 cut straight across Missouri, Oklahoma, and north Texas on its way to Los Angeles—a direct, modern, and inviting pathway west.[96]

Ease of transportation was the key both to the volume of migration and to the special frame of mind with which the newcomers began their California stay. The automobile gave these and other twentieth-century migrants a flexibility that cross-country or trans-oceanic migrants of earlier eras did not share. By reducing the costs and inconveniences of long-distance travel, it made it easy for those who were tentative or doubtful, who under other circumstances would have stayed behind, to go anyway. They went knowing that for the price of a few tanks of gasoline they could always return.[97]

Such tentativeness was common among the 1930s migrants. Some families departed the Southwest resolving to make a permanent home in California, but most set out armed with more provisional strategies. A few left property, even farms, behind, intending to return; most left so many relatives and memories that any sort of initial commitment to remaining out west was unthinkable. A significant number went merely to explore work prospects, or for a short visit with relatives.

Pink Allen testified before the Tolan Committee that he and his wife went to California because "we just wanted to run around." They had heard "how much money a man could make out there and we wanted to go."[98] A young couple interviewed by anthropologist Walter Goldschmidt admitted to having been just as impulsive."When we decided to get married," the wife explained, "we just thought we would come out to California to work in the crops for a season and then go back. . . . We didn't think much about it—looking back it seems we were awful dumb."[99] Another couple, Texans, headed for Los Angeles on a whim. Offered a chance to drive a caravan car across country, they accepted. They would see California and perhaps find work there, they later explained. When they could not find jobs, however, they were ready to return home.[100]

Nothing so readily reveals the accessibility of California as the pattern of annual migration that a few families adopted. In a gigantic interstate loop, they would follow the cotton crop through Texas, Arizona, and into California, returning home at the end of the year. A group of lumber workers and their families maintained a different annual circuit, journeying each year from their homes in eastern Oklahoma to a mill town in northern California where they were assured regular seasonal employment.[101]

The actual trip west posed few problems for most migrants. Families left home in all sorts of conveyances. Some rode on trains and buses, others

Figure 5. Bound for California, 1938. Journalists pounced on scenes that showed the migrants to be quaint and colorful. (*Dorothea Lange, © 1982, The Oakland Museum, The City of Oakland*)

hopped freights or hitch-hiked. And quite a few paid a fee, typically ten dollars, for space in a car going to California.[102] The largest number, however, set out in their own automobiles, and usually the trip was fast and uneventful. In a good car families could make it to California in as little as three days. Nights were spent either in auto courts or camping by the roadside.

Many remember the trip fondly. For Jewell Morris and her sister Gladys, both in their teens when their parents decided to move to California in

1937, the trip took on the features of a vacation. "We never done no traveling back there," Jewell explains, so it was "fun" to cook and camp outside. Their father had hitched a large livestock trailer to the ten-year-old family car and piled into it every sort of family possession and several of the children as well. The rest of the nine family members rode in the car, and though it took them a week, the group reached California without mishap.[103]

Still, some encountered difficulties. Ancient vehicles broke down, families ran out of funds for food and gasoline, travelers became stranded in the Arizona desert—poverty sometimes complicated what should have been a simple journey. Flossie Haggard, mother to country-western singer Merle Haggard, tells a colorful tale of her family's trip west two years before her son's birth.

> In July, 1935, we loaded some necessary supplies onto a two wheel trailer and our 1926 model Chevrolet which Jim had overhauled. We headed for California on Route 66, as many friends and relatives had already done. We had our groceries with us—home sugar-cured bacon in a lard can, potatoes, canned vegetables, and fruit. We camped at night and I cooked in a dutch oven. The only place we didn't sleep out was in Albuquerque where we took a cabin and where I can remember bathing.

Things went well until they hit the desert. Then the car broke down.

> We were out of water, and just when I thought we weren't going to make it, I saw this boy coming down the highway on a bicycle. He was going all the way from Kentucky to Fresno. He shared a quart of water with us and helped us fix the car. Everybody'd been treating us like trash, and I told this boy, "I'm glad to see there's still some decent folks left in this world."[104]

The Haggards made it to California in four days, but for others the trip sometimes took longer. Those who ran out of money had to find jobs before they could continue. Heading west in 1937 with his family of six in a 1929 Hudson, Marvin Montgomery found that the car was using so much gas and oil that "I got to where I had to blindfold it to get it past a filling station." When the car finally broke down, the family had to spend five weeks picking cotton in Arizona to get enough money to continue on towards California.[105] Others made the same stop intentionally, planning their itinerary to coincide with the Arizona cotton-picking season in order to make some money en route. In some cases the brief layover in that state turned into an unplanned stay lasting months and even years. Arizona acquired thousands of new citizens that way. Singer Buck Owens's parents set out for California in 1937 only to have to stop in Mesa, Arizona. Fourteen years later, Owens finally reached California.[106]

However long it took, the trip west was usually not the ordeal that so many popular accounts have made it out to be. It was not the journey itself which posed a challenge to the Southwesterners who decided to go to California during the Depression decade; it was what they would find when they got there.They were arriving at a time when California was beset by serious political as well as economic problems, some of which the migrants would unwittingly aggravate. Their struggle to make a living and in some cases new homes for themselves would prove far more difficult than they expected.

2

The Limits of Opportunity

CALIFORNIA IS A PUZZLE OF MANY PIECES. IN TOPOGRAPHY, ECONOMY, AND culture it duplicates much of the scope and diversity of the nation as a whole. Americans knew best the two metropolitan centers, which by the start of the Depression had still not resolved their contest for leadership of the state. San Francisco, the old commercial capital, maintained what passed for history in California. Rebuilt a scant twenty-five years earlier, after the great earthquake and fire, it had the architecture of a city caught between past and present, between Victorian buildings and skyscrapers, happiest perhaps with the neo-classic grandeur of its "City Beautiful" era civic center. Its economy and social structure read similarly. It was a city of trade, finance, and manufacturing, of white gloves and blue collars, of old wealth and tough labor unions, a city whose proudest days were now behind it. Los Angeles belonged to a different era, the age of automobiles, stucco, and film. The prototype sunbelt city, it answered San Francisco's historicism with unreflective modernism. Sprawling, unconventional, it knew little of charm or tradition. Mad population growth had been until the 1930s its dominating concern.[1]

The two major cities, however, could only begin to suggest the scope and scale of the state. The newcomer to California might also choose between an array of nonmetropolitan zones. Mountains claimed the eastern and northern parts of the state, offering their residents an economy based on lumber, mining, and, by the 1930s, the beginnings of dam building and recreation. Deserts occupied the southeastern corner. Still in the early stages of tourist appreciation, they remained a refuge for part of California's Native American population and for the various seekers and wanderers who valued isolation.[2]

Then there were the valleys. Source of food and fiber, here was the driving force in the California economy, producing more agricultural wealth than any other state in the union. The state's coastal and transverse mountains subdivide the alluvial landscape into a number of discrete plains and valleys, each with somewhat specialized agricultural capacities, some of them no longer realized today. They begin in the south with the Imperial Valley, a desert turned into a year-round vegetable garden with water diverted from the Colorado River. Next comes the Los Angeles basin, already by the 1930s beginning to cut down the orange groves that had made southern California famous. Further north the plains and valleys of the Central Coast yielded lemons, avocados, peas and a dozen other vegetables. Lettuce ruled the Salinas Valley, though sugar beets and other row crops thrived as well. The Santa Clara Valley now produces silicon and suburbs but knew mostly fruits and nuts until World War II. The Napa and Sonoma valleys, north of San Francisco Bay, have been more consistent. Vineyards were important in the 1930s, but shared the landscape with apples and other orchard products. The state's giant Central Valley had no need to specialize. A 450-mile-long trough that is watered by the Sacramento River in the north and the San Joaquin in the south, this is the mother lode of California agriculture, capable of commercially producing more than a hundred different crops, everything "but coffee and boll weevils," the boosters insisted.[3]

The people of California echoed some of the diversity of economy and landscape, though not in the same measure as today. The state's population in 1930 was overwhelmingly white and American-born. Blacks, Asians, and indigenous Americans together comprised less than 5 percent of the population; persons of Mexican ancestry accounted for another 6 percent. Foreign-born whites claimed an additional 14 percent, and children of immigrants another 14 percent. Still, the state sustained a reputation for heterogeneity, partly because of the large variety of racial and ethnic groups and partly because observers also had in mind the enormous volume of migration from other states. California, they liked to say, was a society of strangers. Two-thirds of the population and three-quarters of the adults had come from somewhere else, mostly from other parts of the United States, and mostly within the last decade or two.[4]

The population mix and especially the drama of population growth figured strongly in the outlooks and institutions making up California's regional culture. Here we move into a subject of many dimensions. To speak of California's culture is to raise first the question of *which* California and then to stumble into a thicket of mythic images, most of which assert the state's unique relationship to American civilization. Ever since the Englishman James Lord Bryce visited in the 1880s and devoted a chapter of his influential *American Commonwealth* to the proposition that "California more than any other part of the Union is a country by itself," residents have enjoyed the notion that they and their state stand apart.[5] An enormous literature has been devoted to this proposition, the impact of which may well have been self-fulfilling. Certainly by the 1950s there was reason to pay attention to novelist Wallace Stegner's assertion that California was the cutting edge of a mass-culture-driven consumer society:

> In a prosperous country we are more prosperous than most; in an urban country more urban than most; in a gadget-happy country more addicted to gadgets; in a mobile country more mobile; in a tasteless country more tasteless; in a creative country more energetically creative; in an optimistic society more optimistic; in an anxious society more anxious.[6]

But these are imprecise descriptions, and may or may not have applied equally to the 1930s, a time when California still seemed more a curiosity than a cultural powerhouse to most Americans. We can do better by examining some of the historically consistent perspectives that Californians, despite their diversity, have been said to share. First was the spirit of optimism, a gift of the benign history that Kevin Starr describes in his continuing studies of the "California Dream." The confluence of event and myth that began with the Gold Rush convinced residents and would-be residents that California was a lucky place, a land of opportunity and good fortune. It was a powerful belief, underlying many of the accomplishments of the state, and equally potent when threatened.[7]

The second outlook was a posture of openness towards newcomers and new social experience. As late as the 1960s, California retained something of the aspect of a permanent frontier, ever engaged in the business of absorbing new peoples. Fluidity was both the state's major challenge and in flush times its operative solution. California communities accepted the turn-over of population as a natural condition, accommodating newcomers —with some important exceptions—with an ease and tolerance other parts of the country often still had to learn. The exceptions were mostly the standard ones for Americans, based, that is, on race. The small nonwhite populations and the larger Hispanic group realized little of the tolerance that whites, even the foreign-born, found notable. And especially during times of economic difficulty, the uncertain stability of this society of strangers revealed itself in mass campaigns of race hatred, the community of hatred sufficing when other sources failed.[8]

The third perspective has been less frequently noted by those who examine the ways of the Golden State. It concerns a commitment to progress and sophistication, to urbane if not always urban standards of culture. This may be the one really inflexible standard Californians set for themselves, and it is the matter that most determined relations with Southwesterners. The outlook was evident as early as the 1850s in the confident exertions of brand-new San Francisco, an "instant city" convinced from the outset of its greatness. The early role of New Englanders may have been decisive. Gentility softening into an urbane worldview was their special contribution. Californians, despite their isolation, would never succumb to provincial backwardness. Even rural California insisted on up-to-date outlooks. The booster spirit that raged throughout small-town America in the late nineteenth century seems to have lasted longer in California as rural areas continued to absorb population through the first half of the twentieth. And even where growth slowed, the commercial, informational, and political links between metropolitan and nonmetropolitan worlds were so well developed that rural Californians rarely lost their commitment to keeping up, if sometimes selectively, with urban trends.[9]

Prosperity, of course, was central to the urbane outlook. So was the state's relationship after the turn of the century to the consumer revolution. Hollywood pushed southern California and to a lesser extent the state as a whole to the forefront of that great change in mentality, teaching the pleasures of fad and fashion, imprinting the fear of falling behind, establishing the religion of the "new." Californians thus became consummate modernists. In the absence of a shared past, they embraced the future. The conviction that the future was unfolding around them became one of the myths that held them together.

Two Migrant Streams

Southwesterners filtered quite selectively into California's various settings in the 1930s. Since 1900 the orientation of most newcomers to California had been strongly metropolitan, that being the way of the twentieth century. Los Angeles, followed by the San Francisco Bay Area, had attracted the largest share of foreign and interstate migration, including most of the Southwesterners who entered California during the first three decades of this century. The 1930s migrants, however, were different. In a major departure from standard migration patterns, almost half (48.4 percent) settled in nonmetropolitan areas of the state.

The distribution had much to do with previous background. People from urban areas of the Southwest followed customary patterns. Census data show that 79 percent of those who had lived in large Southwestern cities in 1935 settled in either Los Angeles, the Bay Area, or San Diego. The destinations of migrants of rural background were different. Like farm people elsewhere during the problem 1930s, these rural Southwesterners shied away from large cities, choosing instead the more familiar settings of California's agricultural valleys. Sixty-nine percent of all migrants who had lived on farms in 1935 made that choice, along with about 50 percent of those from towns and small cities. So pronounced is the correlation between origin and destination that it becomes necessary to talk of two separate streams of migration from the Western South: one from the cities of the region to the metropolitan areas of California, the other from the distressed rural areas to the fertile valleys of the state.[10]

Los Angeles was far and away the most important destination of those intent on settling in one of California's major urban areas. Census figures reveal that nearly 100,000 Oklahomans, Texans, Arkansans, and Missourians settled there during the second half of the 1930s, and we may presume that several tens of thousands of others had preceded them in the more difficult early years of the decade. Much less popular were the Bay Area and San Diego, which together attracted only about one-quarter of the metropolitan-oriented newcomers.

If Los Angeles was the main draw for Southwesterners interested in the big cities, the San Joaquin Valley lured the rural-oriented. The southern and most populous half of the Central Valley, the San Joaquin attracted more than 70,000 Southwesterners between 1935 and 1940, 60 percent of all migrants settling in the nonmetropolitan areas. The numbers piled up heaviest at the southern end of the valley, especially in Kern County where an economy based on cotton and oil echoed Oklahoma and Texas.[11]

Map 4 provides a closer look at the destinations of migrants from the Western South. A quick glance indicates the heavy concentrations in Los Angeles and the San Joaquin Valley. Two-thirds of the Depression-era inflow went to those two areas. We might almost suspect there were but two signposts on Highway 66, the road that brought most families west. Migrants either stayed on that highway all the way to Los Angeles or turned off at Barstow and followed the still partially unpaved road that led over the Tehachapi Mountains into the valley of the San Joaquin.

The signposts actually posed a fateful choice. Los Angeles and the San Joaquin Valley offered different futures. Not just economic prospects but the social dynamics of resettlement would take shape differently in the two settings. In Los Angeles (and the other metropolitan areas) the structures of opportunity for white newcomers from the Western South were relatively diverse. Part of a much larger stream of interstate migrants, Southwesterners would for the most part follow a rather conventional pathway of economic and social adjustment. Encountering few situations which inspired distinguishing behaviors, in short order they would be absorbed into a complex metropolitan landscape that had long since learned the high art of population ingestion.

MIGRANT DESTINATIONS 1935-1940

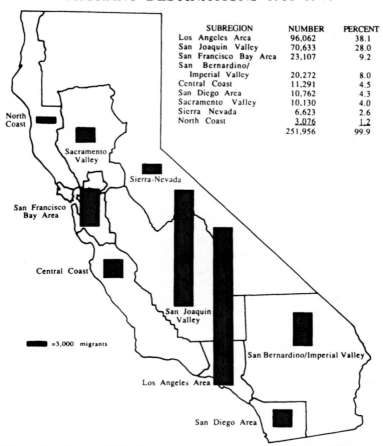

SUBREGION	NUMBER	PERCENT
Los Angeles Area	96,062	38.1
San Joaquin Valley	70,633	28.0
San Francisco Bay Area	23,107	9.2
San Bernardino/ Imperial Valley	20,272	8.0
Central Coast	11,291	4.5
San Diego Area	10,762	4.3
Sacramento Valley	10,130	4.0
Sierra Nevada	6,623	2.6
North Coast	3,076	1.2
	251,956	99.9

North Coast

Sacramento Valley

Sierra-Nevada

San Francisco Bay Area

Central Coast

San Joaquin Valley

■ =3,000 migrants

San Bernardino/Imperial Valley

Los Angeles Area

San Diego Area

Map 4. Residence in 1940 of Southwesterners moving to California, 1935–40. Data from Donald J. Bogue, Henry S. Shryock, and Siegfried A. Hoermann, *Subregional Migration in the United States, 1935–1940*, Vol. 1, table 1.

California's Okie subculture is primarily a product of the other destination, the state's agricultural counties, especially the San Joaquin Valley.
There the opportunities and obstacles dictated a more exceptional pattern of adjustment. There, instead of dispersion and absorption, much
of the group would be channeled into situations that reinforced their ties
to one another. In the limited economic structures of the valleys they

would find job opportunities largely in one stigmatized occupational category—farm labor. From that would flow patterns of residential congregation and habits of social separation which in turn would provide the medium for the preservation of certain features of the migrants' regional culture.

Los Angeles

Southwesterners made up less than a quarter of the interstate migrants settling in Los Angeles during the Depression decade. Despite an overall reduction in the volume of migration since the 1920s, people continued coming to southern California, 40 percent from the Midwest, 18 percent from the Far West, 14 percent from the Northeast, 5 percent from the Eastern South, and 23 percent from Oklahoma, Texas, Arkansas, and Missouri.[12]

As a group, Southwestern adults tended to be slightly younger, their families slightly larger, and their educational level slightly behind that of other newcomers. Some of these differences are attributable to the fact that Southwesterners included somewhat more farmers (23 percent compared with 11 percent of other migrants) and somewhat fewer previous residents of metropolitan areas (42 percent versus 51 percent). In short, migrants from the Western South included larger representations of rural and small-town folk than did the migrants from other regions. Still the distinctions were not as significant as the similarities. Southwesterners settling in the cities fell mostly into step with both the look and the adjustment patterns of other newcomers.[13]

Which is not to say that resettlement came easily. It is never a simple proposition for a family to reestablish itself in a new locale, particularly half a continent removed. And rarely has there been a worse time to attempt such a move than during the 1930s. For its part, Los Angeles was probably neither the best nor the worst city in which to try to make a new start. Equipped with an unusual urban economy based on film, tourism, oil, and agriculture as well as manufacturing and trade, the city emerged from the trough of the Depression in better shape than many major metropolitan areas. Still, recovering from an unemployment rate which had peaked near 30 percent in early 1933 was a slow and uncertain process. Joblessness, homelessness, and associated problems plagued Los Angeles throughout the decade, necessitating massive relief expenditures by local, state, and federal agencies. The summer of 1935 found nearly 350,000 residents, roughly 15 percent of the population, dependent on public assistance programs, and it can be assumed that an additional 5 percent were unemployed without assistance. Five years later as the decade drew to a close, the city still counted one in seven members of the labor force (14 percent) unemployed. With numbers like that, Los Angeles was not going to be an easy place to make a new home.[14]

The difficulties started with the initial drive into the city. Few Southwesterners, not even those from metropolitan settings, had ever seen anything like Los Angeles. Spread thinly over 450 square miles, geographically one of the largest cities in the world, Los Angeles appeared to most visitors as endless, incomprehensible suburban sprawl. "The map of the city," observed one writer, "resembles nothing so much as an amoeba gone berserk."[15] And he was referring only to the city proper, merely half the story. More than a million of the metropolitan area's 2.3 million residents lived outside the city limits in dozens of suburban communities spread over still greater territories.[16]

To those experiencing the vastness of this metropolitan landscape for the first time, the effect was staggering. Melvin Shahan recalled his first disorienting journey through the endless chain of suburbs. Coming from the little town of Guymon, Oklahoma, population 3,000, it was like "going into an entirely different world. . . . It seemed like you could drive forever and never get out of a town."[17] Woody Guthrie, no stranger to cities, was first awestruck then intimidated as he hitch-hiked through the outer rings of Los Angeles.

> I'll see the Pacific Ocean, go swimming, and flop on the beach. I'll go to Chinatown and look around. I'll see the Mexican section. I'll see the whole works. But no, I don't know. Los Angeles is too big for me. I'm too little for Los Angeles.[18]

Wofford and Ruth Clark had spent most of their lives in Oklahoma City, but they too were unprepared for Los Angeles. Heading for the downtown area because "we didn't know where else to go," they could not believe all the people and traffic. They felt "scared and sick." The city was just too immense."It was terrible. . . . All these millions of people out here." By the end of their first day they were almost ready to return home.

Confusion was only part of the experience. Some of what the Clarks saw as they drove into Los Angeles for the first time on a late November day was thrilling. Ruth Clark remembers the Christmas decorations and the spectacular displays in the downtown stores. Even more exciting were the flowers everywhere."What really made me happy," she recalled, "was coming out and seeing the flowers in November and December. Oh, I just loved those flowers."[19]

The Clarks' mixture of confusion and wonder was typical of many first impressions. The city's size was disorienting, but there were also marvelous things to see. Some drove straight through Los Angeles, all the way to the beach for their first glimpse of an ocean. What a thrill to stand on Santa Monica Pier and feel the Pacific pounding underneath. Others had to find

Hollywood or buy a crate of oranges on their first day. There were many ways to sample California's legendary attractions.[20]

More serious concerns soon asserted themselves. With but thirty dollars and a hungry child, the Clarks knew the priorities. "The first place you see with a rent sign, we'll stop and give it a look," Mrs. Clark instructed her husband. Fortunately, lodging was reasonably easy to find in Los Angeles. Thanks to the previous decade's tourist boom, the boulevards leading into the city were lined with auto courts, forerunners of today's motels. Many were used as semipermanent housing during the 1930s. For as little as $10 a month a family could rent a one-room, kitchenless, bathroomless cabin. Usually this would serve as a temporary stopping place while they looked for better quarters. Sometimes, however, that same cabin became home for several years.[21]

Southern California's famous bungalows offered another type of housing for those who could afford them. A nice cottage renting for $25 to $40 a month was probably beyond the means of anyone without a steady job, but apartments might be found for less, especially in the poorer neighborhoods. Many newcomers turned to the racially mixed and run-down sections of central and east Los Angeles and to the belt of white working-class suburbs immediately to the south of the city in their search for housing. The central city neighborhoods were anything but attractive. A 1937 housing study noted that although Los Angeles lacked the density of eastern cities, certain areas were almost as squalid as the deteriorating sections of older cities. The Clarks found their first apartment in such a neighborhood. "We were lost. We just took what we could get," Ruth Clark explained. What they got was a roach-infested flat and neighbors who were mostly "foreigners." They were not happy. Even though they had come from one of the Southwest's major cities, the congestion and the racial and ethnic diversity of Los Angeles were new and disturbing.[22]

People accustomed to life in smaller communities were often still more uncomfortable. An elderly Oklahoman, his comments betraying his unfamiliarity with the world of street signs and address numbers, took one look down a street of identically shaped houses and observed that "You'd have to be right sober to find your home if you lived on this here street." Beyond that, "they're too close together . . . we-uns from Oklahoma has got to have room for chickens, a garden, and a rabbit hutch or two."[23] Younger migrants, even those of rural origins, knew better, but still the close quarters sometimes bothered them. Frank Manies, who had grown up on farms and lived almost all of his twenty-five years in low-density settings, found even the relatively uncongested beach community of Santa Monica too crowded for his liking. A mechanic by trade, he remembers feeling "like I didn't have the freedom to get out and pound on fenders or do what I wanted to do."[24] If some missed the spaciousness, others longed for the social familiarity of small-town life and found the impersonal relations of the city disheartening. Wanda Shahan concluded that neighbors in her new community of Compton were "very unfriendly":

> It took us quite a while to get used to the fact that we lived on a block with people we didn't even know. We didn't know who they were, and they didn't even care who we were. They didn't want to get acquainted. They had their own lives to live, and they weren't interested in being neighbors with you.[25]

But difficulties such as these should not be overemphasized. Symptoms of urban shock of the kind students of migration sometimes record were unusual. Partly that was because of the migrants' background. Few were completely naïve about the elements of modern urban civilization. Most of the rural Southwest had been learning important lessons about city life from films, magazines, radio, schools, and automobile trips. And those who were not prepared, principally the backcountry inhabitants of some of the more isolated Ozark areas, were unlikely to head for Los Angeles.[26]

Equally important, the city they had chosen offered little of the highrise intensity and ethnic complexity which complicated the adjustment experiences of rural Americans following other migration streams. Its decentralized layout, low-profile architecture, and preponderance of detached single-family housing made Los Angeles the least urbanized of all the nation's major metropolitan areas: "an enormous village," wrote Louis Adamic.[27] Likewise its ethnic mix proved less intimidating than the cities of the industrial North or even northern California would have. Los Angeles in the 1930s was, as one report put it, the "most American of all our great cities." Fully three-quarters of its population were American-born whites, mostly transplanted Midwesterners. Compared with most metropolitan settings, the social and spatial dimensions of this one posed few challenges.[28]

The chief obstacles were economic. Would they be able to find work? In the job-scarce climate of the 1930s, it depended variously on skills, connections, determination, and luck. Once the worst had ended and the economy began its post-1933 recovery, certain skills came back into demand. Professionals and white-collar workers typically had fewer problems than most finding work. Robert Kessler was selling tractors within a few weeks of arriving in the outlying community of Redlands in 1934. A clever salesman, his son recalls, "he seemed to have a knack to run onto good deals all the time." Before long he was running his own sales office and had moved the family into a beautiful rented home, complete with a forty-acre orange grove.[29]

Some experienced blue-collar workers fared almost as well. Jess Williams, an Oklahoman who had tried his hand at both cow punching and oil work before drifting west in the early thirties, got a job first helping to build the giant Boulder Dam on the Colorado River. After that his experience with earth-moving equipment helped him to get steady work on construction projects in the L.A. area.[30] Similarly in demand were experienced workers in aircraft or auto assembly, those being the two most rapidly expanding sectors of southern California manufacturing. Jobs in construction or oil—the most common blue-collar backgrounds for Southwesterners—were harder to come by, since neither industry regained its pre-Depression employment levels until World War II. The month that one young carpenter spent trying to find a job in his trade was probably standard; some looked much longer.[31]

Those without specific skills faced greater problems still. Unskilled laboring jobs and semi-skilled positions either in factories or in transportation were the most glutted of all in L.A.'s Depression-weakened economy. Many Southwesterners, including most who had come directly from farms, struggled to find any sort of work. To get by during the first precarious months, a number looked for casual laboring jobs, hiring out on a day-to-day basis on short construction projects, digging ditches, clearing fields, or picking fruit in the area's still numerous citrus groves. Art Williams, who had farmed, worked for the railroad, driven trucks, and even for a time owned his own business back in Oklahoma, went through a succession of casual labor jobs at minimal wages when he first arrived in the Los Angeles area. He fumigated orange trees, worked in a lemon-packing house, tried gardening, and then did part-time work in a service station before finally finding steady employment in construction.[32]

For those with marketable skills and even more for those without, personal connections were often the key to obtaining steady employment. More critical than in times of full employment and loose hiring procedures, networks of personal relationships determined much about the economic adjustment experiences of individual migrants. Those without them were likely to have the hardest time finding jobs or for that matter learning their way around the city. Indeed, the likelihood is strong that few besides the very adventurous or the very confident dared to settle in an unfamiliar city without knowing someone beforehand. Sherman Coleman knew little besides farming when he left Missouri at age twenty in 1936, but he had an uncle and cousin in California both working in the Southern Pacific Railroad yards in the town of Colton, east of Los Angeles. Within a month they got him a job as a laborer in the shop and six months later he was an apprentice mechanic, building refrigerator cars. He was not the only one to benefit from such connections. Three-quarters of the 800 men who worked in that shop were Southwesterners, Coleman estimates, "most of them all relatives . . . uncles, fathers, sons . . . everybody knew everybody." For years much of the hiring had depended upon family ties.[33]

Melvin Shahan's father also found personal connections helpful. After several months of casual labor, he took the advice of a couple of old friends from Guymon and applied for work with the Los Angeles streetcar company. With their help and a good deal of persistence he soon had a job as a conductor.[34] For Frank Manies, who had trained as a mechanic in the Civilian Conservation Corps (CCC) but had yet to work at the trade, membership in the Seventh-Day Adventist Church opened the door to employment. After a full month of scouring Santa Monica for work, his funds nearly depleted, he got lucky. A church member heard of his plight and offered him a position at his Buick dealership.[35]

Personal contacts, however, were not always an aid to economic advancement. The jobs to which friends or relations had access could also funnel newcomers into poorly paid, dead-end occupations. This is precisely what happened to so many of the migrants who settled in the agricultural valleys. Many followed personal connections that provided easy access to farm labor jobs, an occupational category which in significant ways became a social and economic trap. Frank Manies in time escaped, but for two years he set aside his mechanic's training in order to join his brother-in-law doing agricultural work in the San Joaquin Valley. Another Oklahoman made the same choice. When he came to California in 1938, he was "thinking of some kind of factory work." But his father was working the crops, so the young man stayed on until World War II finally opened the doors to a new occupational world. Thousands of others, including many with developed industrial skills, were similarly drawn into the fields and canneries because that is where their personal contacts, so vital in those difficult times, led.[36]

Women sometimes worked for wages too. Opportunities, however, were generally more restricted in the 1930s than in previous decades as public opinion rallied around the primacy of the male breadwinner. What openings there were typically were limited to such traditional female preserves as clerical, service, and extremely low-wage factory and food processing work. Equally traditional, most of the female wage earners in the migrant group were single, divorced, or widowed. Census takers found 38 percent of Southwestern women in these marital categories employed, but only 12 percent of married women. This breakdown of employment and marital status differed little from that of other white women in California's metropolitan areas.[37]

Married women generally worked outside the home only in the case of exceptional need or exceptional opportunity. Lucinda Coffman found herself responsible for earning most of the family income shortly after arriving in southern California in 1937. A grandmother with several younger children still in tow and a couple of married ones living nearby, she took charge because her husband's health prevented him from working regularly. Initially she worked in a pea-packing plant, and later took a job as a maid in a Fullerton home near where she lived. All the while, like Ma Joad in Steinbeck's novel, she held her multi-generational family together, a source of strength and leadership now recalled proudly by younger family members.[38]

As Robert and Helen Lynd discovered in their follow-up study of Middletown, Depression-era emergencies sometimes brought about changes in work roles and family authority systems. But there is little evidence that this was particularly widespread among the Dust Bowl migrants. Women like Lucinda Coffman were the exception in both metropolitan and valley contexts. Families often pulled together to meet the special challenges of resettlement, all members contributing perhaps more deliberately than ever before to the family's well-being. But the stresses and strains seem to have intensified old rather than fashioned new patterns of family organization. Male authority and responsibility for income remained the rule.[39]

Those who found work quickly usually encountered few resettlement difficulties. But many did not find work. And life then could become quite complicated. Despite the state's reputation for generosity, newcomers who had been in California less than a year were ineligible for most kinds of public assistance. Except for the two-year period between 1933 and 1935, when the Federal Transient Bureaus were providing cash assistance to migrants, those in need could expect help from public relief agencies only if they agreed to return to their home state. But many rejected those terms. "We try to send them back home," a social worker explained, "but they won't go. It's better to starve here for a year with a home here than to return to nothing where they came from."[40]

A Missouri couple were among those who sought desperately to remain. In 1936, Mrs. Austin wrote to President Roosevelt pleading for help but begging not to be sent home since "there is nothing there for us." Explaining that her husband "walks from morning till night trying to find some [work] to do," and reminding the President of his promise that "no one will go hungry or with out shelter," she begged him to "help us get work or relief but we prefer work afore anything if there is a way to get work." Whether or not her plea was answered is not recorded, but the couple's plight illustrates the kind of difficulties that some newcomers faced in their first year in Los Angeles.[41]

Provided they passed the first year's test, the means of support then steadily improved. At least they would be eligible for public assistance, either a monthly check from the State Relief Administration or a job with the WPA. How many were forced to rely on these services is difficult to determine. Census figures from the end of the decade indicate that unemployment rates among Southwesterners were comparable to those of the general population: 17 and 16 percent respectively for males in the labor force. Another 17 percent of Southwestern males seem to have been

Table 2.1. Occupational and Income Distribution for Males in the Metropolitan Labor Force, 1940*

	Southwestern Migrants 1935–40	Other Migrants	Pre-1935 Southwesterners	Other White Californians	Hispanics/ Nonwhites
Professionals/ proprietors/ managers	13%	21%	19%	26%	13%
Clerical/sales/ police and fire	13	19	20	21	7
Craftsmen/ foremen	22	21	24	20	9
Operatives	22	19	20	17	15
Service workers	9	8	7	6	24
Laborers (non-agr.)	14	9	9	9	22
Farm labor	8	3	1	2	10
	101%	100%	100%	101%	100%
N =	(399)	(1,334)	(986)	(10,223)	(1,079)
Occupational index	3.3	3.7	3.7	3.8	3.0
Median individual income**	$850	$950	$1,400	$1,375	$755
Median family income**	$1,145	$1,460	$1,720	$1,770	$985

*Military personnel and family farm workers omitted from occupational sample.

**Wage and salary income only. Individuals without wage or salary income were eliminated from the income calculations, as were families without a male wage or salary earner.

Source: 1940 Census Public Use Microdata Sample (see appendix A).

underemployed, reporting less than 35 weeks' work in 1939. Approximately one-third of the group thus would have been eligible for relief assistance at least part of the year. We can assume that the number actually using those services was quite a bit smaller.[42]

The Census Public Use Microdata Sample allows a more comprehensive look at the economic adjustment experiences of Southwestern newcomers (see Table 2.1). The overall picture is one of progress. By 1940, a substantial majority of newcomers to Los Angeles and the other metropolitan centers had attained the basic goals which had brought them to California: a job and an improved standard of living. Eighty-three percent of adult males eligible to work were employed. Most worked with their hands; only about a quarter held white-collar positions. However, blue-collar workers were distributed fairly evenly between skilled, semi-skilled, and unskilled occupations. Incomes also varied. A few were rich, while roughly one family in five made $2,000 or more in 1939, a figure which should have provided close to a middle-class standard of living. More significant, 60 percent of all households had earned at least the $972 that social welfare experts deemed a "health and decency" budget for a family of 4.5 persons. Three-quarters earned the $780 per annum that the State Relief Administration considered "minimum subsistence" and most of the rest probably reached that same income level with the help of public assistance programs.[43]

Compared with what they had left behind, all this was impressive. If we are correct in assuming that the migrants were drawn disproportionately from unemployed and underemployed sectors of the home-state populations, then most had gained some ground during their few years in California. By 1940, the median income for Southwesterners recently settled in California metropolitan areas exceeded that of the resident population of the Southwest's cities, and a much smaller percentage of the California settlers languished below the subsistence income line.[44] Presuming that many of the migrants had formerly been part of that least fortunate urban class and that another portion had come from the still more destitute ranks of rural folk, this means that the years in California had boosted incomes and doubtless also spirits. Certainly that was true for Sherman Coleman. His three years in California had brought him not only a steady income at a job he enjoyed but also a brand-new car and a new love. Soon to be married, he closed out the Depression era in 1940 with one last trip back to Missouri. It was his way of saying goodbye.[45]

Impressive in its own terms, the economic situation of Southwesterners was somewhat less so when compared with other segments of the population. Southwestern newcomers (those settling in California after March 1935) were more concentrated at the low end of both the occupational and income scales than white long-term residents of metropolitan California. Males in the migrant group held roughly half the proportion of white-collar positions and earned a median individual wage and salary income less than two-thirds that of the resident group ($850 compared with $1,375). Nor did their economic standing approach that of Southwesterners who had settled in California before 1935. These earlier settlers, most of them residents since the teens and twenties, were essentially indistinguishable from the rest of the established white population. Only in comparison with Hispanics, Asians, and blacks—groups plagued by severe racial discrimination—did the migrants' economic performance look good.

None of this, of course, is the least bit surprising. It stands to reason that newcomers will face disadvantages in the job market. A more revealing comparison is with migrants from other parts of the country. An index of group occupational status will aid the analysis. It uses a five-point scale where farm workers are counted as 1; unskilled laborers as 2; semi-skilled operatives and service work other than police and fire protection as 3; skilled labor, clerical work, sales, and protection service as 4; and professionals, proprietors, managers, officials, and farmers as 5.[46]

Though the differences were not dramatic, migrants from other parts of the country fared better than Southwesterners. Occupationally the other migrants included more white-collar workers and fewer unskilled laborers, resulting in an index (3.7) that was closer to the resident white population (3.8) than to newcomers from the Western South (3.3). On the other hand, unemployment rates and wage and salary incomes of the two newcomer groups were less discrepant. The $950 median income for individual male earners from other regions was higher than the $850 annual earnings of Southwesterners but nowhere near the $1,375 median level of resident white males.

The census data thus indicate that newcomers in general remained economically disadvantaged by the close of the 1930s and that Southwesterners lagged further behind than most. This was even more true, as we will see, in the valleys, where dramatic occupational differences between Southwesterners and other whites became the norm.

What explains the poorer showing of migrants from this region? Differential job skills had something to do with the pattern. The Bureau of Agricultural Economics's massive survey of interstate migrants disclosed a larger representation of former farmers and unskilled and semi-skilled laborers among Southwesterners than other newcomer groups. Moreover, census data reveal a definite lag in educational background. Forty percent of Southwesterners settling in metropolitan areas never entered high school, compared with 23 percent of other migrants.[47] This may not explain all of the difference, for, as we will see, Southwesterners remain to this day somewhat behind other whites in economic performance. Economic discrimination and particularistic job networks clearly played a role in some settings—most notably the valleys. Cultural understandings also had bearing on economic performance. As will become clearer later, many of the migrants embraced standards of ambition that led more naturally into blue-collar rather than white-collar job sectors.

All this may be tangential. Though it is important to understand what distinguished Southwesterners from other migrants, the more salient feature of these economic profiles is the essential similarity in the experiences of all white newcomers in the metropolitan areas. The increased concentration in blue-collar positions shown by Southwestern migrants was an incidental distinction; the fact is that the majority of all interstate migrants—and resident whites as well—found themselves in that occupational class. Indeed, nothing about their initial years in metropolitan California made Southwestern newcomers distinct in any important way, any more than their predecessors had been in previous decades. Both had found jobs in all sorts of industries and in a considerable range of statuses, dispersing widely throughout the complex economy of the big cities.

Residential dispersion was also the rule. No substantial neighborhood concentrations of Southwesterners were to be found in the metropolitan areas at the close of the 1930s. The overwhelming blue-collar composition of the group did lead to overrepresentation in lower-priced neighborhoods, especially in some of the newer subdivisions that sold cheap cottages or undeveloped lots to white working-class families in the late thirties. The largest and best known of these was Bell Gardens, an unincorporated community just south of L.A. city limits, which by 1940, seven years after it was first subdivided, boasted a population of nearly 14,000 people. Advertisements were aimed at poorer families hungry for property of their own and anxious to escape the more densely populated and racially diverse city neighborhoods:

$20 DOWN, AND $10 A MONTH!
Good schools, Churches, Race restricted. Transportation. Outside city limits. Rich sandy-loam soil. Deep wells; fine water at $1.25 a month. Ideal climate. Sunshine, fresh air, room for children to grow. Give their eager hands something to do and make fine citizens of them.[48]

Many Southwesterners who had attained at least a modest income found the combination highly attractive, but so did a large number of others in their economic circumstances. A 1938 survey of the community by sociologist Charles Spaulding disclosed that 21 percent of Bell Garden's adults were Southwesterners. This was the nearest thing to an Okie enclave in 1930s Los Angeles. Not until World War II would metropolitan California witness any substantial examples of residential concentration, and even then Southwesterners never became a clearly defined population group.[49]

The San Joaquin Valley

The experience of those who settled in the state's agricultural areas, and especially in the San Joaquin Valley, was quite different. Occupational options, financial conditions, residential distribution, and the response of the rest of the population all combined to highlight and isolate the migrant group. The process was rooted first and foremost in the economic structure of these settings. With nowhere near the range of work prospects enjoyed by metropolitan settlers, migrants who made their way into California's valleys were funneled primarily into farm labor, where low wages and social disesteem created lasting obstacles to interaction with the rest of society.

A few end-of-the-decade census numbers will help to establish the contrast between the metropolitan and nonmetropolitan experiences. In the

San Joaquin Valley the median 1939 income for families who had arrived from the Southwest in the previous four years was $650, not much more than half of the $1,145 earned by their big-city counterparts, and below the subsistence-level income used as a guide by welfare authorities. Fifty-eight percent of the recent migrants listed their occupation as farm laborers, and another 13 percent were at the time of the census engaged on WPA work relief projects, an indication that many of them also normally worked in the fields.[50]

Chosen precisely because of its familiarity—because of cotton and oil and relatives and the expectation of ready employment—the San Joaquin Valley proved stranger and more complex than most imagined. Some newcomers may have sensed this as they wound their way down from Tehachapi Pass into Kern County. The land had an odd, empty look. Everything was so vast, orderly, and vacant. Fields extended hundreds, sometimes thousands of acres, in perfect rows that gave the appearance, historian Ernesto Galarza later noted, "of being laid out with dividers and carpenter's square." And the geometry was only occasionally interrupted by signs of human habitation. "Where are the farmers?" another visitor wondered. "Where are the farmhouses?"[51]

More than miles separated the San Joaquin Valley from the rural areas these newcomers had left behind. The Western South, especially Oklahoma, scene of the spectacular land rushes of the 1880s and 1890s, had been the last great homestead frontier, the last expression of nineteenth-century democratic agrarianism. Settled at about the same time, California's valleys opened the book on what Donald Worster calls the "hydraulic frontier" and the twentieth-century's mode of professionalized agriculture.[52]

The largest and most productive of California's agricultural areas, the San Joaquin Valley was the model of that new age. Sixty years earlier, the area had been among the least populated and least economically significant sections of the state. Nature had intended the area for something other than farming, equipping the valley with rich soils but a climate and watershed good mostly for the propagation of grasses. Early man had lived gratefully on what was provided, harvesting fish and fowl from the half-dozen rivers, and seeds, acorns, deer, and small game from the valley floor. The handful of Mexican ranchers who claimed parts of the valley in the 1840s had been scarcely more intrusive. For them and the trickle of Americans who stopped on their way to the gold fields in the 1850s and 1860s, pasturage was what the valley had to offer, no longer for deer, now for cattle and sheep. Such were the limits of nature and the limits of low-capitalization rural enterprise. A different system based on the energies of large groups of men and women, collected and directed by organized capital, and responsive to the plans of various experts would be needed to bring agriculture to the valley. Before it learned the feel of the farmer's plow, the land would first know the much deeper furrow of the engineer.

The work of transformation began in the 1870s. First came the railroad builders, representing the mighty Southern Pacific, pushing their line straight down the valley, laying out towns, recruiting settlers, selling off tens of thousands of government-granted acres, opening an isolated land to the markets of the world. Close behind were the canal builders, huge land syndicates mostly, with capital to dig the miles of irrigation ditches, the political pull to claim the water, and of course the vast acreages to make it all profitable. It was a work of giant enterprise, this business of turning dry grasslands into orchards, vineyards, and productive fields, a work headquartered in San Francisco in the offices of the Kern County Land Company, the San Joaquin and Kings River Canal and Irrigation Company, Miller and Lux, Bank of California, Southern Pacific, and other major investors.[53]

The valley never lost the imprint of its corporate beginnings. Most of the land was in time sold, some in small parcels, some in large acreages, a few hundred thousand acres still maintained by the land companies today. But the mode of development dictated the basic patterns of use. Expensive to purchase and expensive to farm because of irrigation, the land demanded efficiency. Driven by costs, by potential profits, and by the guiding hand of various governmental and corporate godfathers, agriculture in this and in California's other irrigated valleys became a thoroughly modern enterprise. By the early twentieth century California farmers led the nation in their reliance on irrigation, modern equipment, chemicals, hired labor, and scientific experimentation. California led too in the rate of farm capitalization and the value of its products. In 1929, the average California farm produced crops worth two and a half times the national average, three times the Oklahoma average, and the land itself was valued at three to four times the per-acre cost of Southwestern farm land.[54]

The scale of farm operations was another distinctive feature of California agriculture. In an age not yet accustomed to the notion, California pioneered corporate farming. Among its industry leaders were multimillion-dollar companies such as the Tagus Ranch, the world's largest grower of peaches and apricots, and the DiGiorgio Corporation, which included among its international holdings 8,000 acres of Kern County vineyards and orchards employing hundreds, sometimes thousands, of workers. "Factories in the field," critic Carey McWilliams called them, and he had in mind as well the thousand or so largest privately owned farms. Whether corporate- or family-operated, California claimed more than a third of the richest farms in the country in 1929: 2,892 out of the 7,874 farms nationwide producing crops worth more than $30,000 that year.[55] Of course not all farms were large or prosperous. Statewide some 135,000 farms were in

Figure 6. Pea pickers of many backgrounds worked on this vast San Joaquin Valley ranch, 1938. (*Dorothea Lange, The Bancroft Library, Berkeley, California*)

operation in 1929, 90 percent of them yielding crops worth less than $10,000, and 30 percent earning less than the $1,000 that was the national median for all farms in 1929. But while numerous, these small and modest holdings counted for relatively little. The big operations dominated the industry, controlling more than half of the prime lands, hiring three-quarters of the wage labor, and contributing over half of the production.[56]

Whether large or small, long before the 1930s California farming had become an integrated industry governed by rules of interdependence and expertise that the nation's other farming regions were only just beginning to emulate. The fabric of coordination had initially been woven by corporate outsiders, land syndicates, water companies, railroads, canneries, and marketing concerns anxious to insure the orderly and prosperous development of their investments. Then, partly in response, the farmers had added new layers in the form of public water agencies, cooperative marketing associations, and networks of local and regional growers' organizations, many operating under the umbrella of the state Farm Bureau.

Organization proceeded unevenly, varying according to crop. Citrus and raisin growing were by the 1930s tightly integrated. Cooperatives not only handled marketing but assumed responsibility for various production tasks. Cotton was less organized, but with four firms ginning two-thirds of the crop, it was centralized far beyond the understanding of Southwestern farmers. Operating through industry forums such as the San Joaquin Valley Agricultural Labor Bureau and maintaining discipline through the financial leverage of crop loans, the ginners, finance companies, and corporate growers insured product uniformity (only highest-quality Acala cotton was permitted in California), expanded or contracted production, and organized the labor market, annually determining the wage rates for chopping and picking.[57]

Modern agriculture supported a complex social structure. Strictly speaking, the San Joaquin Valley by 1930 was no longer a rural area. Despite the preeminence of agriculture, most of the population neither lived nor worked on farms. Agriculture directly employed 38 percent of the labor force with another 10 percent counted in ancillary activities such as food processing, trucking, and transport, and financial and management services. A vigorous oil industry, a smaller mining sector, and a few manufacturing concerns employed some of the remainder, but most of the nonfarm jobs were in construction, commerce, and services—sectors that were closely tied to the health of the region's primary industry.[58]

If less than half of the valley's 540,000 residents in 1930 earned their livelihood directly from agriculture, only a third of the population lived on the farms that drove the economy. The majority lived in towns, many of them bustling service communities of several thousand residents (see Map 5). The area also boasted four medium-sized cities: Stockton, the valley's gateway to the Pacific, with 47,000 people; Modesto, focal point for the orchards and dairies of the northern valley and home to 13,000; Fresno, the valley's central city and raisin capital (52,000); and Bakersfield, nerve center for the southern cotton and oil lands (26,000).[59]

Much of this was quite new. The cotton areas in particular had been settled only recently, the crop having been introduced in the 1920s. Thus Arvin, McFarland, Buttonwillow, and many of the other towns that would soon be inundated by the Dust Bowl migrants counted as pioneers men and women whose tenure predated the Depression by less than a dozen years.[60]

It had always been a prosperous society, this valley of industrialized agriculture. But the prosperity rested on a profound division of labor. The wealth of California's agriculture came from specialty crops that depended upon large quantities of imported labor. By 1930, for every farm operator and family member employed in agriculture, at least one and a half paid workers were required, for a total of more than 200,000 farm laborers statewide. A portion were permanent employees, year-round farm hands like those common in other agricultural regions. But California's greatest need was for a reliable pool of temporary workers who could move about the state with the rhythms of the growing season, descending upon particular crop areas at key periods to perform the cultivating, thinning, pruning,

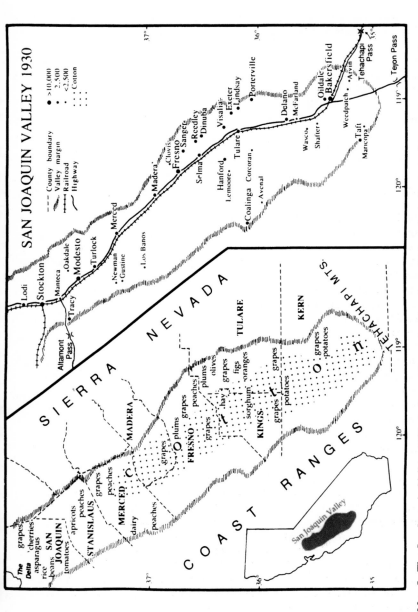

Map 5. The San Joaquin Valley, 1930. *Left*: counties and major crops. *Right*: principal towns, cities, and transportation routes.

and, most important, harvesting tasks needed to bring the diverse agricultural products to market.[61]

Developing that labor force and keeping it cost-efficient required no less
engineering than did the water resources. Early on the industry had learned
to look to outside sources. The Chinese established the pattern. Driven
from industrial work by the campaign of race-hatred associated with the
Workingmen's party, Chinese immigrants helped in the 1880s to tend the
infant orchards that were just then replacing wheat as the focus of California
agriculture. Other immigrants had followed: Europeans of various kinds,
but most notably the Japanese, who by the turn of the century occupied
the central place in the labor system. After World War I, restrictive immigration laws and the tendency of some of this second wave to graduate
to farm ownership sent growers looking for new workers. Immigrants from
Mexico and the Philippine Islands met much of the need in the 1920s.[62]

Native-born whites also participated in the farm labor force. Indeed, at
all points they comprised the largest single group represented, accounting
for 43 percent of all farmworkers in 1930, compared with 21 percent for
Mexicans, 17 percent European whites, 8 percent Filipinos, and 7 percent
Japanese. Preferred as year-round employees, the role of whites among
seasonal harvest workers was limited primarily to the so-called "ladder"
crops, mostly fruit. With the exception of cotton, growers preferred Asians
and Mexicans for the arduous tasks associated with vegetables and other
ground crops.[63]

In a culture that had historically associated agriculture with independence, California's farm labor system broke the rules, so much so that
Carey McWilliams called it the state's "Peculiar Institution." He exaggerated, of course. There was nothing compulsory about seasonal farm work.
Nor was it permanent; in time individuals and whole immigrant groups
tended to work their way out of the fields. But the system did impose one
of the sharpest class structures found anywhere in American society. Moving from place to place, strangers in nearly every community, seasonal
farm workers were a class apart, the mostly invisible underside of generally
prosperous rural California.

Such was the world that beckoned to a large portion of the 1930s migrant
stream. In better times, it would have offered them a greater range of
options. But the Depression had squeezed the flexibility out of the area's
economy. Knowing that relatives and friends had found opportunities of
various kinds in the previous decade may have allowed some migrants to
hope for something more than farm work, or to expect that an initial season
in the fields would then lead to something better. Some, it seems, chose
the valley thinking that they might find a way to get hold of a few acres
to farm for themselves.[64]

With a few exceptions it proved an impossible dream. At roughly $200 per acre (five to ten times the cost in Oklahoma), improved cotton land was clearly way beyond the means of all but the wealthiest of would-be farmers. Leasing land held a bit more promise. Some 20 percent of California farms had been operated by tenants before the Depression, with the rate somewhat higher for cotton farms. A number of Southwesterners had found it possible to rent land in the 1920s, but the competition became steeper as foreclosures left local farmers landless and as consolidation reduced the number of available sites. Then too California landowners usually required cash rents, not the share tenancy so common in the Southwest.[65]

A few newcomers defied the odds, but only because they had substantial resources to start with. Byrd Morgan's parents decided to come to California in 1934, chiefly for his stepmother's health. Back in Muskogee County, Oklahoma, his father had been farming successfully and received $800 when he sold his land. After two years' work in a California dairy farm he had enough capital and a good enough credit reputation to lease 160 acres in Madera County, though without much left for the necessary equipment. That first tough year Morgan and his father plowed their new land the "hard way . . . with horses and mules."[66]

Albert and Velma Davis, who had come west temporarily in the 1920s, tried California again in the 1930s and managed to rent some land. To get started they needed their savings, the incoming rent from their 160-acre farm back in Oklahoma, and Albert working a full-time extra job. All this gained them 26 acres in Kern County in 1931. A succession of larger rentals followed, and in 1943, finally selling their Oklahoma property, the couple bought their first California acreage.[67]

Like these others, the Newsome family also had money when they arrived in California in 1935, profits from the sale of their Oklahoma farm. But as Charles Newsome explains, his father shrewdly decided to work a year learning the techniques of California cotton farming before leasing lands of their own. In 1937 they started off with 40 acres near Visalia and a tired old tractor. A good crop made it possible to expand to 145 acres the following year, and then two more successful years allowed them to buy the land. "At the end of 1939 that place was paid for," Newsome recalls proudly. "He hadn't paid too much for it, I think $16,000."[68]

These were uncommon stories. Only 2 percent of recent migrants to the San Joaquin Valley had become farm owners, tenants, or managers by 1940 compared with 10 percent of earlier Southwestern settlers and 18 percent of other white males in the population (Table 2.2). Opportunities would improve, as we will see, during World War II. Even so, farming never became an option for most. At mid-century only 5 percent of adult Southwesterners living in the agricultural areas of the state owned or operated farms.[69]

Table 2.2. Occupational and Income Distribution for Males in the San Joaquin Valley Labor Force, 1940*

	Southwestern Migrants 1935–40	Other Migrants	Pre-1935 Southwesterners	Other White Californians	Hispanics/ Nonwhites
Farmers/farm managers	2%	6%	10%	18%	9%
Professionals/ proprietors/ managers	2	12	11	15	4
Clerical/sales/police and fire	3	9	9	12	4
Craftsmen/foremen	10	14	14	14	5
Operatives/service workers	10	18	21	21	9
Laborers (non-agr.)	14	15	8	7	11
Farm laborers/ foremen	58	26	27	12	57
	99%	100%	100%	99%	99%
N =	(210)	(106)	(255)	(1,349)	(213)
Occupational index	1.9	2.9	3.0	3.6	2.1
Median individual income**	$425	$760	$775	$1,190	$400
Median family income**	$650	$1,000	$1,070	$1,510	$555

*Military personnel and family farm workers not included in occupational sample.

**Wage and salary income only. Individuals without wage or salary income were eliminated from income calculations, as were families without a male wage or salary earner.

Source: 1940 Census Public Use Microdata Sample.

There were some opportunities to be had in the nonagricultural economy. A few migrants (5 percent) found jobs in the white-collar sector. Young, bright, and ambitious, J.R. McClintock left Missouri in 1934 shortly after graduating from high school to work on his uncle's farm near the town of Hanford in Tulare County. Two years later he talked his way into a sales job in the local Montgomery Ward store—the start of a long career with that company.[70]

A few opened small businesses, usually catering to their fellow newcomers and typically operating on the narrowest of margins. Grocery stands, lunch counters, and repair services located near the labor camps and migrant neighborhoods opened and then folded with regularity. Albert Woods invested the proceeds from the sale of his Texas farm in a service station not long after arriving in California in 1939. The location was poor and he was soon at work in the fields.[71] Others were more successful. Two families who had set up a fruit stand near the Arvin Farm Security Administration camp generated enough business to later turn it into a full-fledged grocery store.[72] Oleta Wever Belezzuoli's father worked in the fields for a year or two after leaving Oklahoma, managed to rent a small farm briefly, and then invested his profits in a gas station and grocery store in the town of Poplar. By the end of the 1930s the family was doing well.[73]

With more frequency, the newcomers found jobs in the valley's blue-collar sector. The oil industry offered some openings; the construction industry many more. Nearly half of all recent Southwestern migrants not working in agriculture were employed in construction in 1940. It was a natural avenue out of the fields, since many migrants were experienced in the work and others—farmers accustomed to building for themselves—readily acquired the skills. To the chagrin of building trades unions who accused the newcomers of undercutting wages, Southwesterners acquired a substantial foothold in the industry. Counting both earlier and new settlers, they made up 29 percent of all construction workers in the San Joaquin Valley by 1940. Some also went into the contracting business for themselves, usually building cheap homes for other migrants. In Salinas, a pair of previously unemployed carpenters from Oklahoma made a fortune in that manner. By the end of the decade they had put up more than $100,000 in new housing.[74]

Still, the majority had to look elsewhere. For most, the constricted nonagricultural economy of the valley combined with their own often limited job skills to make farm labor their only opportunity throughout the 1930s. Indeed, quite a few men with blue-collar skills slipped into agricultural work. The Bureau of Agricultural Economics's interstate migration survey disclosed a significant decline in aggregate occupational standing for valley settlers compared with pre-migration occupations. With some variation depending upon particular occupations, roughly one-third of surveyed males failed to regain their previous occupational status. Those of white-collar backgrounds were most likely to drop into blue-collar work, while those of industrial backgrounds often fell into farm labor. This does not mean that people were worse off economically, for many had been unemployed at their pre-migration occupations, but it does tell us something about the occupational adjustment that settlement in the valley often imposed. In contrast to the cities, where the same data set suggests that migrants usually regained their pre-migration occupational levels, the non-metropolitan settings offered severely restricted job opportunities and equally restrictive social prospects.[75]

The agricultural labor force, meanwhile, had acquired a new look. The number of Mexicans and Asians working in the fields remained much the same in the Imperial Valley and some of the coastal basins, but in the interior valleys farm work was becoming more and more the province of Anglos and especially Southwesterners. Non-Hispanic whites accounted for 76 percent of the farm workers in the San Joaquin labor force in 1940, and almost half of them (38 percent) were Southwesterners. They were joined in the fields by a mix of old-timers, some of them foreign-born, and newcomers from other farm states, principally the Midwest. That was the farm labor profile for the valley as a whole. In crops that Southwesterners knew well, such as cotton and potatoes, surveys from the late 1930s found Okies in a clear majority, up to two-thirds of the seasonal labor force at some points. A stunning change had come over the valley, and one that would last the better part of a generation. Not until the large-scale reentry of Mexicans in the 1950s would white Oklahomans, Arkansans, Texans, and Missourians cease to be the largest component of the San Joaquin Valley's agricultural work force.[76]

The Challenges of Farm Labor

Despite what had been for most a lifetime familiarity with farms and farm work, there was to be nothing easy about the migrants' entry into California's agricultural industry. A tough livelihood in the best of times, the shifting market conditions of the 1930s made farm labor a more complicated proposition than perhaps at any time in the state's history.

Early fall, just before the start of the two-month-long cotton-picking season, was the most common time for agricultural families to come to California. Whether they planned to stay in the state or return home after a short work trip, this was the prime earning period, a chance to make a significant amount of money. A skilled picker could make $3 to $4 a day in the highly productive cotton fields of California, more than twice the normal earnings in the harder-to-pick fields of the Southwest. At such wages and with husband, wife, and older children working, families were often able to accumulate a sizable sum by the time the season ended in December. Many migrants were therefore initially quite impressed with the earnings potential of California farm work. And on that basis a number who had intended only to visit decided to stay.[77]

Regret sometimes followed. If they were not prepared for the lean winter months ahead, they were about to learn that California could be something other than a land of milk and honey. By late December agricultural work ended, for all intents and purposes. Not until March would there be an appreciable revival of employment. Newcomers consequently faced several months without work, months which were the coldest and wettest of the year. Those who had relatives to help them usually managed to get by, but for many who did not, the first winter in California became a test. It was then that journalists and social workers discovered the scenes of hard-

Figure 7. Child care in the cotton fields. By age six, children would be able to help with the picking. (*Dorothea Lange,* © *1982, The Oakland Museum, The City of Oakland*)

ship and suffering which John Steinbeck depicted so powerfully in *The Grapes of Wrath.*

In a pamphlet published before his famous novel, Steinbeck described some of the difficulties people faced when the winter "dead time" set in:

There is no work. First the gasoline gives out. And without gasoline a man cannot go to a job even if he could get one. Then the food goes. And then in the rains, with insufficient food, the children develop colds because the ground in the tents is wet. I talked to a man last week who lost two children in ten days with pneumonia. His face was hard and fierce and he didn't talk much. I talked to a girl with a baby and offered her a cigarette. She took two puffs and vomited in the street. She was ashamed. She shouldn't have tried to smoke, she said, for she hadn't eaten for two days. I heard a man whimpering that the baby was sucking but nothing came out of the breast. I heard a man explain very shyly that his little girl couldn't go to school because she was too weak to walk to school and besides the school lunches of the other children made her unhappy.[78]

Shelter was the most immediate problem. Winters in the San Joaquin Valley were mild compared with many areas of the country, but not mild enough to spend comfortably in a tent. The temperature dips into the thirties, and it rains frequently. To their credit, many of the cotton growers, recognizing that their pickers had no place to go, allowed them to stay on rent free in the labor camps. In some cases the camps furnished cabins, tiny one-room shacks which at least offered some protection against the elements. But in other cases, they provided nothing more than a platform or a patch of muddy ground on which to pitch a tent. Sanitation facilities in the growers' camps were notoriously inadequate even in better seasons. In rainy periods, flooding outhouses sometimes contaminated drinking water and created health problems.[79]

Migrants who managed to find a spot in a labor camp did well compared with those who literally had nowhere to go for the winter. Setting up tents by the side of the road, in unused fields, or next to irrigation ditches, these people tried as best they could to get through the off-season. Some families camped by themselves, but more commonly they found others in similar circumstances and huddled together. Squatter villages varying in size from a few families to several hundred persons could be found throughout agricultural sections of the state, sometimes located near an outlying service station or grocery store where residents obtained water and supplies. Estimates of the number of families living under such conditions ranged well into the thousands during 1937, when the squatter problem was at its worst.[80]

Health problems proliferated under these conditions. A few newcomers may actually have starved to death. Disease also killed, especially infants. Health authorities in the San Joaquin Valley counties reported increases in infant mortality rates associated with the migrant population.[81] Fatalities, however, occurred nowhere on a mass scale. But nutritional defects did: a study of children in the cotton camps in 1938 reported 17 percent suffering from malnutrition and others from rickets.[82] A larger study of more than a thousand children in labor camps throughout the San Joaquin Valley found smaller numbers seriously afflicted but said that 28 percent of all children lacked an adequate diet.[83] Dr. Anita Faverman, who worked with a migrant health project for several years, noted that many parents simply did not know what to do or where to turn for help. "Reckon they're not eatin' too much," one father admitted forlornly. "Maybe it's my fault, as I've not been working. I still have $2 and we have a few more potatoes. I haven't asked for help; haven't been here a year, and it's no use."[84]

The winter of 1937–38 was especially severe. Migration had reached its

Figure 8. California had not been kind to this family. Their two-year-old died of exposure during the winter. They have asked relief authorities to help them return to Oklahoma. (*Dorothea Lange, The Bancroft Library, Berkeley, California*)

prewar peak during the cotton season immediately before, and as the wet season approached thousands lacked adequate shelter. When January and February brought unseasonably heavy rains, what had been a problem became a disaster. Rivers and creeks overflowed their banks, washing out squatter encampments and flooding labor camps. Families were forced to flee, often abandoning their few possessions to the rising water. Hundreds were left without food or shelter.

Private groups and government agencies rushed to their aid. Emergency shelters were set up at various locations, and soon afterwards several valley counties committed themselves to building permanent labor camps and eliminating the squatter settlements. More significant, the floods spurred the federal government into action. The Farm Security Administration, already constructing a string of farm labor camps in the valleys, now launched an emergency program of relief assistance and medical care for those agricultural workers who did not meet the state's one-year residency requirement. Thereafter, families in need could apply for food and sometimes cash grants. From then on, as a result, the problems of getting through the winter months would be considerably less severe.[85]

Migrants with nearby relatives were usually spared these difficulties. Kinfolk could normally be counted on to provide help in emergencies and thus played a critical role in the early resettlement process. Those with already settled relatives in the vicinity also enjoyed substantial labor market advantages, because experience was the key to making a living in California's fields. Starting in March with the pea harvest, California's crops would mature sequentially over the next nine months, presenting an opportunity for harvest hands to make a nearly year-round living, provided they knew the crops and the migratory system.

Only a few crops were familiar to most Southwesterners. When it came to picking cotton, many of the newcomers were expert. They knew how to move quickly down the long rows, backs bent, pinching off the puffs of fiber and stuffing them into the enormous tow-sack trailing behind. If the fingers moved fast enough and the knees and back held up, an adult could gather 300 to 400 pounds of the seemingly weightless fiber in the course of a day, enough to make the hard hours pay. Not everyone could. A Kansan who lacked the proper background told of his difficulties in the unfamiliar cotton fields: "I had never tried that before, and you sure could tell it when I got out there because I picked about 80 pounds that first day, and I worked hard all day long. I finally got so that I could pick about 200 pounds, but you can't make any money out of that at a cent a pound."[86]

Though they had advantages in cotton, Southwesterners faced problems in other crops. Many knew how to harvest potatoes and peas, crops frequently grown in their home states, but fruits and other vegetables were new to them. "These people know cotton but they cannot make a year-round living in cotton alone," the manager of the San Joaquin Valley Agricultural Labor Bureau sympathized. "They are learning sugar-beet work, and in potatoes they are doing well. They can squat and sort, but they cannot squat and walk, like a Mexican; hence they are not good in asparagus. They do not know how to handle fruit as yet—but they will learn."[87]

Fruit they did learn, but vegetables rarely. Having already violated the racial boundaries between ladder and stoop labor, most Southwesterners avoided field crops other than the ones they already knew. And those who felt otherwise were often shocked to find that they were not wanted. So entrenched was the industry's habit of ethnic stereotyping that many growers hired only certain groups for specific crops.[88]

The migratory system posed additional challenges—ones that the newcomers were generally less willing to meet. Earning a living from harvest work required almost constant travel. It meant spending six to nine months of the year in a succession of labor camps. It meant giving up a settled

Figure 9. A family at work in the pea fields, San Luis Obispo County, 1937. (*Dorothea Lange, The Bancroft Library, Berkeley, California*)

existence for the life of the road. A typical harvest circuit might cover 700 to 1,000 miles in the course of a year, perhaps beginning with peas in the Imperial Valley in the spring, moving north into the San Joaquin for potatoes, then over to the Salinas or Santa Clara valleys for apricots, from there up into the Sacramento Valley for the various fruits that ripened in the summer, and then back to the San Joaquin Valley for grapes and, finally, cotton picking in the fall.[89]

Some took readily to the demands of migratory work. When one knew the crops and their seasons, and had the right sort of connections so as to be assured of a job with the same growers year after year, it was possible to make a fair income on the harvest circuit. A 1937 survey of families who had followed the crops for at least a year found a wide variance in earnings. While the median family income was low, $658 a year, and while some families reported meager earnings of only a few hundred dollars, one-quarter of those surveyed earned more than $900 and a few families up to $1,600 a year.[90]

Given the low housing expenses of migratory workers (probably low enough to offset the high transportation costs), some families were clearly able to make the work pay. Roscoe Crawford was one. After coming to California from Oklahoma in 1938, he went to work in the fields, and with the exception of a short stint during the war when he worked in a factory, he spent the next quarter of a century following the crops:

> I just enjoyed it, and I could work and make piece work by the box or the pound. I was awful fast with my hands gathering fruit . . . I could make better than most could and I was practically my own boss. I could get a job for a month or better then move to another job. . . . We would go north in the summertime, south in the wintertime.[91]

If this itinerant way of life appealed to some, most felt differently. Accustomed to a settled lifestyle, they sought alternatives, usually developing ways of searching for work that allowed them to establish permanent domiciles. The Bureau of Agricultural Economics's interstate migration survey makes clear the widespread refusal to participate in the migratory lifestyle. Half of the families whose income derived primarily from agricultural work reported that they had settled in a particular county immediately after arriving in California and had remained there ever since. Another 25 percent established permanent residence within a year of arrival, and many of the remaining families did so soon after. Only a small minority of the newcomer group migrated with the crops for more than a year or two.[92]

Partly it was a matter of pride. In their home states, not unlike California, itinerant labor had been held in disdain, viewed mostly as the province of blacks or Mexicans. Before the Depression, few white families had followed the crops. Some men had worked for wages, but usually that meant becoming a year-round farm hand on someone else's farm or doing assorted odd jobs in the area in which one lived. A man might leave home for a month or so to work in the wheat harvest in Kansas, but it would have been rare for him to take the family along or to travel for any extended period of time.[93] Itinerancy itself was seen as a mark of failure. "None of our folks—neither side—never lived like gypsies, and we sure never set out to," a Texan who had been on the road for several years apologized, adding that "we ain't never owned nothin' much, but then we ain't had to move every time a crop was laid by neither, lessen we was a mind to."[94] "When I was a fruit tramp I thought I was like a jew without a country," another Southwesterner explained, drawing on a different ethnic stereotype.[95]

For families especially, the way of life of the road contrasted sharply with what was considered a proper mode of existence. Parents worried about their children. "They'll be just nomads, not caring for anything except their eats—no home life, church or school. All this is enough to worry me to death," a mother explained.[96] "Everyday life in a migratory camp will actually disgust you," a young Oklahoman summarized. "There are everyday hardships in living this type of life that no one can understand without actually experiencing it."[97]

But it was not easy to defy industrial tradition. Settling down and refusing to follow the crops made it difficult to earn a living from agricultural work. Some areas offered more employment than others, but not even the southern San Joaquin Valley, where potatoes, grapes, and cotton all matured at different times of the year, could support settled harvest workers year-round. Supplemental income sources thus had to be found. For most families that meant struggling to find odd jobs within a twenty- to thirty-mile radius of where they lived. In addition to working in the fields whenever possible, the husband tried to fill in the months between harvests with packing-shed work, construction jobs, and anything else that might come along.

Wives often worked too, but primarily in seasons when the demand for labor was high. Canneries hired females during the summer months, and wives might also work in the fields picking certain crops. During several weeks of the cotton season, not only women but also children often joined in. A whole family might work together with considerable efficiency in the cotton fields, with even seven- and eight-year-olds doing their share. Child labor during cotton-picking times had been traditional in the Southwest. In California, though bemoaned by school authorities, it remained common practice in many migrant households.[98]

Many families adopted a compromise plan of settlement, staying put most of the year, but taking to the road during the summer to add to their income. Work was plentiful in the fruit orchards of the Sacramento Valley during that season, and with school out, one reason for staying home was eliminated. Every summer the Ballard family would leave their home in Lindsay and follow the fruit crops north. "We didn't go til school was out," Dellar Ballard clarified. "We never taken the kids out of school. And we always tried to get back in time for them to start the first day."[99]

If summer expeditions were often essential to supplement income earned the rest of the year through intermittent employment near home, public assistance, once families became eligible, was more important still. More than anything else, relief checks made it possible for most Southwestern agricultural workers to establish a settled existence. Between picking seasons, if no other work was available, eligible families counted on either a job with the WPA or help from the State Relief Administration. A report by the Kern County Health Department summarized with only slight exaggeration the pattern of work and relief that became typical for agricultural workers in that county. Working within a radius of thirty miles, the report explained, the men and women "harvest cotton in the fall, go on relief until May, harvest the potatoes in the spring, work the vegetables and fruits in the summer and rest on relief until cotton harvest again."[100]

Although today few former migrants will admit it, the quest for a settled home life in the 1930s very often made relief a necessity. A 1939 survey underscores the pattern of dependence. Investigators interviewed nearly one thousand settled newcomers who worked in agriculture and asked them about supplemental sources of income. Two-thirds had accepted public assistance during some part of the previous year, with the average family receiving one-eighth of its annual income from that source.[101]

Little Oklahomas

Like work, housing accommodations fell way behind the requirements of the 1930s influx. Some families found houses to rent, but tiny incomes forced many others to make their homes in auto courts, trailer parks, or in the private campgrounds usually located just outside established towns. There for a few dollars a month a family rented a tent, a cabin, or a patch of ground and gained access to toilets and showers.[102]

Even cheaper were the Farm Security Administration camps, more than a dozen of which were scattered throughout the state's different agricultural valleys. Clean, generally well managed, with tent platforms, sometimes metal cabins, and assorted recreational facilities for up to 300 families, these were the federal government's principle answer to the problems created by the Dust Bowl migration. But opposition from many of the important growers, who saw the FSA as a meddlesome liberal agency and worried that the camps would provide haven for union organizers, kept their popularity limited. Mostly they served new arrivals and the highly mobile elements in the farm labor force. A one-year residency rule and the stigma of living in a "government camp" kept the more fortunate and established away.[103]

Buying property of their own was an option for those with somewhat more resources. Despite their frequently marginal economic situation, a substantial number of farm workers acquired their own homes during the 1930s. It was possible because of cheap land values on the outskirts of many valley communities. Understanding the potential market, developers subdivided unused land and sold it in tiny lots with only minimal improvements. Some of the new subdivisions lacked even a water supply. More were without paved roads, sewers, gas, and electricity. But on the other hand the price was right. For as little as $5 to $10 down and a similar amount each month families getting by on minimal incomes could become property owners.

Of course that was just a start; the next step was building a home. Some paid others to do it for them, but a surprising number, equipped with

Figure 10. Highly touted by New Dealers, the Farm Security Administration camps were as much a political symbol as a practical answer to the problems of farm labor. Intended to foster cooperative values as well as provide emergency shelter, the design called for platform camp sites surrounding a common washroom and recreational center. (*Dorothea Lange, © 1982, The Oakland Museum, The City of Oakland*)

carpentry skills from years on the farm and burdened with lull periods between jobs, took on the challenge themselves. Funds for building materials—estimated at $135 for "a good, three room, wood-framed house with cellar included"—were often an obstacle, but ingenuity sometimes sufficed.[104] Scavenging or trading for materials, people built all sorts of dwellings: sound or unsound, attractive or unsightly, usually beginning with a crude shack and working from there on a real house. "The houses have been built jist a piece at a time," a resettled Oklahoman noted proudly of the Modesto-area subdivision where he lived. "If a man saves any money he adds a little more on. Them two houses down yonder across the field is two good examples: one of them is just beginnin' and the other is bein' added on to. At one time nearly everybody in here lived in tents but they have built little houses and have kept addin' on."[105]

Another Oklahoman, who managed to finance his home out of a $44 monthly WPA paycheck, described the process as "jest like the cat eatin' grindstone—a little bit at a time."[106] It took more than a decade for Dellar and Jim Ballard to finish building their house. Having bought a lot in the town of Lindsay in Tulare County in 1933 for $100, the family camped there in a tent for almost three years before beginning construction. Then working on it whenever they could, a small house slowly took shape. "Jim done most of it. Me and him. Well it's not modern by a whole lot, but then I was never used to a modern house no how, so what's the difference. I get by with it."[107]

Called "Little Oklahomas" or "Okievilles" by Californians who resented their makeshift, typically squalid appearance, the migrant subdivisions appeared wherever there were concentrations of Southwesterners eager to buy property, landowners willing to sell, and no building codes to interfere. Huge developments spread around the outskirts of Bakersfield, both on the east side of town and north in the area called Oildale. Similarly, just beyond the city limits of Modesto, Little Oklahomas emerged first on a tract of land near the airport and then across the river in South Modesto. Fresno, Stockton, and Sacramento watched similar developments spread out beyond the incorporated limits, as did Salinas, which labeled its new subdivision "Texhoma."[108] City officials were often concerned. The Kern County Health Department noted the new developments and sounded the alarm:

> Bakersfield has experienced the creation of new subdivisions almost completely inhabited by people from Oklahoma, Texas, Arkansas, and Missouri. Many have purchased lots for as low as $3 per month; houses have been constructed of any materials that can be salvaged from the alleys or retrieved from dismantled structures in exchange for labor. Some of these communities have no satisfactory water supply, poor sewage disposal, no gas nor electricity . . . crude, often offensive, toilets . . . threaten to leach their contents into the same strata of sand and subsoil from which comes the water supply.[109]

If the major valley cities had reason to worry about these "boom towns of destitution," many of the smaller towns had more. Small, established communities sometimes found themselves encircled and overwhelmed by migrant subdivisions. In Kern County, towns like Shafter, McFarland, Delano, and Arvin saw their populations double, triple, even quadruple as subdivisions spread out around the original core. Arvin, a struggling outpost until fruit magnate Joseph DiGiorgio brought in deep well pumps and laid out his 8,000-acre farm in 1919, found itself by the 1930s in the midst of Kern County's expanding grape and cotton region. Its population exploded. By 1944, the community's residents numbered 6,200, two-thirds of them from Oklahoma, Texas, Arkansas, and Missouri.[110]

Like the migrants' occupational clustering, the growth of these migrant subdivisions was part of an economically driven process that would give definition to the Okie group. Both in the labor camps and in the Little

Figure 11–12. Little Oklahomas under construction. *Top:* Framing a new home in Olivehurst, Yuba County, 1940. *Bottom:* Varieties of housing in a Kern County neighborhood, possibly Oildale. (*Dorothea Lange, © 1982, The Oakland Museum, The City of Oakland, and the Bancroft Library, Berkeley, California*)

Oklahomas, the newcomers were finding housing that was physically and socially removed from the host society. Unlike their counterparts who settled in Los Angeles, newcomers to the valley were moving into settings that conditioned separation rather than interaction with earlier residents.

It is important to be clear just how this process of residential clustering unfolded, for it was different in certain respects from the community formation experiences of most immigrant groups in the nation's major cities. The Southwestern character of the Little Oklahomas was to a large extent accidental, or, more acurately, powered by class rather than regional discriminations. No housing covenants or other forms of systematic discrimination forced Southwesterners into their own neighborhoods. Nor was it typical of newcomers to specifically seek out former residents of their own state or region, as was customary among foreigners who found their American surroundings alien and who thus longed for the companionship of fellow countrymen. In fact, substantial numbers of Southwesterners, especially those in better economic circumstances, found homes among the host population in established neighborhoods. Similarly some non-Southwesterners settled in the Little Oklahomas. Regional origins mattered relatively little. The salient criterion was economic. Families sought housing where they could afford it and in neighborhoods whose socio-economic complexion made them feel comfortable.[111]

The class basis for settlement is suggested in Lillian Creisler's survey of a Little Oklahoma located just beyond Modesto's city limits. Established in 1935 when owners of a large tract of land near the city's airport decided to subdivide and sell, the area became home to over 300 families by early 1939, most of whom paid $5 a month for their small, initially empty lots. The residents represented a cross-section of the new farm-worker class in the northern San Joaquin Valley. Exclusively white and almost as uniformly from out of state, less than 4 percent of adults were native-born Californians. Fifty-four percent claimed Oklahoma, Texas, Arkansas, or Missouri as their birthplace, another 8 percent came from Kansas, and the rest from various Midwestern, Southern, or Far Western states. Occupationally, better than two-thirds did farm or cannery work, while most of the remainder listed blue-collar trades like construction, truck driving, or auto mechanics. Moreover, as of the April 1938 interview date more than half were out of work. Thirty-one percent said they were currently receiving relief assistance or held a WPA job, and another 22 percent reported no job or income at all at that particular time.[112]

Here then was a substantially but not exclusively Southwestern residential area shared principally with other newcomers of similar socio-economic standing. Like the immigrant neighborhoods of turn-of-the-century American cities, the Little Oklahomas were not as exclusive as they often seemed, deriving their reputation from a certain critical mass of Southwesterners, one that in this case was rather unintentionally assembled. But volition notwithstanding, that critical mass would insure that the migrant neighborhoods developed along lines familiar to their Southwestern residents, becoming settings for the re-creation of Southwestern institutions and values. Home to neither the most nor the least successful migrants, these were the central staging grounds for the emerging Okie subculture.

What finally do we make of the economic adjustment experiences of the migrants who settled in the valleys? Compared with their metropolitan counterparts, not to mention most white Californians, the economic position of these Southwesterners on the whole seemed far from enviable. The fact that steady work, either farm or nonfarm, eluded the majority and that nearly half finished the decade earning less than a standard subsistence income speaks poorly of the adjustment experiences of the group. So did virtually every report by outside observers. Varden Fuller and Seymour Janow, investigators for the Bureau of Agricultural Economics, calculated the financial progress of a sample of nearly one thousand migrant families as of 1939. Counting the equity in new homes and property, they found an average increase in family net worth of only $140 and concluded that "for the group as a whole there has been little measurable financial progress during the period of residence in the State."[113]

But there are other issues to consider. For one thing, this assessment overlooks, as did all such investigations, newcomers who, although a minority, filtered into the better neighborhoods and the better jobs. It is also true that questions of success and failure are rarely measurable just in dollars and cents. Ultimately, it was up to the migrants themselves to evaluate their experience. And judging from the comments recorded by investigators or printed in the camp newspapers, the range of opinion included more expressions of hopefulness and satisfaction than an "objective" assessment might lead us to expect.

A substantial number, as we have seen, had been able to purchase property, and whatever the financial calculations of the BAE analysts, many clearly felt that this represented an important economic breakthrough.[114] "This is the way I figured it," one man told Creisler, "I'd get a few months' work and then I'd lay by enough for a down payment. Once we had our own place, we'd be all right."[115] For some that was success. Property, even just a vacant lot upon which a house would someday stand, symbolized much of what had recently eluded them. It was the land they no longer or had never been able to own. It was the home that economic conditions back east and migratory compulsions out west tried to deny them. It was the security that they along with so many other Depression-era Americans craved. No wonder that so many visitors found the Little Oklahomas "teaming," as one report misspelled it, "with hopeful life." In the chance to own their own home, many Southwesterners found something that made the trip to California worthwhile.[116]

And what of those who were not privileged to be purchasing a home or plot? Here assessments varied considerably, depending both on the individual economic situations and on the particular set of conditions and expectations that had inspired the move to California.

Many were seriously disappointed. California was not what they had expected. "It's different out here to what I thought it was," complained Homer Towney*, who had spent four years finding out. "You are broke practically all the time."[117] Anthropologist Walter Goldschmidt interviewed a former tenant farmer who was equally disconsolate. He had been doing well back in Oklahoma but thought he might make enough money in California to buy a farm. Now he was going back empty-handed. "People in Oklahoma just don't live like this," he said, pointing to the tent that had been his family's home for the previous year.[118] Frank Kline, another Oklahoman getting ready to return to better prospects back home, put his thoughts into verse:

> If you ever had the blues,
> You know just how I feel.
> Now talk about the scenery,
> I guess it can't be beat.
> There is just one thing against it,
> It is not so good to eat![119]

But the same standards of living that these individuals regarded as a downward shift others perceived differently, having known more serious privation before coming west. Living in the Visalia Farm Security Administration camp, Bill Robinson supported his wife and six children on the usual minimal combination of farm work and relief. But the former timber worker remembered what it had been like nearly starving back in Oklahoma trying to make do on occasional work at 10 cents an hour. "I left there and come to Californy to try to support my family and to school it," he announced plainly. "And I'm proud to come and don't have any intention of going back, cause I can make a living here so much easier than I could there."[120]

After three years living in tents and drifting from farm job to farm job, Marvin Montgomery felt more or less the same way. "I can't say that I like this country, but then there isn't anything back in the East."[121] Camped illegally in a field near Wasco, living in conditions he described as fit only for "dogs or pigs," another migrant similarly maintained that his family was better off in California: "People just can't make it back there, with drought, hailstorms, windstorms, duststorms, insects. People exist here and they can't do that there. You can make it here if you sleep lots and eat little, but it's pretty tough. . . ."[122]

Pitiful and extreme, this is nevertheless an example of the sort of evaluation process which led even some of the poorest Southwesterners to view

their stay in California with a certain sense of optimism, or at least res-
ignation. Precarious though their livelihood might seem to middle-class
investigators, it was often better than what they had left behind. More
important, there was still hope for further improvement. Ed Morrow*,
whose year in the West had brought him only occasional employment,
examined prospects as he saw them in Oklahoma and California. Back
there, he said, the only work was "maybe a little cotton pickin' once in a
while," but in California there was more:

> There's a lot of people here to do it, but at the same time it makes you feel
> a little better settin' around near where there is work. You live in hopes of
> gettin' a little of it. But in a country where there is no work you've not got
> a damn thing to look forward to. No way to take care of your family, nuthin'
> to do but just set there and mold over.[123]

3

The Okie Problem

ECONOMIC DIFFICULTIES WERE ONLY SOME OF THE CHALLENGES THE MIGRANTS faced in Depression-torn California. More serious and more enduring were the social barriers that arose in that decade. Many Californians reacted with hostility to the Dust Bowl migrants. Calling them "Okies" and "Arkies," residents in some settings treated the Southwesterners like an alien social group. More than anything else, this reaction shaped the migrants' subsequent experience in the state. Long after attaining the economic stability they had hoped for, they would wrestle with the lingering effects of California's initial hostile response.

That response had several dimensions. In part a product of regional prejudices that almost always leave people of Southern backgrounds at a disadvantage outside their home region, it built as well on the migrants' association with farm work, poverty, and rural backwardness—all invitations to disesteem in California. But as Walter Stein has shown, the intensity of California's reaction to the Dust Bowl migration was first of all a feature of a special time. The Depression created the climate of fear and conflict that nourished California's mistreatment of its newest settlers. Concerns that in another context would have meant little became charged and significant in this troublesome decade as worried Californians fought over their state's economic health and political future.[1]

Migration was one of the matters that worried them most. Symbol of the state's glory in flush times, interstate migration became an immediate source of concern once the economy soured. Although the particular regional background and social characteristics of the Dust Bowl migrants would also figure in their troubled relations with the Californians, the core of the problem was the state's protectionist mood. Long before anyone had heard of Dust Bowl migrants, Californians had adopted the exclusionary outlooks and drawn up the political battle-lines that would determine much of their response to the influx from the Southwest.

California was not the only state to fall victim to migration anxiety or to attempt to limit ingress during the 1930s. Perhaps because the generations-long debate over foreign immigration restriction was still fresh, a number of states adopted measures in the early years of the Depression to discourage impoverished fellow citizens from settling within their borders. California's response, however, was the most lasting and severe, and that was only partly attributable to the scale of the problem. It is true that no other state absorbed anything like the number of newcomers who poured into California during the 1930s. But it is also the case that California claimed certain traditions conducive to the florescence of migration anxiety.[2]

The state was well practiced in the politics of exclusion. The flip side of its fair-weather openness was a mean-spirited habit of hostility towards certain outsiders during times of stress and uncertainty. Nonwhites had borne the brunt of it. During the state's first major depression in the 1870s, the issue of Chinese exclusion had become first a rallying point for the white working class and afterwards a basic touchstone of state politics. Opposition to Japanese immigration after the turn of the century, and campaigns against Filipinos and Mexicans still later, had followed a similar logic. When economic opportunities narrowed or when war or political struggles raised anxieties, immigrants were often singled out for exclusion.[3]

Less frequently the targets had been whites, usually the hobos and tramps who proliferated in the sunny state during depressions. In the 1870s and again with more potency in the depression of the mid-1890s, the state had worried loudly about the "tramp menace." Warned by public officials that thousands of idle men and boys were on their way west, a number of communities had passed intemperate vagrancy laws. In the years before World War I, tramps had again become a source of public anxiety. At that time not just swelling numbers but the activities of the radical Industrial Workers of the World contributed to the alarm.[4]

These were the precedents that fed California's migration crisis of the 1930s—and more specifically the state's response to the Dust Bowl migrants. The instinct to protect scarce resources from outsiders is probably manifest in all societies, and there is no reason to ascribe any particular strain of selfishness to residents of the Golden State. But a society that turns frequently to exclusionist solutions in times of crisis will find that an easy course to repeat the next time around. California claimed such a pattern, and the Dust Bowl migrants would not be its last victim. Not until the World War II internment of California's Japanese-American population would the cycle finally end.

Transients and Migrants

The 1930s migration crisis came in two stages, the first having nothing specifically to do with Southwesterners. The initial anti-migrant campaign originated in Los Angeles, which almost from the start of the Depression shouldered more than its fair share of the burden of the nation's transient unemployed. An accurate count is not available, but particularly in the winter months of the early 1930s city fathers reported alarming increases in the homeless population. The situation became more serious in mid–1935 when the federal government revamped its relief programs, shifting some responsibilities to the states and closing down the Federal Transient Service, an agency that had aided up to 70,000 individuals a month in California, about half of them out-of-staters.[5]

Goaded by exaggerated reports that "between 25 and 40 percent of the nation's transient unemployed are already in California" and worried especially about the tax burden and the political implications of further migration, Los Angeles authorities declared "war" on the "indigent influx" and demanded state intervention to stem the flow.[6] The state legislature then considered a bill that would have closed the state border to "All paupers and persons likely to become public charges." It failed by a small margin. Sure that he had the support of the city's newspapers and public officials, Los Angeles police chief James E. Davis then took matters into his own hands. In an extraordinary move that quickly captured national headlines, Davis in early 1936 dispatched 125 city policemen to patrol the state's major border crossings, including those shared with Oregon, some 800 miles north of the city limits.[7]

Portrayed in the national media as another example of California theatrics, Chief Davis's "bum blockade" demonstrated the seriousness many Californians attached to the migration issue. Initially, support for the blockade was strong, and state officials did little to interfere despite the clear usurpation of authority. But as the weeks passed, the withering ridicule of the national press and a legal challenge by the American Civil Liberties Union changed some minds. By the time Davis recalled his "foreign legion" after six weeks' duty, the affair had become something of an embarrassment. The migration issue then temporarily slipped from the headlines, especially in southern California, where unemployment rates and relief case loads were steadily dropping. But even as the first crisis came to a close, stage two was about to begin. This time the anxiety would be rooted in the rural areas of California, and directed not just at the generic "transients" but at people from a particular part of the United States.[8]

Southwesterners, of course, had been coming to California all along, and were well represented among the indigent newcomers who elicited concern in Los Angeles during the middle years of the decade. But it was not until the first paroxysm of anxiety had passed that the migration of Southwesterners was recognized as a social phenomenon in itself.

Agricultural economist Paul Taylor was responsible for initially calling attention to what became known as the Dust Bowl migration. He had noticed the growing number of Southwesterners while observing a major cotton strike in the San Joaquin Valley in 1933, and when he returned two years later he realized that a significant demographic transformation was under way. In a July 1935 article for *Survey Graphic*, he described the "westward movement of rural folk from Oklahoma, Texas, Arkansas and adjacent states . . . to California." He told of them fleeing "drifting dust clouds" and called them "Drought refugees," a term which other writers transposed into "Dust Bowl refugees."[9]

Taylor's report attracted immediate interest. Long had he labored to publicize the plight of California's farm labor force. Now he discovered the empathetic value of white skin. The news that old-stock white American families were joining Mexicans and Asians in the fields had human interest potential, and all the more as Dorothea Lange's photographs began to circulate. Local journalists were soon at work on the story. In dozens of mostly sympathetic newspaper articles published during 1936 and 1937, Californians were told about the terrible conditions which had driven the migrants from their homes and about the "battle for life, for food, health, homes and security" that the newcomers waged in the labor camps and shack towns of the agricultural valleys.[10]

Urban Californians became familiar with a new social concept: the "migrant family," "Dust Bowl refugee," or simply "Okie." "You may have seen some of them on the highway," a statewide radio broadcast began, moving into what had become a stereotypic description: "often a whole family with bedding, luggage, cooking utensils, and other miscellaneous possessions crowded into a battered and wheezing jalopy."[11]

Rural California needed no such introduction. By 1936 the impact of the growing migration stream was everywhere evident, and while some Californians might empathize from afar with the plight of the newcomers, valley residents found the situation more complicated, especially because there were different interests involved. The agricultural industry welcomed the migrants, convinced until late in the decade that they were needed to forestall labor shortages in the fields. But the rest of the valley population—the town-dwelling majority—was becoming more and more alarmed. Apart

Figure 13. All the important emblems of the Dust Bowl migration (broken-down car, mattress, tent, and barefoot children) are present in this famous photograph. (*Dorothea Lange, © 1982, The Oakland Museum, The City of Oakland*)

from the widely held dictum that what was good for farmers was good for the valley, most residents were having trouble seeing the benefits of continued migration.

The sources of concern are easy to understand. Los Angeles had spent the early part of the decade worrying about relatively small numbers of newcomers. By comparison, the valley faced a major problem. Walter Stein estimates that most San Joaquin Valley counties added at least 50 percent to their pre-Depression populations by 1938. He bases that on the

Table 3.1. Residence in 1935 of Interstate Migrants Living in the San Joaquin Valley and the Los Angeles Metropolitan Area in 1940

1935 residence	San Joaquin Valley		Los Angeles	
	Number	Percent	Number	Percent
Oklahoma	37,133	32	27,068	6
Texas	14,219	12	29,333	7
Arkansas	10,400	9	10,059	2
Missouri	8,881	8	29,602	7
Southwest	70,633	61	96,062	22
Kansas	5,269	5	22,586	5
Arizona	5,026	4	11,722	3
Nebraska	3,234	3	22,128	5
New Mexico	2,906	3	5,006	1
Colorado	2,873	2	17,387	4
Iowa	1,860	2	20,197	5
Illinois	1,747	2	35,013	8
New York	902	1	31,009	7
Other states	21,005	18	162,224	38
Total All States	115,455	101	423,334	98

Source: Donald J. Bogue, Henry S. Shryock, and Siegfried A. Hoermann, *Subregional Migration in the United States, 1935–1940, Vol. 1: Streams of Migration Between Subregions*, table 1, pp. vii–cli.

assumption that many migrants departed in the decade's last two years when jobs became tight and hostilities strong. What we know for certain is that, by the 1940 census, the valley's population had grown by 39 percent, compared with 26 percent for Los Angeles County and 21 percent for the state as a whole. The rate was highest in the cotton-growing areas. Kern County, adding some 52,000 new residents, saw its population jump almost 64 percent. The birth rate and the reshuffling of Californians accounted for some of these increases, but at least two-thirds of the new residents had come from out of state—and largely from one particular region. If the pattern for the years 1935–1940 held for the entire decade, then 61 percent of interstate migrants settling in the valley had come from the four Southwestern states, 32 percent from Oklahoma alone (Table 3.1).[12]

The numbers themselves were not the problem. These counties were accustomed to absorbing new population—they had grown by almost the same rate throughout the previous quarter of a century. Indeed many of the "old-timers" had settled in the valley just ten or twenty years before. But the context now was totally different. Economic uncertainty, political divisions, and the impoverished conditions of the newcomers turned a challenge into a crisis.

Most of the problems were predictable: not enough jobs, housing, schools, medical facilities, police, and welfare services, and not enough of a tax base to support the necessary expansion. But there were some peculiar elements. Job competition, so often the seedbed of intolerance, was less critical in this instance because of the way authority was distributed in the valley. In the fields, Southwesterners competed for work with the most powerless and least organized sector of society. Few noticed when old-time farm workers lost job opportunities or had to accept lower wages, especially since many of them were Mexicans.

Certain whites, however, also felt the competition. A farm hand complained to a local newspaper that he had lost his job to a newcomer who undercut his wages: "I have worked for the last three years for a man who has lots of money and has been in business here for years. He paid me $2.50 a day and one meal and the work was only part time. Several months ago he asked me if I would work for a dollar a day and I said, 'No.' " So he hired a new man who "had been sticking around for weeks looking for work."[13]

The complaints did not always come from the ranks of the powerless. Students and housewives, some of them respectably middle-class, worked in the canneries and packing houses during the summers. By the late 1930s, the flood of hungry Southwesterners willing to work harder for less had disrupted these summer work patterns and had driven most resident workers out of food processing. Interviewing students at Modesto Junior College, Lillian Creisler recorded the anger. Among other complaints, the newcomers were condemned because they "Cut wages" and "Take other's jobs."[14]

The response was slightly different in the construction trades where, as we have seen, the migrants established an occupational foothold. Feeling the pressure, Kern County's Building Trades Council initially joined the chorus of resentment against the Okies, claiming that without them "every man in Bakersfield would be working today."[15] But this was ground that the unions tread softly. The late 1930s were a time of high idealism for organized labor, and neither the newly emergent CIO nor the more conservative AFL unions then competing in the valley's construction, canning, and oil industries liked the sound of protectionist rhetoric.[16]

In any event this was not the most critical issue. With approximately 40 percent of the resident white population earning their living as farmers, proprietors, or in white-collar positions, the matter of job competition was bound to be secondary. Taxes and the transformation of communities were the central concerns of the middle-class residents who in concert with agriculture controlled the valley's towns and cities.

These were not superficial matters. The newcomers did cost the taxpayers money. A study published in 1940 by the state Chamber of Commerce tried to detail some of the migration-related expenses for the southern half of the San Joaquin Valley. It reported that between 1934 and 1939 school expenditures in one county went up 172 percent, outlays for health and sanitation services doubled, while the cost of free hospitalization for indigents nearly tripled. For the five southern San Joaquin Valley counties together, these new expenses resulted in a 100 percent jump in tax levies over a five-year period, almost twice the rate of increase for other parts of California. More concretely the study found that in several San Joaquin Valley counties the individual taxpayer had been hit with a 50 percent increase in property tax rates.[17]

Still, the Chamber of Commerce's figures do not specify how much of these additional costs was attributable to the newcomers settling in those areas and how much was due to other factors—questions which a 1940 Bureau of Agricultural Economics study of the finances of Kern and Yuba counties hoped to answer. On the basis of a detailed examination of county expenditures for public services such as schools, welfare, and health, the BAE estimated that Kern County spent $3,335,448, or 28 percent of its total budget, on interstate migrants who had settled in the county in the previous decade. Further north in the Sacramento Valley, newcomers claimed 21 percent of Yuba County's 1940 budget. Though the study's authors were careful to point out that in both cases less money was spent on the new settlers than was warranted by their representation in the population, it was a message likely to impress few taxpayers. The fact remained that all of these impoverished newcomers seemed to be costing them money.[18]

There was, of course, another side to the equation. Resettled Southwesterners were paying taxes too. More important, they were contributing to economic growth in the areas in which they settled. Not only did they provide needed farm labor and then use their wages to buy local goods and services, but they also brought in massive doses of federal and state money in the form of relief funds. However, neither contribution was likely to be viewed as such by most valley residents. In fact, the tendency of the Depression migrants to settle down instead of taking their harvest earnings and leaving the area, and their use of the state's unemployment relief system were two of the things that most bothered longtime residents.

The relief problem was especially critical. Californians everywhere worried about mounting relief costs in the last third of the 1930s as the economic downturn of 1937 increased unemployment and the federal government began cutting back WPA projects. Between 1937 and 1939, the California State Relief Administration reported a 77 percent caseload increase statewide. But in the San Joaquin Valley the increase was a whopping 344 percent, and investigation showed that more than half of the recipients had lived in the state less than five years.[19] County welfare costs were on the rise too, and no one knew how much the Farm Security Administration was spending on emergency grants to agricultural workers unable to meet the one-year residency requirement for state aid. Newspapers kept the populace informed of the mounting relief problem and drew special attention to local expenses. "Kern Spends Millions to Take Care of Needy," "Kern Relief Load Highest on Record," headlines in the *Bakersfield Californian* reported; "County Welfare Aid Increases 31.5%," echoed the *Fresno Bee.*[20]

The matter came down to more than dollars and cents. The valley may have gained more in federal and state funds than it paid in taxes or local outlays. But few were prepared to make those calculations. Relief was also a moral issue. Valley residents could not watch the relief rolls increase without concluding that it bespoke some fundamental flaw in their community. For the area to have so many welfare dependents meant that something was wrong, something unsound.[21]

What was happening, of course, was that the valley was finally experiencing in fuller range the social implications of the system of agricultural employment upon which the residents had long depended. Unlike their farm labor predecessors, Southwesterners were not taking their winter problems elsewhere. Where before the burden of winter unemployment and farm-worker poverty had fallen heavily on other areas of the state— San Francisco, whose "skid row" absorbed much of the white "fruit tramp" population during the cold months, and Los Angeles and the Imperial Valley, to which Mexican farm workers returned—now the San Joaquin, Sacramento, and Salinas valleys confronted the massive off-season unemployment and slum housing problems which were the byproducts of the state's farm labor system.

A report by the Kern County Health Department summarized the new social costs that the valleys were paying for their labor. "Growers have lost their fluid Mexican workers who miraculously appeared on harvest day and silently slipped away after the work was done," the author began. Now "the large family of the Southwesterner harvests the cotton of the Kern Valley; when the cotton harvest is over, the family hangs on . . . swelling our emergency relief load" and expanding "suburban slums" which pose a "serious threat to the health and welfare of the entire county."[22]

The chief problem was poverty. The question of costs and economic inconveniences was secondary. What most bothered the residents and drove them towards action were the brutal evidences of new poverty that everywhere marred the familiar landscape. Wherever they looked, they saw the disturbing scenes: rusty old cars chugging along the highways, ragged families living in tents along the riverbanks, unsightly shack towns and do-it-yourself slums. It was pathetic and terrible. There were so many of these downtrodden families, the problem seemed so enormous, that normal feelings of compassion were overwhelmed. Kind people looked

Figure 14. Farm labor poverty was not new, only the ethnic dimensions had changed. A Mexican family in the Imperial Valley called this shack home. (*Dorothea Lange, The Bancroft Library, Berkeley, California*)

upon the scenes of hardship and shuddered. And perhaps because their own hold on the recently settled area felt tenuous, the anguish turned to fear: What do they want? Are they dangerous? The prescription read panic.

The brush with poverty became especially threatening because of the public health implications. Medical authorities monitoring the labor camps reported a range of health problems and issued periodic warnings about potential epidemics, mentioning malaria, typhoid, smallpox, tuberculosis, diphtheria, and other serious diseases.[23] Under headlines proclaiming "Plague Averted" and "Health Problem Because of Migrants," newspapers insisted that only timely vaccination programs had forestalled major outbreaks which might easily have spread to the resident population.[24] Over the radio, residents learned that "on several occasions whole communities have been threatened by the spread of communicable diseases such as smallpox and typhoid, having their source in some squatter camp existing without benefit of proper sanitation and health regulations."[25] Whether or not these claims were completely true, many believed them.

All of these factors—the increased taxes, the changing complexion of communities, the migrants' poverty, the enlarged relief rolls, and the threat of disease—contributed to a growing sense of apprehension as residents watched more and more people, most of them poor, and most of them Southwesterners, filter into the valley. Smoldering at first, in 1938 these apprehensions suddenly flared into the open. In a public campaign more pointed and personal than the earlier efforts, many of the valley's residents turned angrily against the people they called Okies and demanded that steps be taken to limit migration into California.

Political Cross Fires

Politics and the strategic calculations of the valley's major agricultural interests had a great deal to do with both the timing and intensity of the anti-Okie campaign. As long as agricultural leaders felt that additional labor was needed, there was little chance that anything concrete would be done to discourage migration into the valleys. California growers, represented by several powerful organizations including the California Farm Bureau Federation and the Associated Farmers, wielded enormous political muscle at both state and local levels, and it was rare for their interests not to hold sway in the valleys. Thus through the middle years of the decade and even as late as 1937 political leaders and newspapers in agricultural areas remained largely unresponsive to those voices which demanded action to stem the influx of newcomers. However, in 1938, when the needs of agriculture suddenly changed, the stage was set for the state's second anti-migrant campaign.[26]

The reason, as Walter Stein has shown, was the federal government's second Agricultural Adjustment Act, which introduced major new crop controls for California cotton. A dramatic cutback ensued: cotton acreage declined nearly 45 percent, dropping from 620,000 acres harvested in 1937 to only 341,000 acres in 1938.[27] Now there was no longer any question of needing more farm workers. Indeed, the oversupply of labor at the start of the 1938 cotton season made it possible for growers' organizations to cut wages more than 20 percent, thereby adding to the already sizable economic problems facing farm workers. Only the timely introduction of the FSA's emergency grant program and the expansion of state relief rolls staved off genuine disaster.[28]

The crop control program also made it possible for growers to examine some of the consequences of further immigration. Two concerns loomed especially large: the threat of labor unions and the prospect that the migrants might help to upset the political balance of power in Sacramento and turn California over to the liberal wing of the Democratic party.

The labor threat seemed to be coming from two directions in 1938. An American Federation of Labor union, founded the year before, had already made considerable headway among cannery and packing-shed workers. More ominous from the standpoint of most agricultural leaders was the news that the newly launched Congress of Industrial Organizations was preparing an ambitious organizing drive among cotton and other field workers.[29]

Unions had never been tolerated by California's major industry. On practical and ideological grounds growers had always maintained that freedom to control the farm-labor force was essential to their financial survival. That perspective was particularly emphasized during the 1930s, partly because the industry remained fearful of a return to the devastating market conditions of 1931 and 1932, and partly because of the equally worrisome memories of the strike wave of 1933.

Growers had not been prepared for the campaign that the Communist-led Cannery and Agricultural Workers Industrial Union had mounted that year, the first season of agricultural price recovery. Asked to work for starvation wages little changed from the previous year, harvest hands, mostly Mexicans and Filipinos, struck a succession of crops, culminating in a three-county cotton strike involving some 18,000 pickers. Desperate to get in their crops, growers had fought back with fearsome violence in some instances but had caved in or compromised in several others. More successful than any previous farm labor uprising (or the one that followed), the CAWIU effort helped to push up wages during the next couple of seasons. But the industry had also learned the importance of vigilance. In early 1934, with the blessing of the California Farm Bureau Federation, many of the state's prominent agriculturalists came together to form a new organization, the Associated Farmers, whose primary mandate was to combat unionization. The immediate target was the CAWIU, which succumbed rather quickly to a campaign of violent harassment and criminal syndicalism prosecutions. But that, everyone knew, would not be the end of the story.[30]

Several matters worried industry leaders as they awaited the next union offensive. The changing composition of the farm labor force should have been reassuring, but some observers reasoned that white workers would be more susceptible to unionization than their predecessors. Dr. George P. Clements, for years the Los Angeles Chamber of Commerce's expert on agricultural labor, warned that "the white transients are not tractable labor." Lamenting the disappearance of Mexicans, whose recent militancy he evidently overlooked, he cautioned that as American citizens the newcomers were going to "demand the so-called American standards of living," and offer "the finest pabulum for unionization."[31] Supporters of the labor movement sometimes shared these ethnocentric assumptions, John Steinbeck among them: "Farm labor in California will be white labor, it will be American labor, and it will insist on a standard of living much higher than that which was accorded the foreign 'cheap labor.' "[32]

A more realistic concern stemmed from the realization that the new farm and cannery unions had allies in high places. Growers were used to dealing with friendless, easily isolated organizations like the Communist CAWIU, or in earlier decades the Industrial Workers of the World and various small immigrant unions. It was going to be a different story facing CIO or AFL organizations, particularly in an era when joining unions was becoming almost a patriotic exercise. By the mid–1930s organized labor had significant friends in the Democratic party, and that set up a triangular relationship that greatly worried many of the valley's leaders. The migrants were being courted by political reformers as well as unionists. It looked to some as if they might play a pivotal role in deciding the future not just of California agriculture but of the state itself.

Underlying the whole migration crisis just then brewing was the fact that California was poised at the edge of a difficult political transformation in 1938. An election contest was under way that was going to make history. California's Democratic party, after decades of frustration and six Roosevelt Administration years out of office, was finally headed for victory.

It has been argued that the United States, unlike much of western Europe, handled the Great Depression with relative equanimity. The 1930s, says Melvyn Dubofsky in a slightly different context, was a "not so turbulent" era.[33] One would not say that about California. Having spent the previous third of a century as a virtual one-party state—without a Democratic governor since 1899, a Democratic senator since 1919, and as of 1931 claiming only one Democratic congressman in its eleven-member House delegation—California spent much of the decade locked in a pattern of uncompromising political conflict that at times seemed reminiscent of the political situations in Paris or Madrid.

The terms of the battle had been set by the 1934 gubernatorial election. Democratic party regulars, confident of Roosevelt's popularity and looking forward to bringing the state into the New Deal camp, had been ambushed and overwhelmed in the primary election by the surprise candidacy of Upton Sinclair, author and perennial Socialist party candidate. Taking advantage of the party's factional tensions, Sinclair had re-registered as a Democrat and mounted an outsider's campaign based on an elaborate plan to "End Poverty in California." Even the candidate was amazed at the response. The EPIC promise to set up a state-financed system of cooperative farms and factories, tax the wealthy, and give pensions to the elderly caught the imagination and won the votes of some 400,000 California Democrats, swamping Sinclair's mainstream Democratic opponent, New Dealer George Creel. The general election was a different matter. Mercilessly red-baited by supporters of incumbent Governor Frank Merriam and abandoned by elements of his own party (including President Roosevelt, who offered no endorsement), Sinclair doubled his primary vote but lost decisively.[34]

Figure 15. Olson, Okies, and the CIO—for conservatives the 1938 election held a triple threat. This former Oklahoma farmer was one of the leaders of the 1938 Kern County cotton strike. (*Dorothea Lange, The Bancroft Library, Berkeley, California*)

The election left the state with a Republican adminstration, a divided Democratic party with the EPIC faction predominant, and the way cleared for continued political bitterness. Absent the moderate New Dealers who in federal politics bridged many of the potential chasms of that troublesome decade, California became a battleground, contested passionately throughout the remainder of the 1930s by frightened conservatives and frustrated liberals. The Dust Bowl migrants had the misfortune to get caught up in that polarized atmosphere. Victims of California's economic chills, they also came to know the consequences of the state's feverish politics.[35]

The EPIC Democrats had been registering gains all through the middle years of the decade. Despite Sinclair's defeat, a slate of liberal Democrats had won election to Congress and the state legislature in 1934. More followed in 1936, giving the Democrats for the first time in three decades control of the assembly and a majority of the congressional delegation. Leadership of the party had meanwhile shifted. Taking over from Sinclair, who had largely withdrawn from active politics, was Culbert Olson, who had won election to the state senate with EPIC backing in 1934 and had since established himself as the most effective of the legislature's liberals. By late 1937 it was pretty clear that he would be a candidate for governor in the upcoming election, and also clear that Republicans would find him a more formidable opponent than his predecessor. A respected political professional, Olson had none of Sinclair's image problems. Moreover, while embracing the basic principles and slogans of the EPIC program he had backed away from features that critics had called dangerous or impractical. Converting, in essence, a visionary movement into a reform program closer to the formulas of the New Deal, he stood a very good chance of finally bringing California into the Democratic column.[36]

The issue of migration was woven into the political context at several junctures, and almost always in ways that made conservatives uncomfortable. Associated on the one hand with mounting relief costs and the growing welfare apparatus, migration also raised the specter of thousands of new voters likely to support radical candidates and new welfare schemes. These fears had already played a role in the 1934 campaign. Sinclair himself had raised the migration issue. In an unguarded moment he had speculated that his election would mean that "one-half of the unemployed in the United States will hop the first freights to California." A reporter caught the remark, and Sinclair's delighted opponents then spent the rest of the campaign beating him with the issue, helping in the process to stir up the first episode of anti-migration fervor.[37]

The notion that migration might affect electoral outcomes had also surfaced in 1934 when the ultra-conservative *Los Angeles Times* accused EPIC of importing transients to steal the election.[38] It became a much more serious concern in the years that followed, particularly after it became clear

Figure 16. The *Saturday Evening Post* echoed the fear voiced by conservative Californians that a victory by Upton Sinclair would trigger a mass immigration of undesirables (November 2, 1934). (Reprinted from *Saturday Evening Post*, © 1934, The Curtis Publishing Co.)

that so many of the migrants were coming from the Southwest, a region that effectively knew only one political party. The 1936 election raised Republican fears. "No wonder we went Democratic," a San Bernardino County grower commented bitterly after the results were counted.[39] The approaching 1938 contest, with the governor's office at stake, doubled those fears. "Next year these dustbowlers will be voting," a *Times* editorial column warned. "Yes, they'll be voting . . . the Democratic ticket."[40]

It was not an idle worry. Partly perhaps as a way to document residential eligibility for relief purposes, the newcomers were registering to vote as soon as they could—spot surveys indicated upwards of 65 percent registration in some Little Oklahomas.[41] The migrants "may hold the balance of power," *Business Week* warned as the election neared. While voter registration had increased little more than 7 percent statewide, the magazine noted that the San Joaquin Valley counties had recorded a nearly 20 percent increase.[42]

If the state's conservatives thus decided that they had political reasons to fear the migrants, California's liberal and left communities had reasons for becoming their friends and defenders. The Dust Bowl migrants seemed to embody the kind of quest for economic justice which formed the emotional cornerstone of 1930s reform ideology. Here was a highly visible segment of Roosevelt's "third of a nation" engaged in a desperate struggle for survival, not just against unfortunate economic circumstances but also against what the left regarded as a vicious right-wing conspiracy of greed, the corporate chieftains of the state's agricultural industry.

It was an interesting formulation, and a somewhat new one. California farmers, like their counterparts elsewhere, had traditionally enjoyed a much warmer relationship with liberalism. One of the primary constituencies for radical and reform agendas in the late nineteenth century, many farmers had voted Populist in the 1890s and had supported still more vigorously the Progressive Republican movement that transformed California politics after 1910. The San Joaquin Valley had been prime Hiram Johnson country before the Great War, rallying behind the crusading governor's campaigns against railroad, land, and water monopolies, applauding the applications of government funds and expertise in matters of irrigation, credit, crop improvement, and marketing organization, endorsing his vision of a scientific farm sector dominated by efficient, prosperous small producers. The valley was still Johnson country in the 1930s, but both mentor and constituents had by then changed. Now senator, Hiram Johnson had long since surrendered his reforming zeal. Still not comfortable with genuine conservatives, he wandered through the 1930s a half-hearted New Dealer, comfortable with neither Roosevelt nor his enemies.[43]

California agriculture had taken a similar political turn. Since World War I, it had become a sophisticated, integrated industry, acquiring the organizational structures that analysts would later label "agribusiness." Chief among them was the Farm Bureau Federation, the industry's highly effective political voice. Officially nonpartisan, the Farm Bureau pursued an opportunistic policy which in the 1930s featured support for Roosevelt and most of the New Deal agricultural programs, but opposition to California's liberal Democrats. The labor issue and the strikes of 1933 had created the rift. Committed to anti-unionism, the farm bloc subsequently found most of its friends on the right and, apart from a handful of conservative valley Democrats such as Tulare Congressman Alfred Elliott, saw only foes among the state's Democrats.[44]

Thus both out of genuine compassion and also as a way to attack what Carey McWilliams was calling "farm fascism," California's New Dealers cast themselves as the migrants' protectors. Even before the 1938 campaign, a veritable army of radical activists and liberal sympathizers had been trying to aid and organize the newcomers. Nurses and doctors joined volunteer health teams to minister to the newcomers' considerable medical needs. Support groups such as the Simon Lubin Society and the John Steinbeck Committee to Aid Agricultural Organization collected clothes, food, and money to send to the valleys, all the while publicizing conditions there. Meanwhile scores of similarly motivated young men and women went to work for the Farm Security Administration, helping to set up the system of farm labor camps and migrant aid programs which that New Deal agency administered in the valleys. By 1938, these activists had also been joined by CIO labor organizers and cadres of Olson supporters intent on registering the migrants for the upcoming election. To conservatives, it seemed clear that the Southwesterners were being courted by a dangerous collection of enemies.

The California Citizens Association

Conservative concerns gave way to purposeful action in the months leading up to the 1938 election. Popular resentment, which had been building steadily as tax rates had risen, as communities were transformed, and as more and more strangers poured into the valleys, was now turned loose in a crusade that had as much to do with keeping Olson out of office as with its stated purpose.[45]

In June 1938, a group of San Joaquin Valley business and agricultural leaders meeting in Bakersfield launched the California Citizens Association for the purpose of coordinating efforts to solve the state's "migrant problem." They quickly captured press attention with a carefully worded petition to Congress. The document defined the essentials of the conservative solution. It began with the assertion that "California is faced with economic chaos and financial ruin through the influx of thousands of families, displaced in other states and pauperized by the depression." Arguing that there were neither jobs nor housing for them, the statement turned to what conservatives held to be the main reason for the influx: California's too generous relief systems. Not yet ready to criticize the State Relief Adminstration, which after all still remained in Republican hands, the CCA laid the blame on federal agencies, especially the newly initiated Farm Security Administration emergency grant program, but also blamed WPA jobs that paid more in California than in other states. The petition then demanded three remedies: that the federal government "provide relief for these people in their home communities," that "information be disseminated . . . that there will be no relief available for them if they emigrate to California," that the government provide funds to "aid and encourage the return of the idle thousands now here to their respective states."[46]

While the document, which was eventually signed by 100,000 Californians, was fairly restrained, the campaign to gather signatures and publicize the migrant threat was not. Quickly winning the support of the state Chamber of Commerce, the American Legion, and the Associated Farmers, the CCA took its petition into the communities of rural and, to a lesser extent, metropolitan California. School children gathered signatures door-to-door, while their elders discussed the migrant problem (or, as some liked to say, the "migraine problem") in civic and service clubs.

Sympathy for the newcomers, who were generally portrayed as "reliefers," "freeloaders," or "chiselers," found little place in these efforts. CCA secretary and Bakersfield businessman Thomas W. McManus set the tone, telling a committee of the legislature that "no greater invasion by the destitute has ever been recorded in the history of mankind" and demanding that "California jobs go to Californians and not to the horde of empty bellies from the Southwest who come in answer to the tribal call 'there's food in California.' "[47]

Conservative publications joined in condemning the newcomers. Under the headline "Kern County's Battle," the *Los Angeles Times* claimed that "the whole county is being smothered in indigents" and called on the FSA to end its relief program and close its labor camps.[48] Expanding the attack, the *Pacific Rural Press*, the state's leading farm journal, announced that "something like a quarter of a million migrants have come to California to add to our unemployment, our relief burden, and our disease and crime troubles." Offering just a touch of sympathy ("We feel sorry for them, but we also have to feel sorry for ourselves") the editorial went on to explain that "these migrants mean trouble in many ways." They bring disease, have taken over the schools, are "clay" in the hands of Communists, and "the crime record of these migrants include a lot of sordid, depraved acts."[49] *California*, the magazine of the state Chamber of Commerce, endorsed much the same list of particulars, explaining that the "ever oncoming horde of undesirables . . . brings slums to prosperous countrysides, unmorality to schools, and the threat of financial disaster to valley counties."[50]

And not to be overlooked was the political threat. "200,000 are here—more keep coming—they'll soon be voters—what can we do?" asked an article in the Chamber of Commerce magazine.[51] Warning that the state was being turned over to radicals and "crackpots" by the legions of "relief seekers" who had been lured west by those who stood to gain politically from their support, the conservative press hoped to forestall an Olson victory in November. That was the clear intent of an article appearing in *Business Week* during the summer of 1938. Only a year before, the magazine had reported in measured and at least partially favorable terms about the Dust Bowl migration's impact on California's valleys.[52] Now it told of the great fear of California businessmen who waited to learn what the thousands of eligible "Dust-bowlers" would do with their votes. "The destitute hordes who have come from Oklahoma, Arkansas, and Texas

. . . in response to reports of free food, free medical care, generous relief and the more abundant life generally, can be depended upon to vote almost as a unit for any and all 'handout' proposals that may come up at this and future elections."[53] The Chamber of Commerce went further, charging that the migrant problem was part of a Democratic party conspiracy. There is "a smell of political manipulation in so great a population coming into a State that is still in the doubtful column as to party dominance."[54]

The tactic failed to achieve its first political objective. Culbert Olson was elected governor by a healthy 220,000-vote margin, more than the number of votes attributable to the newcomers. Still, it was obvious that the migrants had helped. Olson piled up his largest leads in the southern San Joaquin Valley, winning up to 71 percent of the vote in precincts where Southwesterners were concentrated.[55]

But victory did nothing to resolve the migration issue. The controversy continued to build through the first two years of the Olson administration, helped along by the now altered conservative strategy of blocking the new governor's reform plans. The charge that Olson imperiled the state's economy by maintaining generous relief policies and catering to the nation's riffraff was one of the better weapons in the conservative arsenal.

The left also kept the issue burning. One of the many state agencies now under Democratic control was an obscure and inactive body called the Division of Immigration and Housing, which had been set up in the Progressive Era to monitor conditions in the farm labor camps. Olson turned it over to an intensely capable young journalist-attorney who was completing a book on California's farm labor system. Carey McWilliams soon had the agricultural industry up in arms. Publicizing the appalling conditions of life in camps and shack towns, the future editor of *The Nation* also used the Division to support the union organizing drive under way in the fields. With the publication of *Factories in the Field*, his exposé of industrial agriculture's history of "theft, fraud, violence and exploitation," he solidified his reputation as the state's "number one agricultural pest."[56] Actually, he had a close competitor. In March 1939, Viking Press published the first copies of *The Grapes of Wrath*. Within weeks the novel was a national best seller, and less than a year later it was an even more popular film. Suddenly the Dust Bowl migration was no longer just California's problem. Now the nation, even the world, would watch and judge the way the Golden State treated its newest and poorest.

Congress was soon involved. The CCA formally presented its petition in January 1939, but the divided California delegation could not concur on a course of action. Liberals and conservatives agreed that the situation in the valleys was deadly serious and that interstate migration was a matter for the federal government to handle, but disagreed strongly on what measures were needed. Where the right blamed relief benefits and advocated a "send-em-home" policy, the left accused growers of luring the migrants and called for expanded federal aid both in the migrants' home states and also to help people already in California. In the end, Congress did relatively little, though the liberals came away with part of their program. In early 1940, the House established the Select Committee to Investigate the Migration of Destitute Citizens and handed the chairmanship to John Tolan, a liberal Democrat from Oakland. If nothing else, Congress at least was prepared to continue publicizing the issue.[57]

Conservatives made more headway in Sacramento. Olson had no sooner taken the oath of office than he faced the first of several challenges involving the migrants. Resurrecting the defeated 1935 proposal, Assemblyman Frederick Houser (R-Los Angeles) introduced a bill making it a punishable crime for paupers and other undesirables to enter California. The legislature killed it, but conservatives came back with a stronger strategy, going after the State Relief Administration, which critics claimed was "pushing the State . . . into bankruptcy."[58] Olson dodged the first blows, but by the end of 1939 his control of the legislature, shaky to begin with, was gone. An "economy bloc" coalition of conservative Democrats and Republicans took charge the following year and began to dismantle the SRA. Adopting the logic of Republican State Senator William Rich, who called for an end to all assistance for newcomers ("If they come to this state, let them starve or stay away"), the legislature forced the agency in early 1940 to raise its eligibility requirement to three years' continuous residence in the state, a move which within a year had reduced the caseload by more than 50 percent. The following year, the economy bloc demolished the agency altogether, refusing to appropriate funds and in effect turning relief responsibility over to the separate counties, which then shed additional thousands from the rolls.[59]

Local authorities had also been carrying out their own anti-migrant campaigns. Boards of supervisors up and down the state and especially in rural counties had followed closely the 1939 battles in Washington and Sacramento, mostly supporting the restrictionist position of the CCA, and sometimes indulging new levels of hysteria. The Tulare County supervisors, for example, went on record condemning the "crooks coming into our county from the dust bowl."[60] As the climate worsened some officials explored the possibilities for taking action on their own. In Santa Barbara, the supervisors experimented with a county border blockade. In Kern, the grand jury followed up Thomas McManus's charges of voter fraud by indicting several FSA camp residents for illegally voting in a hotly contested special election.[61]

Then as 1939 drew to a close, the district attorneys in Tulare, Kings, and Yuba counties introduced still another tactic. The state's Indigent Act, first passed in 1933 and then revised in 1937, had made it a crime for someone to bring indigent persons across the state border. It had never been enforced, but now these officials decided to use the law to prosecute individual Southwesterners who helped their relatives enter the state. By the time the American Civil Liberties Union stepped in to challenge the constitutionality of the law, at least two dozen people had already been convicted of violations. The issue ultimately reached the United States Supreme Court, which in 1941 issued a landmark decision (*Edwards* v. *California*) that resolved the legal confusion that had contributed at least marginally to California's decade-long migration debate. Henceforth it would be understood that states had no right to interfere with the free movement of persons across their borders.[62]

The decision came too late, however, to have much impact on the crisis itself. Even as the justices deliberated, larger forces were bringing the state's migration anxiety to a close. World War II, still a distant nightmare for most Americans in 1941, was nevertheless beginning to rearrange the economy and political priorities, especially on the strategically important West Coast. Midway through that year the anti-migrant campaign, built upon a mood which dominated an entire decade, slipped into history. With the defense industry drawing workers to the coastal areas, with relief rolls shrinking and the price of crops rising, with the threat of farm labor unions diminished since the failed strikes of 1939, and with the Olson administration battered and looking towards probable defeat in the upcoming 1942 election, there were no longer reasons for Californians to worry about the issue of interstate migration. Indeed within months the state would find itself with a quite different problem: finding the labor force to man the defense industries and to grow the food to feed an embattled nation.

Overnight, the economic dynamic and its attendant mood had reversed itself. Leaving behind the mentality of scarcity and exclusivity, California after Pearl Harbor regained its more familiar booster frame of mind. Once again, the doors were thrown open to all comers—save, of course, the state's Japanese residents, now on their way to internment. So abrupt was the turn-around that, after months of taking testimony on the problems of destitute migration, Congressman Tolan's investigating committee became irrelevant. A new name and new assignment fixed that. In late 1941 it was recommissioned the House Select Committee to Investigate National Defense Migration, and charged with finding ways to improve the smooth flow of labor to the industrial and defense areas of the country.

So complete were the changed circumstances brought on by the war that only a few months after Pearl Harbor many Californians had trouble understanding their earlier anxieties. Growers especially had reason to think back fondly on the days of labor surpluses and wonder why they had not appreciated them at the time. Sam Maxcy, secretary-manager of the Visalia Chamber of Commerce, was almost contrite when he talked with James

Wilson in September 1942. "The Okie is the best deal the farmer ever had and he didn't know it," he explained. "The farmer had few worries with respect to him. It is different now. Where is the Okie? The farmer is caught without his Okie.... The farmer sure wants him."[63]

The Okie Stereotype

The fickle winds of political and economic fortune had created and then abruptly canceled California's fear of interstate migration. Yet as the language of Sam Maxcy's statement suggests, certain stereotypes remained. Long after the anti-migrant campaigns had ended, Californians would harbor demeaning images of the people they called "Okies." In the course of the Depression decade, many had learned to perceive the newcomers not merely as intruders, not merely as impoverished fellow citizens whose quest for scarce opportunities was resented, but as a separate and alien social group.

The label "Okie" conveyed that understanding. Long used as a casual synonym for Oklahoman, the term acquired broader and more sinister implications in California in the 1930s. Sometimes used in conjunction with its equivalents "Arkie" and "Tex," at other times as a generic term for Southwesterners or still more broadly for poor whites, its imprecision was part of the insult. John Steinbeck, often wrongly blamed for coining it, understood the term's ugly flexibility: " 'Well, Okie use' ta mean you was from Oklahoma. Now it means you're a dirty son-of-a-bitch. Okie means you're scum. Don't mean nothing itself, its the way they say it.' "[64]

Mostly what the term meant was that these people were different and inferior. Anthropologist Walter Goldschmidt observed the pattern of prejudice in the Kern County town of Wasco where in 1941 he was completing the research for his study of the social consequences of large-scale agriculture. Townspeople, he noted, attributed various character traits and sometimes physical traits to "the Okie," usually describing him as "ignorant and uneducated, dirty of habit if not of mind, slothful, unambitious, and dependent. He may be viewed now as emotional, again as phlegmatic; sometimes as sullen and unfriendly; again as arrogant and over-bearing. Not rarely is he accused of being dishonest. These characteristics are sometimes considered innate ... sometimes lack of education is held responsible."[65]

For several years now "Okies" had been the targets of one ugly slur after another, usually uttered carefully out of earshot. A King City bartender called them "no-good bastards" and refused them service.[66] To a prominent San Joaquin Valley businessman, they were "ignorant filthy people" who should not be allowed to "think they're as good as the next man!"[67] A Madera County doctor insisted that they were "shiftless trash who live like hogs, no matter how much is done for them," while a Kern

County physician held that they are "a strange people—they don't seem
to know anything. They can't read at all. There is nothing especially wicked
about them—it's just the way they live. There is such a thing as a breed
of people. These people have lived separate for too long, and they are like
a different race."[68] A grower from the same county was certain that most
of the migrants were too dumb to care for themselves: "You take some
of these guys and give them the best land in the Garden of Eden and they'd
starve to death."[69] Said another: "If you treat them like you would children
you pretty well get the idea how they should be handled."[70] A school
teacher concurred, calling the migrants "Adult Children." "They are not
an ambitious stock," she observed.

> I can spot a migrant on the street every time by watching him walk. He shuffles.
> He doesn't hold up his shoulders and face the world. His glance is often timid
> and wandering. I say these things, not harshly, but with sorrow. Generations
> of living as the underdog has made him like a scared bush rabbit.[71]

To be sure, these were not the views of all Californians, and especially
not those resident in the state's major metropolitan areas. Los Angeles,
San Francisco, and San Diego had not figured strongly in the migration
tensions of the later part of the decade and thus had little stake in the
resulting Okie stereotypes. As the Dust Bowl migration became front-page
news, metropolitan Californians began to use the terms "Okie" and "Arkie," but usually without the same mean edge found in the valleys. Missourian Sherman Coleman who came to southern California at age twenty-
one in 1937 recalls that people sometimes called him Okie, but "I didn't
mind," they were "just teasing."[72] Melvin Shahan remembers some difficulty in the high school he attended after moving to Los Angeles in the
mid–1930s, but he did not take it very seriously. "You were razzed a lot
about being an 'Okie' and coming out here," he says.[73] His younger sister,
Wanda, reacted more strongly. "There was a lot of talk about 'Okies.' . . .
I felt that they resented the people from Oklahoma."[74]

None of this compares with the hostile images circulating in the San
Joaquin Valley. We get a sense of the dimensions of the prejudice there
from an innovative opinion survey taken by one of Paul Taylor's University
of California graduate students. In the spring of 1938, just as the campaign
against the migrants was becoming daily news, Lillian Creisler arranged
to have more than one hundred students in English classes at Modesto
Junior College write essays detailing their attitudes towards a nearby Little
Oklahoma and the people who lived there. Analyzing the responses of
these sons and daughters of the local middle class, some of whom had lost
summer cannery jobs to the newcomers, Creisler concluded that roughly
half expressed feelings of bitterness and resentment and the other half
some kind of tolerance towards their migrant neighbors.

The essays in the first category contained the usual litany of charges about the migrants: They "are a relief problem," "lower the standards of living," "take jobs away," "give bad impression of Modesto," and "cause strikes." Others used stronger language, describing the Little Oklahoma residents as a "disgrace to [the] community," "uneducated and ignorant," "shiftless," "dirty," "not ambitious," "a source of disease," and "degenerate." Still others cruelly characterized the migrants as "lazy, dirty, poor white trash," the "scum of [the] earth," or "the lowest class of humans in U.S." And some proposed solutions such as "tear down the shacks and kick them out," "let them starve," and even, put them "on reservations."

The responses of the "tolerant" students are no less revealing. Many who expressed sympathy for the migrants nevertheless regarded them as a social problem. Typical of this attitude was the student who wrote that they "drag down [the] morals of California," but concluded that "they can be assimilated," or the one who said, "they are ignorant. They should be helped." Condescension of one sort or another marked the vast majority of essays. Only a few students would have agreed with the writer who declared that "Oklahomans are as good as anyone else."[75]

That Californians should say such things about fellow human beings was, of course, nothing new, provided that the subject's skin color was something other than white or their natal culture something other than Anglo-American. But these were white, old-stock American natives, Protestant Americans, rural Americans, heartlanders, who were now bearing the brunt of prejudices traditionally addressed to "foreigners."

The explanation for this development goes beyond the tensions of the 1930s, beyond calculations of economic impact, volume of influx, even beyond the problem of fearsome poverty. Not just any group of impoverished white interstate migrants would have excited these sorts of passions and prejudices. It took a special combination of background and present circumstances to trigger this response. It took, first, a close association with the heavily stigmatized occupation of farm laborer, and second, association with the equally stigmatized background of Southern sharecropper. These were elements out of which the Okie stereotype emerged.

As several scholars have observed, the prejudice against Okies was in large measure a feature of the valley's caste-like social structure. Though they were whites, the migrants inherited many of the social disabilities previously associated with the nonwhite farm labor force—much of this was simply the price of farm labor in California.[76] This explains one important feature of the Okie stereotype: it was never meant for all Southwesterners. Middle-class newcomers encountered little resentment or disesteem. Even in the midst of the anti-migrant campaign most were accorded the same basic respect as other whites of their economic station. The Okie stereotype was not in the first instance a matter of regional prejudice.

It could hardly have been otherwise. Some of the most respected families in the valley traced their origins to the Southwest or other parts of the South. Southerners had been conspicuous in the area since before the Civil War and in fact had made the southern portions of the valley a hotbed of Confederate activity during that conflict. The introduction of cotton after World War I had, as we have seen, attracted more, including some wealthy Southern investors. No one enjoyed more prominence in the valley than W.B. Camp and his brother Sol, South Carolinians who by the 1930s were two of the most powerful figures in California's cotton industry.[77]

The 1941 edition of *Who's Who in Kern County* provides a broader view of the position of Southerners and Southwesterners in the upper reaches of the area's social structure. The capsule biographies of the county's 1,000 most prominent men and women suggest a society of great fluidity, a new society whose elite mostly shared the experience of growing up somewhere else. Only 6 percent were native to the county or the surrounding area, but Californians from other parts of the state were numerous, accounting for 26 percent of the entries. Foreigners accounted for only 6 percent of the social elite, though Italian, German, and Scandinavian names were reasonably common among the American-born. Every region of the country was represented in the list, with the Midwest the leading birthplace (25 percent), followed distantly by the Southwest (11 percent).

Missourians and Texans and, less frequently, Oklahomans and Arkansans made the list of Kern County's important figures. Included were two Superior Court judges, both Missourians who had come to California prior to World War I; two Justices of the Peace, one of them an Oklahoman; the assistant Chief of Police of Bakersfield, a Texan who had come west in 1926; and the Kern County Treasurer, who had left Missouri in 1924. The list of prominent growers included T. Albert Davis and M. Finis Permenter, both Texans, and S. E. L. Wharton, from Missouri, all active in the right-wing Associated Farmers. Joseph Sears, a native of Arkansas who had come west in 1926, owned a chain of grocery stores; Walter Buaas, a Texan, owned an oil drilling company; Dixie Williams, an Oklahoman living in California since 1922, owned the Delano Hospital; and Tom M. Shafer, a Texan, published the *Wasco News*.[78]

No one called these people Okies, at least not seriously. Indeed some of these men and women participated wholeheartedly in the cycle of hostility directed at the less fortunate newcomers. Class was the essential dividing line. The Okie outgroup included people who were not Southwesterners, and the socially respectable ingroup included some who were.[79]

Sharecroppers All

But if class was the primary issue, it cannot be wholly separated from the matter of regional prejudice. While it is clear that the migrants inherited the opprobrium historically associated with farm work, it is wrong to assume, as most analysts have, that this would have happened in the same way to people of another background. The fact that these men and women were Southwesterners—and Southwesterners of a particular rank—made a difference in the eyes of the host society. Most of the migrants from the Southwest were presumed to be sharecroppers, and that, Californians readily believed, meant they were "white trash."

Oscar "Scotty" Kludt understood the subtleties of California's system of social status. As a teenager living in the migrant camps and working in the orchards and fields, he suffered the disdainful remarks of Californians who sometimes called him an Okie. But like the other non-Southwesterners who joined the farm labor force in the 1930s, the Kludts enjoyed certain prestige advantages when their background became known.

> Being from South Dakota wasn't as bad as being from Oklahoma but it was still pretty bad because we talked different. We spoke with German accents and most of us were German . . . but if you were from Oklahoma you were really bad because they were considered trash. Being from South Dakota and North Dakota was just a little bit better than being from Oklahoma.[80]

In Wasco some of the leading citizens thought the distinctions more than minor. Differentiating between Midwestern wheat farmers, whom he saw as the genuine "dust bowlers," and Southwestern sharecroppers, a prominent grower maintained that "the dust bowl people who came out here have settled down and become real citizens. There isn't one of them that hasn't gotten a steady job and settled down. But these Oakies who came out here, who weren't anything before they left, don't amount to anything. They are filthy dirty—you give them a decent house, and in a couple of weeks they are spitting through the cracks."[81] The town Justice of the Peace echoed the distinction. "The people who were blown out from the dust bowl in Kansas, Nebraska, and the Dakotas are as good a class as you'll find anywhere. But those from Oklahoma, Arkansas, and Texas . . . are made up of the so-called 'poor white trash' which even the Negroes consider to be below them. . . . About 95% of them are of that poor class."[82]

Underlying these discriminations were both old and new perceptions about regional character, understandings based on the recognition that the Southwest was part of the broader South. White Southerners (not to mention blacks) have probably always been subject to a certain level of unfriendly stereotyping in other parts of the United States, especially if they were poor. The historic tensions between North and South had much to do with this, but ancient understandings of Southern social structure were also involved. Since colonial times, Southerners themselves had used caste labels like "lubber," "tarheel," and "white trash" to mark off the least fortunate segments of the privileged race. The term "poor white" itself had those implications, suggesting images of social and perhaps physical degeneracy, connoting, as one writer put it, "something more than a white who is poor."[83]

What the South invented, Northerners and Westerners had readily used. As early as the 1850s, Gold Rush Californians—the large majority of them from Northern states—actively deprecated Southerners, whom they called "Pikers," a name derived, much like the later "Okie," from the large representation of migrants from a single area, Pike County, Missouri. Pictured as congenitally ignorant, filthy, slothful, and improvident, of base morals and minimal pride, as either rank backwoodsmen or aimless drifters, but in either case endowed with an endless supply of similarly destined children—this was California's first application of the white-trash stereotype.[84]

There would be others. A group of Texans who founded the town of El Monte seem to have enjoyed a similar reputation among neighbors in the Los Angeles basin through the 1870s.[85] So did some of the early twentieth-century migrants from the Southwest. A 1920 report on the recruitment of Oklahoman and Texan harvest hands for the new cotton farms in the Imperial Valley referred to them as "poor white stuff," while an article on the same subject claimed that residents called them "Texicans" in recognition of the migrants' presumed low educational and moral character.[86] Similarly in Los Angeles, a 1924 report on life in a municipal auto-camp spoke of a "Texas" section of the facility where poor families from Oklahoma and Texas had taken up semi-permanent residence. Many of them, the author decided, "seem to have no ambition to better their present condition, and are . . . satisfied to live in the filth of their hovels."[87]

Clearly, few of the images later to be applied to Okies originated in the 1930s. To some extent, rural Southwesterners settling in California had always contended with the "poor white" syndrome. No less a visitor than Lyndon Baines Johnson has testified to that. Seventeen years old and newly graduated from high school, Johnson and three friends left home in 1924 for a Model-T tour of California. It came as a surprise to the young Texans that Californians should look on them as "hillbillies."[88]

But before the Depression era none of this was particularly serious. Migrants who remember California during the 1920s are quite clear on that point. Ruth Criswell first came west with her parents in 1922, at the sensitive age of thirteen. "I saw none of this discrimination that people later suffered who came from back there. At that time, it was very pleasant. They treated you real nice. There was no stigma attached to the fact that you came from Oklahoma." The family stayed a year and then returned to Texas, and it was not until 1937 that she came back, this time with her own husband and children. Everything was different. Her husband could not get a job in the construction trades: "They would be very favorable until they found out he was from Oklahoma." There was this new word, "Okie"—before

"I never heard of such a thing." And most painful of all, she had to watch her daughters, not much younger than she had been on her first visit, contend with hurtful comments by school mates and teachers: "My oldest girl would come home so mad everyday she could hardly stand it."[89]

This change, as we have seen, had its primary basis in the complex of migration anxieties, but important too was an heightened awareness among Californians of the white-trash concept and the problems of Southern tenant farmers. The years between Criswell's moves had seen a great deal of national attention focused on both matters.

The 1920s and 1930s, historian George Tindall reminds us, were the decades during which Americans discovered the "Benighted South," the South of lynch mobs, political corruption, Bible-thumping, and dirt-poor illiterate sharecroppers. After decades of mint and magnolias, of literary, song, and film images of the mannered South of the "Lost Cause," the region now found itself with an additional reputation for backwardness, bigotry, and unreason.[90]

The new image of the South had much to do with the self-conscious modernism that the nation's leading cultural figures had embraced by the 1920s and with the highly charged political-religious contests that seemed to set rural against urban America in that decade. Determined to liberate the culture from its rural mainsprings, northern luminaries such as Sinclair Lewis and H.L. Mencken spared no effort to tarnish the heretofore cherished image of small-town and agricultural life. Mencken in particular helped to make the South symbolic of the worst of those "forlorn backwaters." The region, as he portrayed it, was a place "with darkies snoozing on the horseblocks, pigs rooting under houses and the inhabitants full of hookworm and malaria." It was the "bunghole of the United States, a cesspool of Baptists, a miasma of Methodism, snake-charmers, phoney real-estate operators, and syphilitic evangelists." The South, he told his appreciative Northern audience, was a dried-up civilization inhabited exclusively by "Holy Rollers," "hill billies," and "ignoramuses" who share a "peasant-like suspicion of all book learning that a plow hand cannot grasp."[91]

But Northerners were not alone in stirring interest in the South and its problems. A number of Southern-born academicians, journalists, and novelists—Howard Odum, William Faulkner, Erskine Caldwell, James Agee, and Thomas Wolfe, to name only the most famous—also began to write critically about their home region. Modernism was part of the issue. Focusing on evidence of the South's poverty, illiteracy, and disease, many were convinced that the region had locked itself in a vise of economic underdevelopment because of its historic commitment to the production of cotton. But mixed in also was a newer interest in folk life, in simple lives honestly led, that was one of the hallmarks of Depression-era literature.[92]

Through the efforts of these writers, the American reading public during the 1920s and 1930s learned a great deal about the Southern tenant farming system and its victims. With racial questions not yet part of the nation's public policy agenda, most of the attention centered on the region's poor white population, a development that had consequences for Southwesterners migrating to California.

The quality of this work varied considerably, and out of some of it came misleading images of the South and its people. In their eagerness for impact, some journalists and novelists used overly broad strokes to portray the scope and depth of Southern poverty. Spared the important distinctions, Americans outside the South came to believe that nearly all cotton farmers, and certainly all tenant farmers, shared the fate of the lowliest sharecropper. In his novel *The White Scourge*, Edward Everett Davis, a professor of agriculture at the University of Texas, draws a nightmarish portrait of rural Southerners damaged by generations of cotton-induced poverty.

> Below us lies a cotton field, the great open air slum of the south, a perennial Hades of poverty, ignorance, and social depravity. . . . Too much of America's worthless human silt has filtered into the cotton belt. . . . The most serious rural problem in the South is . . . that of the biologically impoverished tribes of marginal humanity—black, white and Mexican—subsisting on cotton. . . . The human creature of weak body and moronic mentality who would perish without reproducing his hideous kind amid the blizzards and wheat fields of the Dakotas can survive successfully and populate half a schoolroom in the mild cotton regions of Texas.[93]

The best example of such writing and the work that did the most to convince a wide public of the degeneracy of Southern tenant farmers was Erskine Caldwell's immensely popular 1932 novel, *Tobacco Road*. Like the others, Caldwell's purpose was laudable: the book was intended as a radical critique of the ravages of an unjust social and economic system. But to make his point he crafted a caricature of a white sharecropper completely debased by generations of service to worn-out Georgia cotton land. His main character, Jeeter Lester, along with his dim-witted wife and their moronic children, represent humanity at its most depraved. Filthy, diseased, totally illiterate, driven by uncontrollable sexual lusts, they lack basic concepts of morality and even the will to survive. As the novel ends, the family is starving, the whole lot of them so lazy and incapacitated they fail to make even the most basic efforts to obtain food.[94]

Caldwell's novel was a parable, but it was often taken literally. Overnight, the book and its main character, Jeeter Lester, became household words, symbols for Southern rural poverty. As millions of Americans devoured the novel and more flocked to see the stage play, images of social maladjustment that formerly had been associated with relatively small numbers of poor Southerners began to be loosely applied to the whole class of Southern tenant farmers. "The nation has become Tobacco Road conscious," a sociologist reported in 1938. Explaining that the concept of poor white has been "revivified," she noted that everywhere "a relatively new and almost universal caricature of the great body of poor Southern rural and industrial folk as 'poor whites' " had taken hold. Nowhere was this more true than in up-to-date California, where backwardness had long been a cultural sin. The "poor white" concept found ready application: the thousands of rural families arriving in the state from the Southwest.[95]

"Tobacco Road has come to California," a journalist reported in 1938. He went on to explain that he had personally "thought that play, with all its poverty and filth, was a gross exaggeration—until the same kind of folks landed here on us."[96] Taking all their clues from the migrants' current poverty, many Californians concluded that the Dust Bowl migrants were the kind of ignorant, uneducated poor whites about whom Caldwell had written. The newcomers were obviously dirt poor, they worked in the cotton fields, and dressed in faded overalls and cheap cotton dresses. And when they spoke, their distinct drawl and rural Southwestern phraseology often sounded illiterate to California ears.

But the clues were misleading. Most of the newcomers had little in common with the white-trash stereotype. Poverty they knew; degeneracy was something else. Tenant farmers they may have been, but not at the cost of dignity or respectability. In education and sophistication some did lag behind California norms, but few were illiterate or ignorant of modern standards. Eighty-five percent claimed at least a sixth-grade education. As for morality, their definitions were often stricter than those of their hosts. But blinded by the powerful imagery of two stigmatic associations—farm labor and tenant farming—the Californians understood little of this.[97]

Nor were the mistaken assumptions about the migrants' background limited to those residents who were upset and angry about the migration. On some level most Californians accepted the idea that the migrants were Southern "poor whites." Even those who cast themselves as the migrants' defenders often shared the presumptions about the newcomers' background. One need only glance through the stacks of reports and articles written by various doctors, nurses, social workers, and teachers who ministered to the migrants to see just how many were convinced that the newcomers from the Southwest suffered from the kind of severe social and cultural deprivation implied in the stereotypes of cotton sharecroppers. In their eyes, the Southwesterners were basically an uneducated, unsophisticated, backward people with curious homespun ways, a people who, in the words of one sympathetic Farm Security Administration investigator, "seem almost child-like at times, as indeed they are."[98]

The condescending attitudes of those who sympathized with the migrants are nowhere better illustrated than in the reports of Tom Collins, the dedicated camp manager who did so much to establish the Farm Security

Figure 17. Tom Collins visiting a family in Kern County's newly opened Farm Security Administration camp, 1935. John Steinbeck relied heavily on Collins's colorful vignettes about the migrants, and dedicated *The Grapes of Wrath* "To Tom, Who Lived It." (*Dorothea Lange, © 1982, The Oakland Museum, The City of Oakland*)

Administration's migratory camp program in California. A tireless worker who cared deeply about the people who sought shelter at his camp, Collins nevertheless saw them as quaint and helpless, an impression he conveyed time and again in his weekly reports to FSA headquarters. In little sketches of camp life made especially condescending by his tortured attempts to transcribe Southwestern accent and grammar, Collins presented a portrait of the migrants as simple people unaccustomed to the complexities of modern life. He particularly enjoyed describing their encounters with such symbols of civilization as the flush toilet:

> There was our new neighbor from Arkansas—sitting on the concrete floor, legs stretched on both sides of the toilet bowl. Beside her was a pile of "freshly laundered" clothing. In the bowl was more clothing. . . . The new neighbor broke the silence—"The fella who dun build this air tub must a thot that all wimin be plenty short. Why this air tub aint big 'nuf ter hold my man's pans for me to wash." [99]

Other vignettes purported to show the primitive beliefs and superstitions of the migrants:

> When word reached the camp that the new baby had been born to one of our families "Aint a gal be it? Well I swan. I allus athot that fella was astronger than at. His littl wom'n aint that a strong alooker." We found that they have the belief that a "gal baby" is a sign that the mother is the stronger of the family. In this case our new arrival was a gal.[100]

Collins was not being intentionally scornful, and his frame of reference was not the anti-ruralism of H. L. Mencken. An aspiring novelist, he shared instead the fascination with folk culture and documentary expression that many of the nation's leading artists and writers had turned to in the 1930s. Compensating for the failures of modern economic systems, they now looked for grounding in the traditions and lives of ordinary Americans. It was a quest that animated some of the signal cultural accomplishments of the decade, including many of its finest novels, the documentary journalism of James Agee and Walker Evans, and the monumental efforts of the WPA to compile folksongs and life stories in communities all across the country. But in the hands of less skilled observers this perspective yielded exaggerated images. To Collins, the people seeking shelter in his labor camp were colorful relics of the nation's rural past.[101]

And he was not alone in propounding those images. Prepared to find evidence of backwardness, doctors and nurses apparently noticed little else. Barely acknowledging the hundreds of families who came to them anxious for the best in modern medical care, health workers preferred to describe at length the occasional mother who insisted that her "Black Draught Purgative" had served her family for generations or who believed in weaning babies "by the sign of the moon."[102] Teachers and social workers likewise all too often seem to have noticed only those families where illiterate parents insisted their children work rather than go to school, and failed to realize that these comprised a minority of the migrant group.[103] Writing for the *New York Times* about their song-collecting trip on behalf of the Library of Congress, folklorists Charles Todd and Robert Sonkin followed the same course. Ignoring the fact that most of what they recorded derived from commercial radio, they emphasized the migrants' supposed affection for old English ballads and "tunes that a more prosperous America has forgotten in the process of growing up and getting rich."[104] A sympathetic Oakland journalist carried the pre-modern romanticism still further, stressing the curious antiquity of the migrants' linguistic habits. "To me their speech, with its limp, drawling tone, its queer old-English usages, its odd expressions, like 'plumb wore out,' its mak-ens, and tak-ens and go-ens and do-ens, are a constant delight."[105]

Genuine sympathy underlined these efforts, making them in no way comparable to cruelly administered white-trash characterizations. It is also true that much of what registers as condescending in the 1980s passed unnoticed in the less sensitive 1930s. But recognized or not these images compounded the sense of otherness and inferiority that California seemed in so many ways to impart.

The well-meaning version of the stereotype is also discernable in the novel which made the term Okie a permanent part of the American vocabulary. Falling into the trap of pre-modernism that snared many other sympathizers, John Steinbeck in *The Grapes of Wrath* crafted a portrait that many former Dust Bowl migrants have long regarded as demeaning.

The Joads, heroic in their life-and-death battle with an irrational economic system, are cast as uneducated dirt farmers bereft of many of the moral and social graces that sophisticated Americans of the period valued. Steinbeck may have invested his characters with an underlying human dignity which won the hearts of millions of readers, but to many Southwesterners who read the novel what stood out was the graphic sexuality, the crude living habits, the illiterate-sounding speech, and the general lack of modern sophistication. Using vignettes straight from Collins's notebook, Steinbeck kept his characters close to nature, close to the soil, so as to realize his critique of the machine and its civilization. Poignant and powerful it is; but some former migrants wish it had never been written.

"I think the stigmatism of Steinbeck's *Grapes of Wrath* will always be with us," says one woman, adding that she has "spent a lot of years hating him."[106] As Wofford Clark sees it, the book made Oklahomans "look like a bunch of ignorant people who had never seen a pencil or a piece of paper." "There were poor people and ignorant people back there," his wife Ruth adds, "but they were every place; that's the thing. [The book] made it look like too many people were like that, but they weren't."[107] The Clarks are right. It is not that there were no semi-literate, backward folk among the migrants who came to California, but rather that Steinbeck, like so many other observers, failed to convey that the majority were different. *The Grapes of Wrath*, for all its good intentions, ironically helped to solidify some of the unfortunate images which Californians already associated with the newcomers from that region.

Critics and defenders of the Dust Bowl migration each tended to see the migrants as ill-prepared for California society, even if they disagreed on what to do about it. Those who regarded the migration as a political and economic threat obviously felt little inclination to help the newcomers adjust, and to the extent that they embraced the white-trash construction probably agreed with the school principal who argued that elevating "these

Figure 18. Art and life come together in many layers in this 1940 photograph. As if to acknowledge the media attention that so shaped their experience, several migrant families camp in the shadow of a billboard that advertises the film based on the book about their lives. Brilliant photographer then captures the entire ironic scene. (*Dorothea Lange,* © *1982, The Oakland Museum, The City of Oakland*)

simple, helpless people . . . to even a degree of responsible citizenship is going to be a long heartbreaking job—a process of evolution that probably will require several generations."[108] On the other hand, their liberal counterparts were more sanguine about the migration's consequences and more optimistic about the prospects for educating and uplifting the newcomers. Nurse Mary Sears conveyed the confident view of the task ahead when she compared the Southwesterners to their broken-down automobiles and prescribed a full regimen of social repair for these "flat, tired people." "Just as surely as they can fix those old jalopy tires," she explained brightly, "we shall pump into these people the medicines, the vitamins, the calories, the teaching, and with it the courage to rebuild their lives in a new and difficult environment."[109]

These evaluations—the helpful as much as the hostile—comprised the major challenge that Southwesterners would face in California. In the course of the 1930s Californians had fashioned a set of associations into a troubling stereotype laden with suggestions of inferiority. It was something that virtually all Southwesterners would have to confront. Even the prosperous ones, themselves never really the target of prejudice, were likely to be haunted by the stigma that now attached itself, however inconsistently, to their regional background.

4

The Dilemma
of Outsiders

LIKE MOST WHO CAME WEST IN THE 1930S, ERNEST ATCHLEY HAD NOT BEEN PRE-
pared for the hostility he encountered. He had assumed that as a white,
Anglo-Saxon American he would be welcome in California. Now the "old
Texican" was writing a goodbye letter to his friends at the Yuba City FSA
camp:

> This is a great day, although it is raining, because what we have been waiting
> for patiently here three months for, has come to pass. We're leaving today
> for home, sweet home, and if we ever come back, we'll have a round trip
> ticket tucked securely away.
>   California is all right for Californians, but we're going back to "Big D"
> where the long-horn cattle roam, where the "gen'ral sto'keeper treats yo'all
> lak humans", and where hospitality reigns. A fellow don't appreciate home
> until he comes to California.[1]

Atchley's was one of several responses that suggest the pain and alienation that many migrants experienced. Confusion was often the first reaction; few had ever before felt the sting of prejudice. Several newcomers
registered their bewilderment in letters to the editor of the valley's major
newspapers. "The Californians rave, they slur, criticize, gossip, swear and
demean the Eastern people. What kind of world is this?" an angry Althes
Robbins demanded.[2] "Why is California so bitter toward migrants?" an-

other letter-writer asked. "Are we not human? . . . After all, this is supposed to be a free country."[3]

Expectations were part of the problem. Other groups, especially non-whites, routinely dealt with discrimination more serious than anything Okies faced. But to native-born white Protestants this was new. "May I ask if this is not supposed to be a free country and cannot natural born American citizens come and go as they please if they break no laws? . . . is not California still part of the United States?" a woman wanted to know.[4] "I was born and raised in Oklahoma and until I came to California I had no cause to regret it," G.A. Cody informed the *Fresno Bee*. "I would like to know who Californians think they are when they put themselves on a pedestal. Oklahoma is a full fledged state within these United States and as this is a free country we have every moral and legal right to be here that you have."[5]

Most had always assumed that their race and heritage guaranteed a certain basic respect and were shocked to learn otherwise. "This family truly thinks all American citizens are worthy and should have a home anywhere in the good U.S.A. free from prejudice and illwill," wrote one resettled migrant who signed himself "American citizen."[6] "We have the Right to live in Calif if we Want to," a Missouri woman wrote to President Roosevelt, "For the U.S.A. Belong to the American peopl[e] and I am a Real American."[7]

Statements like these suggest the psychological challenge that accompanied resettlement in the late 1930s. Prejudice always hurts, but in different ways depending upon content and context. For Southwesterners, the attitudes of the Californians raised fundamental issues of dignity and identity, calling into question the prerogatives of a "real American" heritage long taken for granted. In the years to come that tension would figure strongly in their efforts to regain social composure.

There was no single strategy. The newcomers reacted in diverse ways to the stigmas and challenges California imposed, some looking for acceptance through careful acts of conformity, others avoiding contact with the host population and developing an independent cultural community. But whether they tried to hide their background or moved to emphasize it, a legacy of pain and awkwardness and a certain unresolved quality in their relationship with California seems to have remained.

Ernest Atchley was resolving his relationship by ending it. Like the migrant poet who announced facetiously, "I'm tired of life in this heavenly place," he headed back, figuring that, whatever the economic problems, the situation back home was preferable to the bigotry of California.[8] There is no way to know precisely how many others made the same choice, but there are indications that the number was large. Border officials routinely counted "tin-can tourists"—their name for poor people traveling in overloaded old cars—both entering and leaving the state. By the end of the 1930s, the flow back across the border was averaging 22 to 30 percent of the inflow.[9]

Another clue comes from one of Robert McMillan's Oklahoma migration studies. Tracing the movements of more than 8000 persons who lived in five rural Oklahoma townships during the 1930s, he found that 574 people had moved to California in the course of that decade and that, by 1940, 91 had returned, a ratio of roughly one in six.[10] For the region as a whole the return rate must have been higher. Given the lack of opportunity in rural parts of Oklahoma, it is likely that more returnees ended up in towns and cities than in open country areas of the sort he was studying. Moreover, it is not clear whether he counted migrants who stayed only briefly in California. Probably a large minority of those who tried California returned. One cannot travel far in the Southwest today without meeting people who lived in California during the 1930s or 1940s. Some are like the man who tells of kneeling in a California church and praying, "Lord, if you'll just get me back to Texas, I promise I'll never go back to California again." Just once in forty years has he broken that vow, and only because his sister in Modesto was seriously ill.[11]

Those who returned for good were part of a larger contingent of migrants who would have easily made the same choice if it had been at all financially feasible. Many tried. "We went back to Oklahoma," recalls Paul Westmoreland, who goes by the name "Okie Paul." "Every good Okie left more than once—and tried again and failed again. Did that more than once until we finally left for good."[12] Lois Judd also tried. After several months in California she was so upset and homesick that she wrote a poem entitled "Back to Arkansas," which pledged "someday soon, we can't be wrong/ we're going back where we belong."[13] But when she and her husband did go back, they realized that there was still no way to make a living, so they returned to California, this time ready to stay. Oklahoman Myra Pipkins knew the syndrome well. "Well I'll tell you," she volunteered, "they come out here," find they do not like it, so go back home, "and they're not there over a month or so until . . . they find that things is so bad, rundown, . . . as far as work is concerned . . . they just decide they'll come back" to California.[14]

And not everyone learned their lesson on that first return trip home. Walter Goldschmidt talked to an Oklahoman whose travels back and forth to California were a study in frustration. Originally he had come to California in April 1937, but five months later he returned to Oklahoma. After a short stay he returned to California in time for the cotton harvest. This time he remained for two full years. But in 1940 he once again went back to Oklahoma. For nine months he managed to earn a living there, only to decide that prospects after all were better in California. He had been back less than six months at the time of the interview.[15]

The return flow did not stop with the close of the Depression decade; in a sense it has never stopped. One of the distinctive features of the Okie experience in California is the persistence of strong emotional ties to places left behind. Especially in their retirement years many have moved back, taking pension checks and settling down once again near places they left four or five decades before.

Elsie Blagg came to California at age twelve in 1936, her family having been dusted out of the Oklahoma panhandle. Ten years later her parents returned to Oklahoma, but Elsie stayed on in California, by this time raising a family of her own. Three decades passed. Then in 1982, anxious to be near her aging parents, she and her husband sold their business and moved back to the old hometown of Hardesty, Oklahoma. With the still more recent addition of Elsie's California-born daughter, the family's re-migration cycle is now complete—three generations all back where they began.[16]

As the Blagg story suggests, family and kin relations generally provide the primary incentive for these moves—and that would have been true as well for those who returned in the 1930s. But kinship alone does not explain the long-lasting commitment to old homes that remains common among California's Okie population. Interstate migrants from other regions also leave relatives behind, but usually without the same psychological consequences. Helped by certain features of their regional culture, especially homesick themes of country music, Southwesterners in California made the concept of "back home" a central leitmotif of their communal experience.

Whether or not they have any desire to return to the Southwest, many former migrants today retain a pronounced dual loyalty. "Our children have grown up here, bought and built homes, and are raising their kids here although a part of them will always be in Old Oklahoma," one elderly woman explains.[17] "I have learned to love California. It is home now," says another who left for a time after her first experience in the state. But she still visits Oklahoma each year, and is adamant that "I am an Okie and I'm proud of my heritage."[18] Joyce Vernon Seabolt was only eight years old when he moved to California in 1936, but return visits and other contact with relatives have kept his Oklahoma heritage firmly in focus. "I never forget that I am from Oklahoma," he says firmly.[19] Maggie Mouser had been in California much longer. It was 1925 when she and her husband settled in Kern County. Yet even after all those years her identification with her old hometown of Stigner, Oklahoma, was obvious at the time of her 1982 interview. She still made occasional trips back to visit relatives. Moreover, each week she read the copy of the *Stigner News* that arrived by mail. "I get all the news of the younger generation," she explained.[20]

Not everyone shares this orientation. Some migrants quickly lost all meaningful ties to their old homes, either as the entire family relocated to California or because they did not feel that it was important to maintain close connections with those who stayed behind. Nevertheless, in numbers large enough to influence the normative standards of the entire group, a substantial number of former migrants maintained strong attachments to old home settings. This goes beyond the normal parameters of homesickness that persons relocating generally feel. The difference is that Okies, like some foreign immigrants, answered the special psychological challenges of resettlement by making homesickness something of a community project.[21]

Accommodation or Isolation?

Those who did remain in California found all sorts of personal solutions to the social difficulties they faced, but two rather distinct strategies of adjustment can be observed. Some Southwesterners directly pursued the goal of assimilation, trying, often more vigorously than other interstate migrants, to adopt California styles and standards and to gain entry into the social circles of the host population. Others worked much less at assimilation, their sense of dignity dictating a contrary strategy of avoidance. Remaining apart from the world of middle-class California, they turned instead to people of their own background for social contact and mutual support, and set the course for the development of a separate Okie subculture.

Location had something to do with these patterns. Metropolitan settlers were more readily absorbed in the surrounding society than their valley counterparts. The difference can be seen in the marriage patterns of Southwesterners living in these settings (Table 4.1). In Los Angeles County there is no indication of any significant social barriers. Almost three-quarters of Southwestern-born brides and grooms marrying in 1939 chose spouses of different regional backgrounds. Most Southwesterners seem to have interacted freely with other non-Hispanic whites. The valley case is strikingly different. The majority of brides and grooms in Kern and Stanislaus counties married endogamously, and, what is more, would continue to do so as late as 1959. The rate was highest in Kern County, where 65 percent of Southwesterners marrying in 1939 chose spouses of the same background, followed by 62 percent in 1949 and 68 percent in 1959. Stanislaus County was less consistent, the in-marriage rate moving from 51 percent to 62 percent and back down to 45 percent over the three decades.

Interpreting these figures can be tricky. Knowing little about the availability of potential spouses in particular communities, it is difficult to say whether these marriage choices show the effects of discrimination by other whites, self-selection by Southwesterners, or simply ecological factors. Certainly, the growing population of Southwesterners and their uneven class and residential distribution account for much of the valley in-marriage,

Table 4.1. Marriage Choices of Southwesterners in Three California Counties, 1939–59

Spouse	Los Angeles	Kern	Stanislaus
1939			
Southwesterner*	27%	65%	51%
White Californian**	13	14	21
Other white	58	20	27
Hispanic/nonwhite	1	1	1
	99%	100%	100%
N =	(183)	(343)	(215)
1949			
Southwesterner	22%	62%	62%
White Californian	17	14	17
Other white	60	22	21
Hispanic/nonwhite	2	2	0
	101%	100%	100%
N =	(129)	(318)	(303)
1959			
Southwesterner	—	68%	45%
White Californian	—	19	28
Other white	—	12	26
Hispanic/nonwhite	—	1	2
		100%	101%
N =		(154)	(133)

*Includes second generation: California-born of two Southwestern-born parents.
**White native-born Californians excluding second-generation Southwesterners
Source: See Appendix D.

particularly in the later years when the stigma of the Okie background was much reduced. Still, whatever the reason, the fact that the majority of Southwesterners were marrying one another was significant. In the overall pattern one glimpses the coming-together process that permitted the replication of outlooks and values that would comprise the Okie subculture.[22]

However bold the contrast appears in the marriage data, the social adjustment experiences of Southwesterners in the valleys and cities were not discontinuous. In both settings there were tensions associated with the Southwestern background, and in each migrants were divided in their personal strategies. The difference was that social acceptance was more readily available in the metropolitan areas, and Southwesterners were more dispersed. In the San Joaquin Valley, opportunities for assimilation were fewer and group resources greater.

In both zones some migrants made deliberate efforts to fit in, often at a cost of significant personal change. Indeed, part of the misfortune of the Dust Bowl migration experience can be measured in the number of Southwesterners who felt compelled to dissociate themselves from aspects of their background.

The label "Okie" was something nearly everyone sought to avoid; only the most confident and defiant in those early years relished the term as a form of self-identification. Although Californians used the Okie label loosely, the migrants themselves relied on narrow definitions to get out from under the stigmatic associations. Texans and Missourians, for example, were quick to assert that the term applied only to Oklahomans ("Arkies" had their own problems). Goldie Farris recalls her reaction when somebody called her an Okie. "You let them know right away that you were from Texas. There was just a feeling that maybe you were just a little bit better, maybe you were just a notch above them."[23] So too when a reporter addressed Mrs. Willis using the offending label, she responded tartly, "That's not right. We're Texans. There's a difference."[24] Interviewed in 1968, Mrs. Claude Botkins was still distancing herself from the label in the same manner. "There's been a lot of investigation about Okies but I never knew who they were talking about because I happen to be born in Texas, my husband was born in Missouri."[25]

Oklahomans used other devices to dissociate themselves from the troublesome term. Insisting that the appellation pertained only to the Dust Bowl era settlers, earlier migrants "object strenuously to being classified with the present 'Okies and Arkies,' " said one report.[26] Typical was the foreman of a lemon orchard near Santa Paula. "I'm from Oklahoma," he clarified, "but I got here a little ahead of the rest of them, so now I'm a Californian."[27]

Treating the term as a synonym for "no-account trash," other Oklahomans took refuge in their own feelings of respectability, assuring themselves that the label applied only to those who lacked ambition or morals or some other quality central to their particular understanding of decency. Not even the fact that she and her family endured the ragged life of a squatter encampment could bring one Oklahoma native to identify with "those Okies." Like many others, she ducked the label by pinning it on someone else.[28]

All this was quite common. The label Okie would remain a source of embarrassment for a long while, becoming a thing of pride only gradually and mostly since the late 1960s. Until then most Southwesterners were happy to leave the term to the Oklahomans, and the Oklahomans in turn were usually anxious to escape it when they could. At least in public, few wanted to be identified as Okies.

But self-labeling was one thing; efforts to change personal habits and disguise backgrounds were something else. Growing up in the Los Angeles suburb of Pomona, Ted Gehringer felt quite sensitive about his Oklahoma origins. None of his friends were from the Southwest, and even though they used the term jokingly, when they called him "Okie" it made him feel different and uneasy. Not wanting to be thought of as one of the Dust Bowl migrants everyone was reading about, he stopped wearing bib overalls and started losing his Oklahoma accent.[29] Living in nearby Ontario, Oklahoman Robert Kessler felt it necessary to make the same changes, especially in speech. "I had an awful accent," he recalls. "I wasn't really happy about the fact that I had a drawl and was from the Midwest because possibly they looked down on some of us."[30]

Peggy Staggs went through a similar process. Ten years old when her family moved to San Diego, she was surprised and hurt when her teacher announced, "My, you are really smart for an Okie." "This was my first experience of being considered part of an inferior group," she later explained. "It was really a shocker. . . . [Back home] we were used to thinking of ourselves as superior." To avoid further embarrassment, Peggy soon learned how to fit in. When the family moved to Fullerton, near Los Angeles, she did everything possible to act, dress, and, above all, talk like a Californian.[31]

Depending upon the context, certain adults also felt pressured to become "Californianized." Shortly after Ruby Barnes arrived in Long Beach with her husband in 1941, she was admonished by an earlier migrant to get rid of her Oklahoma accent. She had too much pride to try to hide her background, but she remembers others who following the advice.[32] Beverly Barrett's parents were the type who would have responded. She describes the personal transformation they undertook after settling in San Diego: "My dad joined the Masons, went from being a Southern Baptist to a Presbyterian, and just generally worked to cut himself off from his past. . . . Us kids were sent to speech class to get rid of our accents, forbidden to listen to Okie music, given music lessons and encouraged to date the sons of local doctors and attorneys."[33]

Some went further still, denying their origins altogether, hoping to "pass" as Californians. A woman who was a baby when her parents moved to Los Angeles in 1927 never told anyone that her birthplace was Oklahoma. Her own children have grown up believing her to be a native Californian. A man who came of age in the valley uses the term "closet Okie" to describe the deception that he maintained through years of adult life. An elderly former Oklahoman remains careful to this day about revealing his background. Declining to be interviewed for this study, he explained that public disclosure might embarrass his grandchildren.[34]

It is hard to say whether the valley context was more or less conducive to purposeful assimilation efforts than the metropolitan context. What is clear is that in both settings these responses generally had something to do with class and ambition. Those hoping to gain access to white-collar jobs and middle-class social circles realized that it was important to shed behaviors that identified them as Okies. This is understandable. Middle-class standing has always been predicated on certain standards of behavioral conformity, and in succumbing to them Southwesterners were doing nothing more than what socially ambitious Americans of immigrant stock had long felt compelled to do. Whatever their heritage, if it was closely associated in the social system with lower- or working-class standing, those who aspired to higher status in the dominant society often found it difficult to retain full allegiance to their roots.[35]

It was a relatively simple transformation, this business of becoming a Californian. No indelible racial features, foreign names, or inflexible religious commitments stood in the way of assimilation for Okies. Virtually all of the migrants' distinguishing characteristics were subject to willful change. Even their regional accents could in most cases be modified. Bruce Berryhill's study of linguistic patterns of former Oklahomans living in Visalia in 1976 shows that those with an incentive to do so learned to speak "Californian." That meant avoiding double negatives, "ain'ts," and "might coulds," adding the "g" sound to their "fixin's" and "goin's," and shortening the diphthongal vowels that give Southwestern speech its characteristic twang, making "saaat" into "sat," "doawg" into "dog." This was, of course, easiest for children, but Berryhill's interviews with former migrants who arrived in California as adults also show that of those who attained middle-class socio-economic positions, nearly all became proficient in the California accent, while Oklahoma speech remained standard for the working class.[36]

Upward mobility was not absolutely predicated on these sorts of transformations, and over time, as the Southwestern influence increased in the valley, the pressures shifted. Even in the early years there were some job sectors where cultural conformity was less critical. Farming was one. Those Southwesterners who managed to become landowners or farm operators often enjoyed an independence not allowed those who sought entry into white-collar occupations. Walter Goldschmidt interviewed several farmers who had become relatively prosperous by 1941. They seemed to have some difficulty aligning themselves socially. While avoiding activities, including churches, that would have linked them to the Okie population, they were also cautious about their relations with Californians, refusing to join the Associated Farmers and other organizations. What is more, in contrast to their Californian neighbors, these successful Southwesterners seemed openly sympathetic to the plight of the more recent migrants, recalling how much easier it had been when they first came to California.[37]

The example of Kern County's Texas-born deputy sheriff shows the more common position of the middle-class Southwesterner in settings where class and regional background had become closely associated. His career demanded that he distinguish himself from the Okie population. He demonstrated his willingness to do so, and also a bit of the conflict it caused him, in an incident involving an argument between a Californian rancher and a migrant farmworker. The farmworker had taken exception to a rude remark, prompting the rancher to call for assistance. The deputy immediately arrested the Oklahoman. A short while later he let him go, admonishing him to be careful with the Californians and not to take their insults so seriously. "I'm from the East too," he revealed. "I've been here from Texas sixteen years. You'll just have to learn to put up with a lot of that. They don't mean no harm."[38]

Disengagement

The incentive for cultural conformity diminished considerably at lower socio-economic levels. In the blue-collar neighborhoods of Los Angeles and the Bay Area, Southwesterners fit in without major personal changes, though most were soon packing away overalls, bonnets, and other items of farm dress. For the farm-labor class in the valley there was still less reason for purposeful change. With little prospect for winning acceptance in the dominant society, newcomers of this station frequently followed a strategy geared to the maintenance of self-esteem rather than social ambition, a strategy essentially of separation and avoidance.

Disengagement became the first line of defense for most poor Southwesterners, just as it is for many groups which find themselves socially outcast. By minimizing external contacts, the migrants limited the potential for painful confrontations. It was a reaction quickly learned. Shirley Cox has never forgotten the shock of her first confrontation with prejudice. Newly arrived in California, she was sitting with her mother and brother in front of a store near Porterville when suddenly "this man came out of the store and yelled at us. 'You Okies get out of here! I don't know what you Okies are doing here; get out.' " It was brutal and scary. "My brother and I went across the street and watched the airplanes," Cox explained, "my mom just sat there and cried."[39]

Open hostility of this kind was not, however, particularly common. Whatever they thought of the migrants, few Californians made a practice of insulting them face to face. What the newcomers were more likely to experience were little acts of rudeness or condescension that told them they were not welcome. Those who thought about joining organizations or churches or participating in activities dominated by older residents often quickly changed their minds. Some of the new residents of Modesto's Little Oklahoma looked into transferring their Odd Fellows and Masonic memberships to the local lodges but came away discouraged after an initial meeting. The California lodges seemed "uppity."[40] Migrants who wandered into California churches sometimes left with the same feeling. Asked

Figures 19–20. The issue of respectability and media representation is highlighted in these two maternal scenes. Journalists and the public fastened upon images that suggested earthiness and ragged poverty, images that seemed to set the migrants apart from contemporary social standards. But given a chance to prepare for the

photographer, most of the newcomers would have presented themselves in the clean and modern attire of the woman at right, a Tulare County relief client. (*Dorothea Lange, The Bancroft Library, Berkeley, California*)

whether his church would accept members of the migrant group into the congregation, a Wasco minister said he really did not know, because none ever came: "they don't feel comfortable."[41]

Awkwardness and a certain wariness also colored one-on-one encounters as the migrants prepared themselves for the occasional snub. A Kern County grower enjoyed teasing the newcomers about their accents. "I will go up to one of them and say 'What part of Oklahoma did you come from?' and they will say, (imitating accent) 'Naow hain't that sumpn, Haow did you-uns know I's from Oklahomey.' "[42] Sensitivity began to build up after a few such incidents. "The biggest part of these native Californians won't give you a square look," one Oklahoman observed. "That's the damn truth. They are always wonderin' what relief office you are stoppin' in next or where you are beggin' your next meal. You can see it writtin' all over their faces."[43] Others claimed that the Californians seemed "cool" and vaguely unfriendly. An Arkansan found it difficult to deal with the ranchers upon whom he depended for work: "They are just a little distant and make you feel like they just don't want to talk. Sort of cut you off short. They don't seem to want to mess with me. I usually apologize and get away." "It don't make a feller feel quite right," he added.[44]

Depending upon the provocation, the migrants responded in various ways. The relative infrequency of direct insults owed something to their reputation for reacting with their fists. Ed Morrow* was not about to tolerate any snide comments from the Californians he met. He described an encounter with a native rancher:

> When I asked him fer a job he said to me, "What part of Oklahoma are you from?" That's the first thing he said. I was tard of bein' asked that all day. . . . I said, 'It's none of your damn business." . . . Boy I had blood in my eye. . . . I'd a fought him in a minute.[45]

Lonnie Nelson*, who had been a railroad man back in Oklahoma, was equally quick to take offense when a caseworker at the local relief office made a comment about the number of people coming to California from Oklahoma. Nelson* was on his feet in a flash. "If you don't shut your damn mouth," he told the startled young man, "I'll shut it fer you."[46]

More typically, the newcomers just walked away. Don Jackson* described a trip to a J.C. Penney's store and the ordeal of listening to a store clerk making cracks about relief clients using their checks to buy shoes:

> Of course, that hurt my feelin's because I happened to be one of them. That's not the only time I've run into such occasions, but each and everyone hurt and there are things that will never be forgotten. That's all. There's not much I can do about a situation like that, but just try and shield myself, fer no man is proud of relief, and I happened to have my wife with me. It hurt her, too. I just looked at him and didn't laugh with his remark as he did, but just turned

and walked out. We kinda dropped the subject, however, my wife suggested that we never go in there agin.[47]

This was quite common. Growers who wanted to keep their employees learned to be careful how they addressed them. So did Farm Security Administration officials, one of whom explained that if the migrants suspected they were being talked down to or "in any way offended" they "will quietly and politely leave the camp and go elsewhere."[48]

Noting the pattern, some observers decided that the migrants were "timid" or "taciturn" by nature.[49] If by that they meant that many had been taught to be circumspect in relations with strangers, they were probably correct. But even more, such caution was appropriate to the situation, a way to ward off unpleasantness in an unfriendly setting. An Oklahoman who settled in Bakersfield in 1936 summarized the strategy: "There was a lot of hatred for the Okies who came when we did. We soon learned it was best not to say too much."[50]

By staying away from the natives, many Southwesterners were able to avoid ugly incidents that would have reminded them of their despised position in California. Clara Davis and her husband came to Kern County from Oklahoma in 1937 and lived there throughout the worst period of anti-Okie sentiment. Yet she insisted that she never felt any prejudice or had trouble with the native Californians. "But then I never knew any," she added significantly. Except for the few ranchers the couple had worked for, she had nothing to do with the Californians.[51] Another woman said much the same thing when asked how she got along with people in California. Fine, she said, "people are just the same as back home. Course most of them are from Oklahoma. I haven't gotten to know any of the wealthier class here."[52]

We get a comparable sense of social isolation and its shielding benefit from interviews that Lillian Creisler conducted in Modesto's Little Oklahoma. When asked about their relations with the Californians, some complained bitterly, describing incidents of discrimination or antagonism. Others said they had been treated "coolly" or "not so friendly" by the Californians. But surprisingly, the majority of the resettled migrants had no complaints at all, telling Creisler that their treatment at the hands of the natives had been "satisfactory." And when asked specifically about incidents of prejudice or discrimination in that particular community, fully 70 percent said that they had never encountered any.[53]

In view of the fact that Creisler's own survey of Modesto Junior College students had disclosed a great deal of local animosity towards the Little Oklahoma residents, the migrants' answers were, to say the least, curious. Some of the denials need to be discounted. Creisler herself suspected a lack of candor from some of her respondents, partly for cultural reasons.

Believing that adversity was to be overcome not bemoaned, and priding themselves on being able to "keep taking it on the chin," few were inclined to explore moments of personal embarrassment with a stranger, particularly a well-dressed graduate student with a California accent.[54]

But some of the denials were genuine. The valley did not offer much to its farm-worker class, but it did allow them a considerable measure of protective isolation. In the camps where they paused temporarily and in the fringe neighborhoods where many built homes, the migrants found refuge from some of the more demeaning interactions with members of the dominant society and the space to create their own social life.

The Younger Generation

If the strategy of social withdrawal had an important shielding effect for the adults, it was of less value to their children. Where the older generation will today frequently discount reports of difficulties with the natives, those who grew up and went to school in the valleys in either the 1930s or the 1940s almost uniformly tell a different story. Migrant youngsters encountered a more direct challenge to pride and identity than their parents. Going to school made avoidance impossible and left no room for misunderstanding the demeaning social evaluation foisted on Southwesterners by California society. Yet at the same time, the schools offered a broad avenue for overcoming that disability. Young people thus confronted a world from which many of the ambiguities had been eliminated, and their responses would in turn be more emphatic than those of their elders.

It is in the stories of school experiences that one hears the most dramatic tales of confrontations between natives and newcomers. Depending upon where they lived, elementary school could be either a sheltered refuge or a trying experience for Southwestern youngsters. Some Okie subdivisions and labor camps had their own elementary schools, which spared children the problem of interacting with native youngsters. But more children started off in integrated elementary schools, where their Californian classmates were sometimes predictably cruel. Teased because of their strange accents and poor clothes, the newcomers contended as well with hurtful nicknames like "maggie" and "maggot" (allusions to "migrant") and, of course, "Okie."[55] It has been more than forty years, but one former Oklahoman cannot forget "the humiliation of the school children who called me and my sister 'Okies,' and asked us to speak 'our language.' " Bitterly, he recalls the scene at their new school in the town of Oakdale in Stanislaus County as a gang of kids "followed around . . . [and] taunted until we agreed to speak 'okie.' We spoke 'pig-latin,' and the other students seemed satisfied and finally let us alone."[56]

Many youngsters had educational problems which compounded their social difficulties. While some Southwestern children had gone to schools back home which matched the standards of California institutions, more had attended schools of much poorer quality. And bounced from school to school while their parents followed the crops, quite a few fell behind the normal pattern of grade advancement. That provided useful ammunition for their native classmates. "Oh, he's from Oklahoma—he's dumb" was heard frequently on the school grounds.[57]

The activities of teachers and administrators at times posed an equally serious challenge to the youngsters' feelings of self-worth. Some teachers shared the prejudices and anxieties of the general populace. Shirley Cox recalls one teacher in a Porterville school whose resentment of the Southwesterners showed in the way she continually addressed the children as "you migrants."[58] Wayne Rogers also remembers what it was like to be a youngster confronting the bigoted attitudes of certain school personnel. "The school nurse used to check us for lice," he explains. "And as she looked through our hair and our ears, she would tell us, 'Okies have lice.' That really made me feel terrible."[59] Going to school in Modesto made twelve-year-old Myrle Dansby feel the same way. She described her sense of the classroom in a little poem:

> The teachers nag
> And look at you
> Like a dirty dish rag.[60]

Most teachers and administrators were not deliberately cruel; and there are many stories of sensitive, caring teachers who went out of their way to help and inspire the migrant youngsters. But schools, as they often do, challenged the identity and family loyalties of these poverty-stricken children. School personnel who saw their job as uplifting educationally and socially handicapped pupils often focused on that task without giving much thought to the ways in which their efforts might be damaging to the youngsters' self respect. Hoping that "the things the kids were learning in schools were carrying over into the homes," educators rarely considered the possibility that their efforts might introduce tension and conflict into the family life of the child. Youngsters went off to school and learned that much of what they did at home was wrong: that the standards and way of life of their parents were backward and inferior. They learned to be ashamed of their family's poverty, of how they dressed, how they talked, and even of what they ate. In school they were taught that they should bring sandwiches for lunch instead of the cornbread or biscuits and beans which may have been all their family could afford. They were taught about proper clothing and sometimes even taken on field trips to clothing stores, only to return home to a family which may not have been able to buy new clothes.[61]

The schools, as a consequence, placed themselves in the position of competing with parents for the respect and loyalty of the Okie children. Sometimes educators even tried to win the youngsters away from beliefs and practices that their parents valued highly. One study noted that many teachers tried to discourage the evangelical religious commitments of Southwestern families. Feeling that the children needed "fewer emotional religious experiences," the teachers argued that "the school is handicapped when children repeatedly participate in long, highly emotional services in the evening during the school week."[62]

More emphatic were the schools' attacks on the children's accent, vocabulary, and grammar. Okie youngsters were told in no uncertain terms that their way of speaking was improper, even defective. Many educators felt that next to cleanliness, it was most important to teach the migrant children proper English, and that meant disposing of the Southwestern accent. As late as 1949, the Yuba County school system classified the accent of children from Southwestern backgrounds as a "speech defect" and targeted it for special educational programs.[63]

All this created conflict and confusion. The social pressure and ridicule of classmates and the insensitivity of many teachers made it hard for some children to face going to school and hard for others to face their families. Young children from poor families going off to schools dominated by well-dressed native youngsters were sometimes seriously intimidated by the experience. Each day was an embarrassment. A father described the problem:

> Picture how you would feel with two or three children headed for school, almost barefoot, with ragged or ill-fitting clothing. You see them going down the road with a paper bag in their hands, with two baking powder biscuits maybe, and some beans in between. And if you were a little child, how would you feel going to school in that way—and when it comes noon you sit down in your little bunch and drag out those two sandwiches full of beans, when the rest of the little ones are sitting around you there, children of more fortunate people? How do the children feel? It is almost impossible to keep them in school![64]

Other parents told similar stories. One explained that "They said of my child on the school ground, 'He's from the county camp.' Don't you see how it hurts? Makes it hard. Pretty soon the children begin to think they're not equal. That's a draw-back to this education."[65] A mother also worried. "How do you think . . . children feel," she asked, "when they go to school dressed a little poorer than the other children. To be made fun of and called dirty magats from the Migrant camp."[66]

A report by the Kern County Mental Hygiene Society suggested one of the consequences. Among the very young children, some were so "abused" by their school experiences that they appeared to have almost no positive

Figure 21. Three generations of Texans in a California camp, 1935. Note the differences in attire. (*Dorothea Lange*, © *1982, The Oakland Museum, The City of Oakland*)

131

sense of themselves. "No one likes me, I'm an Okie," some were heard to say, while one pitiful youngster told his teacher, "We ain't people we are sharecroppers."[67]

Nevertheless, some youngsters readily adjusted to the school experience and learned to be the kind of students the schools wanted. Those who found the work easy or gained the encouragement of their teachers often became model students. They studied hard, learned to talk "Californian," and perhaps won favor with a circle of native peers. Teachers pointed proudly to migrant pupils who were at the top of their classes academically. The school superintendent for Sutter County explained that in her schools "some migrant children excel the others and are winning their way by virtue of their talents."[68] A resident of Modesto's Little Oklahoma noted with pride that several of the most brilliant students at Modesto High School were Okies. They are "active in everything," he claimed.[69] Athletic prowess helped others gain access to the privileged group. Because of his success on the playing field, Wasco High School's star football player was gradually admitted to the social circle of the native students at the school.[70]

Accepting the standards of the natives and doing well in school could, of course, be the key to mobility out of the Okie underclass. Quite a few Southwestern youngsters graduated from high school and went on either to college or to a well-paid and respectable job, thus leaving behind the poverty and social stigmas of their youth. Dale Morrison's experience shows how it could be done. Entering high school shortly after his family arrived in Kern County in the early 1930s, Morrison responded to the discomfort of being "looked down upon" by trying to make good. "There were two girls in my class who used to make fun of me because of my Oklahoma accent," he later recalled. "But their taunts and jibes . . . forced me to correct my language and study harder than ever." He studied hard enough to graduate at the head of his class in 1936, went on to business college, and then into a successful business career in Bakersfield.[71]

But the struggle to win approval was loaded with emotional pitfalls, especially in the teenage years when children become acutely conscious of status differentials. Some Southwestern young people felt compelled to hide the circumstances of their home life in order not to be embarrassed in front of their wealthier peers. Alpha Arnold recalled an incident in high school: "One day in home economics class, the teacher asked all of us girls to draw a floor plan of our homes. I was too embarrassed, so I dropped the class." She had not wanted the others to know that the self-built house her family lived in had no indoor plumbing.[72]

Stories such as this were common. Willodine Winningham rode the school bus everyday from Porterville High School to her home in one of the Farm Security Administration camps. A girlfriend, however, would always get off well before the camp and walk the rest of the way so as to hide the fact that her family lived in a tent.[73] Dr. George Gleason, a minister investigating conditions among the migrants, told of meeting a teenage girl, a top student in her school in Tulare County, who was so embarrassed to be living in a small cabin that she tried to hide when Gleason came to visit.[74] A self-described "second generation Oakie" who succeeded in school and went on to become an engineer tells a similar story about embarrassment and deception.

> When I was growing up around Lamont, Weedpatch and Arvin, there were but a few who would admit to being an Oakie. I myself would not admit to it, I even invented other names to describe what my parents did for a living. Whenever someone I didn't know well dropped me off from school, I would have them drop me off a block away for fear our house would be easily recognized as an "Oakie shack." It was only after I left home and became somewhat successful that I could admit or talk about being an Oakie.[75]

As these examples suggest, the pressures to conform and the hope of winning the respect of more privileged peers carried the potential for family conflict. Trying hard to be Californians, they were embarrassed by anything about their home life that bespoke either poverty or less than "up-to-date" ways. Folklorists Charles Todd and Robert Sonkin noticed that some young people disliked their parents talking about their life back home. One sixteen-year-old girl did not want her mother to show them the family photographs brought from Texas because in several shots family members were barefoot. Other young people seemed uncomfortable when their parents sang old folk songs, embarrassed by the backwoods imagery.[76]

Many teenagers found the tensions unbearable. To succeed in the school environment required too much self-denial, too much pretense, and too much of a break with their own families. Defiance and withdrawal were the usual alternatives. Where their elders sometimes appeared cautious and retiring, teenagers, and especially young males, were often sullen and angry. Both because of the developmental imperatives of their age group and because of the circumstances which made separation from the natives difficult, their strategy for dealing with California tended to be more aggressive than that of the older generation.

Throughout the late 1930s and 1940s, high school and intermediate school authorities often characterized Okie youths as hard to handle, citing absenteeism, insubordination, fighting, and juvenile delinquency. A 1940 survey of 87 teachers in a dozen different valley schools found that teachers in the upper grades almost unanimously regarded farm-labor class youths as more of a "disciplinary problem" than native youngsters. Many complained that the Okie boys were "obstinate and overbearing." DeVere Stephens, who authored the study, amplified these observations. Migrant youths, he said, were inclined to adopt an attitude of "haughtiness" and "resistance." They "pride themselves on being 'tough,' " cultivate a "fighting spirit," and "hold others in disdain."[77] James Wilson interviewed a fourteen year old who fit the bill and who also illuminated the motivation for his defiance. "Sometimes a teacher will say to one of us, 'You ain't had good bringin' up.' . . . When they act like that we say, 'Do you know what they do with insane people in Oklahoma and Texas? They send them to California to be school teachers.' "[78]

Complaints about the rebellious outlook of Okie youths did not soon abate. Testifying before a state commission investigating farm labor problems in 1950, a school superintendent from Tulare County asserted that migrant youths were obstinate, rude, showed no respect for their elders, and "violate a regulation for the pure and simple fact that it is a regulation."[79] A young Southwesterner told the same commission that the reports were true. The schools, he said, caused many of his fellows to feel "left out and excluded," and as a result, "they develop a natural anti-social attitude, a belligerent attitude, and they get in trouble and cause a high juvenile delinquency rate."[80]

Legal authorities were saying much the same thing, blaming migrant youths for significant increases in crime in the valley. In 1939 the chief probation officer for Kern County claimed that "our records indicate that about 60% of the children who come before the Probation officers and Juvenile Court of this County have been in the state less than two years."[81] And similar reports were heard throughout the 1940s, with incarceration statistics indicating that Southwesterners had more than their share of trouble with the law.[82]

The behavior of this segment of the younger generation thus added another element to the image of Okies in the valley. Toughness, defiance, and delinquency came to be associated in the public mind with the Southwestern population for the same reasons that often leave socially and economically disadvantaged groups with similar reputations. Partly a matter of middle-class bias or even paranoia, there was also a basis in reality. Poverty and the difficulties of maintaining self-esteem often counsel rebellious behavior, particularly when there are conducive cultural factors, which were clearly present, as we will see in the next chapter. Inclined by background to maintain an outlook of toughness, many Southwestern youngsters gained a measure of pride and a sense of control by defiantly contesting an emotionally troublesome environment.

Leaving school altogether was one solution. Southwesterners of high-school age recorded an unusually high drop-out rate. Table 4.2, based on the 1940 Public Use Microdata Sample, shows the patterns for children of various ages living in nonmetropolitan areas. The sample size for individual years is small but the results show a consistent trend that is also confirmed by other sources.[83] At age fourteen, nearly all Southwestern youngsters

Table 4.2. School Enrollment Rates by Group and Age

| | Nonmetropolitan Areas | | | | | | Metropolitan Southwesterners | |
| | Southwesterners | | Other whites | | Hispanics/ nonwhites | | | |
Age	%	(N)	%	(N)	%	(N)	%	(N)
14	97	(29)	95	(188)	92	(40)	97	(36)
15	91	(31)	94	(213)	99	(30)	97	(26)
16	69	(21)	91	(222)	73	(32)	82	(32)
17	46	(12)	82	(184)	60	(24)	72	(31)
18	27	(14)	54	(128)	52	(22)	30	(13)
19	14	(6)	36	(84)	29	(12)	23	(14)

Source: 1940 Census Public Use Microdata Sample

were enrolled in school. At age fifteen, the enrollment rate dipped slightly to 91 percent. Age sixteen, however, marked an important change, as the rate fell to 69 percent, well under the 91 percent enrollment of other white children and lower even than the 73 percent of Hispanics and nonwhites. The drop-out rate accelerated through age seventeen, when less than half of Southwestern-born youths were enrolled, and through age eighteen, at which point a mere 27 percent continued in school, precisely half the 54 percent enrollment rate for other whites of that age.

The drop-out rate had many sources, including the family economy. Clearly for some families the need for supplemental earning power had much to do with the decision to leave school. And yet, quite a few drop-outs did not immediately join the work force. In the Farm Security Administration camps where in 1940 only 41 percent of high school age children attended school, officials reported that the majority of the teenage drop-outs were not seeking employment.[84]

Relevant, too, were culturally derived attitudes towards education. The fact that metropolitan-settled Southwestern teenagers were also under-enrolled (Table 4.2) in comparison with other whites of their age leads us into the next chapter's examination of cultural values. As we will see, many of the migrants shared a vaguely populist outlook which directed expectations towards manual occupations and away from extended schooling.

But none of this completely explains why a student like Willodine Winningham should leave school. Always a promising pupil back in Texas, she eagerly enrolled in the local high school when her family settled down in the FSA camp near Porterville. She was one of the few young people from the camp to do so. Again she did well, winning commendation in the camp newspaper for her grades. But the attitudes of the native children troubled her, and unlike some, she refused to hide who she was or where she lived.

Ultimately the pressure was too great, and at age sixteen she quit school—not to work, just to get away. It seems to have been a frequent solution.[85]

Like their elders, young people moved in various directions depending upon personality, family environment, stresses, and opportunities. The two major options, struggling for acceptance or pulling back into the migrant milieu, were not always mutually exclusive and would become still less so in the decades to come as tensions eased and Okies became a larger and more confident portion of the population. But initially the choice was rather stark, at least in the San Joaquin Valley. And class was the major correlate. Valley society accepted with relative equanimity those who passed the dual test of occupational status and cultural conformity. But a large portion of the Southwestern population was drawn towards a different orientation. Meeting the animus of the host society sometimes stubbornly, sometimes retiringly, they found an alternative to assimilative striving in the social milieu dominated by their fellow newcomers.

II

THE OKIE
SUBCULTURE

5

Plain-Folk
Americanism

THE PATTERNS OF ALIENATION BUILT UP IN THE 1930s ENCOURAGED THE PROCESS of cultural adaptation that gave California its Okie subculture. Regional cultural differences that in other circumstances had meant little took on expanded significance in this one. Although some Southwesterners consciously abandoned distinguishing characteristics, others fell back on the cultural resources of their upbringing, creating community systems laced with values and institutions of Southwestern origin. The remaining chapters will concentrate on the portion of the migrant group who followed this second course. The primary locus of this subculture was the San Joaquin Valley, but in weakened form it also developed in the metropolitan areas, especially during the 1940s when new waves of migrants created for the first time substantial enclaves of Southwesterners in the cities.

Some definitions are needed. The term subculture is quite elastic, which is useful in this case. A subculture is a social formation with a distinctive set of norms and values that offers members a significant sense of identity and locus for social interaction. Subcultures come in many forms, based on ethnicity, class, religion, political ideology, peer group, even consumer interests. But the Okie subculture does not fit neatly into any one of these categories. Depending upon where we look and also what time periods we examine, the formation seems to take on different shapes.[1]

Social science has never supplied the right tools for categorizing the process of cultural adjustment that accompanied the Dust Bowl migration. Initially it was not seen as a cultural process at all. Apart from the concern that the migrants came from a "backward" area, few contemporaries gave much thought to questions of regionalism, assuming that differences between native-stock Americans were minor, that culture carried social consequences only when linguistic, political, religious, or moral traditions were sharply differentiated. Trained social scientists were especially reluctant to find significance in the regional backgrounds of the migrant population. In the usual view class and its many complications alone defined the group.

Anthropologist Walter Goldschmidt best expressed this assessment. After close consideration he concluded that the migrants were not really a group in any coherent sense. A "disorganized aggregate" sharing conditions of poverty and hostility, they lacked "mechanisms by which they could be organized into a community." Though he described in detail the separate Okie neighborhoods, social life, and religious institutions, he assumed these to be transitory developments attributable to the vicissitudes of class. To the extent that the migrants demonstrated divergent values and customs, a history of rural disadvantage or more recent poverty was to blame. Otherwise, the newcomers seemed to share in the basic standards of the host society and appeared most anxious to win acceptance within it.[2]

Stuart Jamieson saw matters differently and, for his time, singularly. In 1942 the Berkeley-trained labor economist published the results of his study of Olivehurst, one of several Okie communities in the Sacramento Valley. Struck by the similarities between the social position of the "new American migrants" and the foreign immigrant groups they had largely replaced in the agricultural labor force, he observed that the newcomers take on the "appearance of a distinct 'ethnic group.' " Despite cultural backgrounds that are "fundamentally the same" as their hosts, he argued, the economic and social context contributed to the migrants' "quasi-segregation" and had the "effect of perpetuating some old traditions and customs of the settlers," among which he listed speech, dress, paternalistic family relations, and religious institutions.[3]

Although he was essentially alone with this formulation in the 1940s, a time when conventional definitions of ethnicity envisioned only national, religious, and racial groups, the redefinition of ethnicity in the last few decades has made his argument increasingly plausible.[4] Indeed, it is consistent with what regional sociologists John Sheldon Reed and Lewis Killian have been saying recently about the ethnicity of white Southerners. In a long list of books and articles published since 1972, Reed catalogues the similarities between Southern whites and conventionally recognized ethnic minorities, stressing the region's persecution complex, enduring sectional identity, and persisting differences in social, personal, and religious values. Killian introduced some of the same points in his 1970 book *White South-*

erners, which was published in Random House's Ethnic Groups in Comparative Perspective series. He also examined the process of Southern outmigration and argued that it was among the "hillbillies" of Chicago and other northern cities that the evidence of minority group behavior was strongest. Caught in an urban context of stereotypes and hostilities not much different than that experienced by their Okie cousins, the working-class Southern whites Killian studied engaged in a process of group formation and cultural retention typical of ethnic minorities.[5]

It is a tempting argument, but there are some complications, at least in the case of the California migrants. The issue of group definition is one. Until recently, few Southwesterners of the middle class identified themselves as Okies. On the other hand, a number of people from states other than the Southwest associated with and were perceived to be Okies; and some today embrace the term. There is something similarly fuzzy and flexible about the cultural materials, the institutions and symbols, that in time gave the group a sense of community and identity. These, too, have not been consistently and exclusively Southwestern.

While in the end it may be valuable to talk about Okie ethnicity, it is important first to deconstruct the experience, to understand that the subculture has operated in several guises. Being an Okie for some Southwesterners is a straightforward matter of regional heritage, and for them the ethnic concept is relevant. They celebrate their state origins and proudly proclaim symbols and distinguishing cultural elements of that background. If ethnicity refers to a sense of peoplehood rooted in a perception of common history and ancestry, some Okies qualify.[6]

But for other participants the subculture expresses something different, either experiential pride (as veterans of the migrant experience) or, most interesting, allegiance to a set of social-political perspectives that might be labeled plain-folk Americanism. This ideological persuasion was part of the cultural system of the Southwest—or more properly of a particular class of Southwesterners—but it was not exclusive to that region. Other white Americans, particularly other rural Protestant-stock Americans, shared many of these interests and values, and still others later found them attractive. Here it is harder to talk about ethnicity, since regionalism was not the central issue. In this guise the Okie subculture was an ideological community of uncertain and, indeed, expanding dimensions. For those who identified with this version of the community, being an Okie was a matter of experiences, standards, and values.

A Framework of Understandings

California's Okie culture derived largely from the outlooks, habits, and institutions of Southwestern "plain folk," a broad social category encompassing most rural and blue-collar whites. As in other parts of the South, the social structure of the trans-Mississippi states divided most obviously into three basic categories: blacks; whites of the business, professional, and land-wealthy strata; and the majority white population of modest means. Some scholars insist on subdividing this last group into its wage-working, tenant farmer, and yeoman components, while others confuse the issue with labels like "poor white" or "redneck." Those distinctions are not helpful here. Tied together in many instances by kinship, rural and formerly rural working-class Southwesterners shared a wide range of life-ways, values, and outlooks. Most of all they shared a seasoned political culture.[7]

Southwestern plain folk claimed a set of social and political commitments that had once flourished widely in nineteenth-century America. Heirs to anti-monopoly and citizen-producer ideas that in earlier periods had guided both agrarian and working-class radicalism, they stood also in the shadow of generations of white Protestants who had fought to preserve the Republic's ethnic and religious integrity. These perspectives tracked through a long line of neo-populist campaigns aimed at rural and working-class audiences. From the days of the powerful Farmers' Alliance through the resurrected radicalism of Huey Long, "Alfalfa Bill" Murray, and "Ma" Ferguson, those constituencies responded best to shirt-sleeved campaigners who talked about the dignity of hard work and plain living and promised deliverance from the forces of power, privilege, and moral pollution, near and far.[8]

Southwestern plain folk brought these and other outlooks to California and made them the basis for their subculture. What they built, however, was not merely a replica of what they left behind. The Okie subculture evolved through a process of cultural negotiation involving many participants. Partly a dialogue between Southwesterners and their new California setting, there was also a speaking role for non-Southwesterners who associated with the migrant population. The resulting synthesis expressed some of familiar ways of the Southwest, but other elements were changed or newly emphasized.

The subcultural construction occurred in stages. It was not until the 1940s that the more obvious institutions—churches, saloons, and country music—began to solidify and make an impact on the surrounding society. Until then the subculture was harder to locate. In the 1930s, the group was taking shape informally and more or less unintentionally in the neighborhoods, camps, and job sites where migrants gathered. Through the act of socializing, men and women discovered common understandings and worked out the new meanings that would give the group its sense of identity and cohesion.

We are fortunate to have a source which identifies some of the more important values that were affirmed in those interactions. The "Pea-Patch

Press" was Charles Todd's name for the collection of newspapers emanating from the FSA camps during the last years of the 1930s. *Tow-Sack Tattler, Pea-Pickers Prattle, Covered Wagon News, Voice of the Migrant*—the colorful, free-form titles say much about the style of these tiny mimeographed publications. Supported by camp fees and published whenever someone volunteered to serve as editor, the format was usually wildly eclectic. More community bulletin board than newspaper, they published a hash of contributions from residents and management. Letters, recipes, poems, jokes, stories, editorials, complaints, homilies, political opinions, discussions of current issues, reports of camp gossip, notices of meetings, lists of rules and regulations, jeremiads by camp managers—whatever was available went out in the next issue.[9]

Many of the contributions were original, but residents also sent in remembered bits of verse, Bible passages, riddles torn from other publications, anything that seemed meaningful enough to share. It is this participatory aspect which makes the camp newspapers so valuable. We hear from children, parents, and grandparents, men and women, union activists and Pentecostal worshippers, those who liked California and those who hated it. They wrote not only about issues but also about day-to-day life. We witness their attempts at entertainment, their approach to humor, their sense of propriety. In letters, poems, and gossip notes, they argued and agreed about community standards, about morals, about right and wrong as they wrestled with the meaning of their California experience and reminded themselves what was important in life.

Were these camp residents typical of the broader population of Okies? Those who lived in the camps were often poorer, more transient, newer to California than residents of the migrant subdivisions where the lasting social networks were being strung. But any distinctions between the populations of these settings were minor and temporary. Residents of camps and Little Oklahomas came from the same background, occupied the same farmworker class, and faced similar adjustment challenges. In both settings large numbers of mostly Southwestern newcomers explored the basic business of living together. The difference is that the camp residents left us a record of the process.

Cult of Toughness

Reading that record for its core values, one concern stands out. A favorite poem expressed it.

> If the day looks kinder gloomy
> An' the chances kinder slim;
> If the situation's puzzlin',
> An' the prospect awful grim,

An Perplexities keep pressin'
Till all hope is nearly gone
Just bristle up and grit your teeth,
An' keep on goin' on.[10]

The message of persistence, determination, of "try, try again" defined one of the essentials of what the migrants considered good character. Learned in school, in church, from parents and friends, courage and determination were the special forte of these plain people. Struggle, they assured themselves, was what they and their ancestors did best. Persistence was more than the key to success—there could be no dignity, manhood, or self-esteem without it. No other theme was expressed as frequently or as passionately as the need to never let up, never quit, to always "keep on goin' on." Winnie Taggart shared her composition "Migratory Grit" with fellow residents of the Brawley camp near the pea fields in the Imperial Valley:

Forget the grouch, erase the frown.
Don't let hard luck get you down.
Throw up your head, thrust out your chest,
Now at a boy! Go do your best.
. . .
It's hard to laugh, and be at ease,
When the darned old peas all start to freeze.
But a pea tramps always full of grit,
He never does sit down and quit.
. . .
To laugh, should be the pea tramp's creed
For that is what we greatly need.
It does not take great wealth to laugh
Just have the grit to stand the gaff.[11]

These calls for courage, determination, and "grit" reflected a preoccupation with toughness that became one of the cornerstones of the Okie subculture. The values involved were in no way unique to the migrants, but in the process of emphasizing and reinforcing them, they were beginning to forge the normative standards of the group and a myth that would anchor expressions of group identity.[12]

Toughness meant, first of all, an ability to accept life's hardships without flinching or showing weakness, a standard applied to both males and females. Displays of weakness were actively discouraged in the camp newspapers. "Complainers," "grumblers," "gripers," and "whiners" came in for frequent criticism. "All's not well that is the talk;/ A grumbler being the worst of the lot," one poet chided.[13] "'Taint no use to sit an' whine," cautioned another version of "Keep On A-Goin'."[14] "Now come on everybody, quit that complaining," a letter writer at the Indio camp in the Coachella Valley urged. "Every cloud has a silver lining. If you don't like things here in camp and the relief you get, be nice enough to keep it to yourself."[15]

Toughness also meant a willingness to fight, metaphorically for women, in all senses of the word for men.

> It takes a little courage;
> And a little self-control;
> And a grim determination;
> If you want to reach the [goal];
>
> It takes a deal of striving;
> And a firm and stern-set chin.
> No matter what the battle,
> If you really want to win.
>
> You must take a blow and give one.
> You must risk and you must lose
> And expect within the battle.
> You must suffer from a bruise.
>
> But you musn't wince or falter.
> Lest a fight you might begin.
> Be a man and face the battle.
> That's the only way to win.[16]

An Arvin camp resident thought his fellow campers might benefit from that untitled poem, perhaps remembered from childhood, a personal credo now being shared. Its message was a familiar one in the migrant communities. It mentions goals but is mostly about struggles and manliness. A man has courage and self-control, he fights his own battles, facing each with "stern-set chin." And, significantly, he prepares not so much to win as to lose, steeling himself to "suffer from a bruise."

Another poem, labeled "A Man's Creed," repeats the same themes:

> Let this be my epitaph
> Here lies one who took his chances
> In the busy world of men
> Battled luck and circumstances
> fought and fell and fought again
> Won sometimes, but did no crowing
> Lost sometimes, but did not wail
> Took his beating but kept going
> And never let his courage fail.[17]

In both of these contributions a man's creed is courage, not as a means to something but as a goal itself. What is important is the ability to fight and fall and fight again, to take a "beating" and keep going. There is an understanding of life here that lies outside the Franklinesque formulas of aspiration and success that are the core of middle-class American culture.

These invocations speak to a worldview in which struggle is the only verity, in which society is divided not into winners and losers but into those who fight and those who quit, men and cowards. They speak to a system of honor which, Bertram Wyatt-Brown and others suggest, may be a special feature of the culture of Southern whites. More definitely we can say that these values flourish outside the middle-class mainstream of twentieth-century American society, in working-class and rural contexts where symbols of prestige are hard to come by, where money and occupation cannot be everything. This was a context Okies knew well.[18]

Physical courage was a central part of the creed, and not just for males. Both children and adults were expected to know how and be willing to fight. Fist fights occurred frequently in the camps, in the schools, and in nearby saloons and were a continual source of concern to camp authorities, among others. Most involved males, but girls also fought with surprising frequency.

Young people have a "strange code," the Shafter camp manager complained in his regular column. "A young lady was called into my office for fighting and she said she had to fight or the other children would call her chicken."[19] He need only have read his own camp newspaper to begin to understand that the "code" was promoted by parents as well as the younger generation. Aside from crime or base immorality, no more serious charge could be leveled at another person than the charge of cowardice. "The world will forgive you for being blue, sometimes forgive you for being green, but never forgive you for being yellow," a Yuba City camp philosopher intoned.[20]

The words were meant to be taken seriously, and elsewhere were backed up with punishing ridicule. A boy who walked away from a school fight was mercilessly taunted as a crybaby in the Arvin camp newspaper: "Bill Jones got his feelings hurt in the school room the other day, he went home to get his [baby] bottle but his mother was not home so he came back crying."[21]

The migrants' support for the values of toughness and courage which comprised that "strange code" can also be seen in the enormous popularity accorded the sports of boxing and wrestling. Amateur bouts were staged weekly at many of the FSA camps and quickly proved to be the best attended of the camps' many recreational activities, attracting Okies living outside the camps as well as residents. On some nights, crowds of up to 500 people would assemble to watch what the Shafter *Covered Wagon News* described as "plenty of good fighting and lots of action."[22] The matches featured contests between boys of several age levels up to the early twenties and nearly always included at least one pair of girls.

Figure 22. Never too young to learn. Boxing was part of the nursery school program at the Tulare FSA camp. (*Arthur Rothstein, The Bancroft Library, Berkeley, California*)

The Shafter paper's description of a fight between two teenage girls shows something of both the enthusiasm for the sport and the importance attached to displays of toughness:

> A rough and tumble exhibition was put on by Mildred Searcy and Aldyth Aust, two of our promising young ladies. Mildred sure protected her pretty face all during the two rounds, and bucked like a ram with her head. Both girls displayed good sportsmanship by taking their punishment with a smile.[23]

That fighting between girls should be sanctioned in this way suggests a significant departure from the standards of comportment absorbed by generations of middle-class American women. Nevertheless, as the passage itself implies, fighting was primarily a test of male honor. For women, toughness had more to do with the ability to shoulder burdens, withstand pain, and bear up under life's trials. Female toughness was preeminently a matter of fortitude.

In several respects the migrants' cult of toughness represented an adjustment of old values to a new setting. In their efforts to deal with the formidable challenges of resettlement, the migrants appear to have emphasized courage and determination even more than they had back home. Beyond that, these values took on new social implications. At home toughness was a matter of individual concern; in California it became a badge of group pride, something that Okies believed made them collectively special.[24]

To listen to former migrants today is to encounter again and again this proprietorial claim to toughness. It takes various forms, emerging sometimes in proud tales of Okie fighting prowess. In his book *Okies*, a collection of short stories, Kern County native Gerald Haslam, a second-generation Okie on his father's side, sees fighting as one of the major themes of the group experience. His male characters are frequently locked in combat, proving their courage and manhood to themselves and each other, rising to each challenge instinctively, obsessively, even as they sometimes wish they could turn a cheek and walk away. In the story "Before Dishonor," a battered "good old boy" moves from one teeth-shattering fight to another as other males test the truth of the "Death Before Dishonor" tattoo on his forearm. "There's things a kid does just haunts a man," the protagonist says of the tattoo he must defend. For Haslam it is all part of a particular system of honor which haunts and therefore helps to define Okies.[25]

If Haslam is intrigued by the Okie reputation for violence, he is not alone. Many of his contemporaries and elders relish stories about fighting, particularly accounts of fights between resilient Okies and insolent Californians. The understanding is that Okies were singularly proficient with their fists, more than a match for their native detractors. "About the time they'd say, 'Okie,' I'd put my fist in their mouth," Byrd Morgan recalls.[26]

Charles Newsome uses the same proud tone in telling of his school-yard fights:

> As the Missourians always said, "It was show me time." . . . Well, the Okie was the one that could show them so that's why there were a lot of little tough Okie kids running around the schools because they had to be tough.[27]

James Lackey was an adult when he arrived in California, and evidently a good fight never came his way. But he witnessed many and sees courage as an Okie trait. "I've never seen an Okie run from trouble at all. If you corner an Okie he's going to fight."[28] Hadley Yocum likewise takes pride in the fights won by others. "I'll tell you one thing," says the former Arkansas and Oklahoma sharecropper whose land holdings now make him a millionaire, "the native Californians weren't no match for the boys coming from Oklahoma when it came to fist fights."[29]

This celebration of combat skills is part of the mythology of the Okie subculture. By mythology I do not mean the claims are untrue—indeed, there are good reasons to believe most of them—but rather that, true or not, such ideas form an important element in the framework of the group's identity.[30]

The toughness myth extends beyond physical combat, however. In its most important manifestation, Okies find meaning in the belief that they or their parents or grandparents were part of a special encounter with suffering, a special exercise in perseverance and hard work, a special triumph over adversity.

Listen to Francis Walker, who looks back proudly on the years she and her family spent in the cotton fields of the San Joaquin Valley. "The Okies were invincible, they won, they are here, they own land, houses—and are comfortable," she insists.[31] "Okies were resilient," echoes Dee Fox, a third-generation Okie whose pride in her heritage comes from "hearing all the stories" from her grandparents and parents.[32] Okies "were willing to work," says Charles Newsome, "they'd work long hours trying to get ahead" while the "big shots" who settled the area earlier "had learned to live on a silver spoon and . . . didn't know how to compete."[33]

Okies are people "who tried to stay alive and managed," explains Lester Hair, who was born in Arizona as his parents made their way west from Texas in 1924. And struggle, he continues, gives them a sense of pride "that is more important to that person than anything else."[34] Hard times, hostile treatment, persistence, and struggle—"*that's what made Okies out of us*," concludes Texas-born Bernie F. Sisk, who worked his way out of the fruit orchards to become congressman from Fresno County.[35] Whether all this struggle was in fact unique is unimportant; the belief that it was continues to shape a group identity.

A Shifting Populism

Related values of a more political nature also helped the newcomers feel themselves part of a special enterprise. The process turned on their understandings of American heritage and character. As they took a close look at the residents and the reigning values of their new state, they found a basis for rethinking their inferiority complex. California had some significant flaws. Maybe the migrants were not the ones who should be making the concessions and changes.

Plain-folk Americanism found its central bearings in a neo-populist perspective that understood but two great social classes, producers and parasites. Once key to a far-reaching radical critique of the economic order, the perspective had been changing political coloration since the turn of the century as adherents added anti-communism, racism, nativism, and the resilient individualism evident in the toughness code to their list of political priorities. By the 1930s, many plain folk embraced an ideological construction which seemed to cross the conventional boundaries of Northern (and Californian) politics. Ever sympathetic to appeals on behalf of the common man or against the "interests," they responded with equal vigor to symbols that recalled a white Protestant and intensely patriotic vision of Americanism. This parochial populist combination matched neither the business conservatism nor the urban liberalism that had become dominant in California's Depression-era political life. A lens through which the migrants judged their surroundings, it became as well one of their contributions to their new state.[36]

The outlook was evident in the camp newspapers, in the way camp residents dealt with questions of ambition, privilege, and equality. Invocations to personal ambition were curiously muted. For all the talk of determination and fighting, no Andrew Carnegie models appeared on these pages; few indeed were the discussions of competitive striving. This is striking when we consider the didactic nature of many of the contributions and the fact that they were often aimed at the younger generation. Reading closely we can see that particular standards of ambition were being employed. Exhorting one another to be the best they could be, contributors urged also that limits be recognized. Be your own man, proud but no better than anyone else—this was what contributors seemed to want for themselves and their children.

What occupational references there were suggest unfamiliarity and some distrust of white-collar work. Bankers seem to have been hated, businessmen mostly ignored, bureaucrats and intellectuals widely lampooned. A joke about an "old Texas farmer" who uses common sense to outsmart a pretentious college professor reveals a sense of distance from the world of higher education. Underlying these evaluations was a basic belief in the primacy of manual labor. Real work meant creating with one's hands either

in the fields or in the factories, ideally in a setting where one was independent, "his own boss."[37]

Clearer than the migrants' occupational discriminations was their intolerance of social snobbery or elitism. Residents frequently blasted those
who put on uppity airs, acted "high hat," or who tried to become "better
than other people." "In Oklahoma and Texas where we folks come from
one person ain't no better than another," an angry Shafter camp resident
wrote after learning that elected camp council members were to be henceforth exempt from the task of cleaning bathrooms.[38]

Outsiders found that a democratic demeanor was essential to any sort
of effective dealings with Okies. Eleanor Roosevelt passed the test. After
she paid a brief visit to the Shafter camp, the newspaper exuded: "No
more gracious lady, no kindlier lady have we folks ever seen. When she
talked with us she was so common, so plain, so sincere. Said a man in Unit
Five, 'She is plain like all of us—not stuck up or stuffed.' "[39]

On the other hand, some of the camp managers, most of them young
college graduates, ran afoul of the migrants' standards. Oklahoma-born
Wiley Cuddard, Jr.*, criticized the string of previous managers at the Arvin
camp—all "educated men, who have never done any real work"—for acting
like "Dictators." The last one, he said, was "the professor type, he didn't
associate with the people enough, too much business about him." Cuddard
had nothing but praise, however, for the new manager, Fred Ross: "he is
an educated man but when he came here he acted as one of the boys. . . .
He didn't act one bit better than his staff or the people in the camp. And
he's always got time to say a few words to you."[40]

This commitment to social equality and resentment of pretension and
authority had implications for the migrants' adjustment. Strictures against
social snobbery dampened status ambitions that otherwise might have lured
young people out of the working class and hence out of the Okie milieu.
Here may be one of the factors in the high drop-out rate among high school
students. If the camp newspapers are any guide, young people were taught
at home to set modest life goals. Mrs. V.E. Langley passed along this piece
of advice to residents of the Brawley camp in the Imperial Valley:

> We all dream of great deeds and high positions. . . . Yet success is not occu-
> pying a lofty place or doing conspicuous work; it is being the best tha[t] is in
> you.
>   Rattling around in too big a job is worse than filling a small one [to]
> overflowing. Dream aspire by all means; but do not ruin the life you must
> lead by dreaming pipe dreams of the one you would like to lead. Make the
> most of what you have and are. Perhaps your trivial, immediate task is your
> one sure way of proving mettle.[41]

"The secret of happiness is not doing what one likes, but in liking what
one has to do," a Yuba City camp resident argued.[42] That was the message

also of a popular poem entitled "Be What You Is" that appeared in print
in several different newspapers:

> If you're just a little tadpole
> Don't try to be a frog
> If you're just a tail
> Don't try to wag the dog
> You can always pass the plate
> If you can't exhort and preach
> If you're just a little pebble
> Don't try to be the beach.
> Don't be what you ain't
> Jes' be what you is.
> For the man who plays it square
> Is a-goin to get "his."[43]

Reinforced, as we will see, by the teachings of some of the churches they
attended and also by important themes in country music, messages of
restrained ambition doubtless helped to sustain the class integrity of the
Okie group.

This sort of class consciousness also had political implications. Politics
loomed large in the catalogue of fears inciting native hostility. Residents
assumed the newcomers to be Democrats, and worse, probably radical
Democrats. They were not far from the mark. Missouri, north Oklahoma,
and parts of the Arkansas Ozarks knew something of the Republican party,
but most Southwesterners had been raised in areas that acknowledged only
one legitimate party. And since the onset of the Depression, major elements of that Democratic party had become reacquainted with radical-
sounding rhetoric and proposals which harkened back to the 1890s. Leading
Southwestern politicians such as Thomas Gore and "Alfalfa Bill" Murray
of Oklahoma, Jim and Miriam ("Pa" and "Ma") Ferguson of Texas, Hattie
Caraway of Arkansas, and, of course, the broadly influential Huey Long
of Louisiana had greeted the economic crisis of the 1930s with a resurrected
language of angry opposition to Eastern money and corporate greed, with
dramatic calls for federal action to rein in the rich and redistribute wealth,
and with renewed commitment to the cause and dignity of plain hard-
working folks—in short with a neo-populism (a debilitated populism, says
historian Alan Brinkley) that found an eager if perhaps not entirely cred-
ulous audience among the region's distressed rural and working-class
populations.[44]

The same disposition shows itself in the voting habits of many of the
migrants who settled in California. Using the largely Okie town of Arvin
as a gauge, we can see what worried Republicans and conservative Democrats. Arvin, from 1934 through the end of the decade, voted more
strongly Democratic and much more in favor of liberal and radical Dem-

Table 5.1. Percentage Voting for Democratic Candidates and Ham 'n' Eggs
Initiative, for Arvin Precincts and Statewide California

Electoral contest	Arvin	Statewide
1934 gubernatorial (Sinclair v. Merriam)	54%	38%
1936 presidential (Roosevelt v. Landon)	75%	67%
1938 gubernatorial (Olson v. Merriam)	71%	52%
1940 presidential (Roosevelt v. Willkie)	65%	57%
1939 Ham 'n' Eggs	65%	34%

Sources: *Arvin Tiller*, Nov. 6, 1939; Voter Registration and Election Results Arvin Area, Goldschmidt
Records, San Bruno; Michael P. Rogin and John L. Shover, *Political Change in California* (Westport,
1969), 123, 132; Robert E. Burke, *Olson's New Deal for California* (Berkeley, 1953), 33, 112.

ocratic candidates than the state as a whole. While Californians rejected
the 1934 candidacy of Upton Sinclair, Arvin voted for him. Four years
later, when Culbert Olson won the governor's mansion with 52 percent of
the statewide vote, Arvin residents gave him 71 percent of theirs. Olson's
blasts against big business, his calls for public ownership of utilities, and
his endorsement of a watered-down version of Sinclair's "production for
use" proposal may have bothered a good number of Californians, but those
familiar with the anti-corporate, government-as-savior tone of Southwestern electioneering were not among them.

The best indication of the neo-populist mind set of the new voters was
Arvin's showing on the oddly named Ham 'n' Eggs initiative of 1939. Losing
two to one statewide, it won by the same margin in Arvin amidst indications
that the proposal was especially dear to the hearts of much of the migrant
population. Ham 'n' Eggs was a radical welfare scheme derived from the
earlier formulations of Dr. Francis Townsend, the famous Long Beach
geriatric crusader. Among other things it called for the distribution of $30
in special scrip every Thursday to each needy Californian over the age of
fifty. Like the Townsend plans, the goal was to assist the elderly while
stimulating the economy through massive currency expansion.[45]

Denounced as crackpot economics not only by financial experts and
conservative politicians but also by much of the liberal and left community,
including Upton Sinclair, the initiative nevertheless seems to have inspired
more enthusiasm and political activity than any other issue to come before
the Okie group in the 1930s. Letters to camp newspapers and the established press called out their endorsement, often revealing a profound mis-
trust of the experts who opposed it: the self-same bankers alleged to have
brought on and profited from the Depression. "Ham and eggs everybody,"
Arkansan Henry King urged fellow residents of Arvin camp. "Do you
believe it will work, the money Gods say it wont. . . . [Don't] believe those

dirty rich liars that say Ham and Eggs wont work. . . . Ham and eggs wont
work if the rich can help it."[46]

In addition to playing to the migrants' suspicions of bankers, corporations, and pretentious wealth, Ham 'n' Eggs found a responsive echo in
the neo-populist fondness for currency manipulation schemes. Financial
conspiracies were responsible for the economic crisis, financial wizardry
would resolve it. Bill Hammett was the kind of voter who found Ham 'n'
Eggs compelling. Although his comments were made several years before
the initiative appeared, his political philosophy suggests the sort of down-
home radicalism that earned the ballot measure so much support among
resettled Southwesterners:

> I ain't no communist . . . I hold the American flag's just as good here and now
> as when Betsy Ross finished her stitchin' and handed it over to George Wash-
> ington. What's good over in Russia don't mean it's good for us. I ain't edicated
> enough to know whether it's Epic plan or Townsend plan or whatever, but if
> there's plenty folks ready and willin' to raise food and other folks are still
> starvin', don't take no college education to know there's somethin' cloggin'
> the gin feed.[47]

Labor's Dilemma

If the migrants' worldview could take them in radical directions, it also,
as the orthodox left discovered, took them in conservative ones. The plain-
folk ideology circulating in the migrant communities was tinged with much
else beside the old populism of their forefathers. When Okies talked of
social equality, they usually meant equality for whites and often only native-
stock whites. When they sorted out their pantheon of enemies, they frequently figured Communists to be more dangerous than bankers. And when
faced with organizational opportunities that might yield collective benefits,
they typically fell back instead on habits of individualism and family self-
sufficiency. The 1930s marked something of a midpoint in the transformation of the political culture of Southwestern plain folk. The insurgent
potential had been steadily draining away. Even as many Southwesterners
continued to use a class-based terminology of the plain versus the powerful,
more persuasive commitments to patriotism, racism, toughness, and independence were pointing towards the kind of conservative populism that
George Wallace would articulate three decades later.

Suggestions of this trend can be seen in the migrants' response to the
two left-wing unions which tried to recruit them in the closing years of the
1930s. The United Cannery, Agricultural, Packing and Allied Workers of
America, a Congress of Industrial Organizations union better known by
its acronym UCAPAWA, and the Workers Alliance, which called itself

the "union of the unemployed," together tried to organize the migrants in their twin roles as farm workers and relief recipients. Neither was very successful. The plain people's consciousness which found expression in the Ham 'n' Eggs vote fit much less well with the programs and campaigns of radical organized labor.

Strictly speaking, the Workers Alliance was a pressure group rather than a union. A loosely structured organization that enjoyed the support of both the Socialist and Communist parties, it was the chief successor to the militant Unemployed Councils of the early 1930s. Chapters first appeared in the agricultural areas of California in 1936 and quickly began to pick up members among the Okie population dependent upon relief. Sending grievance committees to lobby local relief authorities while backing those efforts with petitions and public demonstrations, the organization gained a reputation for influence and with it a small but significant following in many of the camps and communities. Helpful, too, was the fact that Workers Alliance stewards sometimes controlled the distribution of jobs on WPA projects. Even migrants who disapproved of the organization's radical politics sometimes found it useful to join. "Seems you've might near got to belong . . . to get what's coming to you," one man complained as he contemplated signing up.[48] Membership figures are hard to judge, but it seems likely that chapters in Arvin, Bakersfield, Madera, and Marysville could each claim the support of several hundred members by early 1939, while smaller chapters operated in several other locales.[49]

UCAPAWA first appeared in the migrant communities in late 1937. Part of the newly independent CIO, it pulled together several tiny food-processing and farm-labor locals left over from the campaigns of the early 1930s. Its leaders sought first to build a strong base in the canneries and packing houses (a sector rapidly falling to the American Federation of Labor) but at the urging of state CIO leaders agreed to undertake as well the formidable task of organizing the state's vast armies of seasonal farm workers. UCAPAWA's commitment to the project, however, was inconsistent and greatly hindered by a shortage of financial resources and skilled organizers. Unsure whether it should be setting up dues-paying locals or organizing strikes, the union mostly drifted behind events. Workers Alliance activists took charge of most of the organizing, converting their chapters into UCAPAWA locals during harvest seasons, and at times initiating walkouts for which UCAPAWA leaders were not fully prepared.[50]

Serious strike activity began in the fall of 1938 with a spontaneous walkout by several hundred Kern County cotton pickers, many of them residents of the Shafter FSA camp. Emboldened by the reputation of the mediagenic CIO and angered by the drastic wage cuts that accompanied the federally sponsored acreage cutbacks, a militant minority, consisting of Okies and Hispanics, had initiated the action. The union dispatched organizers to try

Figure 23. Activists gather at the Bakersfield labor temple during the 1938 cotton strike. (*Dorothea Lange, The Bancroft Library, Berkeley, California*)

to broaden and discipline the strike, but after some exhilarating efforts at coaxing other workers from the fields using automobile picket caravans, the strike collapsed, helped to its early end by the mass arrest of some one hundred picketers.[51]

The next year saw a wave of similar walkouts in other crops as cadres of activists spread the union enthusiasm up and down the state. One or two of the strikes resulted in wage increases, but most, like the Kern strike, floundered after dramatic beginnings, either because most workers refused to strike or because other migrants appeared to take the jobs of those who did.[52]

The cotton harvest of 1939 promised to be the major test. UCAPAWA tried a new strategy. Counting on the support of the recently installed Olson administration and the public sympathy engendered by the publication of *The Grapes of Wrath*, leaders were hoping to win bargaining concessions from growers without a strike. But when industry representatives ignored the recommendations of the governor's Wage Rate board the scene was set for confrontation.

The union concentrated efforts in Madera County, where a strong Workers Alliance local had been preparing for months. Initial reports were encouraging. A majority of cotton pickers in the area responded to the strike call and hundreds gathered in the county park for assignment to picket caravans. Despite some early arrests, observers counted the strike 75 percent effective in the first week in that county, though efforts to inspire walkouts elsewhere in the cotton belt fizzled badly.[53]

The Madera momentum was also about to end—the Associated Farmers saw to that. On the strike's ninth day, a mob of several hundred growers attacked a rally of union supporters with clubs, pick handles, and tire irons. Other beatings and arrests followed as local officials cooperated with efforts to break the strike. With the governor unwilling to intervene and most of the leaders in jail or driven from the county, UCAPAWA's most significant farm-labor strike came to a close. The defeat ended serious efforts to organize field workers. Activists maintained some of the locals and kept the threat of further campaigns alive for another year or so, but union headquarters had lost interest and now turned its energies elsewhere.

It is unwise to make too much of UCAPAWA's poor showing. Substantial obstacles stood in the way of any attempt to organize the farm-labor force, an occupational sector that remains largely nonunion to this day. The timing of the UCAPAWA campaign was particularly bad, coinciding with a dramatic drop in farm employment and a growing surplus of workers. The combination made many migrants angry, but left others desperate for work and unable to make the sacrifices a strike demanded.

Slim Phillips's case is indicative of the choices many faced. He had just arrived in California, was out of money, and had not yet heard of the strike when a grower stopped him on the highway and offered him work. He accepted but moments later encountered a carload of strikers. "We want to get a little better price on this cotton," they told him.

> So I says we ain't got nothing to eat. If you got the price of something to eat why we can talk business with you, otherwise we is gonna starve. We just didn't have no money. That was all there was to it. We was broke.[54]

Given the desperation of people like Phillips, the aggravating labor market conditions, not to mention the difficulties of coordinating farm-labor strikes against the obstinate and very powerful agricultural industry in California, UCAPAWA's failure is anything but surprising. Still, one can ask whether the values and disposition of the migrants had something to do with the campaign's problems. Many observers thought so, concluding in the final analysis that Southwesterners were not good union material, that, as Charles Todd put it, they were "immune to the wiles of the organizer."[55] Later writers have also followed this lead. Walter Stein argues that the migrants were unfamiliar with unions and too individualistic to support the campaign. Comparing the UCAPAWA experience with the more encouraging results of the earlier Cannery and Agricultural Workers Industrial Union drive among mostly Mexican field workers, he observes that "precisely because Okies were rural Americans with that streak of individualism, they were less malleable material for union organizers than were Mexicans. Rugged individualism and collective action do not mix well."[56]

Can this be correct? The Western South, historian Lawrence Goodwyn assures us, had once thrilled to the cooperative strategies of the Farmers' Alliance and then with equal vigor had supported the programs of the People's party. Even more distinctively, in the years immediately prior to World War I, Oscar Ameringer, Kate Richards O'Hare, and Thomas "Red" Hickey had built the nation's largest Socialist party membership on the foundation of former Populists. Enjoying the support of thousands of tenant farmers, miners, timber workers, and urban sympathizers, the movement had garnered over a third of the vote in many of Oklahoma's poorer counties, and substantial numbers as well in western Arkansas and northern Texas. Now a mere twenty years later was it possible that migrants from this region were too individualistic to contemplate joining a union?[57]

The story is more complicated than that. First, it is important to understand that not all migrants responded alike to the union campaign. A sizable minority did join or support these organizations. Many of the activists who agitated in the fields and camps, triggered the walkouts, and mounted the picket caravans were Okies, as were the hundreds and occasionally thousands who responded to their calls. Though definitely in the minority, the number of union supporters was by no means negligible. Just how many there were is not clear, but three small surveys perhaps provide a clue. Approximately one-quarter of the 60 men James Wilson interviewed were UCAPAWA members or supporters; 30 percent of Lillian Creisler's 100 Modesto respondents, not all of whom were farmworkers, belonged to some sort of union; and 39 percent of Walter Hoadley's 117-family Salinas area sample said they might like to join a union, though UCA-PAWA was not specifically mentioned. To estimate, then, that one out of every three at least sympathized with the union would not be irresponsible.[58]

Many belonging to this pro-UCAPAWA segment seem to have had prior experience either with unions or radical causes. Arthur Brown*, active in UCAPAWA in Kern County, learned his unionism working in the oil fields of Oklahoma. Carrie Morris and her husband, mainstays of the Marysville local and leaders of several walkouts, claimed thirty years of unionism in various industries before coming to California. Likewise, the president of the Wasco local, who looked back on careers in both mining and railroad work, liked to tell visitors that he had "been a Union man all my life." Given the number of farmworkers who had previously worked in nona-gricultural jobs, these backgrounds were not unusual. Some 28 percent of residents in Modesto's Little Oklahoma claimed previous union experience.[59]

Other sympathizers came to UCAPAWA via the Southwest's radical movements. Like Jim Ballard, an Arkansas tenant farmer who grew up reading the Socialist weekly *Appeal to Reason*, some of the people settling in California were veterans of the prewar Socialist campaigns. Others, too young to have participated in the glory days of the Debsian movement, had been involved in such Depression-era leftist ventures as the Southern Tenant Farmers' Union, the Oklahoma-based Veterans of Industry (an organization of the unemployed), or, for that matter, the Workers Alliance, which had chapters in the Southwest as well as California. Tex Pace, editor of the Visalia camp *Hub*, is a good example. His penchant for items about Commonwealth Labor College at Mena, Arkansas, suggests his roots in the radical subculture of his home region.[60]

These radicals, however, no longer enjoyed the sympathy that would have once made them welcome in a large percentage of the region's rural households. The two decades since World War I had indeed seen a major transformation in political consciousness. The patriotic fervor and uncom-promising repression of the war and Red Scare years had begun the process. Next came the nativist, fundamentalist, and moral reform crusades of the 1920s. The Ku Klux Klan attained for a time major influence in the region, taking power in Texas and Arkansas and coming close in Oklahoma. The experience helped even Klan opponents learn to equate radicalism with treason, anti-Communism with Americanism.[61]

The region's farm population had been especially affected. Even though the Klan found more enemies than friends among the region's plain folk, the organization's preeminent lesson took hold in the 1920s. Henceforth, patriotism would remain the foremost proposition for the majority of Southwestern farm folk. All other impulses, including their continued interest in economic justice, would be subject always to qualms about the proper activities for loyal Americans. For the organized left, this proved an insurmountable burden. Still a force in the Southwest's cities, oil fields, and mining camps, radicals usually encountered an aroused and suspicious majority opinion in rural and small-town settings. Despite the turmoil and discontent that the 1930s brought to the region's farm population, patriotic concerns channeled most energies away from the radical left, sometimes into the election campaigns of neo-populist candidates such as Murray and Carraway, sometimes into apathy.[62]

It was to be the same in California. Chief among the obstacles that the unionists faced were the strong anti-Communist sentiments of many of their fellow migrants. Both UCAPAWA and the Workers Alliance were vulnerable on that score. As grower representatives and major newspapers never tired of pointing out, both organizations had important links to the Communist party. For people like Oklahoman Clint Powell* there was nothing more to be said. Probably unaware that he was inverting the Populists' famous challenge to raise less corn and more hell, he refused to have anything to do with a "damned red outfit" which "just raises more hell than anything else."[63]

Even migrants who otherwise claimed to be interested in unionization were sometimes deterred by the Communism issue. An old-timer who felt that unionization was definitely "in my interests" nevertheless insisted that "it won't do us a bit of good unless it's 100 per cent, and unless all the radicals are killed off." "The radicals," he continued, "are so unreasonable, it hurts rather than helps us."[64] A twenty-seven-year-old Oklahoman who felt "we need some form of pullin' together to prevent goin' into slavery" was also wary. Though he thought UCAPAWA "is the best thing we've got now to keep wages up," he was not a member. "I don't knock on the CIO but I do say let's be careful lest we join an organization that's influenced by some foreign government."[65]

The scope and vehemence of this concern seems unusual for the late 1930s. Most sectors of the American public probably shared the migrants' antipathy towards Communism, but not in the same measure. At least in urban settings, the CIO found its Communist allies more help than liability, as tens and hundreds of thousands of industrial workers ignored red-baiting campaigns and picked up the union card. But anti-Communism had become a more serious proposition in heartland regions like the Western South where the nativist-fundamentalist fires of the 1920s had burned so brightly.[66]

Figure 24. This barn in Arvin served various segments of the migrant population in 1940. A church group met there on Sundays, the Workers Alliance on a week-night. Shown here, it serves as a relief distribution center. (*Dorothea Lange,* © *1982, The Oakland Museum, The City of Oakland*)

Religious and racial concerns also had something to do with UCAPA-WA's difficulties. The evangelical churches that claimed the attention of a significant minority of the migrant group often spoke against union membership, sometimes quite vehemently. "They get up and tell the people that the CIO is wrong, and that those who are wearing the CIO badges have the mark of the 'beast' upon them," a UCAPAWA leader charged, and he suspected the preachers were "paid by the ranchers."[67] They did not need to be bribed. Many of these churches belonged to Pentecostal or Holiness sects that taught that all forms of political action were wrong because they distracted from the pursuit of individual salvation. Worldliness of any kind was to be avoided. Even the conservative American Federation of Labor "had trouble with these holy rollers." A frustrated Cannery Workers Union official complained, "They have screwy ideas. Some of them don't want to belong to any organization and will quit their jobs rather than join a union. Their preachers won't let them belong to any organization, but their own."[68]

Again, it had not always been so. Evangelical groups had played a different role in the era of Southwestern radicalism before World War I, says historian Garin Burbank. The Socialist movement, he argues, gained the support of preachers and deeply religious farm folk who found a resonance between the promises of Socialism and chiliastic Christianity.[69] But that link had largely dissolved by the 1930s. Among the ministers and religious-minded migrants who came to California one finds only scattered examples of sympathy for radicalism: a Nazarene minister active in the Olivehurst chapter of the Workers Alliance; a Pentecostal preacher known as Brother Theodore who reconciled his belief in Socialism saying, "Ah have to seek the truth, Brother, an' after ah've found that truth then ah've gotta preach it"; and Lillie Dunn, who discovered Jesus at age thirteen and the Communist party twelve years later and never found the two in conflict.[70] They were exceptional. Most of the migrants involved in the union campaign were not necessarily irreligious, but rarely were they closely involved in a church.[71]

UCAPAWA's policy of racial inclusion may have also limited its appeal to white Southwesterners. Like most left-wing CIO organizations, the union insisted that workers of all colors and national origins be included, though not always within the same local. Bowing to the logic of language groups, UCAPAWA divided them into Spanish- and English-speaking locals. Still, the fact that Hispanic farmworkers, some of them veterans of the 1933 strikes, played prominent roles in some strikes kept certain whites on the sidelines. Even more troublesome was the presence of a small number of black unionists. The Wasco local evidently defied headquarters and discouraged interested blacks from attending most functions. The local's president denied this and assured Walter Goldschmidt that all races were welcome, but his wife interrupted to insist, "You can't equalize me with no nigger—I don't care what."[72]

The issue of individualism remains to be considered. Much depends on the definition, whether an ideology or a condition is meant. The notion that rural Southwesterners were "rugged individualists" unfamiliar with the rudiments of cooperation is another one of the mistaken stereotypes generated by a society that was uncomfortable with its rural shadow. Here is the *New York Times* quoting a Farm Security Administration official's characterization of the migrants: "These are men who got a shotgun and guarded a stalk of cotton that was hanging over the fence so that the farmer on the other side of the fence wouldn't pick it." "They're the greatest individuals on earth," he went on. "They'd die in a factory."[73] This is nonsense. Okies were neither loners nor frontiersmen, and they did as well as anyone else in the factories. Cooperation was certainly nothing new. The churches that many supported and attended before coming to California were proof of that.[74]

On the other hand, it was true that plain-folk culture gave considerable emphasis to issues of self-reliance and personal or family autonomy, and true that even today symbols of independence rank highly in the honor scheme of the Okie group. That makes the union question complicated, because it is not necessarily true that unionism and the spirit of independence are incompatible. Over the years a good deal of American labor activism has been generated in defense of principles of self-reliance, manhood, and personal integrity. From railroadmen in the 1880s to teamsters in the 1980s, the collective discipline of unionism seems often to be marshaled in favor of symbols of pride and independence.[75]

The notion that Okies were unprepared for or ideologically opposed to unions breaks down as soon as industries other than agriculture are considered. In the oil fields and canneries, or in the shipyards and aircraft factories that many entered during World War II, Southwesterners showed little reluctance and in some cases considerable enthusiasm for workplace organization. Confronting faceless corporations, they were readily persuaded that the exercize of group power was not only practical but honorable.

But a union of farm workers seemed a different proposition. Farming was too sacred an endeavor for the tactics of the factory. Whatever their current social station, the majority of these former farmers could not but remain loyal to the enterprise of their ancestors. And whatever their current economic interests, they thus found it hard not to identify with their employers.

UCAPAWA faced an impossible public relations problem. Organizers tried to convince the newcomers that California agriculture was not what they were used to, that independent farming was a fiction in an industry controlled by giant concerns, and that in any event the union had no quarrel with the small growers. "All the farms around here are financed, and the finance companies wouldn't allow but so much [for wages], and they couldn't pay more," explained a Missourian who found the lessons persuasive. It galled him that "a bunch of these Chamber of Commerce, White Collar fellows, who never farmed in their lives, go up to Fresno every year and set the prices."[76]

But even as many of the migrants agreed with the union's characterization of the system as "monopoly agriculture," it was difficult for UCAPAWA to break the bonds of sympathy that these former farmers often felt for their particular California employers. Many are the stories of workers who stuck by their bosses during the strikes because "he was a good fellow." Ed Crane, who allows that "I never was too much on strikes," worked through several in the 1930s. "If I'm working for a person I owe my allegiance to my employer until it becomes patently unfair and then I'll go somewhere else to go to work. That's been my theory of the whole thing."[77]

Particularly if they worked for a grower of modest scale, the migrants were quick to identify with him. A young father from Kansas was barely feeding his family on his 25 cents per hour wage. But though he knew it "is a little too low, a man should have 30 cents," he was not complaining. "Under present prices these California farmers are payin' about all they can stand fer wages. . . . Last year a good many farmers went broke."[78] Martin Childs* sympathized with the aims of the union but was too much of a farmer at heart to fully accept the logic of opposing interests implicit in the union strategy. "The ranchers have done pretty well [by us]," he allowed. "Our main drawback is too many people. We've rustled pretty hard in my family and got quite a bit of work. They seem to pay a reasonable fair price. Some folks don't think they do, but I figure they pay a reasonable fair price."[79]

And with less frequency the same logic worked for even the wealthiest of growers. James Lackey is today a stalwart member of the pipefitter's union, but in the late 1930s he made his home on the gigantic DiGiorgio ranch, most famous of the "factories in the field." And he had no interest in the union: "I didn't see anybody taking advantage of anyone. . . . It was friendly and the bosses were good. In fact I talked to the old man Di-Giorgio, the one that owned it, and little Joe. . . . they was just like common people. All the bosses were swell." Here was the unions' dilemma. A farmer (even a millionaire California grower with international corporate interests), if he acted like a man of the soil and treated his employees with dignity, was more of a kindred spirit than were some of the allies the unions proposed: nonwhites, Communists, educated middle-class sympathizers.[80]

The significance of all this for the UCAPAWA campaign was limited. Farm-labor unionism in the late 1930s was defeated by market conditions that would have undermined even the most determined constituency. But the migrants' response helps us to see both the variation in their political orientations and the majority trend. If we seek the central tendency in this emerging subculture, we will find it among those who were suspicious of the left and impressed with gestures of independence and toughness even while they retained a faith in programs that promised economic justice. This was a political culture in transition, lodged somewhere between the agrarian radicalism of an earlier era and the flag-waving conservatism of the next. And for the moment it found at best an awkward home in California, fitting only partly under the very liberal banner of California's Democratic party.

True Americanism

Nativism and racism were aspects of the value system of Southwestern plain folk which figured also in the subculture taking shape in California. For all their aggravation at the hands of middle-class white society, nothing bothered the newcomers more than California's system of racial and ethnic relations. It was one of the features of their new surroundings that convinced them that California's standards, not their own, needed changing.

Settlement in California imposed a number of unfamiliar ethnic encounters on migrants from the Western South. Coming from a region where blacks and in some settings Hispanics were the only significant minorities and where white Protestant supremacy was an unquestioned fact of life, the greater diversity and somewhat more tolerant habits of California offered a serious challenge.[81]

Some found themselves working for Italian, Scandinavian, Portuguese, Armenian, or perhaps even Japanese growers; others for Hispanic labor contractors or once in a while a black contractor. They competed for jobs with Hispanic and Filipino workers, sometimes finding that these groups were preferred by certain growers. All this was confusing. "We thought we were just 100 percent American," recalls Martha Jackson, who arrived in California as a teenager in 1937. "I had never heard of an Armenian, I had never met an Italian and I never had seen Chinese or Japanese or Mexican people. . . . We thought their grandparents didn't fight in the Civil War or Revolution."[82]

The new encounters were especially difficult because of the contempt Okies experienced at the hands of so many white residents. Accustomed to a social structure which guaranteed them ethnic privileges, they read California's arrangements as an inversion of accustomed patterns. "I have not noticed the California critics condemning the Filipinos, Japanese, or any other foreigners," William Siefert wrote to Fresno's major newspaper. "But when United States born citizens come here, they say we cut wages and lower their standard of living."[83]

"Just who built California?" another writer asked rhetorically before revealing his ignorance of California's ethnohistory:

> Certainly not the Chinese, Japanese, Hindus, etc., that you let stay inside her borders. . . . The aliens are perfectly welcome, but the real citizens must stay out. . . . Not one word of protest did I hear [about foreigners]. But let a citizen from the East come out here and try to make a home and be a respectable person and one hears plenty.[84]

James Wilson encountered similar complaints among the migrants he interviewed in Kern County. Among those who would speak freely of their feelings of discontent, several blamed Mexicans, Japanese, and Filipinos, all of whom, one Oklahoman claimed, "git the cream of the crop, they git the jobs." "That is where a lot of our trouble is," he continued, "the country is too heavily populated with foreigners . . . the farmers ain't got no business hirin' them fer low wages when we native white American citizens are starvin'."[85] It was bad enough, Clyde Storey* maintained, that

Californians refused to "treat you like a white man," but to encounter a sign reading "No White Laborers Need Apply" at the ranch belonging to former President Herbert Hoover was in his mind the most painful irony of all.[86] A young Oklahoman summarized the fear that pressed heavily on the self-esteem of many migrants: "they think as much of a 'Nigger' uptown here as they do white people."[87] It was not true, of course, but the decline in their own social position, combined with what most Southwesterners saw as a substantial elevation in the rights of racial and ethnic minorities, perhaps made it seem so.

Without question the most troubling feature of the California ethnic system for Southwesterners centered on interactions with blacks. A tiny black population shared the farm-labor occupational strata with Okies in the San Joaquin Valley. Excluded even from the FSA camps, living mostly in isolated enclaves in some of the larger towns, blacks, as always, suffered far more serious economic and social discrimination than any whites. Still they enjoyed certain opportunities not common to the Southwest, and these offended the sensibilities of the newcomers. The superiority of white over black was the bottom line of plain-folk culture, and any change in the status of black people was very deeply felt.[88]

The most obvious breach in segregation etiquette occurred in the schools, some of which admitted black students to the same classrooms as whites. Ruth Woodall Criswell recalls the resulting trauma in her household. It was "the first time in my life I'd ever gone to school with anyone except just white children." Her parents "could hardly reconcile themselves to the fact. At first they didn't seem to mind so much about the Mexican and Chinese but the blacks bothered them."[89]

Noting that "they are niggers back home but colored people here," one of Goldschmidt's informants confessed similar worries. "I thought it would be awful to send our children to school with niggers, but they aren't so bad. The children like the niggers alright—they don't bother any. These niggers around here don't bother us any if you let them alone."[90]

Alvin Laird was one of many Southwestern parents who became embroiled with school officials over the issue. He claims (though it is hard to believe) that education authorities in the Imperial Valley tried to enroll his children in an "all-colored school." "My children ain't going to go over there," he told the officials, and rather than send them he kept them out of school until the family moved north to the San Joaquin Valley. There were problems in the new setting as well. After his daughter was blamed for an altercation with a black teenager, he confronted the school principal, announced that his daughter would not apologize, and threatened that if the youth "don't leave my daughter alone I'll have one of them boys of mine to whop him so you won't know him when he comes to school."[91]

Parents' anxieties were played out in a sometimes violent fashion by the younger generation. Charles Newsome remembers with some embarrassment his first days at an elementary school in Tulare County.

> The teacher assigned me and told me to go sit in this desk . . . it was right behind the only colored kid in the class. So I was a little smart ass Okie and I had never had much school with them so no way was I going to get behind no colored kid . . . I told her "Teacher, I don't sit behind no nigger." So when recess time came naturally that's when a fight got started.[92]

The fighting became more serious in the upper grades. High school teachers sometimes blamed Okie youths for persecuting black students, and knifings and serious brawls were reported.[93] Not all of this was the fault of whites. Juanita Price, one of the few black Oklahomans to come west during the 1930s, recalls some of the violence in the Bakersfield area and blames it on both sides:

> When the white Southerners came here a lot of them got whippings from black people . . . the blacks had a little hostility in them and when they came out to California they thought the situation was different so they could just whip a white fella and forget it. And many fights went on. The blacks had said all their lives, "one of these days I'm going to whip me a white kid," and they'd whip one. It was just stupidity.

Some of it was also bloody. She tells of one particularly violent incident. "Tex's Bar," an Okie hangout in Bakersfield, prominently displayed a "NO NIGGERS" sign on the door. When a black man walked in one day, the owner tried to throw him out. The would-be customer then pulled a knife and "cut him up real bad."[94]

All this needs to be qualified. Racial tolerance was not unknown in the Western South, and some migrants warmly endorsed more equitable racial relations. Despite the example of the Wasco UCAPAWA local, racial liberalism was especially pronounced among the minority who participated in unions and radical politics. And others also came to accept the sorts of inter-ethnic contact that California imposed. James Wilson listened as a group of young cotton choppers discussed their employer, a black labor contractor:

> Harvey Johnson*: That "Nigger" guy is a nice boss, better than a lot of white men.

> Bill Brown*: But I wouldn't let anybody know I was workin' fer a "Nigger."

> Henry Johnson*: He said to me the other day, "Will you please cut the weeds over behind those beets?" He said "Please."

> Boyd Jones*: They think as much of a "Nigger" uptown here as they do white people. I don't even like fer one of them to ask me fer a cigarette. Another thing, they drink out of the same cup.

Angus Dow*: "I don't mind drinkin' out of the same cup if he'll set it down and let it set fer five minutes.

Harvey Johnson*: I've been in ten states and don't like them yet.[95]

As the conversation indicates, this was a process which would take time. Even as some whites were learning new lessons, others clung tenaciously to racial animosity. And if we are looking again for central tendencies, it would have to be said that racism remained the subculture's dominant voice. Many Southwesterners found purpose in speaking out against rather than for interracial understanding.[96]

This became quite evident in the 1940s, when the racial composition of California underwent a fundamental change. Black migration accelerated dramatically during World War II, nearly quadrupling the state's Afro-American population by 1950. Where Okies and blacks met there was continual tension. Sociologist Katherine Archibald observed the conflict in a Bay Area shipyard. Blacks were resented by most whites, she noted, but especially by Okies, who "found it hard to accept the casual contact between Negro men and white women to which Northern custom had become indifferent—sitting together on streetcars and buses, standing together before lunch counters or pay windows, working side by side in the same gangs."[97] Grumbling that "it's the niggers who are taking over California," Okies talked loudly, she added, about lynchings and other bloody remedies. "What you need round here," one Southwesterner told her, "is a good old-fashioned lynching. Back in my home state we string a nigger up or shoot him down, every now and then, and that way we keep the rest of them quiet and respectful."[98]

Apparently it was not all talk. Violent incidents, including cross burnings and even murders, occurred in both the Bay Area and Los Angeles, settings where defense work brought the two groups of Southerners together. At the end of the war a brief florescence of Ku Klux Klan activity in southern California was linked to Southwestern whites.[99]

Southwesterners enjoyed no monopoly on racism, of course. Nor did California, with its legacy of anti-Asian sentiment, need instructions in white supremacy. Black newcomers met resistance from many quarters. But some white Southwesterners brought a heightened militancy to the subject. Both because interracial contacts at work and school were new and because their self-esteem at this juncture was so fragile, vigorous racism became a prominent feature of the Okie response to California. Charles Newsome remembers the transference. "The people out here [Californians] looked down on the Okies but the Okies looked down on other people too at the time."[100]

An outlet for frustration, racism was in subtle ways also a source of group identity—something that made at least some Okies feel special and distinct. While many white Californians shared the migrants' racist outlook, the fact that some features of California law and custom were different than back home allowed certain newcomers to conclude that there was much that was wrong with the state and its citizenry. And some, as we see in Archibald's report, styled themselves guardians of white supremacy, dispensing advice on how to deal with blacks. Here, sadly, was another understanding and shared purpose, another piece of the subcultural framework.

Native Sons

If the debasement of California's nonwhites had therapeutic and group definitional implications, the migrants' concept of Americanism figured more ambiguously in relations with the state's whites, most of whom possessed old-stock credentials not much different than their own. Mostly, Americanism provided a bridge. That so many of the Californians were "Americans" minimized the migrants' defensive reactions and sustained their interest in assimilation, which as we have seen was one compelling strategy of adjustment. But for some members of the group, expectations about the behavior of proper Americans also provided ammunition for criticizing their native hosts. And while this endeavor was but a weak reflection of the disdain Okies knew was directed their own way, it offered some measure of emotional conciliation and group definition.

Southwesterners used several devices to turn the tables on Californians, the simplest of which were snide labels of their own, including "Calies," "native sons," and the curious favorite, "prune pickers," which played on the bathroom humor associated with the sticky, sweet dried fruit. A stereotype accompanied the labels, the thrust of which was that Californians were selfish, arrogant, "privileged characters" who thought they were better than everyone else. As one novice poet put it:

> Some of the Californians go around, with their nose stuck up;
> Like when it would rain, They'd use it for a cup.[101]

This view of rude and haughty natives was often coupled with the notion that Californians had grown soft and lazy, and furthermore that their resentment of the migrants was rooted in jealousy and fear. "If it weren't for Texas, Oklahoma, and Arkansas, there wouldn't be much to California, would there?" a migrant hitchhiker lectured Charles Todd. He figured that everybody else in the state had forgotten the meaning of real work.[102]

As have-nots often do, the migrants also enjoyed suggestions that Californians' lofty social positions rested upon lowly origins and ill-gotten or unearned wealth. A popular ditty that apparently pre-dated the Dust Bowl migration delighted Okies with its irreverent view of the California pedigree.

> The miners came in forty-nine,
> The whores in fifty-one;
> And when they bunked together
> They begot the native son.[103]

The author of a letter to the *Modesto Bee* had different suspicions about California bloodlines. Establishing his own credentials as a "native son of the U.S.A." whose "father and grandfather served in the Civil War," he addressed his challenge "to the native son who owns your big dairies, your big vineyards, your big orchards, look up the records and get the facts. . . . The few I have worked for, I have been informed, got their starts from their fathers, who happened not to be native sons."[104] Here was the plain folks' critique in a nutshell: "big" farms, too big and too cushy; unearned wealth and social position; and possibly immigrant backgrounds. It was quite a brief.

Still, these attempts at denigration, unlike those directed at nonwhites, were not particularly serious. Few Okies really entertained feelings of superiority over white Californians. Most of the jibes were simply attempts to reassure themselves and regain some composure. Nevertheless, the process had bearing on the emerging subculture. In clarifying their definitions of proper Americanism and in laying special claim to that heritage, the migrants were developing an identity capable of sustaining a group experience that initially owed its existence to external forces of class and prejudice.

We will let Ernest Martin restate the proposition that underlay the group identity. An Oklahoman who came to California as a child, grew up in the valley, then moved to Los Angeles and became a minister and religious scholar, he speaks boldly and with insight about the cultural and cognitive parameters of the Okie experience. We considered ourselves "the best Americans in the world," he recalls. "To our people their way of life was America. New York isn't America . . . we were America."[105]

This is no simple statement of regional pride. The Okie subculture was anchored in a group concept that is not reducible to the ethnic formula that scholars sometimes employ in relation to other groups of Southern white outmigrants. Instead of a particularistic definition of the group based on state origins, many Southwesterners laid claim to a nativist conception of national community. Plain-folk Americanism was in some respects a regional enterprise—white Southerners were its core proponents in California—but it also spoke to and for whites of many other backgrounds. Hence, the curious dynamics of the Okie subculture. Southwesterners drew together and gained feelings of pride and definition from this ideological system but never manifested the exclusivity, the insularity, of an ethnic subsociety. Plain-folk Americanism gave their community a different thrust, outward and expansive, open to other whites who embraced the proper values. These heartlanders had come to California with something not just to save but to share.

This would become increasingly clear in the decades to come. The 1940s would simultaneously reduce the structures of social and economic isolation and encourage the proliferation of key cultural institutions. Country music and evangelical churches would become important emblems of the Okie group in the post-Depression decades. And each would function in the dual manner we have been observing, on the one hand solidifying elements of group pride, while also carrying messages of wider appeal that helped to spread the Okie cultural impact far beyond the formal boundaries of the Southwestern group.

6

Up from the Dust

It was 1952, and Oliver Carlson was back in Kern County, trying to find out what had happened to the Dust Bowl migrants. He had spent time there before, in the late 1930s. Much had changed, including the investigator himself. At one time he had been willing to highlight the inequalities of American life; now his eyes were trained on evidence of the self-restorative ability of "America's system of free opportunity for all." And he was sure he had found it. Gone were the dilapidated cars, the roadside encampments, the tents and ragged clothes, the hungry looks that he remembered. The terrible poverty of the 1930s had vanished. The valley seemed more prosperous now, and the Okies with it. "The pariahs, outcasts and social lepers of yesterday have become . . . worthy and respected members of the communities in which they settled. They are honest and industrious. They have better homes, better jobs, and greater economic security than ever before. They have regained their self-esteem; and they walk, talk, work and vote as equals among equals."

Especially impressive was the new look of the communities south of Bakersfield, the little towns of Arvin, Lamont, and Weedpatch in the area that had provided the setting for parts of *The Grapes of Wrath*. Streets of "tar-paper shacks, tents, and trailers" had given way to "modern but modest frame cottages," and men and women who had once drifted in to pick cotton now distributed themselves across many occupations and activities.

"The Texas twang and Arkansas drawl pervade discussions at the cotton gin, the filling stations, the bars and the market."[1]

For all of its self-congratulatory tone, Carlson's report was not far off the mark. The years following the end of the 1930s saw major improvements in the opportunities open to Southwesterners, not just in the valley but throughout California, and not just in economic but also in social terms. And as tensions eased and confidence rose, there were opportunities as well for new expressions of cultural identity. The P&J Cafe in Arvin seemed to speak for the whole area when it advertised itself as "The Home of the Oakies."

The changes began with the onset of World War II and had to do with the new economic and social dynamics that the war brought to California. The war, of course, had a palliative effect on the entire nation's economy, banishing the malaise that had persisted despite a decade of New Deal programs. But the effects were particularly stunning in California, which received more federal defense dollars than any other state, some 10 percent of total war-era expenditures.

The need to fight a two-ocean war dictated the spending policy. By 1945, the state claimed nearly one hundred major military installations through which passed most of the personnel and equipment for the Pacific theater. Defense production centered there as well. California turned out one-sixth of the nation's total output of war materiel. The San Francisco Bay Area, its protected waterways ideally suited for a maritime nation at war, transformed itself into the country's premier shipbuilding center, while southern California assumed the same role in the production of aircraft, accounting for 40 percent of all planes produced during the war. If the United States had become the "Arsenal of Democracy," California was its most important factory.[2]

All this meant jobs. As the defense buildup gained momentum, California's unemployment rate, still 14 percent in early 1940, plummeted. By mid-1942, joblessness was but a bitter memory in most parts of the state. Indeed, once again the lure of employment pumped newcomers into California. Dwarfing the 1930s inflow, exceeding even the 1920s, the war decade attracted nearly three million permanent new residents, helping the state to achieve a stunning 53 percent population growth rate.[3]

California during these years looked straight into its future. The state's new military-industrial economic foundation, its heightened value to a nation increasingly engaged in the Pacific basin, and its revitalized sunbelt appeal would in short order propel it to the first rank among states. "We have sniffed our destiny," proclaimed Governor Earl Warren as the war drew to a close.[4]

For Southwesterners in California, these were equally transforming years. Economic opportunity was not the only reason. Important too were the huge new additions to the resident Southwestern population. In numbers nearly twice that of the Dust Bowl period, at least 621,000 Oklahomans, Arkansans, Texans, and Missourians settled and stayed in California during the 1940s. Both in background and in outlook, these "Defense Okies" differed somewhat from their predecessors. The most notable group of new migrants were Southwestern blacks, more than 125,000 of whom moved west in the 1940s, to be followed by larger complements in the 1950s and 1960s. With others coming from Louisiana and the Eastern South, California was soon to have for the first time a substantial black population.[5]

Southwestern whites, as before, were drawn from both rural and urban settings, but certain sectors contributed in larger measure than before. Outmigration increased from the Ozark-Oauchita upland areas which had been spared the acreage reduction programs that had previously helped depopulate more prosperous farming regions. Now the promise of high wage employment accomplished what poverty alone had not. From the hill counties came migrants like John Pennington, who had spent the thirties in Arkansas scratching out a living on farm jobs and WPA work. Having visited California in 1929, just at the start of the Depression, and later hearing stories of hardship out there, he stayed home during the 1930s, deciding that it was no time to be taking chances. But by the early 1940s the western winds of opportunity were blowing strong and sure. "In that country, in Arkansas, especially eastern Oklahoma and part of Texas, the Depression wasn't over like it was most everywhere else, it went on for several years in a lot of places. . . . I thought I could do better here, so I come out."[6]

Joining him were families who had fared relatively well in the 1930s but saw in California's booming defense sector a chance to improve earnings or accumulate savings. Some, as in previous decades, intended only a temporary stay. An Oklahoma oil worker with an erratic employment history during the Depression counted on earning enough in California to return after the war and purchase a farm. A farm couple from the same state had slightly different plans. With three sons in the military, they decided to lease out their 320 acre farm and work for a time in southern California. Their expected earnings would allow them to refurbish and perhaps expand the farm. Whether intending to stay or return, whether from the poorest or more fortunate segments of Southwestern society, the region's slow recovery and California's speedy one sent a new generation of migrants west.[7]

Following jobs primarily, and relatives secondarily, in the early years of the 1940s migrants usually headed for California's metropolitan areas, not just Los Angeles but now also San Diego and the San Francisco Bay Area. These were the centers of defense production; here lay the shipyards, aircraft factories, and assorted secondary defense contractors hungry for workers. By 1943, recruiters for some of the largest companies crisscrossed the Midwestern and Southwestern states, combing the labor-rich heartland, guaranteeing a job and transportation expenses to anyone willing to sign an employment contract. The recruiters, however, merely accelerated what informal job information networks had long since started. The same grapevines that had facilitated migration in the 1930s had grown dense by the 1940s, multiplying the flow.[8]

Among the Defense Okies heading for the cities were substantial numbers of Southwesterners who had settled in California's valleys during the previous decade. Though the second half of the 1940s would again see growth in these areas, census estimates suggest that many rural counties lost population to the cities during the first three years of the 1940s.[9] For Jewell Morris's brother Chester, frustrated by several years of marginal employment in the fields, opportunity finally beckoned. Hearing of work in Richmond, where Henry Kaiser was laying out the nation's largest shipyard complex across the Bay from San Francisco, he left the San Joaquin Valley for good in 1941, taking a job first with the railroad and later building liberty ships.[10] About the same time, James Lackey made his way to the Long Beach shipyards. A full-time hand at the DiGiorgio ranch in Kern County, he had done well compared with many Depression-era migrants, but defense work promised to pay two to three times more. The early 1940s found thousands of valley residents making the same choice, many of them destined, like Lackey, to return to the San Joaquin at war's end.[11]

As they had in the 1930s, Southwesterners comprised only a portion of the out-of-state defense migration into the metropolitan areas, between 25 and 30 percent depending on the city. This was only slightly larger than their 22 percent representation in the previous decade's inflow to these same areas. Nevertheless, Okies were more noticeable this time and perhaps more cohesive in their social habits, and as a result the decade witnessed examples of residential concentration previously rare in metropolitan settings.[12]

Employment opportunities guided this development. Unlike the scattered job search patterns of the previous decade, many Southwesterners went to work for the major defense contractors, often for companies employing tens of thousands of workers. Employment records for the CalShip facility at Los Angeles's Terminal Island show that 19 percent of the company's 34,000 employees in 1944 were Oklahomans, Arkansans, Texans, and Missourians who had come to California after December 7, 1941. That is far from a complete total for Southwestern employment at that firm, since it does not include the many already present in the state before Pearl Harbor. The overall representation was probably similar to figures at the giant Kaiser shipyard in Richmond. There, 28 percent of the 90,000 workers, including roughly half of all newcomers, were Southwesterners.[13]

Residential clustering followed naturally. With their work located mostly in the fringe areas outside city limits, the defense migrants poured into communities surrounding Los Angeles. As early as May 1941, journalist Ernie Pyle, soon to become famous as a war correspondent, noted that "Aviation Okies" were filling up low-priced south-side communities such as Bell Gardens. On the west side, closer to the sprawling Douglas, North American, and Northrup aircraft plants, the towns of Santa Monica, Culver City, El Segundo, Torrance, and Hawthorne also felt the impact. Shipyard workers meanwhile competed with aircraft employees for housing in the Long Beach area, in nearby Lakewood and the newly developing Orange County communities of Cypress, Hawaiian Gardens, and Buena Park. In each of these settings, new subdivisions, built at a furious pace but hopelessly behind demand, quickly filled with newly arrived defense workers, many of them Southwesterners.[14]

North Long Beach had been quiet and semi-rural when Audie and Walter Moffitt settled there at the start of the Depression. It was already changing rapidly, however, when Ruby Barnes, her husband, and two children arrived from Oklahoma in early 1941. Ahead of the main defense rush, the Barneses were lucky: homes were still available and prices still reasonable. After five weeks of doubling up with relatives, and with a job secured, they were able to buy a small, two-bedroom house in one of the early tracts. Later arrivals would pay much more and look harder, but street by street, ranks of cheaply built stucco cottages replaced the fields of cabbages and oats. Despite the rapid development, the Barneses felt comfortable in their new neighborhood. The neighbors were "very friendly," Ruby Barnes remembers, and it seemed like "ninety percent" were from the Southwest.[15] The actual percentage was not nearly that high. A survey conducted in another defense community near Torrance indicates that between 22 and 30 percent of residents were from the four Western South states.[16]

Near the Bay Area's far-flung shipyards, concentrations of Southwesterners also appeared, in Vallejo, in Brisbane, in the Bayview section of San Francisco near Hunters Point, in Oakland, and, most important, in Richmond. A dull industrial suburb consisting of an oil refinery, a Ford assembly plant, and some 24,000 residents before Kaiser began his shipyard, Richmond became after 1941 the nation's "quintessential war boom town." Two years later, with city services, housing, and transportation crushed beneath what one report called an "avalanche" of newcomers, the population topped 100,000, perhaps a third of the new residents Okies.[17]

Migrants arriving in any of the metropolitan areas during the war stepped into a feverish environment where everything save jobs stood in short supply. Los Angeles, San Diego, and the Bay Area each made the federal government's top ten list of "Congested Production Areas," and it took but one look at the housing shortages, the transportation crises, or the

Figure 25. Richmond, 1942. (*Dorothea Lange, © 1982, The Oakland Museum, The City of Oakland*)

day-to-day frenzy of three-shift life in those areas to understand why. Overcrowding, soaring prices, and shortages were standard. With affordable housing all but impossible to find, people imposed on relatives, crammed into undersized apartments, or made do in trailer parks. With the schools overflowing, they sent their children off for half-day split sessions, sometimes third-of-a-day sessions. With gasoline, tires, and many other goods rationed, shoppers stood in long lines and commuters fought for standing room on buses and streetcars.[18]

Southwesterners shared the challenges of adjusting to this boomtown existence with many others, newcomers and residents alike. The story's central elements are familiar enough. People learned to accommodate not only consumer inconveniences but also significant changes in work lives and family responsibilities. Wives as well as husbands often took factory jobs—a new experience for many Southwestern women, as it was for others. Stella Baxter had never worked outside the home back in Texas, but along with her husband, a brother, a sister, and at least one nephew, she signed on at the Kaiser shipyard. The job may have been somewhat of an adventure, but the 120 mile round-trip commute and the need to leave her four children alone each night were not.[19]

Sherman and Mildred Coleman faced slightly different inconveniences after leaving San Bernardino for the Bay Area. Housing was not a problem. Coleman's mother had come out from Missouri and now owned a house in Oakland. The young couple squeezed in. Still, their lives were hectic. He worked nights as a plate hanger at Moore Dry Dock while she worked days as a welder in the same shipyard. Both found the pace and scale of things initially bewildering. So large was the shipyard that Sherman could not find his work station. For the first six nights on the job, "I just wandered around."[20]

Whatever the difficulties of the new setting, they were of a different order than those that had greeted Depression-era migrants. The desperation of that earlier experience was gone now, replaced by the security of plentiful job opportunities and wage rates beyond memory. Helpful too was the fact that newcomers were so plentiful. It was hard to feel isolated and alone amidst this drama of mass resettlement. And the war itself made everything different. The spirit of patriotism, the call for commitment, cooperation, and sacrifice helped to smooth the anxieties of resettlement, making the process seem more exciting than difficult, an adventure more than a struggle.

Less difficult too, in most instances, were relations with the resident population. The fears that had prompted most of the earlier hostility had dissipated with the economic recovery. Migration, everybody knew, was now in the national interest. Still, there were old reminders and some new sources of tension. The Okie epithet had not and would not disappear, thanks in part to Steinbeck's unforgettable novel. Among Californians, the term came often to mind and almost as frequently to mouth. But the old sting was fading.

Ruby Barnes remembers some teasing but refused to take it seriously.[21] Frank Manies, who had left the Central Valley in part to get "away from the Okie, Dust Bowl accusations," found Santa Monica a great improvement. Occasionally someone would notice his accent and ask, "Are you an Okie?" But the men at work were "all nice people. . . . They treated me like anyone else."[22] Working also in Santa Monica, at the Douglas aircraft plant, Ted Gehringer felt less sensitive about his Oklahoma background than he had a few years earlier going to school in nearby Pomona.[23] So did Ken Griffis, who had spent several years at a central Los Angeles high school. For them as for most Southwesterners who had known first hand the stigmas surrounding the Dust Bowl migration, the war marked a turning point. "There was such a coming together," says Griffis, "that at least as far as I'm concerned by the end of the war that obliterated all feelings about Okies, Arkies, and Texans."[24]

Relations apparently were somewhat less affable in certain parts of the Bay Area, where after several decades of modest population growth residents now contemplated the addition of more than half a million new-comers, a significant number of them from the Western South. A new element in the region's population mix, Southwesterners were greeted with something more than good-natured teasing in some of the more crowded shipyard communities. At Moore Dry Dock, where she worked for two years, sociologist Katherine Archibald observed that Southwesterners bore "their own burden of disapproval and discrimination," less virulent than the hostility directed at blacks, the other major newcomer group. "Scarcely a day passed without my hearing of the Okie and his idiosyncrasies, and though laughter softened the impact of the remarks, the undercurrent of conscious ridicule was steady." She continued:

> "There were jocose tales, for instance, of the money-hunger of the Okies, too avid to be respectable, which led them to travel west and seek employment as family units—husband, wife, grandma, half-grown youngsters, and all. Of an Okie family well represented at Moore Dry Dock one man remarked, "Why, they'd put their five-year-old to work it they could get him through the hiring office as a midget."
> . . . Okie stupidity was second only to sex as a subject for scrawls on bulk-heads and toilet-shack walls. One of the milder examples was the caption, "Okie, this is a door," crudely chalked over an obvious bulkhead passageway. In a rougher vein of satire, shipyard urinals, I was told, were frequently labeled, "Okie drinking fountain," and a tin cup was conveniently placed near by. Half humorously, half maliciously, the symbol of the Okie was elaborated with countless details of stupidity, so that he emerged at last a caricature of a man whose only proper sphere was the outhouse and the tumbledown shanty of the funny-paper Ozarks.[25]

Similar conditions prevailed in nearby Richmond. "The whole damn states of Oklahoma, Arkansas and Texas arrived during the summer," old-time residents were heard to complain.[26] Officials at the Kaiser shipyard noted the proliferation of bulkhead graffiti aimed at blacks and Okies. "Why don't You Okies Take Japan, You Took California Without the Loss of a Man!" someone had written. The company newspaper, *Fore' n' Aft,* called for cooperation and understanding. "What's all the beefing about outsiders? . . . Let's all get together and work for faster production and a quicker victory."[27]

Heavy humor or light ribbing, the Bay Area response to white South-westerners was never as serious or as psychologically threatening as the patterns of the previous decade. The migrants were also much better pre-pared to handle it, both because they had heard stories and knew something of what to expect, and because the war context had given them new sources of pride. More than in the previous decade, Southwesterners seemed to confront their detractors from a position of confidence, usually either dismissing the taunts or countering with expressions of Okie superiority.

Figure 26. Shift change, Kaiser shipyards, 1943. Some 90,000 employees worked in the Richmond yards. (*Dorothea Lange,* © *1982, The Oakland Museum, The City of Oakland*)

Archibald observed that Okies readily "exchanged epithet for epithet" with the inhospitable " 'Calies' or 'Prunepickers,' though these terms, too, were saved from the heaviness of unqualified insult by a large admixture of bantering good humor and conscious satire."[28]

The same combative spirit became evident in other settings. Tired of the Okie jokes but willing to use that label as a signature, a correspondent addressed a Los Angeles newspaper:

> Most of us came here because of the war effort. We're here because you Californians cried for manpower and womanpower. We're here because we are patriotic, because you couldn't handle the job. We're here because this is still a free country. As for sky-high salaries, may I mention the sky-high cost of living? No, that was no incentive for us coming here. We came because we felt it our duty. But as soon as this mess is over with, you can have your goldanged, over-soaked, unsunnied California with its "pumpkin size or-anges," "five pound lemons," your dirty fog, reckless drivers, gestapo atti-tude—and the geraniums, too!"[29]

Another letter writer, also proud to be identified as "just another Okie," responded to Kaiser graffiti artists with a potent blend of defiance and humor:

Sure, we took California without losing a man,
We Arkies and Okies could take Japan!
But while we'd fight that dad-burn foe.
Who would build ships? We'd like to know.
If we swam the ocean, put the Japs to flight,
We'd have to swim back and work all night
To supply ourselves and the Allied nations
With sufficient arms and ammunitions.
We Okies and Arkies are among the best,
We knew how to work before taking the test.
Our force we've combined to help Uncle Sam,
So squawk all you want, we've taken our stand.
We're not ashamed of the old home state,
In fact—we're proud, and think it's great.
And when the war's over and you Callies are safe.
We'll gladly go HOME to that wide open space.[30]

These comments reaffirm the "real American" formula earlier migrants had used to reconcile their social position. Again the point was that Californians were soft, Okies tough, only this time the assertions were made with much more confidence. The war made the critical difference, first because now California needed workers, being unable to "handle the job," second because patriotism was another of those all-American attributes to which Southwesterners laid special claim. With the war on and patriotism the issue of the day, Okies felt more in control, more empowered than the 1930s had allowed.

Key to their new attitude was the perception, reinforced by public opinion, that Southwesterners were contributing their share and more to the war effort. The press deserves much of the credit. Partly in an effort to ease tensions, but more centrally as a means to goad Californians into greater sacrifices, both the press and the defense establishment routinely used the migrants as patriotic models, favoring above all poignant stories about large Okie families with numerous sons overseas. *Fore' n' Aft* profiled one Oklahoma couple whose six children, including a daughter, were all in the military. "When the last son enlisted Pa Reid said to his good wife, 'we're not going to let our kids fight the war alone. We're going to pack right up and go to Californy and the shipyards."[31]

The same images circulated in the Central Valley, as local officials carefully included references to boys from Oklahoma and the other Southwestern states in their paeans to local servicemen.[32] Even critics fell into the habit of conceding the migrants' contributions. "Yes, these people helped in the war effort wonderfully," a woman worried about postwar job and housing shortages began her letter to the *Fresno Bee*, "but now what about the fact that they are still here and seemingly do not intend to return to their own communities?"[33]

For the migrants, the praise was sweet music. But, curiously, it seems they were credited with a distinction that did not exist. The 1950 census asked men whether they had served in the military during the war. The service rates for appropriately-aged Southwestern-born males living in California was only slightly higher than that of other whites, and both were noticeably lower than the service rates for Hispanics, nonwhites, and foreign-born. It was an odd irony. Hurt so often by negative stereotypes, Southwesterners benefited unfairly from this positive one.[34]

Opportunity in the Valley

The war brought improvements to Southwesterners residing in the agricultural areas as well as to those in the coastal zones. Despite a sizable outflow of job-seekers in the early years of the decade, the Southwestern population of nonmetropolitan California soon began to grow again as some families returned from the cities and as a portion of the newcomers from the Southwest turned in the same direction. Both of these trends accelerated noticeably after 1944 with the start of defense industry layoffs and then continued throughout the postwar reconversion period. By the end of the decade, more than a quarter-million Southwestern newcomers had distributed themselves throughout the state's nonmetropolitan areas, far more than in the previous decade.

Though favoring northern California settings (the Sacramento Valley, Napa Valley, and North Coast counties) somewhat more than their predecessors, the forties migrants generally followed the patterns of those of the thirties, not surprising in view of the usual kinship connections. Again the San Joaquin Valley was the primary nonmetropolitan target. The number of white Southwesterners living there nearly doubled between 1940 and 1950 as at least 120,000 newcomers joined earlier settlers. That raised the total number of Southwesterners living in that valley to 255,000, roughly 22 percent of the population. (See Appendix B.)

Despite the increased volume, the 1940s migration occasioned much less comment and made much less impact than the earlier influx. Partly it was because demographic proportions were different. A larger valley population base and a larger resident Southwestern population greeted the new migrants. Significant too was the fact that Southwestern newcomers were now accompanied by larger numbers of migrants from other parts of the country. But most important was the changed economic climate.

Sustained economic growth made feasible the new migration into the valley areas. Less dramatically than the coastal zones but perhaps more consistently because of the smaller reliance on direct military contracts, the San Joaquin Valley produced the jobs that attracted newcomers and improved the lot of residents. A few defense plants and some light manufacturing appeared near Bakersfield, Fresno, and Stockton, but mostly the economy grew with the traditional mix of agriculture, food processing, oil, transportation, construction, and commercial services.[35]

Southwesterners already settled in the valley were among the primary beneficiaries of the war-initiated economic growth. Improvements came steadily to the farm-labor sector. An accelerating demand for agricultural products coincided with the departure of many farm workers to create a labor shortage very much to the benefit of those remaining. Some increase in wage rates and improved labor market was evident in 1941, but the big change came the following year, when rates jumped 30 to 40 percent in most crops, and cotton pickers worked for $1.50 per hundred weight, a 50 percent increase over 1940. Just as important, farm workers might now work as steadily as they wanted, and with less travel required. The result was a dramatic improvement in earnings for those who stayed in the fields. A study of families living in Farm Security Adminstration camps found a fivefold increase in weekly earnings between 1940 and 1942, much of it attributable to the longer work week. Of course, inflation took away part of that. "We are makin' good money, we are also spendin' good money," observed one veteran farm worker.[36]

Farm employers watched these changes with something less than equanimity. The labor shortage was real, and neither appeals to housewives and town folk to join in the harvest work nor the federal government's hastily arranged Bracero agreement with Mexico could bring back the days of surplus. Now, as a result, it was the growers' turn to accommodate. "We've all got to realize that the workers have us over a barrel now," a Modesto area grower cautioned during the summer of 1942. "You can't say a word to them or they will walk off the job and take others with them. They are running the ranches instead of the farmers. The farmers just have to take it."[37] An exaggeration, to be sure, yet there was enough truth to such statements to help explain why some Southwesterners remained in farm work throughout the war. Improved earnings, changes in crop organization that reduced the need for seasonal travel, and an augmented sense of control over the conditions of employment helped to make agricultural employment competitive enough with defense work to keep some of the old work force in the valleys and also to siphon off some of the new migrants streaming into California.

There were instances too of defense workers returning to the fields either because they hated factory work or the urban way of life or because they thought they might do just as well or better in agriculture. Working in a defense plant, Isaac Faught calculated the benefits of such a move:

I'm makin' eleven dollars a day fer ten hours, five days a week, and fifteen dollars fer ten hours on the sixth day. When tomatoes come in pretty soon I may quit this job and go into them fer they will be a good price this year.

I've got four kids who can go into the fields with me and they can pick as much as I can. We can hit it fer seven days a week and make a lot more than I'm makin' now. After that it won't be no trouble gittin' back on defense.[38]

While conditions in agriculture improved dramatically, the more significant news was that jobs other than farm work were also opening up. In the valleys as well as on the coast, the 1940s marked a major leap in occupational status for many Southwesterners. With men enlisting in the military and economic activity soaring, job opportunities appeared in the full range of blue-collar and commercial occupations.

Thomas Smith had tried various jobs back in Oklahoma, including oil and railroad work in addition to farming. But since coming to California in 1937, his only work had been farm labor, mostly for the DiGiorgio Corporation. He was still working there in 1943 and earning just 30 cents an hour when he was introduced to a construction contractor who offered him a job at $1.00 an hour. "I'll be down there in the morning," he replied. A year later he made another move when his employer folded his business and left Bakersfield. Smith and his son-in-law began building houses on their own. "I would do the brick and cement work. He would do the carpentry work and the wiring. We'd both do the plumbing. Then we would sell the house and buy another vacant lot and build another house." For the next six years, they built houses, earning a good living many years, but struggling in others as the unpredictable housing market see-sawed in the postwar period. Opting for greater security, Smith quit in 1950 to take a job as a heavy equipment operator for the county.[39]

Only the details of his story are unique. Hazel Smalling's husband went from the fields to a job making tires for Firestone in one of the San Joaquin Valley's new war-era production plants. After the war he became an electrician. Talmage Lee Collins moved from farm labor to farm-labor contracting; Ed Crane into cotton-gin work. R. M. Dinwiddies, like Thomas Smith, took up carpentry, while Bob Surratt opened a service station across from the Visalia FSA camp where his family had lived.[40]

Others became farmers. Even with labor tight, the war saw a significant expansion of farm activity in the San Joaquin Valley as cotton and food prices rose and irrigation opened new lands. That, plus the internment of several thousand Japanese farmers, made it possible for some Southwesterners to rent or purchase farms. Slim Phillips, who, it may be recalled, had ignored UCAPAWA pickets just after arriving in California because he was broke and needed to eat, by 1941 had done well enough picking cotton and driving a truck to secure a bank loan and buy a farm. By the end of the 1940s, he had branched out successfully into real estate and other businesses. In like manner Wade Miller parlayed his earnings from farm work into a substantial fortune, investing first in a "tourist court," selling that two years later and buying a farm, and then in 1949 exchanging that for a cattle ranch. Hollis Roberts also bought his first land during the war. Working in the oil fields by day, he rented five acres and raised hogs by night. Next he bought fifteen acres and grew potatoes, cotton, and alfalfa. Turning then to farming full time, he began to build an agricultural empire that eventually covered seven thousand acres and made him a multimillionaire.[41]

These three were exceptional, of course. Farming carried no guarantee of great riches, especially on the scale that former laborers were likely to manage. Like Roberts, Truman Mitchell tried to combine oil work with part-time farming, but the fifteen acres that he and wife, Viola, bought never made them wealthy. Ed Crane looks back with considerable regret on his war-era farming venture. For two years, during 1942 and 1943, he owned a sixty-acre farm in partnership with his uncle. But tired of paying out a dollar an hour for labor and figuring that it would be more lucrative to work for wages themselves, they sold the land. "It was the sort of deal that I couldn't see any future in farming, but you know what's happened since. Hindsight is twenty-twenty."[42]

Opportunities also awaited many of those who returned to the valley at the conclusion of the war. James Lackey learned the pipefitting trade in the Long Beach shipyards. But like many who had left the valley when he did, he hated wartime Los Angeles. "Too many people for me. I was used to a small place and during the war they had blackouts. You had to have car pools and . . . if you drove to work you had to get stamps to buy gas and this and that." When the shipyards began to lay off workers, he returned to Kern County to take a job with his brother's new pipeline company.[43] Terry Clipper (appropriately named as it turned out) spent the war years in the Army learning, among other things, the hair-cutting trade. In 1948, after three years of working in Los Angeles, he moved to Bakersfield and opened a barber shop.[44]

The success stories do not apply to everyone. A certain percentage of Southwesterners never left farm labor. In addition, some went into the military or into defense work only to return to the fields at war's end. The huge shipyard and aircraft layoffs caused a renewed glut of farm labor in the postwar years, resurrecting concerns about migrants and poverty. The final year of the decade, 1949, was especially difficult. With an 11 percent unemployment rate, the San Joaquin Valley again witnessed scenes of rural suffering, one reporter warning of "a new disaster so vast that the eyewitness must grope back to the great depression to find anything like it."[45]

But the problem was temporary. Agricultural employment picked up in the early 1950s. Equally important, those Southwesterners who remained in the farm labor force were gradually working themselves into the better-paid and more secure sectors of that industry. More and more they tended to find employment as foremen, equipment operators, and year-round farm

Table 6.1. Occupational Distribution and Income for Males in Metropolitan Areas, 1950, 1940

	1950			1940
	Southwesterners	Other Whites	Hispanics/ nonwhites	Southwesterners
Professionals/ managers/ proprietors	19%	30%	10%	18%
Clerical/sales/police and fire	17	20	9	18
Craftsmen/foremen	27	22	14	24
Operatives	20	16	23	20
Service workers	6	5	18	8
Laborers (nonfarm	8	5	22	10
Farm laborers	2	1	5	3
	99%	99%	101%	101%
N =	(2,352)	(16,435)	(2,598)	(1,385)
1950 occupation index	3.7	4.0	3.1	
1940 occupation index	3.6	3.8	3.0	
1949 median income	$3,005	$3,215	$2,275	
1939 median income	$1,190	$1,320	$ 755	
percent increase	(152%)	(143%)	(201%)	
1949 med. family inc.	$3,565	$3,900	$2,855	
1939 med. family inc.	$1,545	$1,725	$ 985	
percent increase	(131%)	(126%)	(190%)	

Note: Occupational data are for all males age 14 and older in the labor force excluding military personnel and family farm workers. Personal income figures are for males 18 years and older who reported any earnings; family income is for male-headed families. The 1939 figures are for wage and salary workers only; self-employed are included in the 1949 data.

Sources: 1940 and 1950 Census Public Use Microdata Samples.

hands, leaving the seasonal harvest work to the rapidly expanding Hispanic population.[46]

The general picture of occupational and financial improvement for the 1940s can be seen in Tables 6.1 and 6.2. In the metropolitan areas, overall occupational distributions had changed only slightly during the war decade. By 1950, Southwestern males were still employed largely in blue-collar jobs, though the percentage of skilled workers had increased somewhat. Still underrepresented in white collar positions but removed as well from the laboring and service work that occupied so many Hispanics and non-whites, most Southwesterners remained modestly in the middle of the occupational spectrum. Of course to present things in these terms is in

Table 6.2. Occupational Distribution and Income for Males in the San Joaquin Valley, 1950, 1940

	1950			1940
	Southwesterners	Other Whites	Hispanics/ nonwhites	Southwesterners
Farmers	5%	15%	5%	6%
Professionals/ managers/ proprietors	11	21	5	7
Clerical/sales/police and fire	6	12	3	6
Craftsmen/foremen	18	18	5	12
Operatives	23	14	11	13
Service workers	4	5	7	4
Laborers (nonfarm)	8	6	14	11
Farm laborers	25	9	51	42
	100%	100%	101%	101%
N =	(871)	(1,936)	(495)	(465)
1950 occupation index	3.0	3.8	2.2	
1940 occupation index	2.5	3.5	2.1	
1949 median income	$2,420	$2,970	$1,380	
1939 median income	$ 550	$1,130	$ 400	
percent increase	(340%)	(163%)	(245%)	
1949 med. family inc.	$2,970	$3,480	$2,015	
1939 med. family inc.	$ 790	$1,470	$ 555	
percent increase	(276%)	(136%)	(263%)	

Note: Occupational data are for all males age 14 and older in the labor force excluding military personnel and family farm workers. Personal income figures are for males 18 years and older who reported any earnings; family income is for male-headed families. The 1939 figures are for wage and salary workers only; self-employed are included in the 1949 data.

Sources: 1940 and 1950 Census Public Use Microdata Samples.

many ways misleading. The portrait of group stasis is really not that at all. At least thirty percent of these Southwesterners were newcomers whose earlier occupations do not figure in these data. As we have seen, many of them experienced real and in some cases dramatic occupational improvements.

There is no question that incomes rose substantially in the 1940s. During a decade in which consumer prices rose approximately 70 percent, median incomes for Southwestern male wage earners increased 152 percent and family incomes rose 131 percent, signifying a major standard of living improvement. With three-quarters of all families now earning more than

$2,500 a year and half better than $3,500, it was clear that the great body of Southwesterners in metropolitan California enjoyed standards of living associated with that hard-working bedrock strata of the postwar American social structure—the lower middle class.[47]

The changes were more obvious in the San Joaquin Valley. First and most significant, the percentage of Southwesterners engaged in farm labor had dropped in ten years from 42 to 25 percent, the proportion of unskilled laborers (both farm and nonfarm) from 53 to 33 percent. Most had shifted into blue collar positions. By 1950, 41 percent of male Southwesterners made their living in skilled or semi-skilled jobs, compared with 25 percent a decade before. Still seriously underrepresented among farmers, proprietors, professionals, clerical, and other white-collar occupations, Southwesterners now played major roles in the construction, oil and gas, automotive services, and canning industries. In essence, Southwesterners in the San Joaquin Valley were beginning to catch up with their metropolitan counterparts by moving substantially into the blue-collar working class.[48]

The change was made possible by an overall shift in the occupational structure of the valley as agriculture employed a decreasing portion of the labor force. Southwesterners were perfectly placed to take advantage of the transformation. While racial prejudice and language barriers channeled the growing Hispanic population into the fields, white Southwesterners filled the new nonfarm jobs. The occupational index records their rise. As the aggregate status of other whites increased from 3.5 to 3.8, Southwesterners climbed from 2.5 to 3.0. Increasingly distanced from the Hispanics and nonwhites with whom they had previously shared the farm labor sector, by the end of the 1940s the bulk of the group had taken a visible step up the occupational ladder.[49]

Occupational changes, elevated wage levels, low unemployment rates, and an increase in the number of working wives all helped to raise standards of living for valley residents. By 1949, median family incomes for Southwesterners had jumped 276 percent, from $790 per year a decade before to $2,970. Even with the price increases, that represented an enormous financial improvement. Furthermore, it closed considerably the financial gap that had previously separated most Southwesterners from other whites in the valley. Where a decade before the average Southwestern family had earned 54 percent of the income of other white families, now the figure was 85 percent.[50]

The forties thus were a remarkable catch-up period for Southwesterners in the valley. Financially the bulk of the group had escaped the crushing poverty that had entrapped and stigmatized them in the previous decade. Occupationally, too, they were steadily leaving behind the socially burdensome role of farm laborers for the more respectable ranks of the blue-collar working class. No longer separated from other whites by huge differences in wealth and status, no longer outside the occupational categories customarily reserved for whites, they now filled in the low end of that spectrum.

The 1940s paid social as well as economic dividends to Southwesterners living in the valley. With each passing year the indications of prejudice and ill-will lessened steadily. The surface changes were naturally most apparent. Valley residents learned first of all not to talk openly about Okies, reserving that term for private settings. Sensitive to the new pattern, a 1946 Bureau of Agricultural Economics memo suggested dropping the label from future reports. Significantly, the term also failed to appear in a vigorous migration debate that occupied readers of the *Fresno Bee* all through the month of September 1946. Calling for "out of state families" to go home, opponents were careful to avoid offensive labels, usually employing the term "midwesterner" as a respectful alternative to "Okie." Meanwhile, the social columns of the same newspaper reveal further signs of the improving social position of Southwesterners. Appearing with growing frequency in the postwar period were notices of local families hosting visitors from Oklahoma and other Southwestern states or setting off themselves "to spend some time with a sister in Arkansas."[51]

Still, the entrenched habits of prejudice did not dissipate easily. Frank Manies had been glad to escape to Los Angeles after three hard years in the valley, and even as the war drew to a close and his defense industry job ended, he had no desire to return. But his father, living in the Tulare County town of Ivanhoe, convinced him that the farming community would make a good setting for the garage and machine shop Frank planned to open. Initially, Manies had nothing but regrets. Other businessmen and growers shunned his new shop, Manies recalled bitterly, "partly because I was an Okie and partly because I was in competition with these natives who had been there for a number of years." Regardless, his business succeeded because of the loyal patronage of Southwesterners in the area. "I would say that 95 percent of the work I got was from people like myself, people who had come . . . from Oklahoma and Texas." Not until eight or nine years later did the shop begin to attract a more varied clientele, and only then was he invited to join the Chamber of Commerce.[52]

Dale Morrison had a very different experience. Since graduating from a Kern County high school in 1936, the Oklahoma native had encountered few obstacles to advancement. By 1952, he looked back on a varied career that included four years in the military, a position with the Bank of America, a job as office manager for the Bakersfield Chamber of Commerce, and proprietorship of his own successful employment agency. Yet if his own life was testimony to the diminishing burden of a Southwestern background, his line of work at times reminded him that some habits of prejudice remained. "Even to this day," he told a journalist in 1952, "I occasionally have some potential employer (usually a woman) say to me— 'Don't send me an Oakie or an Arkie.' "[53]

The 1940s were an opening, the prelude to further gains in economic and social standing that would come with the rising tide of prosperity of the 1950s and 1960s. And the changes registered beyond the personal lives of former migrants. California's cultural landscape was also affected. Over 1.2 million white Southwesterners had settled in the state by mid-century, and now that the stain of poverty was fading other signs of their influence were becoming more visible.

Like others who had come to California, Southwesterners had been engaged all along in the delicate business of cultural negotiation, changing some of their ways and re-creating others in a give and take sequence that ultimately transformed both newcomers and hosts. Especially but not exclusively in the San Joaquin Valley and especially as the group gained social position and confidence, Southwestern influences would show up in California's politics, religious life, linguistic habits, and recreational interests.

This was not just a function of numbers. Broad changes in American culture in the postwar period were also involved. With its hyper-Americanism and sentimentalization of traditional values, the Cold War era resonated with some of the central perspectives that Southwestern plain folk embraced. As national priorities changed, so did the weighting of some of the key symbols associated with Southwestern and, more broadly, Southern regional culture. In the 1950s and 1960s, increasing numbers of Californians (as well as Americans in other settings) would find value in perspectives and institutions that former Southwesterners had been maintaining.

7

Special to God

ONE NEEDS ONLY BE WITHIN RADIO RANGE OF THE SOUTHERN SAN JOAQUIN Valley today to hear the Southwestern influence. The radio brings in a few Spanish-language broadcasts, some rock and roll of various vintages, a bit of news and listener talk programming, but mostly the dial belongs to country music and religious stations. Here are the most distinctive public voices of the Okie subculture—the drawling heart-of-America songs of the country-western idiom and the soul-saving preaching of evangelical Protestantism. Separated by only a few megahertz, they are the twin keys to the dynamic influence of Southwesterners in California. The story of these two institutions takes us deeply into the process of cultural negotiation that has transformed both Southwesterners and California over the last half-century.

The two voices also suggest something of the variation and range of the Okie subculture. From its inception, it has been a community split between two poles, oriented on the one hand around stern-minded religiosity and on the other hand around hard-drinking irreverence—a community of churches and saloons, of churchgoers and good old boys. While many members move between both camps, or avoid both, the community is preoccupied with this dualism, a habit that reflects the intensely Protestant religious background of the Southwest.

Like its political culture, the home region's religious orientation was distinct but not unique, a concentrated version of patterns widely spread throughout American society. In a largely Protestant nation, the Southwest, along with the Eastern South, was more emphatically Protestant, and emphatically Low Church, evangelical Protestant. The western end of the Bible belt, or more accurately, the Baptist-Methodist belt, the Southwest saw few of the Catholics, Jews, Lutherans, and liberal and non-evangelical Protestants who variegated the religious culture of other regions. "Nowhere else in Christianity's long history," writes historian Samuel Hill, has revivalism-fundamentalism enjoyed the influence it maintains in the American South. Denominations that began centuries ago in dissent there comprise a "virtual establishment."[1] Oklahoma shows the pattern. Ninety-one percent of its church members in 1936 claimed the Protestant faith, 35 percent of them Baptists, 23 percent Methodists, and most of the rest Presbyterians, Pentecostals, Adventists, or Church of Christ—persuasions which in that setting were predictably evangelical.[2]

Beyond the usual compilation of numbers, the precise dimensions of evangelical Protestant influence have not as yet been adequately plotted, but there is every reason to suspect that, as in the Eastern South, this religious culture infused nearly every aspect of life in the Southwest. There are some obvious clues. The area participated vigorously in the moral reform crusades of the early twentieth century, passing in many jurisdictions not just prohibition legislation but also tough laws limiting divorce, outlawing prostitution, and prohibiting the teaching of Darwinism in public schools. Texas nearly passed an anti-evolution law, while Oklahoma and Arkansas became two of only five states in the country actually to do so. Oklahoma's 1923 law forbade references to evolution in textbooks; Arkansas's more comprehensive 1928 statute banned the subject from both textbooks and classrooms.[3]

As elsewhere, the crusade for moral and religious legislation waned with the 1920s, but the forces of moral rearmament put up a longer and stronger fight in the Southwest than in most other regions. Prohibition repeal, for example, was vigorously contested everywhere but Missouri, whose large urban and immigrant sectors made it a special case. Amidst feverish debate, Texas and Arkansas both lifted statewide prohibition in the mid-1930s in favor of a county option plan that still today leaves sections of those states dry. Oklahoma, which claimed the distinction of having been "born sober" by reason of its 1907 constitutional provisions banning alcohol sale and consumption, legalized 3.2 beer in 1933 but held firm against hard liquor until 1959 and then only for off-premises consumption. A county option law permitting the sale of liquor by the drink was not approved until 1985.[4]

More lasting than public policy accomplishments, however, and more revealing of the depth of Protestant influence, was the ability of the evangelical establishment to define ideal standards of behavior for broad segments of Southwestern society. The pluralism which permitted subgroups to maintain a variety of moral, religious, and ethnic perspectives in Western and Northern cities flourished only weakly in Southwestern urban areas and not at all in small town and rural settings, where as one Missourian put it, the churches "control everything." What they controlled was not so much behavior as the standards by which behavior was socially evaluated. In the Missouri town which anthropologist Carl Withers called "Plainville," he observed that people did violate norms—by not going to church, using alcohol or foul language, attending dances at distant clubs, even taking sexual liberties—but generally they did so surreptitiously and usually they lost prestige when found out. Conformity or nonconformity thus were the only real options; one could break the rules but not escape them.[5]

Breaking the rules was precisely the defining dynamic of the mostly male, alcohol-using counter-culture. Drinking was an act laden with serious social significance. From the timid group of males Withers spied sharing a bottle of rye in the Missouri town's produce house to the hard-bitten denizens of some "blood and guts" Texas road house, alcohol consumption signaled defiance. But it was a kind of ritualized, guilt-ridden defiance which in the end reinforced the religious-based moral codes. Men, especially young men, were more or less expected to break the rules, expected to exhibit a wild streak that might involve any number of ultimately forgivable "sins." It was all part of the rhythm of growing up and the larger rhythm of sin and repentance that tied together this culture of moral opposites. The religious and the rowdy, the sinners and the saved, were connecting pieces of the same puzzle: often members of one family or aspects of one life. Paul Westmoreland, "Okie Paul" to his country-music fans, penned a song whose ironic refrain delighted audiences who understood its several layers of truth:

> Drink a little beer in a honky tonk,
> Stomp the boards hard Saturday night.
> Go to church on Sunday,
> That makes everything alright.[6]

The Religious Challenge

Neither half of the moral divide would be reconstituted in precisely the same way in California. The rowdy would find expanded opportunities and new meanings for their endeavors, while the religious struggled against long odds to recapture the authority to which they were accustomed. We begin with the religious side of the process.

Relocation often drastically alters religious behavior, either disrupting or intensifying it. In this case it did both. Especially in the 1930s, most migrants found it difficult to maintain the patterns of church involvement that had been customary back home. That is hardly surprising. Even in the best of circumstances, people are often shy about introducing themselves into a new church. The economic conditions of the 1930s complicated matters further, either because families were forced into an unsettled existence which virtually precluded steady church attendance or because poverty introduced priorities and insecurities which distracted in other ways. "It seems like a fellow can't be very religious and live in California," a young Texan who had been in the state for two years complained. Telling of one man who upon reaching the state border supposedly "got down on his knees and said, 'Good-bye, Lord, I'm goin' to California,' " he explained that "you never get to stay in one place long enough to be religious. You move too fast to belong to a church."[7] For another man, an Oklahoman, the problem was money. He felt he should get his financial life in order before worrying about church. "I used to be religious but I just fell down on it," he confided to James Wilson. Here he was "tryin' to feed a family of six on a dollar a day. Can you feed them on that and keep your mind on religion at the same time?"[8]

Social factors also posed a major problem. Some churches deliberately made laboring-class Southwesterners feel unwelcome, "freezing" them out, as one minister put it. Others let routine class barriers do their work. The pastor of the Presbyterian Church in Visalia talked proudly of the wealth and standing of his large congregation.

> None of them are of the migrant class, they are far from it. You look over my congregation on any Sunday morning and you will see the social and spiritual leaders of Visalia. It is a white collar crowd. I am not used to speaking to people from the Dust Bowl.[9]

The story was the same at the First Baptist Church in Shafter, the minister reporting that "the people who come to my church are the kind who like to dress up and dress up their kids too. I know only one migrant woman who comes."[10]

These ministers were not necessarily unsympathetic to the migrants, and some preached occasionally in the labor camps or, more typically, directed resources into the ecumenical Home Missions Council which maintained a migrant ministry in California. But their congregations were apt to be less friendly and as a rule quite intimidating. Oklahoman Jesse Carter*, a faithful Baptist before coming to California, would not go near the Shafter church:

> The average migrant out here is broke and can't git good clothes, so when they go down to church among the natives you feel they are saying, "Here comes a damned Oklahoman." If we went to church back home with our poor clothes on, knowin' the ways of the people as we do, we wouldn't feel that

way. But to go down here with our clothes among the high-ups and all their
fine cars, it makes you naturally feel like you ain't in their class.[11]

A former Baptist living in Wasco echoed this assessment, explaining that
her family avoided the Baptist church there because "We don't have the
clothes. Back home there were little old meetings and you could go any
old way. When you're just raised up among folks its different from the
way it is here."[12] Similarly, when a neighborly Californian invited another
Wasco newcomer to join her at the Baptist services, the woman declined,
saying that, "We are poor people and everybody that goes there are up-
to-date people."[13]

In keeping with the generally more open social atmosphere in Los Angeles and the other metropolitan regions, Southwesterners settling there
in the 1930s were less likely to feel shut out of the churches. This was a
reflection of the greater heterogeneity of the population. The metropolitan
areas boasted a multiplicity of religious institutions, many of them tailored
to the socio-economic character of particular neighborhoods. Accordingly,
the chances were good that migrants looking for a church would find one
where the poor were readily accepted.[14]

Migrants in the valley did, of course, join native churches too. Some,
knowing that they had a right to be in God's house, braved the stares and
refused to be intimidated. In other settings, socially conscious ministers
managed to create an atmosphere in which the migrants felt welcome. But
in general, the major valley churches remained class-specific, catering
largely to relatively well-heeled, older residents while ignoring the vast
majority of newcomers. Usually only those migrants whose economic position provided some confidence of social acceptance had the courage to
attend.

The 1940s provided the key to much greater Southwestern participation
in these churches. As incomes rose and tensions fell, thousands who had
previously stayed away from the organized religion now began to attend
church. Grover Holliday did not wait until the 1940s, but the tentative,
step-by-step way in which he became involved with the Union Congregational Church in Arvin shows something of the relationship between
socio-economic advancement and involvement in one of the erstwhile native churches. Holliday, an Arkansan who had come to California in 1937,
probably would not have approached the Congregational Church but for
the influence of his employer, a respected grower who took an interest in
the religious well-being of his employees and introduced several of them
to the church. About a year after going to work as a year-round hand on
the ranch, Holliday and his family started attending Sunday services. For
a long time, however, their involvement remained limited, reflecting the
family's tentative social position in a church dominated by farmers, mer-

chants, and long-term residents. Not until nine years had passed and Holliday had worked his way into a position of some authority on the ranch—and thus in his community—did the family formally join the church.[15]

Beyond the social challenge, joining one of the California churches often required changes in certain patterns of religious observance. The state's Baptist and Methodist churches in fact belonged to different denominations than the churches back home. California was Northern Baptist (later called American Baptist) and Northern Methodist territory. Most Southwesterners had known only Southern Baptist or Southern Methodist worship. There were important differences.

Each of the major Protestant faiths (including Presbyterians) had split in the 1850s as a result of the slavery/sectional crisis. And in the decades that followed, divisions born of politics had been reinforced by ecclesiastical and theological issues. As far as the actual denominational creed was concerned some of these matters were relatively technical and, in the case of the Methodists, ultimately resolvable. But beneath the level of denominational policy a more substantial divergence had been taking place, one that became quite apparent in the early decades of the twentieth century. The Northern denominations by then were deep in the crisis of modernism, with many of their leaders and congregations turning away from evangelical enthusiasm to embrace religious and social liberalism. The Southern churches, on the other hand, held more uniformly to the main tenets of evangelical Protestantism: revivalism, scriptural literalism, piety, and above all the commitment to individual salvation through Jesus Christ. The fundamentalist movement helped to bring the differences between Northern and Southern Protestantism to full light. Flourishing in all parts of the country, fundamentalism had its greatest strength in the South, where its chief provisions were largely taken for granted. While Baptists and Methodists in the North and West wrestled with the issues of liberalism versus literalism, modernists remained an easily isolated minority in the Southern denominations, each of which maintained a very substantial, if never completely uniform, commitment to "old-time religion."[16]

Thus despite the familiar-sounding church names, Southwesterners were treading on somewhat foreign ground. Wofford and Ruth Clark were initially impressed with the First Baptist Church in Los Angeles. It was grand and imposing, "like a great big beautiful mansion," far larger than their old church back in Oklahoma City. But the services were also different, and before long a misunderstanding led to their departure. Following Southern Baptist practice they had made a financial contribution during the Sunday School meeting instead of waiting for the regular service as was customary in Northern Baptist churches. When the "offering" went unreported in the next week's church bulletin, the Clarks were hurt. "That broke my heart, because you know my money was dedicated to the Lord, and I didn't like that," Ruth Clark recalled. They never went back. There were too many things, once they thought about it, that were wrong about that church: "it was just different . . . just something you didn't know."[17]

Maggie and George Mouser felt the same way about services at the First Baptist Church in Shafter. "We were over there quite a while . . . but then that didn't satisfy we Baptists from the South, from Oklahoma, because it wasn't like we were used to."[18] Some of the differences were matters of polity and probably of little concern to most laity: Northern Baptists exercised somewhat more denominational control over churches, formed ecumenical relations with other denominations, and were not as strict about re-baptizing converts from other Protestant faiths.

But often there were noticeable differences in the content and style of worship. Back home most Baptist and Methodist preachers were strict on moral issues and took their lessons straight from the Bible. And services were conducted in a fervent, revivalistic style that emphasized the search for personal salvation while allowing for a good deal of enthusiastic group participation. With much singing and eagerly appended "Amens," and with the minister pounding out a sermon that let you know that "God was near and heaven was real," religion back home had been vigorous and emotional. On the other hand, much of what California seemed to offer was in comparison cold and formal. It is hazardous to generalize about the California churches, for revivalism and fundamentalism found voices among that state's Baptists, Methodists, and Presbyterians. But more often the major congregations departed from the religious standards of the migrant group. Most churches seemed to be too liberal in what they taught and too restrained in the manner of their worship—offering "brain" religion to people accustomed to a religion of the "heart."[19]

It is hard to say how much these differences would have mattered had they not been compounded by the social question. Even the Mousers, who had always been active in church affairs and were more knowledgeable about matters of practice and doctrine than most laymen, traced part of their alienation to social factors. Stressing that the Shafter Baptist Church was not "to our liking and what we felt [it] should be," Maggie Mouser also makes it clear that "they didn't care about us either. . . . They really didn't accept us very well."[20] For those, like Ruth Criswell, who were less familiar with the issues, problems of acceptance were more important:

> We didn't attend church for several years because we were Southern Baptists and there weren't any Southern Baptists . . . in the state at that time. We went to the First Baptist Church there in Visalia and realized that it wasn't a Southern Baptist Church. It was an American Baptist Church. We just went a couple of times and they were very cold. They weren't very friendly people. I don't know whether they were that way to every outsider that came in or

what. We didn't go back. It was several years before we attended church regularly.[21]

California was not entirely without the sort of churches the migrants did know. In fact, if there is one generalization to be made about California religion it is that it offered a little bit of everything. If the South was the most religiously homogeneous of regions, California was probably the least. Despite its head start, Northern "mainstream" Protestantism had never conquered the Golden State; nor had any other tendency. Demography, always the complicating element in California's cultural scheme, had not allowed it. "So many people," writes historian Eldon Ernst, "of so many kinds from so many places have so rapidly moved into and about California so continuously for so long, that a distinctive [pluralistic] religious environment has emerged." A large Catholic population figured in that heterogeneity. Important too was the state's developmental mythology. The rough and tumble Gold-Rush antecedents of northern California and the Xanadu dimensions of southern California's civilization both had impeded standard religiosity, encouraging a turn to secularity on the part of some Californians, towards religious innovation and extreme pluralism on the part of others. With one of the lowest rates of religious participation in the nation, California also claimed the greatest diversity of religious institutions.[22]

Well before the 1930s Southerners and Southwesterners had contributed to this diversity. Southern Baptist preachers had been forming congregations in California at least since the 1860s. However, by arrangement with the Northern denomination none of those congregations had been allowed to affiliate with the Southern Baptist Convention. Most remained independent or joined one of the small Baptist movements such as the American Baptist Association (Landmark), an Arkansas-based group that had begun as a highly doctrinaire faction within the Southern Baptist Church. By the 1930s, a sprinkling of these independent fundamentalist Baptist churches stood ready to receive the tens of thousands of migrants arriving from the Southwest.[23]

Unlike the Southern Baptist Convention, Southern Methodists had established an official foothold in California. In theory at least, incoming Methodists should have been able to find a church of their own denomination. However, Methodism was in the midst of a national merger just at the time of the Dust Bowl migration, and for that reason and others, the migrants found little haven in California's Southern Methodist churches.

In point of fact, the resident Southern Methodists showed little interest in the newcomers from the Western South. Founded in the 1850s and maintained across eighty years in California, the denomination had long since lost its missionary zeal. Overshadowed by the 113,000 Northern Methodists in the state, the Southerners, with a mere 18,000 members and 60-odd churches in 1936, had seen little growth in decades. Neither the 1920s, when California added several hundred thousand Southwesterners to its population, nor the larger influx of the 1930s had brought the denomination out of the doldrums. Not a single new church opened in either southern California or the San Joaquin Valley during the latter decade, and many of the existing congregations declined in number. The reason is evident. These mostly wealthy churches (the denomination ranked third after Presbyterians and Congregationalists in the per capita value of church property) wanted nothing to do with the impoverished newcomers, regardless of their faith. Still, had the two major Methodist bodies not been talking merger, and putting it into effect in some California communities well in advance of the official 1939 agreement, the Southern Methodist hierarchy might eventually have responded to the growing constituency of unchurched members gathering in California. Merger ultimately denied the resettling Methodists the same chance the Baptists would eventually get to reestablish religious institutions in the manner of their upbringing.[24]

The Pentecostal Conversion

Until the Southern Baptist Convention changed its policy in 1941 and allowed California congregations to affiliate, the major religious alternative to the mainstream churches was to be found among the profusion of sects and tendencies on the radical fringe of evangelical Protestantism. The Seventh-Day Adventists, claiming their strongest foothold in California and always looking for new members, welcomed the migrants into their fold; so did many of the conservative Cambellite congregations which identify themselves only as Churches of Christ. But most important were the multitude of organizations belonging to the Holiness and Pentecostal movements. The Assemblies of God, Church of the Nazarene, Pentecostal Holiness, and various Churches of God and Full-Gospel assemblies—these became the primary refuge for Southwesterners seeking religious haven during the 1930s. Yet they were not traditional refuges. Back home the Pentecostal and Holiness sects probably accounted for no more than 5 percent of the region's church membership. But in California they would reap a great harvest of converts, gathering at least as many souls as the Southern Baptists—the natal church for the largest number of migrants—would later reclaim.[25]

This transfer of religious allegiance had several causes, not all of them directly tied to the migration experience. The 1930s and 1940s saw these same groups gaining converts in various parts of the country, including the Western South. But the exceptional rate of growth among Okies suggests that the reasons were perhaps somewhat different in California. Partly the difference was a matter of opportunity: for a time these churches enjoyed almost a monopoly position in the migrant communities. Equally important, they met a need that some migrants felt for heightened, more intense religious commitment. The Pentecostal conversion was part of what historian Timothy Smith would call the "theologizing experience" of migration.[26]

The Holiness movement and its even more radical offshoot, Pentecostalism, stood at the furthest reaches of the evangelical Protestant world during the 1930s and 1940s. The Holiness movement had emerged in the second half of the nineteenth century initially as a reform tendency within Methodism, spreading then to the Calvinist denominations. Theologically the movement's major point of departure centered on the Holiness understanding of the process of sanctification. Taking their lead from John Wesley's writings about his own pursuit of Christian perfection, believers held that sanctification involved two distinct experiences: first a faith conversion, then a "holiness" work of grace, a transforming, perfecting "blessing" of the Holy Spirit. Sustained also by a general conviction that the major denominations were steadily sacrificing spiritual priorities in favor of worldly concerns, the Holiness critics withdrew after years of bitter struggle and formed by the 1890s an independent movement whose chief denomination in time became the Church of the Nazarene.

Hardly had the new movement appeared when it too split, with the new tendency, Pentecostalism, soon overshadowing its parent. Perfection and its manifestations were again the issue. The Pentecostals, guided by the story in the second book of Acts in which the apostles were baptized by the Holy Ghost on the day of Pentecost, argued that sanctification and spirit baptism were separate matters, the latter representing still another "blessing" and one with very definite characteristics. Spirit baptism endowed the soul with supernatural "gifts," including the gift of healing. It also, they held, revealed itself in a very special way. Those who received the baptism would speak in "tongues," foreign or unknown languages whose meaning they would fully comprehend.[27]

From its beginnings in the early years of the new century the Pentecostal movement spread rapidly, but gains in notoriety far outstripped the expanding membership. Indeed, both the Pentecostals and the Holiness groups earned more ridicule than respect, contending from an early date with the derisive label "holy roller." Much about them was unorthodox. Among the only groups to welcome female preachers, a few of the sects also allowed racially mixed congregations. More significant were the theological departures. The emphasis on miracles, healing, and speaking in tongues seemed ludicrous and outlandish to some critics, heretical and dangerous to others. So did the extraordinary emotionalism and seeming disorder of their services. Even by the standards of revivalistic Southern Protestantism, the techniques of worship in Holiness/Pentecostal churches seemed extreme. "Emotional," "ecstatic," "frenzied," "hysterical" were just some of the adjectives observers used to describe services, which might include episodes of screaming and weeping as well as the trademark (for the Pentecostals) babbling in incomprehensible "tongues."

Condemned by other churches and ridiculed by the secular world, Pentecostals, and their Holiness cousins, remained the poor relations of organized Protestantism throughout the first half of the twentieth century. Yet they would grow to major significance among Southwesterners in California. Part of this success derived from the movement's head start in the migrant camps and communities during the 1930s. At a time when other religious organizations were ignoring the Okies, Holiness and Pentecostal activists were busy preaching, recruiting, and setting up churches.

Some of these men and women were Californians. The state claimed a vigorous movement before the Dust Bowl migration; indeed, Los Angeles is cited as the birthplace of the Nazarene denomination and also as the setting of the celebrated Asuza Street revival that launched the Pentecostal movement in 1906. Beginning in the 1920s that city had also hosted evangelist Aimee Semple McPherson's much publicized revivals. With her magnetic style and extravagant staging, the Cecil B. deMille of Pentecostalism gained thousands of converts.[28]

Many of the Pentecostal preachers, however, were Southwesterners. The Assemblies of God, the largest denomination, had its headquarters and most of its strength in the migrant's home region, and that was true as well of some of the smaller groups. Especially in the Central Valley, most of the preachers were recent migrants themselves who thus appealed to potential recruits on the basis of common background and common experience. Professionalism was not a standard feature of the clergy of these faiths, some of which readily ordained nearly anyone who heard the "call" to preach. Nor in the early days was preaching likely to provide much of an income. Socially and economically indistinguishable from the people they sought to serve, many of Pentecostal preachers earned their living in the fields alongside the others.[29]

And they also set to work building congregations. Talking with strangers, gathering an interested core group, at first they met wherever they could, often in private homes or camp tents. When there were enough members to form a congregation, a store front or some other modest facility might be rented. If the congregation reached a sufficient size, eventually the group would build a permanent structure. Scores of Okie churches belonging to a dozen different Holiness and Pentecostal sects sprang from such humble beginnings. By the end of the 1930s nearly every town in the Central Valley boasted at least a Nazarene and

Figure 27. Sunday school pickup near a labor camp, Kern County, 1938. (*Dorothea Lange, The Bancroft Library, Berkeley, California*)

Assemblies of God and often several other Pentecostal churches. Olive-hurst shows the pattern. By 1942 the Yuba County town with its pre-dominately Okie population boasted eight religious institutions, only one of them, a Methodist community center, affiliated with a main-stream denomination. The others, meeting in everything from private homes to a converted dance hall, bore the following names: Nazarene, Free Pentecostal, Pentecostal Holiness, Faith Tabernacle, Church of God (two of them, different sects), and Jehovah's Witness.[30]

Drawn to these churches were all sorts of people who back home had laughed at holy rollers and their extreme ways. California softened that laughter. There were many reasons for the change. Most important was the social context. There were few other religious institutions where poor Southwesterners felt comfortable and welcome, where they knew they could go without being ashamed of their clothes or accents, where they could socialize with "home folks."

Then too, in a context in which all the other religious institutions were new and different, the Pentecostals were at least in some ways familiar. The teachings might be controversial and the worship might seem "wild," but the general tone of the proceedings borrowed much from the summer revivals that Baptists and Methodists remembered fondly. The energy and excitement helped to draw in the skeptics, if only because they found it entertaining. A former Baptist living in Wasco assured Walter Goldschmidt that she was no convert to the Pentecostal faith. "I don't believe that sort of church is anything but ignorance," she professed. But she sometimes attended services anyway "just for fun."[31]

Church leaders were not unwise to this appeal, and many knew the value of a good show. Music played an important part. The Pentecos-tals differed from most other faiths in their emphasis on music and in the range of instruments and arrangements they used in services. In-stead of the traditional organ, piano, and slow hymns, they sang rous-ing, up-tempo gospel tunes backed by guitars, banjos, tambourines, sometimes by whole bands.[32] And there were other sources of excite-ment. "The motive of the entire service is to get the people aroused," James Wilson reported after visiting a Pentecostal church. "This is done through prayer, testimony, songs, sermon, shouting, clapping the hands, and vigorous physical activity on the part of the leader or leaders." The songs, he noted, are especially "emotional in nature." "Choruses are often repeated eight or ten times while bodies sway back and forth, and feet beat out the music upon the floor. Lusty "Amens" and vigorous "Hallelujahs resound all over the room."[33]

But entertainment was only good as an introductory device. The churches won their recruits through more substantial services. Providing a sense of community to people who had grown up in the community of faith and who now very much needed that kind of support was part of it. Generally quite small, counting anywhere from ten to forty families as members, congregations tended to be tightly knit and mutually supportive. Worshipping together several times a week, socializing and helping one another in the interval, the churches encouraged a familial atmosphere that some prospective recruits found quite appealing. Visitors could see the closeness manifest among worshippers at the Wasco Pentecostal church. "We should all pray for one another," a woman instructed the group. "There is no wrong in our acting like one big family, for that's what we are."[34] And within the church family, people found all sorts of assistance, ranging from marathon prayer in times of illness or tragedy to food, clothing, and help finding jobs. Over the years that he has been a member of the Nazarene church in the Los Angeles suburb of Lynwood, Melvin Shahan has participated in a number of "poundings," donating food to help families in need. Not long ago, when the Shahans themselves were having a rough time, "they had a pounding on us." "After church one night the whole bunch came over to the house and brought in all kinds of canned food and stuff like that for us."[35]

Yet the act of conversion bespoke still deeper needs: a desire for a profound religious commitment. Students of twentieth-century religion have often ascribed the growth of the Holiness/Pentecostal movement to socio-economic conditions that breed symptoms of personal distress. Converts, the argument usually goes, turn to this ecstatic, otherworldly faith to find comfort and escape from unusual difficulties, especially from the wrenching problems of poverty and social disesteem. As the title of one recent study argues, Pentecostalism has been a faith for the disadvantaged, a *Vision of the Disinherited*.[36] The fact that the Pentecostal movement (or "Charismatic" movement, as it is now called) today draws converts from many walks of life cautions against the monolithic tone of some of these assessments. But in specific cases, and especially the one at hand, the disinherited argument has considerable value. Here indeed were people in need of religious solace. Lonely, out of place, economically and socially insecure in a difficult new setting, the migrants in California were perfect candidates for the new religion.[37]

What the Pentecostals and Nazarenes offered was a particularly strong version of what Christianity usually offers: a transvaluing world view, a system of beliefs that lightens life's burdens by assuring believers both of happiness in the world to come and of their own superior status in the physical community of Christians. Money, status, power—the things the migrants lacked— were not supposed to matter. "It ain't what's in this life, its what we are goin' to do in the next that counts," believers told one another.[38] There will be "No Disappointment in Heaven," one of their songs promised:

> We'll never pay rent for our mansion,
> The taxes will never come due;
> Our garments will never grow threadbare,
> But always be fadeless and new.[39]

If heaven offered the most profound reward, a Christian life promised to pay more immediate dividends in self-worth. Believers took their place among the elect, took their place as true Christians in a world obsessed with the wrong values. In Wasco, Walter Goldschmidt sat with the congregations of farm laborers in the Nazarene and Assemblies of God churches and watched the messages of reassurance take effect. "The real bluebloods are those who are firm in their faith," a preacher reminded his people. "In heaven everybody is a blueblood—no matter how poor you are."[40] A worshipper took comfort: "Sometimes I think I am worth nothing to the Lord or to anybody else, but when I realize what I am in His eyes, it makes me want to pray all the more."[41] Here then was a value system which provided solutions to some of the migrants' most severe social and psychological concerns. In religion they attained the dignity and position that real conditions, for the time at least, denied them.

Mrs. Will Casey counted herself one of the "full consecrated people." Secure in her relationship with God, she bore daily witness to the joy, peace, and happiness awaiting those who would allow themselves to feel "the power of the Lord." "To git the Holy Ghost and to speak in tongues is the most wonderfulest blessin' you ever had," she eagerly explained. "When you git the Holy Ghost you just commence rollin' and stirrin' inside. You just feel glad all over, you shore do." It's "jist like gittin' shocked with electricity." And she liked the constant demands. Her preacher never let the chosen rest. He was always testing them, calling upon them to replenish their faith.

> We have counterfeits alright but I want you to know that when one of them comes along the rest know it. You ort to been down at our service the other night and heerd the preacher preach on counterfeits. He preached a strong one. He's been trimmin' us down. One of these days we're goin' to be sifted and strained so we've got to be without spot, wrinkle, or blemish.[42]

This demanding regimen made the Pentecostal groups special. Not everyone would receive the blessing, and that gave the faith a certain power and appeal. For migrants looking for a source of dignity and purpose in their lives, membership in such an elite, one so confident of its own righteousness, could be quite attractive.

These then were some of the factors which brought people into the Pentecostal or Holiness churches. Socially accessible and openly interested in the migrants at a time when many avenues were closed to them, the Pentecostal denominations also offered a version of evangelical Protestantism more demanding, more daring, and perhaps more confident than their old faiths. With its doctrine of higher orders of sanctification suggesting new truths revealed, and its frenzied services suggesting a closer relationship to the Lord, many curious Baptists and Methodists could not but wonder whether the Pentecostal way was not perhaps the right way. Enjoying the advantage that often comes to radicals urging a further plunge towards the root of a particular logic, the Holiness/Pentecostal groups dared others to move beyond their customary denominations, to try a more complete, a more radical faith—a religion at once familiar and extreme—suited therefore to the new conditions in which they found themselves.

The Southern Baptist Mission

The concept of intensification also has bearing on the experience of the Holiness/Pentecostal movement's closest competitor, the Southern Baptists. The other major religious institution to find a home within the Okie social networks, the Southern Baptist denomination initially recruited only former members. And yet there was something different about the style of religion that the denomination established in California. In certain ways, they too sought a more rigorous and definite religion than had usually been the case back home.

The Southern Baptists officially began reclaiming members in California only after 1941. Prior to that the denomination had honored a 1912 agreement that left California to the Northern Baptists. But the pressure to enter the California field had been mounting steadily, and unofficially the work had been under way for several years. As more and more Southwesterners headed west during the 1930s, some had written to former pastors complaining about the absence of "true Christian" churches in California and begging them to send someone to help them form churches of their own. A clergyman already in California received this letter:

> Dear Brother:
>
> We live in the town of Madera. You probably do not know where it is located, but we are Southern Baptists and have not found a Baptist Church where the Gospel is preached or the Bible honored.
>
> I wonder if you could come to our town and preach on some Sunday afternoon? We will get the community building for you, if you will. There are several families of us here and we want a church so bad, so that our children can study the Bible and be saved from the ways of the world around us.[43]

A few ministers responded, heading west to "recapture their lost flocks." Operating without the blessing of the Southern Baptist Convention, these first preachers set up churches independent of either of the two major

Baptist organizations. One of those heeding the call was Sam Wilcoxin, pastor of a small church in Arkansas. Contacted by a group of Southern Baptists living in Shafter (led by George Mouser) he agreed to come to California.[44]

Wilcoxin's arrival in 1937 marked the effective start of the campaign by Southern Baptists in California to win official recognition from the denomination and in the meantime to establish unofficially new ministries. Under Wilcoxin's leadership, the Shafter congregation spawned new churches in the nearby Kern County towns of Delano, Oildale, Lamont, Taft, and Arvin. Before long other churches, some of which had previously been independent Baptist congregations, began affiliating with the San Joaquin Valley Missionary Baptist Association that Wilcoxin and R. W. Lackey, a minister from Oklahoma, had founded. Finally in 1941 the association, consisting of fourteen separate churches, was acknowledged by the Southern Baptist Convention.

The newly recognized body quickly expanded the call for preachers, asking for missionaries to help with "the work" in California. "It has been estimated that there are between seventy-five and a hundred thousand Southern Baptists living in the State," the association announced in 1942. "They [are] as sheep scattered abroad not having a shepherd."[45] The appeal registered. Throughout the 1940s in Baptist circles in the Southwest the idea of going to California to build churches became almost a crusade. Preachers who had visited the migrant communities in California returned with reports of the enormous potential awaiting those who "would come west to labor in this white harvest field." They told of former Southern Baptists hungry for religion, and raised heroic images of the pioneering struggle ahead in a nearly pagan land dominated by secular values and apostate churches. Said one, recently back from a California visit, "I have spoken this week in lodge halls, unused barrooms, chicken houses, garages and makeshift tents, but in all of these adverse conditions I have found a power so near to the days of Pentecost that I would come west . . . if I were twenty years younger."[46]

The results were soon evident. Southern Baptist churches sprang up everywhere, not just in the valley but also in Los Angeles and the San Francisco Bay Area where already settled Southwesterners were being joined by thousands of Defense Okies. By 1952, a mere fifteen years after the original Shafter church was founded, the denomination claimed more than 400 churches in California with nearly 75,000 members. A portion of the wandering flock had been reclaimed.[47]

As they set off on their errand into the West Coast wilderness, the avowed intention of the Southern Baptists was to build churches mirroring those in the states from which they had come. Nevertheless, certain changes in religious practice were inevitable. There was, for one thing, the question of which Southwestern state's constitution would be used as the model for the California organization. "Those coming from Oklahoma wanted to build another Fall's Creek Assembly, those from Texas wanted immediately to start a Western Baylor, and those from Missouri had their ideas of things to do," a minister later recalled. The inevitable compromise represented something new for everyone.[48]

Other changes were more significant. Most noticeable, especially for the clergy, was the greatly reduced social position of Southern Baptists in California. Accustomed to prominence and de facto community leadership back home, preachers now catered to small congregations of mostly poor and working-class newcomers, sharing their social problems and often their poverty as well. California demanded almost pioneering adjustments of some ministers. Beyond the financial sacrifices, they had to get used to the fact, said one church report, that Californians regarded them as "a bunch of ignorant Arkies, home-sick Texans, misplaced Missourians, and wandering Okies."[49]

Status problems were compounded by the sometimes fierce resentment of the Northern Baptists who throughout the 1940s attacked the Southerners for violating the territorial agreement and sometimes tried to keep them out of particular California communities. Hostilities raged openly in some settings. In 1946 a group trying to form a new congregation in the town of Calwa, near Fresno, encountered both official and unofficial persecution. First, town officials tried to block a bank loan, then vandals set fire to the church's meeting tent.[50]

These conditions affected the kind of religion practiced in California. It may be that the ministers took cues from their Pentecostal competitors, or that California attracted preachers of a certain theological tendency, or that the bitter conflict with the Northern Baptists encouraged theological rigidity. What is certain is that California churches emphasized doctrinal orthodoxy and evangelical fervency more consistently than did churches in the Southwest. Like the Pentecostals, the Southern Baptists showed a heightened inclination toward revivalistic worship and strict fundamentalist principles. California churches tightened baptism requirements, took a strong stand against ecumenicism and equally strong positions in favor of evangelism and a literal biblical curriculum. In the Southwest, the general pattern of conservatism among Southern Baptists was broken by notable variations, ranging from experimentation with a Social Gospel to committed modernism. Not so in California. A 1963 survey of Southern Baptists in the Bay Area found twice as many holding "orthodox" religious views as in the denomination's nationwide sample (88 percent versus 44 percent). In the same survey 97 percent of the California members took the classical evangelical position that belief in Jesus Christ as savior was "absolutely necessary for salvation."[51]

Baptist scholars who have described these changes sometimes trace them to the influence of newly reintegrated independent Baptist congregations in the state, many of them Landmark Baptists who stressed conservative theology and exclusive fellowship. Others have argued that the intensity of California worship owed much to competition with the Northern Baptists. The hostile atmosphere bred strategies of defense, purity, and isolation. So much animus developed between the two Baptist denominations that the Southerners often refused to recognize Northern Baptist baptisms when members switched denominations.[52]

Whatever the proximate causes, the changes in Southern Baptist practice suggest a desire for intensified religious experience of the sort that was evident in the growth of Pentecostalism. Settlement in California created emotional and social needs which some migrants answered through religion, and very often through a more fervent, uncompromising religious commitment than ever before.

The Evangelical Enterprise

Migration had rearranged the religious affiliations of many Southwesterners and the social status of the transplanted churches. Those establishments in turn were to influence the socio-cultural adjustment of members and the shape of the migrant community. The nature of that influence changed significantly over time. During the 1930s and early 1940s, the evangelical churches, remaining small and isolated, would reinforce the social boundaries and some of the cultural outlooks that helped to define the Okie group. In the postwar period they would gradually gain a different thrust. Emerging from their initial isolation, they would begin to transform the complexion of Protestantism in California. The San Joaquin Valley in particular would respond to the presence of a rapidly expanding and highly assertive conservative evangelical movement.

Especially in the early years, the decision to join one of the new evangelical churches entailed a twofold commitment. The commitment to God was understood; the commitment to the Okie group was not always. Peggy Staggs sees now the significance of her family's religious choices. The Oklahoma-born community college professor spent her teenage years in Fullerton during the 1940s, her widowed mother having settled in the Los Angeles suburb in order to be near an extended group of relatives. But despite those initial intentions, Peggy actually grew up in a different social milieu than her nearby cousins, aunts, and uncles. Her mother had declined to join the small Baptist church to which the rest belonged; the decision rested on an earlier rejection of fundamentalist religion. Peggy and her sister instead attended Sunday school at a nearby Presbyterian church. The different religious affiliations brought a chill to the relationship between the families and swept Peggy and her relatives along different life trajectories. They "thought we were snobbish" for not going to their church, she remembers. And, thinking back, she realizes that the Presbyterian affiliation did become part of a social climbing strategy that contrasted with the experiences of her relatives. In church and also in school, Peggy joined an in-group consisting of the sons and daughters of the town's elite families. Living just six blocks away and attending the same schools, her aunt (her contemporary in age) mingled with a different crowd, working-class and largely Southwestern. This was the social milieu of most of the evangelical churches.[53]

Even more in the San Joaquin, the evangelical churches belonged to and reinforced the Okie group. Partly it was a question once again of snobbery and social distance. The middle-class arbiters of valley society frowned upon the humble little churches, their fundamentalist beliefs, and their revivalistic techniques. Showing the disdain for "excessive" religion which had become the common coin of the sophisticated and urbane during the 1930s, they drew few distinctions between groups (sometimes even labeling the Southern Baptists holy rollers) and saw the migrants' religious proclivities as further evidence of backwardness.

These people "pray and sing so loud and furious all hours of the day and night" that they should not be permitted "in any ordered community," a Kern County grower maintained.[54] A member of Modesto's First Baptist church spoke with equal scorn of services he had witnessed at a nearby Pentecostal assembly. "It seemed to be a crazy house," he averred. "They were all standing and shouting like wild Indians." A junior college student extended the ethnographic metaphor: "I don't see any sense to it. People in Africa jump and carry on like this."[55] Teachers sometimes offered similar evaluations, complaining about "emotional services" that interfered with sleep and studies.[56] Not even in the FSA camps, otherwise so accommodating, could the evangelicals escape the unfavorable assessments. Sharing the general prejudice against enthusiastic religion and convinced that the evangelical preachers introduced "fanaticisms and irrationalities which can seriously disturb the social equilibrium," managers often took steps to discourage them from holding services in the camps, either favoring ministers with Social Gospel views or trying to minimize religious activities altogether.[57]

Thus membership in one of the evangelical churches carried a price tag. It meant a departure from sophisticated standards required of those who sought respectability, a step, at least for the moment, away from involvement with the dominant sectors of California society. But there was a payoff as well. Members and even some nonmembers drew a different lesson from the tensions: California was in serious need of religious instruction. "True Christianity," an integral part of "real Americanism," was in short supply, and it would be up to Southwesterners to deliver it. A Richmond shipyard worker fired off a letter to a local newspaper to let readers know just who the genuine Christians were. "I believe that when the Christ of Calvary makes his appearance back to earth that there will be a goodly number of Oklahomans go back with him to that place He has prepared for the righteous."[58]

The Martin family attended church very infrequently when Ernest Martin was growing up in the Tulare County town of Exeter, yet they shared the "natural inborn feeling of superiority" that many Southwesterners drew from their religious convictions. "It is hard to believe," says Martin, who as an adult turned to Pentecostalism and became an official of the World-wide Church of God, "I mean here they are dirt farmers having nothing whatsoever. They couldn't rub two dimes sometimes between their fingers but they still felt a superiority—the superiority primarily came I think because we considered ourselves better Christians than anybody else . . . 'special to God' in some ways."[59]

One of the important components of the emerging subcultural identity, this claim to Okie religious superiority would not reach its full potential until the postwar period. During the 1930s, many of the religious-minded were too distracted by sectarian battles and too little interested in secular issues to care about the subcultural boundaries of the evangelical camp. Indeed, there was no evangelical movement to speak of in the 1930s; in California as elsewhere bitter rivalries divided the fervent side of Protestantism. Much of this was a product of the demoralizing defeats that fundamentalism had suffered within the major Northern denominations in the 1920s. The Scopes trial had broken the momentum of conservative evangelicals and fastened upon them a reputation for ignorance and intolerance that would linger for generations. The movement splintered in the aftermath. And the emergence of Pentecostalism only further complicated the picture. Condemned by more traditional evangelicals, the upstart Pentecostals were constantly splitting and fighting among themselves. For evangelicals of all sorts, this was a period of intense sectarianism.[60]

Religious discord rather than a sense of collective purpose was therefore one of the evangelicals' initial contributions to the migrant communities. In Olivehurst, the seven small congregations bickered constantly, leaving the town, observed James Wilson, in a state of "chaos." Community projects died in the cross-fire. A Methodist-sponsored community center became one of the casualties when other preachers used their influence to keep their followers away. The pastor of one of the two Churches of God attacked the young minister in charge of the center: "That man don't have salvation. . . . He has too much worldliness going on over there. I don't believe, Brother, that anyone who went there would ever learn anything about salvation." Criticizing the center for showing movies and providing recreational equipment to the children, he added: "Nobody went there but a lot of unsaved people. . . . He might as well a had a small saloon there considering what he did have."[61]

The pursuit of Christian purity fueled the dissension in Olivehurst and elsewhere. The churches battled among themselves over points of theology and practice. When the evangelicals did see eye to eye, it was often with a view to obstructing secular activities that might have helped the migrant community to interact and cohere. Moral issues marked an area of at least partial agreement among the churches but disagreement with other sectors of the migrant group. Alcohol and tobacco use was considered sinful, and so too were dancing, card-playing, movies, and most other recreational activities. Any form of worldliness was condemned in many of the churches. "We don't go in fer recreation at all," a preacher explained. "There ain't no Scripture that tells you to play and have a good time. . . . We don't go to shows and picnics and the like. . . . We love to pray and sing and have a good time like that."[62]

These standards made it difficult for a significant portion of the Okie population, males in particular, to participate. That would later change, and the move towards more forgiving formulas that instructed without driving the errant away would be one of the keys to expansion in the postwar period.

Also due to change somewhat was the posture of fierce detachment from political and social activities that would have brought Southwesterners together. The fight over the Olivehurst center was one example of the 1930s' rejectionist program; opposition to labor unions and political activism were others. "Politics is rotten," the founders of the Pentecostal movement had taught. "I don't believe," the national chairman of the Assemblies of God had said in 1922, "that any Christian is ever authorized by the word of God to put his nose into political business. We shall never get the world converted by legislation."[63] Sectarian and otherworldly, sure of their own righteousness and contemptuous of most everyone else, these small, close-knit congregations showed little interest in the secular well-being of the migrant population. Although their members were mostly Southwesterners, the churches were not yet promoting a sense of Okie community.

This would change beginning in the 1940s. Especially in the postwar period evangelicalism would become more and more a recognized community enterprise. It would be a two-way relationship, with many of the churches deliberately stressing subcultural loyalty, and with large numbers of Southwesterners, including some who did not attend church, taking pride in the accomplishments of these institutions.

The new posture stemmed from several developments, some rooted in the religious realignments occurring on a national level during the 1940s.

We will come back to these. The other significant factor was the increasing role of the Southern Baptists in the migrant communities. Not much of a presence in the 1930s, they began to establish churches in the 1940s with a different organizing scheme than the Pentecostal and Holiness groups had used.

Unlike the other evangelicals, the Southern Baptists were self-consciously a regional denomination. Very clear about its Southern constituency and Southern identity, the organization had a precisely defined purpose in California. Convention leaders assured the Northern Baptists that the goal was simply to reclaim former members, and not "to molest or disturb anyone in his religious life. If one is already a member of some organization and is satisfied therein, we believe he should be let alone."[64] Consequently, the Southerners built regional loyalty into their appeal. Anxious to lure Oklahomans, Texans, Arkansans, and Missourians back into the fold and unconcerned about alienating persons of non-Southern backgrounds, the denomination adopted recruiting tactics which called attention to the migrants' sense of otherness, played upon their homesickness, and helped them to realize that they were culturally different from the Californians.

Nostalgia figured prominently in the Southern Baptist strategy. In their radio ministries, their door-to-door visiting in Okie neighborhoods, and other recruiting activities, church workers liberally sprinkled references to Southwestern states, reminding migrants of home and tradition and stressing the idea that the church was part of that heritage. "[We] looked for people from Arkansas, Texas, wherever," Reverend Buren Higdon recalled of his first West Coast pastorate. "The appeal was that this was just like the church back home." Church suppers featuring favorite Southwestern foods proved to be an effective technique. We would have "potlucks," Higdon explained, with "cornbread, greens, chili." "People really enjoyed that."[65]

The denomination also addressed regional identity directly. One of the few institutions in Okie communities to make connections to the South as a whole instead of simply to individual Southwestern states, the Southern Baptists urged the migrants to think of themselves as Southerners and embrace a quasi-ethnic sense of the Okie group as a cultural minority. Significantly, this promotion of "Southernness" exceeded the normal practices of Southern Baptist churches in the Southwest. Back home there had been little reason for church workers to dwell upon the denomination's historic links to the South. As the only Baptist denomination of any size in Oklahoma, Texas, and Arkansas (Northern Baptists competed in Missouri), the organization was in most cases simply known as *the* Baptist Church. But laboring in the shadow of the Northern denomination in California made the newcomers more aware and deliberate about their regional ties. In bold letters church logos spelled out "Southern Baptist," while preachers took pains to stress that theirs was a Southern church, different religiously and historically from the Northern denomination.[66]

All this seems to have made a difference in the adjustment experiences of loyal members. The Southern Baptist denomination functions to this day more or less as an ethnic church in California, unable, admits Reverend Higdon, to shake its reputation as an "Oklahoma Club." Despite vigorous efforts in recent decades to broaden the base, leaders estimate that at least half of the California members trace their heritage to the Southwest.[67] Moreover, some of the clearest examples of cultural preservation can be seen among members of this denomination. Members often call themselves Southerners, continue, in some cases into the second and third generation, to speak with noticeable Southwestern accents, and retain very close ties to their old homes. Young people are sometimes sent to church-affiliated colleges and universities in Oklahoma and Texas (Oklahoma Baptist and Baylor, typically), while the older generation frequently makes plans to move back to the Southwest when they retire.[68]

These patterns hold true in the metropolitan areas as well as in the valley. Reverend Higdon watched many Bay Area Southern Baptists "count the years until they can retire and go back," although he notes that some who finally got their chance to return to the Southwest "don't stay a year."[69] Similar orientations were evident in the Southern California congregation to which Wofford and Ruth Clark belonged in the early 1980s. Many of their friends had moved back east, and with the Clark's own children living in Oklahoma, the couple often contemplated moving back as well. Of course, not all Southern Baptists display these sentiments. Many have no wish to return to their former homes and today consider themselves happy, well-adjusted Californians. But to a greater extent than in any other definable sector of the Southwestern population in California, Southern Baptists seem to maintain outlooks suggestive of an ethnic group.[70]

The Pentecostal groups have been less regionally consistent. Churches in the valley usually provided the same sort of nostalgia-rich, just-like-back-home ambience that the Southern Baptists engineered. However, these denominations were less interested in explicit subcultural commitments. Aggressive and universalistic in outlook, they sought every sort of convert. And especially in the last thirty years they have grown well beyond the Okie base. No records are kept of such matters, but officials of the largest Pentecostal organization, the Assemblies of God, estimate that Southwesterners and their progeny today comprise somewhere between 25 and 50 percent of the membership.[71]

The composition of congregations varies significantly, with the Southwestern influence still very clear in the San Joaquin Valley. Reverend Bob Friesen, an Assembly of God pastor and a Minnesotan by background, has served several California congregations. His first pastorate took him to Stockton, in the valley, where "about three-quarters" of the members seemed to be of Southwestern heritage, and quite proud of it. They "very dearly call themselves Okies." His current church is in the Bay Area, not far from the Richmond shipyard sites that forty-five years ago attracted so many thousands of defense workers. This congregation has two distinct components. The older members tend to be Southwesterners, but the younger majority come from diverse backgrounds, evidence of the widened appeal that the Charismatic movement has enjoyed in recent decades.[72]

Evangelizing California

Larger forces were also beginning to reshape the Okie churches and their relationship to the migrant community. A mood of religious reawakening swept the nation after World War II, helping the evangelicals to reemerge from the lonely isolation to which they had retreated in the 1920s. Significant changes in organization and emphasis were involved, the first of which was the 1942 founding of the National Evangelical Association. Signaling a close to the period of sectarian struggles, the NEA brought together many of the elements of the evangelical tradition, and for the first time Pentecostal organizations were invited to participate. At the same time, the movement was taking steps to rid itself of the low-brow image that had dogged it since the Scopes trial.[73]

Billy Graham and Oral Roberts were two of the men most directly responsible for the facelift, one representing the Baptist side of conservative evangelicalism, the other coming from the younger Pentecostal movement. Tall and debonair, as erudite as he was smooth and charming, Billy Graham became the mass evangelist par excellence of the postwar period, updating the techniques of Dwight L. Moody and Billy Sunday and bringing revivalism out of the tents and backwoods and into "middle-brow" respectability. Respectability was less the concern of Oral Roberts, who like Graham rose to fame in the late 1940s. Born in Oklahoma, the son of a minister in the Pentecostal-Holiness church, the Tulsa-based evangelist became the best-known leader of the "healing revival" which after 1947 swept tens of thousands of new converts into the Charismatic movement and helped to make it one of the most dynamic forces in postwar Protestantism. Still a source of amusement to nonbelievers, Pentecostalism was nevertheless also adjusting its image, dropping the hayseed look for a coat-and-tie professionalism that expanded its social appeal. Roberts also followed Graham into modern communications media, mastering the techniques of radio and then television evangelism, helping to establish the near monopoly that evangelicals would soon enjoy over broadcast religion.[74]

Figure 28. Located near Richmond's housing projects and shipyards, this Pente-costal church was brand new in 1944. (*Dorothea Lange,* © *1982, The Oakland Museum, The City of Oakland*)

The willingness to embrace "modern technology and modern (middle-class) forms of cultural expression," sociologist James Hunter explains, opened doors to an enormous expansion of the evangelical community. Religiosity in general flourished in the postwar period. In the context of a multifeatured drive for home-centered cultural renewal, Americans re-turned to church and faith in unprecedented numbers in the twenty years following the war. By the early 1960s, 63 percent of the nation's adults claimed church or synagogue membership, compared with 47 percent in 1930.[75]

Although California, as always, lagged somewhat behind, the trend there was in the same direction. And the Okie churches were positioned to capitalize. No sector of the California population participated in the revival more vigorously than Southwesterners. Equipped now with respectable standards of living, many of those who had drifted away in the 1930s now joined the flow back to organized religion. For the evangelicals, it was the beginning of an era of exhilarating growth. By 1952, Southern Baptists and the various Pentecostal and Holiness groups claimed more than 200,000 members. Add to that the Missouri Synod Lutherans, Seventh-Day Adventists, and various other conservative evangelical denominations that were less closely linked to the Southwestern population, and the evangelical community represented at least 23 percent of the state's Protestants.[76]

In metropolitan California, where Catholics figured prominently and where the unchurched outnumbered the religious, the evangelical movement remained relatively insignificant despite its growth. Not so in the valley, where organized religion held greater authority, and where by 1952 the evangelicals already claimed nearly a third of Protestant churchgoers. With almost 18,000 members in those counties, the Southern Baptists were closing in on their Northern Baptist (now called American Baptist) rivals and were fast becoming one of the valley's largest denominations.[77]

Although the evangelicals still attracted mostly Southwesterners in the decade following World War II, a redistribution of religious prestige was under way that would open new possibilities for Okie pride and influence. Growing numerically, the Okie churches were also becoming wealthier and gaining acceptance and influence. Now anxious to participate in community-wide religious activities, the evangelicals often took the lead in joint revival crusades. With undisguised envy, clergy in some of the older churches watched the new churches grow and tried to get their own congregations to duplicate the spirit and commitment of the recently despised evangelicals.[78] The Dust Bowl migration, it was now becoming clear, had changed the face of California religion. Not only had the migration contributed a dynamic religious movement that was now challenging the Protestant establishment, but the mainline churches themselves had also been steadily picking up new members from the same source. By mid-century there was no question which population element was contributing the most to the ongoing religious revival.

Larry Murrell was one of those who took pride in the new religious order. Texas-born and a resident of the Arvin-Lamont area for a dozen years, he no longer felt defensive about his place in California or his relations with Californians when interviewed in 1952. Instead the shoe-store owner felt intensely proud of the impact that he and other "ex-Dust Bowlers" had made on that part of Kern County, especially the religious impact. "We're trying to make this spot a heaven on earth," he volunteered. "I hope you will notice how many churches we have in this area. This is a very religious community."[79]

The passage of time provided still more reasons for pride. The evangelical expansion has continued right up to the present, escalating sharply in the last two decades. And breaking out of the regional niche, each of the major Okie denominations have picked up more and more non-Southwesterners. By 1971 the number of Southern Baptist, Pentecostal, and Holiness worshipers in California had reached 600,000, triple the membership of 1952. Nine years later, in 1980, it crossed the 800,000 mark. Counting other recognizably evangelical denominations, the evangelical camp by that date encompassed 40 percent of the state's Protestants. The Southern Baptists were by then the second-largest Protestant denomination; with 392,451 adherents and 937 churches they were only slightly smaller than the Mormons.[80]

All parts of California—indeed the nation—have experienced this latest surge of evangelical enthusiasm, but predictably the effects have registered most emphatically in the San Joaquin Valley, an area some observers now label the "California Bible Belt." In Kern County, for example, the Southern Baptists had long since emerged as the leading denomination. By 1980 they outnumbered the largest of the mainline groups by almost three to one. Table 7.1 shows the distribution of Protestant church membership in that county from 1936 to 1980. As of 1980, nearly one-quarter of Kern County's affiliated Protestants belonged to one of 49 Southern Baptist congregations. Another 34 percent were members of Holiness, Pentecostal, or small Baptist denominations, or belonged to other evangelical bodies such as the Church of Christ, Seventh-Day Adventists, or Missouri Synod Lutherans. Altogether these denominations accounted for 58 percent of the county's Protestant members.

And that only begins to measure the conservative evangelical influence. Not counted are the many independent Full Gospel and conservative Baptist churches sprinkled throughout the county. Not measured either are the conservative tendencies now manifest in the mainline denominations. In some ways this is the most telling impact of all, for just as in the South, conservative evangelicalism has become so much the dominant theme in the valley that it tends to govern even traditionally liberal denominations. Valley congregations of many faiths—Presbyterian, United Church of Christ, American Baptist, even Lutheran—have become unusually conservative, more committed to revivalistic methods and fundamentalist principle and less interested in social issues than is typical in these denominations.[81]

Professor Meryl Ruoss has observed the pattern in Bakersfield. A former Presbyterian minister and official of the National Council of Churches, he arrived in that city in 1972 to teach public policy and administration at California State College, Bakersfield. The conservatism of the mainline churches surprised him, especially the outlook of the city's major Presbyterian congregation which during the 1960s had attempted to withdraw from the denomination. "They opposed the trend at the national level to get involved in issues like civil rights, poverty, housing." Instead of social reform, they wanted the church to concentrate on spiritual commitment. That focus has sharpened since the 1970s. Today "a lot of the things they

Table 7.1. Protestant Church Membership in Kern County, 1936, 1952, 1980

	1936		1952		1980	
Conservative Evangelicals						
Southern Baptist	—		5,104	14%	19,976	24%
Assembly of God	559	5%	2,268	6	8,364	10
Church of Nazarene	246	2	911	2	3,705	5
Church of Christ	—		—		4,372	5
Foursquare Gospel	—		478	1	1,581	2
Other Holiness/Pentecostal	—		422	1	2,457	3
Seventh-Day Adventist	641	5	1,253	3	2,917	4
Missouri Synod Lutheran	366	3	1,314	4	1,703	2
Other evangelical	—		725	2	2,557	3
Total	1,312	15%	12,475	34%	47,632	58%
Mainline denominations						
American Baptist	1,972	16%	4,608	13%	6,748	8%
United Methodist	2,010*	16	4,243	12	5,920	7
Presbyterian	648	5	5,194	14	3,082	4
Disciples/Un.Ch.Christ	1,813	15	4,095	11	2,128	3
Episcopalian	504	4	1,637	4	2,337	3
American Lutheran	—		336	1	2,539	3
Unitarian	—		18		116	
Total	6,947	56%	20,131	55%	22,870	28%
Other Protestant bodies						
Latter-Day Saints	483	4%	3,024	8%	8,519	10%
Others/unspecified	3,149	25%	1,249	3	3,172	4
Total Protestants	12,391	100%	36,879	100%	82,193	100%

*Includes 61 Southern Methodists.

Source: U.S. Bureau of the Census, *Census of Religious Bodies: 1936* (Wash., D.C., 1941), table 32, pp. 725–27; National Council of Churches, *Churches and Church Membership in the United States* (New York, 1956–58) Series C, No. 58–59, table 128; Bernard Quinn et. al., *Churches and Church Membership in the United States 1980* (Atlanta, 1982), table 4, p. 45.

do are very similar to things Southern Baptists might do," says Ruoss. Bakersfield Presbyterians have "almost abandoned any formal liturgy . . . and Jesusology has just about taken over . . . everybody goes around asking are you saved."[82]

Tod Moquist has watched similar changes overtake the church of his youth, the Congregational Church of Shafter. A former student at the Berkeley Graduate Theological Union, he grew up in Kern County and then returned to live there in 1980. Through the 1960s, the church had maintained a position not too distant from the traditional stance of Congregationalism, a denomination one scholar has called "the most fertile soil for liberalism." But that no longer holds. "In the last fifteen years the church has become extremely conservative," Moquist observes. Like so many other churches it has "taken on a Southern-style religion." Not that the members are necessarily Southwesterners. "Just like everybody in the Central Valley has learned to speak with a bit of a twang, the religious idiom has also become more and more familiar to them."[83]

Ten miles up the road from Shafter stands another Congregational church which has seen still more dramatic changes. Founded in 1907 and the oldest church in town, Wasco First Congregational is no longer affiliated with its parent body, the United Churches of Christ. When Walter Gold-schmidt studied the town of Wasco in 1941, he described the Congrega-tionalists as the town's leading citizens and the prime example of a congregation socially and theologically removed from the burgeoning Okie population. But today the church bears the clear imprint of that cultural group and its powerful religious agenda. In 1970 the congregation voted to withdraw from the denomination and become an "independent Bible" church. Members disliked the direction of the National Council, one of the leaders of the move explains. "The UCC became all Social Gospel oriented instead of Christ oriented. . . . There was not one mention of God in the Sunday school materials they sent us, just things about how we should all love one another. Which is nice but there wasn't anything about our Savior."[84]

These developments are keyed to processes that have been unfolding in many sectors of American society. Evangelicalism has been on the rise everywhere in the last two decades, becoming for the first time since the 1920s the dominant thread of American Protestantism. And it is not only in the valley that the movement has moved into mainline territory. Always a factor even in the most liberal denominations, the born-again movement has captured the initiative in the wake of the confusing social and cultural changes of the 1960s and early 1970s, convincing people of many back-grounds to seek new meaning in spirituality. Less a movement than a "mosaic," according to Timothy L. Smith, the new evangelicalism ranges widely across the political spectrum, from Jerry Falwell and the reborn political fundamentalists to Jimmy Carter and the various expressions of "progressive evangelicalism" that re-blend Social Gospel and evangelical traditions that had fallen out of harmony almost a century before.[85]

If the San Joaquin Valley is any indication, Southwesterners tend to be over-represented on the conservative side of this mosaic as it has developed in California, but they have contributed to the whole enterprise. Fervent, fundamental religion was one of the distinctive offerings they made to their new state. Never the only champions of evangelical Protestantism, they have been right up to the present its most consistent and identifiable con-stituency. And their close relationship to the religious movement has had broad implications for the group experience. Always a controversial com-mitment in a state that had little background in fervent Protestantism and tends to slide away from organized religion altogether, evangelicalism has reinforced the Okie subculture first by solidifying social networks in a climate of disesteem, later by offering validation and pride as the movement's popularity and influence grew. One of several cultural commitments that Southwesterners have sought to share with their California neighbors, it reminds us of the intriguing link between promotion and preservation which has been the central dynamic of the Okie subculture.

8

The Language of
a Subculture

THE NAME OUT FRONT SAID "PIONEER CLUB." A DARK AND DINGY BAR NEAR
the end of Arvin's commercial strip, it was a place respectable residents
made a point of avoiding. The clientele was mostly male, mostly farmworkers. Its unsavory reputation was probably deserved. Drinking was not
the only activity the premises condoned. Men went there to play pool,
gamble at cards, flirt with the handful of women present, and, with some
frequency, to fight.

Every San Joaquin Valley town had its Pioneer Club by the end of the
1930s, though sometimes one had to scout the lonely outskirts to find it.
There the flip side of the Okie population congregated: daring women,
single men, married men with a taste for liquor and independence. Saturday
nights might be a bit different. If the place was big enough a band would
be playing and couples dancing. Women and married couples then felt
more comfortable. The very serious Christians saw no distinction, but
others might sin a little on dancing nights.

Like the evangelical churches, these drinking establishments advertised
their association with the Okie population through sometimes subtle cultural clues. No sign at the door said Southwesterners only (though "whites
only" would have been typical); the place signaled its socio-cultural allegiance in the rude decor, often a Western name (or one like the "Texhoma
Club"), and a jukebox filled with hillbilly hits. Not that the clientele was

exclusive. Some Californians enjoyed the rough style of these places. But mostly these were "Okie joints."[1]

The music was critical. What we today call country music by and large belonged to Okies in the 1930s, a fact that had implications far beyond the honky-tonk scene. A recreational interest traditional to Southwesterners but less popular in California, country music, like evangelical religion, became something of a group enterprise. Southwesterners became its primary agents of dispersion, dominating it as performers and claiming it as consumers. And through this participation the music helped to shape their adjustment to California, conveying some of the political and social values and the regional symbols that sharpened their sense of special identity.

Okie bars were but one arena where the recreational interest was manifest. Thanks to radio the music could also be heard in less controversial settings. Indeed, to some extent the country medium bridged the ethical-religious divisions within the migrant group. The religious faithful, profoundly opposed to the goings-on in the taverns, nevertheless joined in appreciating the gospel and old-fashioned folk songs that comprised two important elements of 1930s and 1940s country music. "The music was a common type of language that everyone understood," says Ernest Martin of his teenage years in the San Joaquin Valley during the 1940s. "It was part of our way of thinking . . . [it] had a powerful influence upon melding together the people."[2] It is a useful observation. Modern America looks more to recreation than to religion to find its working consensus; and the Dust Bowl migrants were no different. Where religion divided, country music at an early date appealed across the moral-religious boundaries to illuminate the common denominators of their subculture, the essential values and symbols that over the years have comprised the Okie identity.

The origins of country music have been closely scrutinized in recent years, much of the investigation animated by the desire to distinguish folk from commercial antecedents. Although the label "country" did not become standard until the late 1940s, a definable commercial medium, usually called hillbilly music, had emerged with the advent of radio and the expansion of the phonograph industry in the early 1920s. Hoping to satisfy a perceived market for "old-time music," the two industries tapped a rich tradition of rural musicianship. The earliest commercial recordings, reports one study, reflected the "assembly tradition" of American rural music, the songs and instrumental tunes enjoyed at dances, parties, community gatherings, and in church. This material in turn derived substantially from nineteenth-century minstrel and vaudeville songs.[3]

Significant variations in musical style attended the early days of radio and recording. As radio stations combed their communities for talent and record companies explored the markets for specialized musical products, diverse strands of musical tradition were uncovered, some of which were later lost as the medium coalesced around a few dominant styles. It was the music of the South, most historians agree, which emerged ascendant as the medium began to consolidate tastes and professionalize in the late 1920s.

Two somewhat discrete styles became prominent, both of them substantially Southern. One was the style that gave the genre its early name. Most prominently associated with the Eastern South and best illustrated by the Carter Family, the hillbilly paradigm featured string-band music, multiple voice groups singing in a pinched, high, nasal style, and emphasized family, religion, and mountain settings in their song lyrics and stage personae.

The three members of the Carter Family—A.P. Carter, his wife Sarah, and sister-in-law Maybelle—recorded for the first time in Bristol, Tennessee, in August 1927. A few days later the same recording session also captured the music of Jimmie Rodgers, father of the second and ultimately more popular paradigm. Country music's first genuine star, Rodgers drew on a variety of musical sources, including the country blues he had learned growing up in Mississippi's black belt, train and hobo tunes reminiscent of his years as a railroad brakeman, and the cowboy songs popular in Texas, his home after 1928. Singing with somewhat greater tonal range, featuring guitar over fiddle, and donning cowboy hat or trainman's cap instead of the bumpkin attire favored by Southeastern groups, Rodgers brought country music down from the mountains. His career lasted a scant six years; by 1933 he was dead of tuberculosis. But well before that imitators were converting his style into an industry formula, one that many scholars feel has been the central trend in country music ever since.[4]

Californians participated sporadically in the initial stirrings of this commercial medium. In the early 1920s, before network programming took over much of the air time, radio stations opened their microphones to a haphazard array of local talent, from barbershop quartets to professional orchestras, and including performers who would later be classified as country musicians.

Johnny Crockett was fourteen years old in 1923 when the announcer for Fresno's new radio station KMJ invited him to perform. Expert with the banjo, guitar, and harmonica, the young West Virginian had performed with his father and five brothers at square dances in the Fresno area. His first radio appearance featured a combination of traditionals learned from his parents and versions of records he had recently heard. Soon the whole family was involved, playing once a week for free on the radio and making a little money performing music and black-face minstrel shows at local theatres. A few years later they moved to Los Angeles, where paid radio work awaited.[5]

Harry McClintock, better known as "Haywire Mac," found a niche at

San Francisco's station KFRC during the same years. Born in Tennessee in 1882, Mac came to radio by way of an extraordinary career as railroad switchman, seaman, longshoreman, hobo, and Wobbly troubadour. He had learned his music watching vaudeville skits and singing in the Episcopal Church choir in his native Knoxville. Taking to the rails at an early age, he spent more than twenty years wandering the railroad yards, hobo jungles, and mining camps, working sometimes, singing for his keep in between. Credited with writing two of the IWW's most popular songs ("Hallelujah I'm a Bum" and "Big Rock Candy Mountain"), he was a natural for the talent-hungry radio station. Combining colorful stories and comedy gags with his "Songs of the Road and Range," he appeared regularly on the station's "Blue Monday Jamboree" variety show from 1925 through 1938.[6]

Despite the following enjoyed by certain early California performers, audience interest was rather weak prior to the Dust Bowl influx. California was not prime country-music territory. Stations used hillbilly performers as novelty acts and insisted on as much humor as music in the show. The state's most famous early country-music group illustrates this expectation. The Beverly Hill Billies were the brainchild of the managers of Los Angeles station KMPC. In 1930 they hit upon a gimmick to boost listenership. The station would "discover" a band of hill folk long lost to civilization in the recesses of posh Beverly Hills. A troupe of musicians, some with Hollywood and vaudeville experience, others brought in from Arkansas, were hired to play the part, and the Beverly Hill Billies became an instant Los Angeles phenomenon. Even in the Southeast the hillbilly image of early country musicians contained a large element of self-parody, but the Beverly Hill Billies carried the joke to extremes. Popular especially with youngsters, their celebrity rested only partly on their music. With their ever-present cornpone routine, they also gave southern Californians an opportunity to indulge comic-page stereotypes of white Southerners.[7]

California's limited interest in country music was another reflection of its urbane mind-set. Along with many other jazz-age and swing-era Americans living in the North and Pacific West, most Californians found the music banal. Accustomed to the lush sounds and bouncy rhythms of the dance band and the rich ornamented voices and violin-backed melodies of Hit Parade popular songs, they found the hillbilly sound with its old songs, garden-variety instruments, and untrained voices dull and amateurish. So said a letter writer to the *Modesto Bee*, who, faced with the rising popularity of the music in the wake of the Dust Bowl migration, protested that "I am a music lover, but when half of the radio stations fill in time with people who name themselves cowboys and who cannot even carry a melody of a simple old song, and to which the accompaniment is a guitar and harmonica, it makes me wonder where music is going."[8]

Views such as these kept country music from achieving substantial popularity in large parts of the United States until the 1940s. The best estimates indicate that country songs accounted for less than 10 percent of nationwide record sales in the two previous decades. However, the music was not marginal everywhere. Record sales and radio format data make it clear that the medium enjoyed substantial popularity in the South and secondarily in the rural Midwest.[9]

Nowhere was the interest keener than in the Western South. Part of what some scholars have called the "fertile crescent of country music," Texas, Oklahoma, Arkansas, and Missouri embraced the young commercial medium at a time when most of California did not. Weekly reports by juke-box owners to *Billboard* magazine in the late 1930s provide a sense of Southwestern musical tastes. Big-band and Hit Parade tunes collected the most nickels—Bing Crosby, Tommy Dorsey, Kay Kayser, Rudy Vallee, Benny Goodman, and Artie Shaw knew how to appeal to audiences in all parts of the country. But Southwestern whites apparently spent almost as much money on the songs of Bob Wills, Gene Autry, Jimmie Davis, Cliff Bruner, and Milton Brown, the region's major country-music stars.[10]

Country music was especially popular among the rural population, whose preferences could not so readily be counted in the nickel slots. Radio stations, however, knew their tastes. While the city stations usually featured one or two country-music shows amidst their daily network-dominated schedules, smaller rural stations filled in large portions of the broadcasting day with performances by local hillbilly and cowboy musicians.

Politicians likewise knew the power of the young commercial medium. In an era when polling organizations were only beginning to survey audience tastes, the Western South announced its preferences in a pair of gubernatorial elections. In 1938, Wilbert Lee "Pappy" O'Daniel, manager and song writer for the Light Crust Doughboys, one of Texas's premier western swing bands, became governor of that state. The feat was duplicated six years later when Jimmie Davis, famous for the song "You Are My Sunshine," harmonized his way into the Louisiana statehouse. At a time when sophisticates in some parts of the country looked upon it as yokel music, a voting majority of Southwesterners viewed country music's leading practitioners with respect.[11]

The Dust Bowl migrants brought this recreational interest with them to California and in doing so helped to change the state's entertainment industry. Observers were quick to notice music's prominent place in the social activities of the migrants. In the camps where they settled, guitars, fiddles, harmonicas, and banjos often appeared, said one investigator, as if "by magic."[12] Dinner over, somebody might pull out a guitar and begin to play. Others might wander up with instruments of their own. Soon a crowd would gather, either listening quietly or joining in the singing. Shirley

Figure 29. Playing for a Saturday night dance at the Tulare FSA camp, 1940. (*Arthur Rothstein, The Bancroft Library, Berkeley, California*)

Cox remembers the way music brought people together in the labor camps where her family stayed. As a young girl she took special pride in the fact that her mother was often asked to sing the old folk songs to the entire group.[13] In another setting, Woody Guthrie watched as the singing of two young girls transformed a huge squatter encampment inhabited by perhaps two thousand people. "People walked from all over the camp and gathered . . . as still as daylight while the girls sang":

> Takes a worried man to sing a worried song
> Takes a worried man to sing a worried song
> Takes a worried man to sing a worried song
> I'm worried nowwww
> But I won't be worried long.

The music was like a tonic, Guthrie observed. "It cleared your head up, that's what it done, caused you to fall back and let your draggy bones rest and your muscles go limber like a cat's."[14]

Recognizing the interest, the management of the Farm Security Administration camps sponsored a variety of musical events, including regular Saturday night dances. Featuring musicians recruited from the camp population, these gatherings ranked among the most popular aspects of the camp program. Attended not only by residents but also by Okies from miles around, the camp dances often drew crowds of up to four hundred people, who appreciated the opportunity to dance in a liquor-free environment.[15]

Radio stations, especially the smaller ones struggling for audiences, picked up the clues as well. As the Southwestern population increased, stations in Los Angeles and the Central Valley added more and more country acts. Lobbying tactics helped to encourage the change. Some migrants wrote letters to local stations asking that they play more of their favorite music.[16] Equally important, the few programs already on the air generated voluminous fan mail. Not yet famous, indeed, just starting his career and the sole hillbilly singer on station KFVD in Los Angeles, Woody Guthrie received more than a thousand letters a month from fans in 1938, many of them migrants who told him how glad they were to be able to hear songs reminding them of home. "We are just plain Texas people," said one, "your talk gives us a thrill and those beautiful songs." Another wrote, "you sing the songs I use to sing 40 years ago." These letters convinced his skeptical employer to keep the show and expand its time slot.[17]

Still, in adding country music to their broadcast format, radio stations were not responding to the Okie market alone. Although Southwesterners were the most vigorous champions of the music, an audience of Californians was emerging as well. The reason had much to do with Hollywood and a singing cowboy named Gene Autry.

"Oklahoma's singing cowboy" went to Hollywood about the same time that the first waves of Dust Bowl migrants were entering California. In a sense they built the country-music industry in California together. Autry became an immediate sensation with the release of his first film, *In Old Santa Fe* (1934), in which he had only a backup part. And he was soon one of filmland's biggest stars. With six-gun in one hand and guitar in the other, he combined the action-hero cowboy role already popular on the screen with the cowboy songs that since Jimmie Rodgers (as well as Carl Sprague, Jules Allen, and others) had become an important component of country music. Singing about dusty trails, blue skies, and purple plains, he brought country music to the attention of vast new audiences outside the South and rural Midwest. His cinematic success also accelerated the medium's stylistic evolution. By the late 1930s the hillbilly look and sound was in decline everywhere except the Eastern South as audiences turned to Autry-style guitar strumming cowboy soloists and to a jazzed-up fiddle dance music from Texas called western swing.[18]

Figure 30. Born in Texas, Gene Autry grew up in Oklahoma. The best of the Jimmie Rodgers imitators, his yodeling and cowboy songs in 1930 earned him a regular spot on the National Barn Dance, broadcast by Chicago radio station WLS. From there he went to Hollywood in 1934. (*Courtesy of Gene Autry, Western Music Publishing*)

The growing appeal of country music meant opportunities of several kinds for Southwesterners, most directly for musicians. In the decade following Gene Autry's film debut, the silver screen attracted a distinguished list of country-music stars, most of them from Oklahoma and Texas. Besides Autry the Hollywood Southwesterners included Tex Ritter, Stuart Hamblen, Bob Wills, Jimmy Wakely, Bill Boyd, Patsy Montana, Tim Spencer, Spade Cooley, Eddy Dean, and Elton Britt. Roy Rogers, an Ohioan, was a notable exception among singing cowboy film stars.[19]

Many of these performers had made names for themselves before moving west, but the singing cowboy craze also provided some opportunities for migrants who had initially come to California with different purposes in mind. Arriving in Los Angeles in 1937, Woody Guthrie found his relatives busy trying to capitalize on the Gene Autry phenomenon. Cousin Jack Guthrie had outfitted himself in cowboy gear and was trying to talk his way into auditions with local radio stations. Several other cousins, an aunt, and an uncle had formed a fiddle band and were hoping to get into the movies.[20]

The same sort of aspirations took root among Southwesterners in the valleys. When folklorists Charles Todd and Robert Sonkin visited the Farm Security Administration camps in the summers of 1940 and 1941, they intended to record old ballads traditional to the Southwest. They found some of what they were looking for, but reported that the migrants were often more interested in singing current hillbilly and cowboy hits. Several were anxious to showcase their talents because they were "goin' on the air soon." A few affected stage names. "I'm Homer Pierce, the singin' cowboy from way down in Missouri, and I'd like to do a couple of my own tunes for you," one young man introduced himself. Another had all the poses of a cowboy singer but had not yet learned to play the guitar. He was working on that, he assured Todd, confident that a bright musical future lay ahead.[21]

For some migrants, music did provide a bright future. Jack Guthrie got his radio show, invited cousin Woody to be his sidekick, and both went on to distinguished careers, one legendary. Oklahoma-born Spade Cooley played with several hillbilly groups on the honky-tonk circuit in California and Oregon before settling down with his own band in Los Angeles in the early 1940s. By the end of World War II he had appeared in several movies, enjoyed a list of hit records, owned a country-music club, and styled himself the "King of Western Swing."[22] Rose Maddox was eleven years old in 1937 when she and her four brothers sang their first audition for a Modesto radio station. The family had come to California four years earlier, mostly riding boxcars. Although from Alabama, they became Okies in California, absorbed along with many other poor whites into that flexible subculture. Within a few years the Maddox Brothers and Rose would have a recording contract and a nationwide following.[23]

Others never achieved national stardom but like "Okie Paul" Westmoreland managed to make a life and a living for themselves in the state's country-music industry. The son of Oklahoma sharecroppers, Westmoreland spent his first four years in California alternately working in the fields and acting with a traveling theater group. In 1941 he got a chance to put his talents as a steel guitar player to work. Moving to Los Angeles, he spent the war years performing, writing songs, and sometimes working in defense plants. 1946 found him in Sacramento with his own fifteen-minute morning radio program. Next he opened a club. "I built me a beer joint and got behind the bar with my guitar and sold beer and sang." The place prospered, and "Okie Paul" became a permanent fixture in Sacramento's country-music scene.[24]

If the growing popularity of country music made it the pathway to fame for a handful of migrants and a career option for others, it meant something almost as important to the thousands of Okies whose relationship to music was that of listener rather than performer. The music's success gave its migrant audience the chance to bask in the reflected glory of musicians from their home states. What Frank Sinatra was for Italians, and Paul Robeson for blacks, nationally recognized country-music stars like Gene Autry became for Okies.

Bob Wills was the real favorite. Perhaps because he seemed to remain closer to his roots than some of the other Hollywood figures, the Texas-born band leader earned unparalleled affection from migrant audiences. Future country star Merle Haggard was too young to attend the dances, but when Wills came to Bakersfield in the late 1940s, Haggard and his friends would stand outside the hall soaking up the stray sounds. These periodic appearances were events of communal significance for the area's Southwesterners, particularly for the younger generation. "We needed a hero," Haggard recalls, "and Bob was certainly that and more . . . it was like he brought some of home with him."[25] Oklahoma-born Ken Griffis speaks in similar terms of Wills's effect on Southwesterners living in Los Angeles. Wills, he insists, "was very important to people like myself. . . . He was one of us Okies and Arkies. People would say 'That's old Bob, that's our boy.' . . . We were on that stage with Bob Wills."[26]

This was audience involvement of a special kind. By no means the only fans of country music, many Okies nevertheless took almost proprietorial interest in the medium and its performers. The attention was often reciprocated. Some musicians catered closely to Southwestern audiences, responding either for practical reasons or because of the common background. Wills did so by peppering his performances with references to "all of us Okies" and by playing tunes with lyrics about Oklahoma and Texas. Spade Cooley came up with an even better device for insuring the loyalty of the mobs of defense workers who jammed the Venice pier each weekend to hear his band. He nicknamed his three vocalists "Okie," "Arkie," and "Tex," claiming that each hailed from the appropriate Southwestern state. It was not quite true. Tex Williams, later a popular band leader in his own right, was actually a native of Illinois. But contrived or not, the names demonstrate the audience power of Southwesterners and the symbolic rewards they sometimes commanded. Musicians often found it profitable to link themselves expressly with the Southwestern community ("Okie" Paul Westmoreland is another example). Okies in a sense by profession as well as background, they became public champions of the migrant group.[27]

It is ironic that the artist who came to be most closely identified with Okies by the general public was relatively unknown to the migrants themselves. Woody Guthrie got his professional start in California and while there wrote many of the Dust Bowl ballads that eventually brought him fame. As classic in their way as Steinbeck's novel and Lange's photographs, songs like "Talking Dust Bowl Blues," "So Long (It's Been Good to Know Yuh)," and "Do Re Mi" provide some of the most enduring images of the migrant experience. There is no better memorial to California's inhospitable 1930s mentality than the lines:

> Now, the police at the port of entry say,
> "You're number fourteen thousand for today."
> Oh if you ain't got the do re mi, folks,
> If you ain't got the do re mi,
> Why, you'd better go back to beautiful Texas,
> Oklahoma, Kansas, Georgia, Tennessee.
> California is a Garden of Eden,
> A paradise to live in or see.
> But believe it or not, you won't find it so hot,
> If you ain't got the do re mi.[28]

But the Dust Bowl ballads were not recorded until Guthrie moved to New York in 1940 and even then failed to gain widespread commercial circulation. Guthrie had sung most of them, of course, on his Los Angeles radio program and also on several trips he made into the Central Valley in 1938 and 1939. Rose Maddox and her brothers heard him on one of those occasions and picked up "Do Re Mi," which they retitled "Dustbowl Blues" and added to their performance repertoire. But Guthrie in those days was a minor figure, just one of many hillbilly performers struggling to make names for themselves. Neither he nor his material made a sustained impression.[29]

Fame when it came rested on a different base. The people who heard and loved his Dust Bowl Ballads and hailed him as the "Okie Troubadour" belonged to the New York–centered world of labor and left-wing activism. When he left California at the end of the 1930s he also in a sense left the country-music medium. He would spend much of the 1940s with Pete Seeger and the Almanac Singers breaking trail for Joan Baez and Bob Dylan, establishing the protest-oriented musical tradition that a later generation would call folk music. But little of this registered in California's Okie communities. Indeed, cousin Jack Guthrie probably enjoyed a larger reputation there. In 1945, Jack recorded a song that he and Woody had written some years before. A standard nostalgia piece loaded with old home references, "Oklahoma Hills" gained the air play and popularity that the Dust Bowl ballads had missed.[30]

The Symbolism of Country Music

The chance to celebrate the success of the industry and its stars was but one aspect of the community's close relationship to country music. The message of this medium also mattered. Easily the most didactic form of twentieth-century popular music, the songs themselves carried meanings relevant to the migrants' sense of self and group. Anthropologist Sherry Ortner talks of "key symbols" that succinctly convey a culture's central values and tensions. It is tempting to suggest something like that in this case. Across two generations, from Gene Autry to Merle Haggard, country music has been to Okies what rock and roll was to young people in the 1950s and 1960s: the symbol, the medium, the "language" that communicated the essence of their subculture.[31]

The format of country songs almost guarantees some of this influence. Although much about the music has changed over the years, some features have remained remarkably consistent, one of them being the heavily lyrical emphasis of country songs. Where other genres stress music or mood, it is the words that count in most country songs. Once described as "three-minute soap operas," most songs sketch a situation of dramatic proportions. And the issues raised are varied and ethically complex. Where much of twentieth-century popular music focuses on the single issue of romantic love (to which rock and roll adds sex and dancing), country songs deal with a much wider range of subjects. Personal relationships are central, but the songs often problematize those relationships, achieving their characteristic "sad" mood within a context of cheating lovers, errant sons, and dying parents. Almost Victorian in their blend of sentimentality, tragedy, and stiff morality, song images are emotional, powerful.[32]

What these images mean is the issue, and a few points need to be clarified before we begin. Country music did not belong to Okies in the way a folk product might. A commercial medium with many diverse national audiences, its songs cannot be taken as an expression of any particular constituency. With New York record companies, professional songwriters, demanding radio station managers, and the canon of convention all factoring themselves into the creative process, it is also impossible to say much of anything about what the songs meant to those who helped to produce them. That, however, is not what is important. What matters here are the meanings that Okies derived from these songs and the ways they made commercially produced materials their own. In the analysis that follows I have looked for resonances between the imagery and metaphor of songs and the values and preoccupations of the group. There are many, enough to suggest that the music played an intimate role in the group cultural system.[33]

One of the themes that resonates most strongly has to with questions of family and place. Long-lasting ties to people and places left behind has remained, as we have seen, a feature of the Okie experience in California, and country music appears to be at least partly responsible. Celebration of the family as an institution and a general tone of nostalgia still play major roles in country songs today. Fifty years ago the two concerns were omnipresent. Like the late Victorian parlor songs that so influenced the early medium, many 1930s compositions examined the issue of home and being away from home. Song after song told of ramblers, hobos, lonesome cowboys, runaway lovers, outlaws on the lam, and other figures cut off from their roots. Contrite or forlorn, they usually looked back wistfully upon treasured moments of youth and longed for the security of home.

Scholars have offered varying interpretations of this preoccupation, most seeing it as a metaphor for uncertainty about general forces of modernization and social change.[34] That may have been the right level of meaning for other listeners, but to Okies in California, a thousand miles from their homes, no metaphor was needed. A song like Jimmie Rodgers's classic "Daddy and Home" spoke pure homesickness:

> Daddy, dear old daddy,
> I'm coming back to you.
> You made my boyhood happy,
> But still I long to roam;
> I've had my way, but now I'll say,
> I long for you and for home.[35]

Nostalgia flowed heavily in the songs popular among residents of the FSA camps. A young man from Arkansas entertained neighbors in the Shafter camp with a tune called "Hillbilly Gal":

> Sometimes I wonder why I have to roam
> My thoughts still linger in the way back home
> How I miss the old folks and my little sister Lu
> Wonder if she misses me too.[36]

James Wilson noticed the transforming power of such lyrics at a dance held at one of the other camps. When the band finished the evening with a mournful rendition of "Home Sweet Home," "a hush . . . falls upon the merrymakers," each listener seemingly absorbed in thoughts of faraway places.[37]

The effect was compounded in the many cowboy ballads that featured references to the Southwest. Texas was by far the most common song setting of the period. Compositions like "Deep in the Heart of Texas," "By the Silv'ry Rio Grande," and "Red River Valley" appeared in great profusion. Songs about the other Southwestern states were fewer, but the Oklahomans in particular could take pride in some very popular tunes, including Bob Wills's "Take Me Back to Tulsa" and Woody and Jack Guthrie's "Oklahoma Hills." These songs kept the home fires burning bright. Stuart Hamblen stoked the flames each day when he began his Los Angeles radio show with the song "Texas Plains":

> Each night in my dreams, somehow it seems,
> That I'm back where I belong;

> Just a country hick way back in the sticks,
> Back where I was born.
> City lights, and city ways,
> Are driving me insane;
> I want to be alone; I want to be back home,
> Back to my Texas Plains.[38]

Songs like this stirred feelings and gave them social validity. Country music expressed the rootlessness and loneliness that most felt and made it into a recognized group sentiment; homesickness or at least a kind of unresolved attitude towards life in California was for many years emblematic of Okies.

In other ways too the music may have compounded feelings of alienation. Beyond the direct invocation of nostalgia, songs promulgated values that helped to set the migrants apart from their California neighbors. Plainfolk Americanism found a strong voice in country music.

The ideological perspective of recent country music—vaguely anti-urban, decidedly white, and rooted in the everyday concerns of common people—was much sharper in the 1930s and 1940s. In that era of green mountain homes and purple plains, songs mostly focused on simple people who often worried about the loss of simple ways. Cowboys rode the range, singing of sweethearts, open skies, courage, mother, and death. Hoboes and railroadmen rode the trains, regretting lives gone bad and remembering the warmth of lost embraces. Paeans to the joys of rural life abounded, companions to the tragic tales of broken homes, dying parents, and abandoned lovers. God too was often near, ready to receive the faithful, watching over the "circles" of life and family, keeping them, as the often recorded hymn promised, "unbroken."[39]

With rural ways, family, religion, and tradition so important, songs of the period contain few positive references to the sort of world that California had come to represent. Cities, as we saw in the Stuart Hamblen lyrics, were alienating; they could also be dangerous and imprisoning, as in the Carter Family's "Behind These Stone Walls."[40] Much of what passed for modern lifestyles was equally suspect. Materialism, greedy ambition, flashy styles, instrumental relationships, and casual morality all drew fire in the country song texts, most of which upheld in one way or another the value of plain living. In "Come Along Home My Darling," Lulu Belle and Scotty drew out the lesson with a jab at college-educated experts:

> That city slicker told me
> As sassy as a pup,
> I'd better take care of my poultry
> Or the chickens would scratch it up.[41]

In other cases, the comparison was more subtle. "I'm back in the saddle again," Gene Autry sang to open his weekly radio show, "Out where a friend is a friend.''[42] Here was the choice. Rejecting the postures and preoccupations of modern urban existence, country music chose the cleansing open spaces, the dignity of "real" work, the genuineness of friendship and family, and the democracy of rural life.

The committed ruralism of the country genre—a feature that in modified form holds today—may have been one of the seminal forces shaping the identity and personal styles of Southwesterners. Here was the clearest counterweight to California's critique of rural backwardness. Here indeed was an influence that in the decades to come would help to convince previously scornful Americans in a number of settings that rural people and ways could be worthy of respect and emulation.

Much of this power centered on the compelling image of the cowboy, who, as we have seen, became the basic icon of the medium by the late 1930s. Actually, the cowboy was everywhere in American popular culture in that period. From magazine to movie house to juke box, Americans of all sorts soaked up tales of the romantic horsemen who in an earlier age of glory and certainty had supposedly won the West. Along with the gangster, who shared the cowboy's penchant for life and death struggle but whose heroism was more complex, the Western knight gained his media following by posing questions that mattered to Americans of the Depression decade. Bringing to life a confident past for people troubled by an intractable present, the cowboy cult also embodied a deep dialogue about the direction of American culture.

At issue was society's commitment to individualism. As usually rendered in popular media, the cowboy stood for independence and rugged strength. Courage and determination were his religion, honor and freedom his reward. A generally unambiguous figure in Western action films, the portrait assumed greater complexity in the country song. No medium as committed to matters of family and place as this one could give an unqualified endorsement to such a solitary, potentially irresponsible, figure. The country-music cowboy wrestled with contradiction, in one song at peace with his role, in another tormented by guilt or loneliness. Several of the most popular and enduring ballads ("The Cowboy's Lament," "Oh, Bury Me Not on the Lone Prairie") found the hero facing a lonely death. Heroic and possibly tragic at the same time, the cowboy tantalized and challenged audiences that perhaps had not fully reckoned the disjuncture between independence and responsibility, between individualism and the needs of family and community.[43]

For Okies in California, facing their own questions of place and dignity, the mythic images resonated strongly. The cowboy modeled many of the traits they believed essential to good character. Like many other Americans of the period, but with special enthusiasm born of their close relationship to the country-music medium, Southwesterners (at home as well as in California) took the cowboy figure to heart.

Figure 31. When Western swing was king. Sailors, defense workers, and their dates jam a Bay Area night spot to dance to the Dude Martin band. (*Dorothea Lange,* © *1982, The Oakland Museum, The City of Oakland*)

There was no missing the migrants' fascination with Western symbolism. It showed up occasionally in their vehicles—trailers fashioned after covered wagons. More numerous were the "pioneer" references appearing in FSA camp newspapers, some of them, like the *Covered Wagon* logo of the Shafter paper, encouraged by the management. Most telling were the cowboy styles of dress and speech which became increasingly evident towards the end of the decade.[44]

Young men were especially drawn to the Western look. Cowboy hats, boots, and belts replaced bib-overalls as the favored style of the younger set, conveying additional status because of the expense entailed. Cowboy lingo accompanied, with terms like "pard-ner" and "dogie" creeping into the casual vocabulary. Here is Katherine Archibald's description of young Okie shipyard workers in 1942: "His dress tended to be flamboyant, and his manner likewise. He fancied himself on a horse and on the wide, uncitified plains of his native region."[45]

Mature men also might adopt the look. Lois Barnes recalls that her father took great care with his cowboy apparel. It was for him more than simple fashion. Strangers would call him "Tex" because they "saw his cowboy hat and figured he came from Texas." Though he was an Okla-

homan, he liked the misidentification. It "made him happy," she recalls—
it was better than being looked upon as a poor Okie.[46]

Southwesterners were not alone in donning cowboy styles. Nor was the
style particularly new. Well before the Dust Bowl migration, rodeos, Western Day celebrations, and a sprinkling of cowboy hats signified rural California's Western heritage. But the look grew significantly more popular in the
closing years of the Depression and became associated with the Okie subculture in the same nonexclusive way that governed most of the group's symbols and institutions. A marker of sorts, it was not the defiant group uniform
adopted by some subcultures (zoot suits, for example, by young blacks and
Chicanos in the same period). Okies sought legitimacy from their symbolic
statements. Choosing references they assumed to be widely respected, the
distinction they valued was that of being the best Americans around.

Country music was the text they often drew upon. All through the difficult resettlement years of the 1930s and the more accommodating 1940s,
the music seemed to provide the resources for a sense of independence
and pride. Like the evangelical churches, it offered possibilities for in-
group social contacts. And in different ways than the religious institutions,
the medium also suggested alternatives to the dominant middle-class value
system. Standard country-song symbols like nostalgia, plain living, and
cowboy courage helped to reinforce the understanding that the migrants
were different from and perhaps better than their California neighbors.

The music seems to have played an especially important part in maintaining the subculture across generations—and, as we will see, in diffusing some
of its features among other Californians. The handing down of valued outlooks to children in the face of competing school and peer influences was easier because of the heroic symbols that came with this influential
entertainment medium. This may be one of the clues to the retention of the
Okie accent, as well as to the continued appeal of a "down-home" style of
self-presentation that utilizes rural aphorisms, elements of Western dress
(hat, boots, or string tie), and abundant references to plain people and plain
virtues. The middle-class critique of rustic mannerisms and the unceasing efforts of teachers to eradicate the Okie accent would have carried much more
weight but for the continuing "good old boy" models presented by the country-music industry. Young people had only to turn on the radio to realize
that they had a choice. If Gene Autry could maintain his "aw-shucks" style
and if Bob Wills could carry on in his high-pitched Texas twang, a second-
generation saw nothing wrong with following their lead.

"Okie from Muskogee"

The year was 1969, and that younger generation's most famous member
was back home, in a manner of speaking. Merle Haggard was in Muskogee,

Oklahoma, not far from where his parents had grown up. At the moment he was on stage, facing an adoring concert audience. "Okie, Okie," they called out whenever there was a break in the music. He smiled but did not respond. Running through his repertoire of hit songs, he was teasing them, denying them the one they wanted so much to hear. Finally, the familiar opening bars and that unforgettable first line: "We don't smoke marijuana in Muskogee." The hall erupted. It was their song.[47]

"Okie from Muskogee" had many fans. One of the best-selling country songs of 1969, it propelled Haggard from country-music stardom to cult figure. Conservatives loved it. Hailing its flag-waving slams at hippies, draft-dodgers, and campus radicals, President Nixon sent him a letter of congratulations. George Wallace thought it captured perfectly the message he had been trying to send to Washington and asked Haggard to sign on for the governor's ongoing presidential campaign. But the performer did not need politicians. The press was already proclaiming him a working-class hero, "the poet laureate of the hard hats."[48]

The song had a special meaning to a particular audience of Californians who shared Haggard's Southwestern heritage. Its patriotic lyrics said nothing directly about them. Haggard and band member Eddie Burris wrote the song while touring Oklahoma, when a Muskogee road sign inspired the stray comment, "I bet they don't smoke marijuana there." But in crafting the song's powerful refrain, "I'm proud to be an Okie from Muskogee," Haggard was touching a different base. It would become a slogan for California Okies, part of a new way of thinking about themselves, a new stage in their relationship to California.

Much had changed by 1969: for Okies, for country music, for the United States. Age had been overtaking the Southwestern community in California. Migration rates had tailed off in the 1950s and 1960s, as oil and defense booms enlivened the economies of Texas and Oklahoma. Thus, even as they were beginning to make their most substantial cultural impact, Southwesterners were losing population share in fast-growing California. That was especially true in the San Joaquin Valley. Twenty-two percent of the valley population in 1950, Southwestern-born whites were down to 12 percent in 1970. Statewide their representation had fallen from 11 to 7 percent (see Appendix B). Of course there was also a second and a young third generation by then, but we know little about their numbers.[49]

Members of the first generation, the Dust Bowl and defense migrants of the 1930s and 1940s were nearing retirement age now, most in a position to feel proud of their accomplishments. The socio-economic progress begun in the 1940s had continued through the next two decades, lifting most into relative comfort and security. The old curse of poverty fell now on only a small minority: just 4 percent of those still of working age in the metropolitan areas, 10 percent in the San Joaquin Valley. A few still made their

Figure 32. Redneck chic was in full flower when Merle Haggard posed for this publicity still in the early 1980s. In 1969, he had been clean cut, usually appearing in a sport coat. (*Norman Seelf, Epic Records*)

living through agricultural work, but mostly this generation closed out its working life in blue-collar respectability (see Appendix C).

Their children, Merle Haggard's generation, had reached maturity by then and had spread out widely across California's social strata. They were doctors, lawyers, nurses, and teachers, truck drivers, farmers, waitresses, and aerospace workers. They lived in suburbs, cities, and small towns, in northern California, southern California, and of course the Central Valley. Mostly they were indistinguishable, except when they wanted to be, from other white Californians.

Merle Haggard had always been among the distinguishable ones. Born in Bakersfield in 1937, fatherless nine years later, he grew up in nearby Oildale with a devoutly religious mother who supported her family as a bookkeeper. A restless youngster, he fell in with that portion of the younger generation who got more out of toughness and juvenile delinquency than out of school. At ten he hopped his first freight train and turned up in Fresno. At fourteen he hitch-hiked to Texas, bought his first cowboy boots, and spent his first week in jail, an adult jail. Juvenile arrests had started earlier, for truancy, theft, fighting, drinking. In and out of reform school more times than he could count, he was every inch the rebel he later sang about in "Mama Tried":

> One and only rebel child,
>   from a family meek and mild,
>   my Mama seemed to know what
>   lay in store,
> 'Spite of all my Sunday learnin'
>   towards the bad I kept on turnin'
>   'Til Mama couldn't hold me anymore.[50]

It was a road that finally led to San Quentin. He "turned twenty-one in prison," to quote another song, serving almost three years for burglary and attempted escape. But the experience had its desired effect. When they released him in 1960 he was ready to change his ways.[51]

He had always loved music—his father played fiddle—and at an early age learned to play the guitar his mother bought him. When not up to some wildness, he made a few dollars singing in the dives and honky-tonks that sprinkled Kern County. By the time he got out of prison, Bakersfield had developed a reputation as an up and coming center for country music. Big-name performers rolled through town on their Western tours, and the area also supported a variety of radio programs, a daily television show, and a couple of fledgling record labels. Most important, Bakersfield was just then producing its first genuine star, a sandy-haired former Texan named Buck Owens who over the next decade would build the city a reputation as "Nashville West." Merle Haggard followed in his footsteps. He made his first record in 1962, hit the charts in 1964, signed with a major label in 1965, and by the time "Okie" appeared in 1969 claimed thirteen albums and almost as many number-one or top-ten singles.[52]

Country music had also been changing during these decades, finding a new niche and new audiences, and adjusting some of its representations accordingly. The diffusion process that California's Okies had participated in during the 1930s had become national—indeed international—during the war years, as GIs and defense workers redistributed musical tastes, carrying the market for country music as far as England, Germany, even Japan. Other audience changes followed in the 1950s as the music industry adapted to the explosive emergence of rock and roll. By the 1960s, country music no longer belonged just to Southerners and Southwesterners. As sociologists Richard Peterson and Paul Di Maggio have shown, the locus had shifted "from region to class." Country was now the favored medium of large numbers of lower-middle-class Americans, almost entirely white, mostly blue-collar, over thirty, and increasingly conservative.[53]

Heard now in clubs in the Italian sections of Philadelphia and Polish neighborhoods of Chicago and widely throughout the white working-class suburbs of California, the spread of country music pointed to a convergence of more than musical tastes. Immigrant-stock working-class Northerners and Protestant Southerners now seemed to mesh on several fronts, including the political one. Northern blue-collar constituencies which thirty years before had been at the very heart of New Deal liberalism were changing political coloration by the late 1960s. Threatened by the civil rights agenda of liberal Democrats, and angered by ghetto riots and campus demonstrations, they were moving towards a politics of racial and patriotic conservatism that had much in common with the formulations of Southern and Southwestern plain folk. The fact that significant numbers of Northern and Western voters had become fans of Alabama governor George Wallace was an indication of the way that institutions formerly associated with the white South had begun to have wider appeal.[54]

The diffusion of country music was certainly a symptom and probably an instrument of this convergence. An already established mass-cultural force, its symbols were flexible enough to be grasped selectively by the diverse audiences who shared its core understandings. Moreover, the music appealed to its new fans with some updated themes and symbols. Cowboy images had pretty well disappeared by the 1960s (though they would repear in the 1970s), replaced by coats and ties on stage and song texts that featured modern-day dramas. Marital relations had become the favorite subject; songs often explored the real-life issues that threatened marriages—country music was well into its "Cheating Heart" phase. Class and rural perspectives had also been adjusted. Still very much dedicated to ordinary people, occupational references had shifted towards the urban and industrial. A half-shift actually, as signified by the new central character of the country song, the truck driver. Tough and independent, yet also part of a proud fraternity, the truck driver synchronized old values with a new context. Part loner, part team player, modern and yet still free to roam the wide spaces, these eighteen-wheel cowboys knew how to manage the machinery of modern life without losing their independence. It was a symbol that worked for both old audiences and new.

Other aspects needed less adjustment, particularly the medium's long-standing traditionalist perspective. Songs raised new problems but generally answered them according to the formula that had always been central: the old ways are best, happiness depends on being true to one's upbringing and to the traditions of community and nation. This too worked for newer constituencies bothered by the disturbing changes of the late 1960s. As the "silent majority" began to find its voice, songs sprang to the defense of God, country, hard work, the patriarchal family, and at least subtextually, the white community.[55]

California's Southwesterners were beneficiaries of these changes, just as they would be from the growing influence of evangelical Protestantism. In both cases, early investments paid off in pride. It helped enormously that a leading figure in the redneck/hard-hat marriage was one of their own, and that he was busy telling their story to the country-music world.

Even before "Okie from Muskogee," Merle Haggard was the central force behind country music's tough new populism. His early reputation had been built mostly on convict tales that played off his rough and rowdy youth ("Sing Me Back Home," "I'm a Lonesome Fugitive," "Branded Man," "Mama Tried"). But after 1968 his interests became more political and he recorded a string of best-selling songs about working-class America. They began with "I Take a Lot of Pride in What I Am," followed the next year by "Working Man's Blues," a proud and bitter anthem to the hard-working family man. Then came "Okie" and its angrier sequel, "The Fighting Side of Me" (1970). Merle Haggard was by then at the top of his industry and a nationally recognized symbol of the ideas he championed.

California's Southwesterners were not uniformly aligned with these sentiments. Former migrants and their offspring could be found in every sort of political camp, from John Birch Society clubs to the Students for a Democratic Society. And among them was no shortage of liberals. Indeed, the state's most powerful Democratic legislator, Speaker of the Assembly Jesse Unruh, was an Okie. A Texan actually, he had settled in Los Angeles in the 1940s and then built a political career modeled after Lyndon Baines Johnson. Bold and crude, "Big Daddy" Unruh wielded power with the instincts of a Texas oil man and with the compassion of a liberal Democrat. The Unruh Civil Rights Act (1959) was one of his legislative trophies.[56]

For most Southwesterners, however, the currents flowed in a different direction, more along the lines of the state's other major Okie politician, Congressman Bernie F. Sisk. Another former Texan, and another Democrat, Sisk had won Fresno County's congressional seat in the 1950s and held it for twenty-four years. For a Californian, he was an unusual Democrat: cool to organized labor, lukewarm on civil rights, strongly opposed to Cesar Chavez and the United Farm Workers. Midway through the 1960s, he parted company with the Johnson Administration and with his own delegation, building ties instead to conservative Southern legislators. When he ran unsuccessfully for Majority Leader in 1970, it was, said one report, "with support more from the South than the California delegation."[57]

Kern County, where the Southwestern vote counted most heavily, had become by the late 1960s too conservative even for a Bernie Sisk. Without abandoning their heavy Democratic party registration, voters had turned the county into a Republican stronghold, giving Ronald Reagan large majorities in his campaigns for governor in 1966 and 1970 and sending a conservative Republican to the Congress and Richard Nixon to the White House, all the while saving 9 percent of their 1968 ballots for George Wallace. Equally telling was the county's record on ballot measures. On the death penalty, school busing, marijuana legalization, coastal conservation, homosexual rights, and farm-labor legislation its tallies were far more conservative than state averages. "I think Merle Haggard summed up our philosophy here," Bakersfield mayor Donald S. Hart would say in the late 1970s. "We respect and love America, its flags and its symbols. We believe in paternalism, a strong family . . . and the merits of good old hard work. That's all—nothin' very sophisticated about it."[58]

Whether or not they shared his political disposition, many former Southwesterners were learning from Merle Haggard new ways to think about their heritage. In his drive to celebrate the virtues of hard-working 100-percent Americanism, Haggard had begun to explore his own heritage and was in the process of resurrecting a subject that had been more or less lost to public scrutiny for two decades. In 1969, he recorded the first of his Dust Bowl ballads, a loosely autobiographical song called "Hungry Eyes" that went back to the themes of poverty, prejudice, and struggle that formed the core of the Okie experience. The opening verses evoke Dorothea Lange's "Migrant Mother" photograph:

> A canvas-covered cabin, in a crowded labor camp,
>   stands out in this memory I revive.
> 'Cause my daddy raised a family there with two hard-
>   working hands,
>   and tried to feed my mama's hungry eyes.
>
> He dreamed of something better there,
>   and my mama's faith was strong.
> And us kids were just too young to realize
>   that another class of people put us somewhere just below.
> One more reason for my mama's hungry eyes.[59]

Other compositions pursued the same basic themes. "Cotton Fields," "Tulare Dust," "They're Tearing the Labor Camps Down," and "The Roots of My Raising," provide further images of people overcoming adversity through fierce determination, adding to the conviction that this was indeed a special heritage. He brought this theme to its sharpest point with the line, "The roots of my raising run deep," from the title song of his 1975 album. The song is about family and tradition, from which he gets "the strength that I need." Okies are not mentioned in that song, but the point is clear enough to those who share his background. It says we share an inheritance of determination and courage, an inheritance of sturdy values and quiet accomplishment.[60]

Haggard's songs broke open the reservoir of group pride and laid the foundation for a renaissance in group consciousness that became especially noticeable in the 1970s. The movement had several faces. Other musicians, mostly based in Bakersfield, by then the thriving Western capital of country music, turned out additional Okie pride songs. A literary circle led by writers Gerald Haslam and James Houston began to publish the poetry and fiction of a dozen or so second-generation Okie authors. Newspapers caught the spirit and commissioned a new round of "where are they now?"

articles about the Dust Bowl migrants. Colleges, libraries, and city admin-
istrations in the San Joaquin Valley sponsored programs to celebrate or
study the Okie experience, and one or two high schools and colleges experimented with Okie Studies programs.[61]

All this attended a more far-reaching change at a personal level. For the
first time it had become acceptable, almost fashionable, to be an Okie. In
working-class communities a proliferation of "Okie Pride" bumper stick-
ers, belt-buckles, and trucker caps heralded the change. But of greater
significance was the meaning for those of middle-class standing, some of
whom had spent the better part of a lifetime hiding from that label. For
Frank Manies, who had at times passed himself off as an Arizonian, for
Peggy Staggs, who had spent her formative years becoming a perfect Californian, for Ernest Martin, who as a young adult had fled the valley so
as not to be "associated with the 'Okie' image," these years brought a new
reckoning with what had been a troublesome background. The old stigmas
had mostly been conquered, though not entirely. Just enough remained to
make them feel triumphant in their newly expressed identity, to make them
feel good about "stepping out," as one former Oklahoman put it, "of the
'Okie closet.' "[62]

Haggard, it must be understood, was the catalyst, not really the cause.
His songs reflected a search for roots which blossomed in many corners of
America during the 1960s and 1970s. His quest and the response to it rested
on recent changes in the way Americans thought about ethnicity and cultural differentiation. Okie pride was closely tied to the new ethnic consciousness that swept the country in the wake of the Civil Rights and Black
Power movements. The "new ethnicity" made it socially acceptable to be
an Okie just as it made it safe to be Jewish, Italian, Chicano, and so on.
In an era that was uniquely and genuinely celebrating pluralism, many
Americans were dragging once-problematic backgrounds out of the
closet.[63]

But it was no accident that country music provided the medium for the
reconstruction of Okie consciousness. All along that industry had helped
to define the migrants' changing relationship with California. A group
project that paid dividends of recognition and validation as it became more
and more popular, it was also a fluid cultural system that again and again
conveyed symbols of great meaning to the group. It remains yet the single
most important source of group integrity, the essential language of the
Okie subculture.

American Exodus

The place and position of Southwesterners in California has changed dramatically in the past half century. Beginning in poverty and social conflict,
saddled with stereotypes for which few were prepared, the migrants even-

tually recovered both their economic balance and their sense of dignity and pride. If their lives thus constitute a success story, it is not the conventional success story about which Americans love to read. This has not been a rags-to-riches tale. For the most part, the migrants' economic progress has been unspectacular. Both first and second generations have moved upward on the rising tide of prosperity that has lifted most white Americans of their ages into a growing middle class. Indeed, they might have done just as well by remaining in the Southwest. The postwar economy that improved the lot of Okies in California created similar opportunities for Southwesterners who remained behind.

But that is not the way to measure this experience. The real issue is culture. The Dust Bowl migration teaches us about the ways American culture is transformed through population movement. Nothing is more basic to our collective history.

The migration of Southwesterners to California was one dramatic episode in a larger twentieth-century population movement that historians have all but ignored. The migration of millions of white Protestant Americans out of the heartland regions of the South and Great Plains to the more cosmopolitan perimeter has had as profound consequences for Illinois, Indiana, Michigan, Ohio, Arizona, New Mexico, and Oregon as for California. Certainly, this is one of the factors contributing to the political redirection of the white working class in those areas since World War II. If the arrival of blacks from the South helped turn the northern Democratic party into the voice of racial liberalism, the influx of white heartlanders has helped spread lower-middle-class conservatism. From Richard Nixon's silent-majority Republicanism to the rekindled political fundamentalism of Jerry Falwell to the anti-establishment conservatism of Ronald Reagan, many of the nation's recent political realignments have had something to do with this heartland exodus.

But generalizations of this sort can be hazardous. The consequences of population shifts vary according to particular circumstances. If there is one thing I hope this study demonstrates, it is that the experiences and impact of the Dust Bowl migrants in California have been governed by specific historical conditions. Southwesterners did not leave home as a coherent cultural group, and it took more than differences in regional culture to make them so. There was nothing fixed or predetermined about their adjustment patterns. Particular configurations of class and politics and of California's institutions and popular moods provided the context for the migrants' interaction with their new state.

Timing was critical. It mattered greatly that so many Southwesterners moved west in the 1930s. That decade, with its particular problems and passions, created the Okie crisis and, perhaps, created Okies. Had the hostile reception that forced many Southwesterners into the position of social outsiders been absent, would there have been an Okie subculture? Certainly not the same one.

So too, the decades since the 1930s have been critical to the increasing influence of Southwesterners in California. Major changes in the way Americans in general and Californians in particular think about issues of modernity have governed the relationship between these former heartlanders and their adopted state. In an age when the mass media worried about rural backwardness, Southwesterners suffered from the association. But as postwar America began to look favorably upon one symbol of traditionalism after another, embracing religion, family, patriotism, and finally rural nostalgia itself, the stigmas fell away. By the early 1970s, a nation caught up in the search for "roots" and indulging a renewed fascination with cowboys, Texans, and country music was ready to romanticize the Dust Bowl migrants.

It is important, too, that we understand the significance of particular institutions in the migrants' changing relationship with California. A group identity may not carry very far unless it is tied to specific institutional vehicles. This may be one of the reasons why Midwesterners have not made the same kind of demonstrable cultural impact on California, despite massive numbers and sometimes avid home-state loyalties (Iowans for example). Of course, the fact that Iowans were never cast as social outsiders made a powerful difference, but so did the Southwesterners' proprietorial control of several institutions that were relatively new to California. Evangelical religion, country music, and the political perspectives of plain-folk Americanism are not merely projects of the Okie subculture, they are what has given the group continuity and influence over the years. Without them, we would be discussing a different experience.

So what finally is this Okie subculture? It remains a historical construction of inexact and changing dimensions. Based partly on regional background, partly on a unique set of experiences, and also independently on this set of religious and political institutions, it encompasses many but not all of the Southwesterners who settled in California and with them a number of other Californians who have joined the good-old-boy or evangelical milieu.

Ultimately, the Okie is an invention, a work of collective imagination. Over the last half century, pieces of group identity have been assembled from many sources: from shared traumas of the Depression era, from ancestral legend, from popular media, from Steinbeck, Lange, and Haggard. And those pieces generally have less to do with symbols of regionalism than with Americanism. In their drive to create a positive self-construction, Okies have dipped again and again into the well of plain-folk Americana, finding there sources of pesonal dignity and, paradoxically, sources of group distinction.

Novelist Ken Kesey, author of *One Flew Over the Cuckoo's Nest* and *Sometimes a Great Notion*, offers a compelling explanation of what his Okie heritage means to him:

> Though my mama came from Arkansas and my daddy came
>   from Texas, and though we all came to Oregon from
> Colorado by way of daddy being stationed at the Mare Island Navy
>   base in California during WWII, I nevertheless must admit that
> I think of myself as an Oakie.
>   Let me tell you what being an Oakie means:
> Being an Oakie means being the first of your whole family to finish
>   high school let alone go on to college . . .
> Being an Oakie means getting rooted out of an area and
>   having to hustle for a toehold in some new area . . .
> Being an Oakie means running the risk of striving out
>   from under a layer of heartless sonsabitches only to discover
> you have become a redneck of bitterness worse than those
>   you strove against . . .
> Being an Oakie is a low rent, aggravating drag, but it does
>   learn you some essentials . . . essentials like it isn't a new car
> that pulls over to help you when you are broke down with the
>   senile carburetor; it is somebody who knows what it is
> to be broke down with a hurt machine.[64]

Regionalism is not the issue here. The references have to do with character, values, and experience. Okies are people who have known suffering, who are tough enough to rise above it, who can be guilty of redneck intolerance, even as they never forget the "essentials," namely, that ordinary folk are the guts and sinew of American society. This is a song of plain folk. The Okie identity has been constructed out of symbols appropriated from the heritage of an entire nation.

APPENDIX A

Public Use
Microdata Samples

THE PUBLIC USE MICRODATA SAMPLES (PUMS) ARE COMPUTER-READABLE DATA files prepared by the Bureau of the Census. This study uses the 1 percent samples from the 1940, 1950, and 1970 censuses. The 1940 and 1950 data sets have only recently become available and are a resource of untapped potential for twentieth-century social historians. Not only do they make it possible to track groups, like Southwestern-born migrants, who cannot be identified in published census reports, but they also allow the investigator to arrange and manipulate the data to fit particular research designs. Two limitations are worth noting. The chief one is the inability to distinguish geographic areas. To guard anonymity, locations smaller than Standard Metropolitan Statistical Areas or State Subregions are not reported. Thus, it was not possible to examine particular communities, something that would have helped this project. It was also not possible to identify second-generation (California-born) Okies. Census questionnaires do ask about parents' places of birth, but that item was not included in the data picked up in the PUMS.

On the technical side, another problem needs to be noted. Each PUMS actually consists of twenty separate probability samples that need to be compiled to reach the full 1 percent sample. The tapes I obtained of the 1940 data had one bad subsample (number 4). As a result, the 1940 figures reported here are somewhat shy of the full 1 percent count. The ommission, however, does not significantly affect the accuracy of the sample.

Southwesterners in California Subregions 1935, 1940, 1950, 1970

THE FOLLOWING TABLE SHOWS THE DISTRIBUTION OF SOUTHWESTERN-BORN non-Hispanic whites in California at selected dates between 1935 and 1970, the net increase in population between dates, and their representation in the population of each area. Since the sources are the Census Public Use Microdata Samples, which are one-percent census samples, the numbers are calculated estimates.

A word about the 1935 figures. They derive from the 1940 Census question, "Where did you reside April 1, 1935?" which, unfortunately, is our only source on the distribution of Southwesterners before 1940. It is not a fully accurate survey since anyone who had left California during the second half of the decade would not have been counted.

It may be noticed that there are discrepancies between this table and the data reported in some of the text tables. Table 1.1 in Chapter 1 reports volume of migration to California and includes Hispanics and nonwhites, which this table does not. The data accompanying Map 4 in Chapter 2 is not precisely comparable because it tracks persons who lived in the Southwest in 1935 as opposed to those born in those states.

Southwesterners Living in California Subregions, 1935–1970

	1935 Southwesterners	1935 % of pop.	1940 Southwesterners	1940 % of pop.	1935–40 increase	1950 Southwesterners	1950 % of pop.	1940–50 increase	1970 Southwesterners	1970 % of pop.	1950–70 increase
Los Angeles	224,300	10%	316,300	11%	92,000	448,100	10%	131,800	464,500	5%	16,400
SF Bay Area	44,400	3	74,000	4	29,600	178,000	7	104,000	194,100	5	16,100
San Diego	19,400	10	29,000	10	9,600	65,500	12	36,500	94,500	7	29,000
All metropolitan	288,100	7%	419,300	9%	131,200	691,600	9%	272,300	753,100	5%	61,500
San Joaquin Valley	62,300	12%	135,100	19%	72,800	254,800	22%	119,700	221,500	12%	– 33,300
Sacramento Valley	13,800	6	23,400	8	9,600	59,000	12	35,600	109,700	8	50,700
San Bernardino/Imperial	34,400	14	60,500	19	26,100	79,400	15	18,900	98,800	9	19,400
North Coast	4,300	3	9,400	6	5,100	23,600	9	14,200	24,100	8	500
Central Coast	18,600	8	32,400	10	13,800	64,700	13	32,300	94,900	7	30,200
Sierras	8,500	6	21,200	10	12,700	29,300	12	8,100	*	—	
All nonmetropolitan	141,900	10%	282,000	14%	140,100	510,800	16%	228,800	549,000	9%	38,200
California total	430,000	8%	701,300	10%	271,300	1,202,400	11%	501,100	1,302,100	7%	99,700

Note: Subregional areas changed somewhat for the 1970 Census. Most important, the Sierra-Nevada counties were divided between North Coast, Sacramento Valley, and San Joaquin Valley subregions.

APPENDIX C

Occupation and Income 1940–1970

1970 Occupation and Income of Males Aged 40–62 in Metropolitan Labor Force, and for All Southwestern-Born Males in Metropolitan Labor Force 1940 and 1950

	1970 Southwesterners	Other whites	Hispanics/ nonwhites	1950 Southwesterners	1940 Southwesterners
Farmers	—	—	—	—	—
Professionals/ managers/ proprietors	28%	39%	15%	19%	18%
Clerical/sales/ police and fire	16	18	11	17	18
Craftsmen/ foremen	27	22	21	27	24
Operatives/ service	24	18	39	26	28
Laborers (nonfarm)	4	3	13	8	10
Farm laborers	1	—	1	2	3
	100%	100%	100%	99%	101%
N =	(1,535)	(12,026)	(2,880)	(2,352)	(1,385)
Occupational index	3.9	4.2	3.5	3.7	3.6

Table (*continued*)

	1970 Southwesterners	Other whites	Hispanics/ nonwhites	1950 Southwesterners	1940 Southwesterners
Median individual earnings	$10,000	$11,400	$7,400	$3,005	$1,190
Income below poverty line	4%	5%	12%	—	—
Welfare recipients	3%	2%	8%	—	—

Sources: Bureau of the Census, 1970, 1950, 1940 Public Use Microdata Samples.

1970 Occupation and Income of Males Aged 40–62 in San Joaquin Valley Labor Force, and for All Southwestern-Born Males in Valley Labor Force 1940 and 1950

	1970 Southwesterners	Other whites	Hispanics/ nonwhites	1950 Southwesterners	1940 Southwesterners
Farmers	3%	7%	6%	5%	6%
Professionals/ managers/ proprietors	14	30	11	11	7
Clerical/sales/ police and fire	10	15	5	6	6
Craftsmen/ foremen	24	21	11	18	12
Operatives/ service	28	19	23	23	13
Laborers (nonfarm)	7	4	10	8	11
Farm laborers	14	4	34	25	42
	100%	100%	100%	100%	101%
N =	(485)	(1,300)	(410)	(871)	(465)
Occupational index	3.3	4.0	2.7	3.0	2.5
Median individual earnings	$7,200	$8,900	$5,000	$2,420	$550
Median family earnings	9,100	12,000	7,400	2,970	790
Income below poverty line	10%	7%	20%	—	—
Welfare recipients	6%	3%	9%	—	—

Sources: 1970, 1950, 1940 Public Use Microdata Samples.

APPENDIX D

Marriage Survey: Sources And Methodology

THE DATA FOR THIS SURVEY WERE OBTAINED FROM MARRIAGE LICENSES ON FILE
in the Bureaus of Vital Statistics in Los Angeles, Kern, and Stanislaus
counties. A two-stage sampling procedure was followed. As a first step;
random samples of 200 to 250 marriage licenses were drawn for each county
and year to be studied. These provided estimates of the representation of
Southwesterners, natives, and other social groups in the marrying population. The number of Southwesterners in these initial samples was, however, too small for reliable analysis. Consequently a second random sample
was taken, consisting only of licenses where one or both of the parties was
a white Southwesterner. Since the pattern of male and female choices
appeared to be quite comparable in the initial survey, I did not sample
them separately. The size of each combined sample of Southwesterners
and the margin of error associated with estimates of their marriage choices
are reported below.

County	Year	Sample size	Margin of error*
Kern	1939	343	±4.2%
	1949	318	±4.6%
	1959	154	±7.3%
Stanislaus	1939	215	0.0%
	1949	303	±3.8%
	1959	133	±7.3%
Los Angeles	1939	183	±7.1%
	1949	129	±8.5%

*At the 95 percent confidence level.

Abbreviations

Charles Todd Collection: Charles L. Todd Okie Studies Archive in Professor Gerald Haslam's possession, Department of English, California State University, Sonoma.

Federal Writers' Collection: Works Progress Administration, Federal Writers' Project, Oakland, California, Collection on Migratory Labor in California, Bancroft Library, University of California, Berkeley.

FERA Records: Records of the Federal Emergency Relief Administration, Record Group 69, National Archives, Washington, D.C.

FSA Collection, Bancroft: Farm Security Administration Collection, Bancroft Library, University of California.

FSA Records, San Bruno: Records of the Farm Security Administration, Record Group 96, Federal Archives and Regional Center, San Bruno, California.

Goldschmidt Records, San Bruno: Records of Walter R. Goldschmidt–Central Valley Project Studies, 1942–46, Record Group 83, Bureau of Agricultural Economics, Western Regional Office, Federal Archives and Regional Center, San Bruno, California.

Haynes Collection: John Randolph Haynes Foundation Manuscript Collection, Special Collections Library, University of California, Los Angeles.

JEMF Quarterly: *John Edwards Memorial Foundation Quarterly* (Los Angeles).

La Follette Committee, Hearings: U.S. Congress, Senate, Subcommittee of the Committee on Education and Labor to Investigate Violations of the Right of Free Speech and Assembly and Interference with the Right of Labor to Organize and Bargain Collectively. Pursuant to S. Res. 266, 74th Congress, *Hearings* (Washington, 1940).

McWilliams Collection: Carey McWilliams Manuscript Collection, Special Collections Library, University of California, Los Angeles.

Odyssey Program: California Odyssey: The 1930s Migration to the Southern San Joaquin Valley, Oral History Program, California State College, Bakersfield Library.

Public Use Microdata Sample: U.S. Bureau of the Census, *Census of Population, Public Use Microdata Samples* (machine-readable data files for 1940, 1950, 1970 censuses). See Appendix B.

Taylor Collection: Paul S. Taylor Collection, Bancroft Library, University of California, Berkeley.

Todd-Sonkin recordings and field notes: Charles L. Todd and Robert Sonkin Migrant Recordings, 1940 and 1941, Archive of Folk Culture, Library of Congress. Collection includes recordings, field notes, and some song transcriptions.

Tolan Committee, Hearings: U.S. Congress, House of Representatives, Select Committee to Investigate the Interstate Migration of Destitute Citizens. Pursuant to H. Res. 63, 491, 629 (76th Congress) and H. Res. 16 (77th Congress), *Hearings* (Washington, 1940, 1941).

Wasco field notes: Walter Goldschmidt's 1941 Wasco field notes, in Professor Walter Goldschmidt's possession, Department of Anthropology, University of California, Los Angeles.

Women Farmworkers Project: Women Farmworkers Oral History Project, interviews by Margo McBane, Mary Winegarden, and Rick Topkins, copies in author's possession.

Notes

Introduction

1. Dorothea Lange, "The Assignment I'll Never Forget: Migrant Mother," *Popular Photography* 46 (Feb. 1960), 42–43; Paul Taylor, "Migrant Mother: 1936," *American West* 7 (May 1970), 41–45; Milton Meltzer, *Dorothea Lange: A Photographer's Life* (New York, 1978), 132–36.

2. See, for example, Dan Fowler, "What's Become of the Okies," *Look* (Jan. 13, 1953), 19–21; Oliver Carlson, "Up from the Dust," *U.S.A.* (Aug. 1952), 97–104; "Grapes of Joy," *Newsweek* (Sept. 3, 1945), 31; or the more recent articles cited elsewhere in this volume.

3. The church listings are from the Bakersfield telephone directory. The area's recent political leanings are discussed in Tony Quinn, "Anatomy of an Electorate: 75% Faithful, 25% Fickle," *California Journal* 13 (March 1982), 100–102; Michael Barone, Grant Ujifusa, Douglas Matthews, *The Almanac of American Politics 1978* (New York, 1977), 77–81; *The Almanac of American Politics 1982* (Wash., D.C., 1982), 100–101; Michael W. Donley, Stuart Allan, Patricia Caro, and Clyde P. Patton, *Atlas of California* (Culver City, Calif., 1979), 54–57.

4. Ernest L. Martin interview, by Judith Gannon, South Pasadena, April 15, 1981, California Odyssey Oral History Program, California State College, Bakersfield, 32–33.

5. These are minimal migration estimates based on the number of Southern and West North Central Division natives living in the West, Northeast, and East North Central Division in 1970. U.S. Bureau of the Census, *1970 Census of the Population,*

Subject Reports: State of Birth (Wash., D.C., 1973), 43–44, 49–50, 55–56, 61–62. On the black diaspora see James R. Grossman, *Land of Hope: Black Southerners, Chicago, and the Great Migration* (Chicago, 1989); Joe William Trotter, Jr., *Black Milwaukee* (Urbana, 1985); Peter Gottlieb, *Making Their Own Way: Southern Blacks' Migration to Pittsburgh, 1916–30* (Urbana, 1987).

6. Like the Dust Bowl migration, the resettlement experience of Southern whites in the North is the subject of a famous novel, Harriette Arnow's *The Dollmaker* (New York, 1954). Scholarly accounts include Robert Coles, *The South Goes North* (Boston, 1967), 313–420; Lewis M. Killian, *White Southerners* (New York, 1970), 91–119, and his dissertation "Southern White Laborers in Chicago's West Side" (University of Chicago, 1949); Todd Gitlin and Nanci Hollander, *Uptown: Poor Whites in Chicago* (New York, 1970); William W. Philliber and Clyde B. McCoy with Harry Dillingham, eds., *The Invisible Minority: Urban Appalachians* (Lexington, 1981). Several dissertations and master's theses have been contributed by University of Chicago students: Don Edward Merten, "Up Here and Down Home: Appalachian Migrants in Northtown" (1974); Edwin S. Harwood, "Work and Community Among Urban Newcomers: A Study of the Social and Economic Adaptation of Southern Migrants in Chicago" (1966); Rosemary Deyling, "Hillbillies in Steelville: A Study of Participation in Community Life" (1949). Also Eldon Dee Smith, "Migration and Adjustment Experiences of Rural Migrant Workers in Indianapolis" (Ph.D. diss., University of Wisconsin, 1953); and Harry P. Sharp, "Migration and Social Participation in the Detroit Area" (Ph.D. diss., University of Michigan, 1954). Two of the earliest reports on Southern white migrants are Grace G. Leybourne, "Urban Adjustments of Migrants from the Southern Appalachian Plateaus," *Social Forces* 16 (Dec. 1937), 238–46; and Erdmann Doanne Beynon, "The Southern White Laborer Migrates to Michigan," *American Sociological Review* 3 (June 1938), 333–43.

Chapter 1. Out of the Heartland

1. Katherine Archibald, *Wartime Shipyard: A Study in Social Disunity* (Berkeley, 1947), 44.

2. Students of regionalism have been no less divided. The Census Bureau groups Oklahoma, Texas, and Arkansas with Louisiana in the West South Central Division and gives Missouri to the West North Central. Regional sociologist Howard Odum parceled out the four states between three separate regions, placing Missouri in the Midwest, Arkansas in the Southeast, and Oklahoma and Texas in the Southwest. "The Way of the South," *Social Forces* 23 (March 1945), 258–69. Cultural geographers, on the other hand, slice up the states, finding large zones of Southern culture in each of them. See Raymond D. Gastil, *Cultural Regions of the United States* (Seattle, 1975); Wilbur Zelinsky, *The Cultural Geography of the United States* (Englewood Cliffs, 1973), 118–25. Sociologist John Sheldon Reed, *One South: An Ethnic Approach to Regional Culture* (Baton Rouge, 1982), 66–70, uses a cognitive test of Southernness to argue that Oklahoma, Texas, and Missouri are not genuine Southern states.

3. D. W. Meinig, *Imperial Texas: An Interpretive Essay in Cultural Geography* (Austin, 1969), 38–56; Terry G. Jordan, "The Imprint of Upper and Lower South

on Mid-Nineteenth-Century Texas," *Annals of the Association of American Geographers* 57 (Dec. 1967), 667–90; Ray Allen Billington, *Westward Expansion: A History of the American Frontier* (New York, 1974, 4th ed.), 392–430; Milton D. Rafferty, *Missouri: A Geography* (Boulder, 1983), 49–73; Howard Wight Marshall, "Meat Preservation on the Farm in Missouri's 'Little Dixie,' " *Journal of American Folklore* 92 (Oct.–Dec. 1979), 400–417; Michael Owen Roark, "Oklahoma Territory: Frontier Development, Migration, and Culture Areas" (unpublished Ph.D. diss., Syracuse University, 1979); Michael Frank Doran, "The Origins of Culture Areas in Oklahoma, 1830–1900" (unpublished Ph.D. diss., University of Oregon, 1974); Douglas Hale, "The People of Oklahoma: Economics and Social Change," in Anne Hodges Morgan and H. Wayne Morgan, eds., *Oklahoma: New Views of the Forty-sixth State* (Norman, 1982), 34–50.

4. Donald J. Bogue and Calvin L. Beale, *Economic Areas of the United States* (New York, 1961), is an extraordinary resource for regional and subregional comparisons. See also Rupert B. Vance, *Human Geography of the South: A Study in Regional Resources and Human Adequacy* (Chapel Hill, 1935), 316–50; Meinig, *Imperial Texas*, 91–108; Doran, "Culture Areas in Oklahoma," esp. 16.

5. Oscar Lewis, *On the Edge of the Black Waxy: A Cultural Study of Bell County, Texas* (St. Louis, 1948), 2.

6. Bogue and Beale, *Economic Areas of the United States*, 355–70, 374–85; Vance, *Human Geography of the South*, 325–32; Meinig, *Imperial Texas*, 50, 107–8; Sheila Manes, "Pioneers and Survivors: Oklahoma's Landless Farmers," in Morgan and Morgan, *Oklahoma*, 106–8; Evon Z. Vogt, *Modern Homesteaders: The Life of a Twentieth-Century Frontier Community* (Cambridge, Mass., 1955), 11–17, 90–93.

7. Varden Fuller, *Rural Worker Adjustment to Urban Life: An Assessment of the Research* (Ann Arbor, 1970), 11–41, provides a helpful overview of many aspects of rural transformation. Studies focusing on the South include Jack Temple Kirby, *Rural Worlds Lost: The American South 1920–1960* (Baton Rouge, 1987); Gilbert C. Fite, *Cotton Fields No More: Southern Agriculture 1865–1980* (Lexington, 1984), 233; Neil Fligstein, *Going North: Migration of Blacks and Whites from the South, 1900–1950* (New York, 1981). Hal S. Barron, *Those Who Stayed Behind: Rural Society in Nineteenth-Century New England* (New York, 1984), 11–15, also has some useful data on rural depopulation.

8. The farm labor force statistics are from Everett S. Lee, Ann Ratner Miller, Carol P. Brainerd, Richard A. Easterlin, *Population Redistribution and Economic Growth: United States, 1870–1950*, Vol. I (Philadelphia, 1957), table L-4, pp. 609–21. Rural farm population data are from U.S. Bureau of the Census, *Fifteenth Census of the United States: 1930 Population* (Wash., D.C., 1932), Vol. III, Part I, p. 30; *Seventeenth Census of the United States: 1950 Population* (Wash., D.C., 1953) Vol. II, Part I, pp. 1–105. Various reports on the modernization of agriculture in the Southwest can be found in Part 5 of the published *Hearings* conducted by the House Select Committee to Investigate the Interstate Migration of Destitute Citizens, Pursuant to H.Res. 63, 491, 629 (76th Congress) and H.Res. 16 (77th Congress) (Wash., D.C., 1941) (hereafter cited as the Tolan Committee). See also Sheila Goldring Manes, "Depression Pioneers: The Conclusion of an American Odyssey, Oklahoma to California, 1930–1950, a Reinterpretation" (unpublished

Ph.D. diss., University of California, Los Angeles, 1982); Paul Faulkner Tjensvold, "An Inquiry into the Reasons for the Post-Depression Migration from Oklahoma to Kern County in California" (unpublished MA thesis, University of Southern California, 1947), 6–22; Garry L. Nall, "King Cotton in Oklahoma, 1825–1939," in Donald E. Green, ed., *Rural Oklahoma* (Oklahoma City, 1977), 37–55; Paul Taylor, "Power Farming and Labor Displacement in the Cotton Belt," *Monthly Labor Review* 46 (March–April 1938), 595–607, 852–67. The best studies of Arkansas depopulation were conducted by rural sociologist William H. Metzler: "Population Trends and Adjustments in Arkansas," *Arkansas Agricultural Experiment Station Bulletin* No.388 (May 1940); "Migration of Farm Families to Urban Centers in Arkansas" and "Population Pressure in Upland Areas of Arkansas," both in Tolan Committee, *Hearings*, Part 6, pp. 1997–2011.

9. U.S. Bureau of the Census, *1930 Census of Population*, Vol. III, Part I, pp. 184–88, 1339–46; Part II, pp. 558–63, 975–80; Judith Anne Gilbert, "Migrations of Oklahoma Farm Population 1930–1940" (MA thesis, University of Oklahoma, 1965), 25–39; J. T. Sanders, "The Economic and Social Aspects of Mobility of Oklahoma Farmers," *Oklahoma Agricultural Experiment Station Bulletin* No. 195 (Aug. 1929).

10. Ray Allen Billington, *America's Frontier Heritage* (New York, 1966), 190; George W. Pierson, *The Moving American* (New York, 1973), 170. This is asserted more than it has been proven, but seems true enough for migration to California. Peter R. Decker, *Fortunes and Failures: White Collar Mobility in Nineteenth-Century San Francisco* (Cambridge, Mass., 1978) shows that post-gold-rush newcomers to San Francisco were predominantly of the middling classes, and observers of the southern California influx up to 1930 were uniformly emphatic on that point. See Carey McWilliams, *Southern California: An Island on the Land* (1946, reprint edition Santa Barbara, 1973), 156–60; Robert M. Fogelson, *The Fragmented Metropolis: Los Angeles 1850–1930* (Cambridge, Mass., 1967), 63–84.

11. Walter D. Davenport, "California, Here We Come," *Collier's* (Aug. 10, 1935), 10. California's image and its meanings for Americans living elsewhere are the subjects of Kevin Starr's two books, *Americans and the California Dream, 1850–1915* (New York, 1973) and *Inventing the Dream: California Through the Progressive Era* (New York, 1985). See also McWilliams, *Southern California*; Oliver Carlson, *A Mirror for Californians* (New York, 1941).

12. Warren S. Thompson, *Growth and Changes in California's Population* (Los Angeles, 1955), 10; Fogelson, *Fragmented Metropolis*, 63–84.

13. Elbert Ray Garretson interview, by Michael Neely, June 25–26, 1981, Palmdale, California Odyssey Oral History Program, California State College, Bakersfield, 3 (hereafter Odyssey Program).

14. Vera Ruth Woodall Criswell interview, by Stacey Jagels, Feb. 24, 26, 1981, Lindsay, Odyssey Program, 10.

15. Audie Moffitt interview, by author, June 5, 1981, Long Beach. See also the Odyssey Program interview with Clarence William Graham. Frederick L. Ryan, *The Rehabilitation of Oklahoma Coal Mining Communities* (Norman, 1935), 73, reports that a substantial number of coal miners moved to Los Angeles as that industry began to decline in eastern Oklahoma in the mid-1920s.

16. Velma May Cooper Davis interview, by Judith Gannon, May 25, 1981,

Delano, Odyssey Program, 9. On the introduction of cotton see Paul S. Taylor and Tom Vasey, "Contemporary Background of California Farm Labor," *Rural Sociology* 1 (Dec. 1936), 413–19; Devra Anne Weber, "The Struggle for Stability and Control in the Cotton Fields of California: Class Relations in Agriculture, 1919–1942" (unpublished Ph.D. diss., University of California, Los Angeles, 1986).

17. Mrs. G, 1941 Wasco field notes, in Walter Goldschmidt's personal files, Department of Anthropology, University of California, Los Angeles (hereafter Wasco field notes).

18. Mr.W.B.B., Wasco field notes.

19. Max Stern, "Cotton Goes West," *Nation* 123 (July 14, 1926), 30; D.J. Whitney, "White Labor Harvested Raisins," *Pacific Rural Press* (Oct. 22, 1921), 416; California State Relief Administration, M.H. Lewis, *Migratory Labor in California* (San Francisco, 1936), 142; Paul S. Taylor, "Again the Covered Wagon," *Survey Graphic* 24 (July, 1935), 349.

20. Exact numbers are not available. The census (see Table 1.1) reported net increases of 243,339 in the 1920s and 315,124 in the 1930s. But these numbers neglect those earlier settlers who died or left the state during each decade. For the 1930s we have an additional bit of data. The 1940 census asked where people had lived on April 1, 1935, and counted 251,989 California residents who had lived in the Western South five years earlier. If the inflow during the first half of the decade was half as great, the total for the 1930s would have been approximately 375,000. This, it should be noted, refers only to those migrants who stayed in California until the end of the decade. Many others, as we will see in Chapter 4, returned home after a brief stay. The migration data are from U.S. Bureau of the Census, *Sixteenth Census of the United States, 1940: Population, Internal Migration 1935 to 1940, Color and Sex of Migrants* (Wash., D.C., 1943), table 16, pp. 105, 112–14.

21. Dorothea Lange and Paul Schuster Taylor, *An American Exodus: A Record of Human Erosion* (New York, 1939). The refugee image also figures in Carey McWilliams, *Ill Fares the Land: Migrants and Migratory Labor in the United States* (Boston, 1942); California State Chamber of Commerce, *Migrants: A National Problem and Its Impact on California*, reprinted in Tolan Committee, *Hearings*, Part 6, pp. 2755–91; Henry Hill Collins, Jr., *America's Own Refugees: Our 4,000,000 Homeless Migrants* (Princeton, 1941); George Gleason, *The Fifth Migration: A Report on the California Migratory Agricultural Worker Situation*, reprinted in Tolan Committee, *Hearings*, Part 7, 2995–3012. Among recent studies of the Dust Bowl migration, Jacqueline Gordon Sherman, "The Oklahomans in California During the Depression Decade, 1931–1941" (unpublished Ph.D. diss., University of California, Los Angeles, 1970), sees the migrants in the same tragic terms. The two major historical works on the subject take a more complex view of the factors promoting migration. Walter J. Stein, *California and the Dust Bowl Migration* (Westport, Conn., 1973); Manes, "Depression Pioneers."

22. I am aware that some migration theorists would conceptualize the matter differently. Subscribers to the wage differential model of migration would argue that the pull of California simply became more pronounced during the 1930s. This is the line of analysis followed by Hope T. Eldridge and Dorothy Swaine Thomas, *Population Redistribution and Economic Growth: United States, 1870–1950*, Vol.

III, pp. 345–67. On the other hand, sociologist Neil Fligstein, *Going North*, has recently argued that throughout the twentieth century Southern outmigration, including the exodus from the Western South, is best understood as an expulsive process. He sees Northern and Western opportunities as a more or less constant factor which became relevant only when local conditions required Southerners to think about leaving home. Though harder to deal with mathematically, I am persuaded that push-pull models are far more adequate for explaining migration scenarios. My thinking on this has been influenced by Donald Bogue's hypothesis as summarized in Clifford J. Jansen, "Migration: A Sociological Problem," in Jansen, ed., *Readings in the Sociology of Migration* (Oxford, 1970), 15–16. Also by Pierson, *The Moving Americans*, 165–89.

23. Works Progress Administration, Division of Social Research, *Social Problems of the Drought Area*, Research Bulletins Series V (Wash., D.C., 1937), remains the indispensable source on the drought. Metzler, "Population Pressure in Upland Areas of Arkansas," 2903–4, documents the drought damage to Ozark counties.

24. The 16,000 figure is calculated from census data found in Donald J. Bogue, Henry S. Shryock, Jr., and Siegfried A. Hoerman, *Subregional Migration in the United States, 1935–1940, Vol. I: Streams of Migration Between Subregions* (Oxford, Ohio, 1957), table 1, pp. lxxxiii- cxxxiii. A number of studies chronicle the Dust Bowl devastation: Donald Worster, *Dust Bowl: The Southern Plains in the 1930s* (New York, 1979); Paul Bonnifield, *The Dust Bowl: Men, Dirt, and Depression* (Albuquerque, 1979); Fred Floyd, "A History of the Dust Bowl" (unpublished Ph.D. diss., University of Oklahoma, 1950).

25. Gilbert, "Migrations of Oklahoma's Farm Population," 42. Gilbert also shows that despite problems and turnover, more Oklahomans moved on to farms than off them during the first four years of the Depression. Marginal areas of eastern Oklahoma and the Ozarks which had lost population in the twenties became temporarily repopulated as a result of the back-to-the-land impulse of that period. For Arkansas examples see the letters and questionnaires in the Pamela Webb Collection, University of Arkansas Library, Special Collections. And for a revealing look at the Depression's impact on an Arkansas farming community see the 1924 and 1936 typescript reports on Nashville, Arkansas, in the Dept. of Agricultural Economics and Rural Sociology Collection in the same library.

26. U.S. Bureau of the Census, *Seventeenth Census of the United States: 1950 Agriculture* (Wash., D.C., 1953), Vol. II, table 75, pp. 628–29.

27. U.S. Bureau of the Census, *Fifteenth Census of the United States: 1930 Agriculture* (Wash., D.C., 1932), Vol. II, Part I, pp. 30–31. On the development of tenancy in the region see Manes, "Depression Pioneers," 50–173. Important contemporary reports include: National Resources Committee, *Report of the President's Committee on Farm Tenancy* (Wash., D.C., 1937); John H. Southern, "Farm Tenancy in Oklahoma," *Oklahoma Agricultural Experiment Station Bulletin* No. 239 (Dec. 1939); J. A. Baker and J. G. McNeely, "Land Tenure in Arkansas: I. The Farm Tenancy Situation," *Arkansas Agricultural Experiment Station Bulletin* No. 384 (Jan. 1940). See also the various documents and reports compiled in the Tolan Committee, *Hearings*, Part 5. The distinction between sharecroppers and share renters was economically, socially, and even legally significant. The former typically furnished nothing in the way of farming equipment and turned over half

of their annual crop to the landlord. Under Oklahoma law they could not claim the contract rights of tenants. For legal purposes sharecroppers were employees, not renters.

28. Lange and Taylor, *An American Exodus*, 80. The AAA's impact on tenant farmers has been examined in several recent studies: David Eugene Conrad, *The Forgotten Farmers: The Story of Sharecroppers in the New Deal* (Urbana, 1965); Donald H. Grubbs, *Cry from the Cotton: The Southern Tenant Farmer's Union and the New Deal* (Chapel Hill, 1971); Fite, *Cotton Fields No More*, 128–62.

29. U.S. Bureau of the Census, *1930 Census of Agriculture*, Vol. II, Part I, pp. 30–31; *1950 Census of Agriculture*, Vol. II, table 21, pp. 968–86.

30. Broadus Mitchell, *Depression Decade* (New York, 1969), 91–96, and John A. Garraty, *Unemployment in History: Economic Thought and Public Policy* (New York, 1978), 167–71, discuss the problems with 1930s unemployment statistics, including the three data sets used here. The voluntary 1937 unemployment census was particularly problematic and is not reported in Table 1.2. The 1937 data in that table comes instead from the follow-up spot survey used to evaluate and criticize the accuracy of the original census.

31. David Ellery Rison, *Arkansas During the Great Depression* (unpublished Ph.D. diss., University of California, Los Angeles, 1974), 34; U.S. Works Progress Administration, *Final Statistical Report of the Federal Emergency Relief Administration* (Wash., D.C., 1942), table xiv, pp. 235–47; Gilbert, "Migrations of Oklahoma's Farm Population," 81; Metzler, "Migration of Farm Families to Urban Centers in Arkansas," 1998–2001. Local and state efforts to cope with the area's economic problems and care for the unemployed and homeless have been detailed in a number of excellent MA theses: Dove Montgomery Kull, "Social and Economic Factors Affecting Unemployment in Oklahoma" (University of Oklahoma, 1940); Bobby Thomas Quinten, "The Social Impact of the Great Depression on Metropolitan Tulsa, 1929–1932" (Oklahoma State University, 1963); John Mitchell, "Greer County, Oklahoma and the Great Depression 1929–1942" (University of Oklahoma, 1962); Norman W. Cooper, "Oklahoma in the Great Depression, 1930–1940: The Problem of Emergency Relief" (University of Oklahoma, 1973). Worster, *Dust Bowl*, 131–36, describes relief activities in Cimarron County, Oklahoma.

32. The data on relief grants is from Works Progress Administration, *Final Statistical Report of the Federal Emergency Relief Administration*, tables vii, viii, pp. 169–76. On WPA wages see California Chamber of Commerce, *The Migrants*, table 9, p. 2784. The "minimal subsistence" budget is an estimate derived from two sources. U.S. Works Progress Administration, Margaret Loomis Stecker, *Intercity Differences in Cost of Living in March 1935, 59 Cities*, Research Monograph XII (Wash., D.C., 1937), 5, suggested that $70 a month constituted an "emergency" budget for Oklahoma City residents. The California State Relief Administration meanwhile used a lower figure ($65) for its "minimal subsistence" guidelines. Adjusting that to reflect the 7 percent cost-of-living differential between the two areas yields the $60 figure. For more on budget guidelines see the Minutes of the Cotton Picking Wage Hearing, Sept. 28–29, 1939, Fresno, Exhibits A-D, in Carey McWilliams Collection, Special Collections Library, University of California, Los Angeles (hereafter McWilliams Collection).

33. Mattie Cal Gibson, "The Dependent Family in the Oklahoma City Com-

munity Camp" (unpublished MA thesis, University of Oklahoma, 1934); Fred
A. Replogle, *Survey of Welfare Activities in Oklahoma City*, Part II (Oklahoma
City, 1936), 31–33; Ruth Fischer Lowry, "An Analysis of One Hundred Families Residing in Community Camp, Oklahoma City, 1941" (MSW thesis, University of Oklahoma, 1945). Housing problems in Tulsa are described in
Quinten, "The Social Impact of the Great Depression on Metropolitan Tulsa,"
26–28.

34. Charles Todd and Robert Sonkin Migrant Recordings, Aug. 27, 1941, Visalia, in the Archive of Folk Culture, Library of Congress (hereafter Todd-Sonkin
Recordings).

35. U.S. Department of Agriculture, Bureau of Agricultural Economics, Seymour J. Janow, "Volume and Characteristics of Recent Migration to the Far West,"
Tolan Committee, *Hearings*, Part 6, table 16-A, p. 2307. Missourians were not
counted as Southwesterners in these data, nor was the survey fully representative.
The information was collected by public school officials from pupils whose families
had come to California since 1930. Individuals and families without school-age
children would not have been counted.

36. The data are from the 1940 Public Use Microdata Sample, a machine-
readable data file produced by the Bureau of the Census (Wash., D.C., 1983) (see
Appendix A). There is some possibility that the number of former farm residents
was under-reported in the census. Enumerators noted that former rural residents
sometimes simplified their answers and mentioned nearby towns or cities as their
earlier place of residence. See U.S. Bureau of the Census, *1940 Population: Color
and Sex of Migrants*, 4.

37. Everyone who has written about the Depression-era migration from the
Southwest overlooks the urban component. Even Walter Stein, *California and the
Dust Bowl Migration*, 16, who is usually very careful, asserts that "only a few city
people" joined the migration. Manes, "Depression Pioneers," 17, and Sherman,
"Oklahomans in California," 72, make the same mistake.

38. Lillie Eva Grose May interview, by Michael Neely, June 2, 16, 1981, Grover
City, Odyssey Program.

39. Robert Lewis Kessler Jr. interview, by Michael Neely, May 26, 28, 1981,
Auberry, Odyssey Program.

40. See Chapter 8.

41. Tolan Committee, *Hearings*, Part 5, p. 2063.

42. U.S. Department of Agriculture, Bureau of Agricultural Economics and
Farm Security Administration, *Population in Farm Security Administration Migratory Labor Camps*, No. 1 (Berkeley, 1940), 15, found that 28 percent of camp
users had at one time or another been farm owners and 51 percent had experience
as tenants. These figures are similar to what Lillian Creisler found in a smaller
survey of resettled migrants living near Modesto: " 'Little Oklahoma' or the Airport
Community: A Study of the Social and Economic Adjustment of Self-settled Agricultural Drought and Depression Refugees" (unpublished MA thesis, University
of California, Berkeley, 1940), 31.

43. Commonwealth Club of California, *The Population of California* (San
Francisco, 1946), table 42, p. 114: Of the 251,989 Southwesterners who settled
in California between 1935 and 1940, only 11,829 were blacks. See also Law-

rence B. de Graaf, *Negro Migration to Los Angeles, 1930–1950* (San Francisco, 1974).
44. 1940 Census Public Use Microdata Sample.
45.

Median Completed School Grade for Oklahoma, Arkansas, Texas, Missouri Males
Aged 25–34 by 1935 Residence and 1940 Migration Status

| | 1940 migration status | |
1935 residence	Non-migrants	Outmigrants*
Rural farm	8.0	8.4
Rural non-farm	8.8	10.3
Urban	10.0	11.8
All locations	8.8	10.3

*Outmigrants to non-continuous states, primarily California.

Source: U.S. Bureau of the Census, *Sixteenth Census of the United States: 1940 Population. Internal Migration, Social Characteristics of Migrants* (Wash., D.C., 1943), table 23, pp. 112–90.

See also Robert T. McMillan, "Migration of Population in Five Oklahoma Townships," *Oklahoma Agricultural Experiment Station Bulletin* No. B-271 (Oct. 1943), 29; Fuller, *Rural Worker Adjustment to Urban Life*, 44–47.
46. 1940 Census Public Use Microdata Sample.
47. Tolan Committee, *Hearings*, Part 7, 2903–4.
48. Letter from Bob Hardie to Tom Collins, Dec. 10, 1936, in Records of the Farm Security Administration, RG96, Federal Archives and Regional Center, San Bruno, California, Box 19 (hereafter FSA Records, San Bruno). A number of investigators surveyed groups of migrants on their reasons for coming. See Walter Goldschmidt, *As You Sow* (Glencoe, 1947, reprinted Montclair, N.J., 1978), 150–51; Creisler, "Little Oklahoma," 11; Walter Evans Hoadley, Jr., "A Study of One Hundred Seventy Self-Resettled Agricultural Families, Monterey County, California, 1939" (unpublished MA thesis, University of California, Berkeley, 1940), 51–54; Stuart M. Jamieson, "A Settlement of Rural Migrant Families in the Sacramento Valley, California," *Rural Sociology* VII (March 1942), 53. James Bright Wilson, "Social Attitudes of Certain Migratory Agricultural Workers in Kern County, California" (unpublished MA thesis, University of Southern California, 1942), 74–105, transcribes the thoughts of some 60 migrants on this and other subjects.
49. Collections of these newspapers, most of which were published between 1938 and 1942, can be found in the University of California, Berkeley, Documents Library, and in Bancroft Library. Other copies are in FSA Records, San Bruno.
50. The two young men were commissioned by the Library of Congress to collect folk songs among the migrants in California during the summers of 1940 and 1941. The results of their project—almost 12 hours of recorded songs, folklore, and personal interviews and an accompanying volume of field notes—can be found in the Todd-Sonkin Recordings. The Archive of Folk Culture also houses a smaller collection of migrant songs recorded by Margaret Valiant, an amateur folklorist, during 1938. A partial copy of the Todd-Sonkin field notes and several unpublished

manuscripts by Todd reside in the Charles Todd Okie Studies Archive, in care of Prof. Gerald Haslam, Department of English, California State University, Sonoma (hereafter Charles Todd Collection).

51. Frank Kline, "Attention, Chamber of Commerce!," *The Voice of the Agricultural Worker* (Yuba City) (March 15, 1940).

52. Imogene Chapin, "The Job's Just Around the Corner," Arvin, Aug. 1, 1940, Todd-Sonkin Recordings.

53. The Prodical's [sic] Return," *The Covered Wagon* (Indio) (Feb. 4, 1940). Mary Sullivan, "Sunny California," Shafter, Aug. 9, 1941, Todd-Sonkin Recordings.

54. Aug. 17, 1940, Todd-Sonkin Recordings.

55. Sung by Gussie Ward Stone, July 2, 1940, Arvin, California, Todd-Sonkin Recordings. Margaret Valiant, Migrant Camp Recordings, also caught a large crowd singing the song at one of the FSA camps in 1938. See also *The Covered Wagon* (Indio) (March 4, 1939). U.S. Works Projects Administration, California, *A Study of California Folk Music* (Berkeley, 1940), 5, reports that variants of the song had been sung for over 70 years on the "westering high roads in America," but since 1933 it had been the song of the Okies in California. For other discussions of the importance of the song see Charles Todd and Robert Sonkin, "Ballads of the Okies," *New York Times Magazine* (Nov. 17, 1940), 6; Sheldon S. Kagan, " 'Goin' Down the Road Feelin' Bad': John Steinbeck's Grapes of Wrath and Migrant Folklore" (unpublished Ph.D. diss., University of Pennsylvania, 1971), passim; Bill C. Malone, *Country Music U.S.A.: A Fifty Year History* (Austin, 1968), 140. Woody Guthrie recorded his own version of the song, entitled "Blowin' Down This Road," as one of his Dust Bowl ballads (Victor P27-P28).

56. Todd-Sonkin Recordings.

57. Photograph, Tolan Committee, *Hearings*, Part 5, 2062f. See "California: No Hobo Utopia; Los Angeles Police Chief Sends Patrolmen to Guard Border," *Literary Digest* (Feb. 15, 1936), 9; "Golden State Insists on Golden Passports," *Newsweek* (Feb. 15, 1936), 15.

58. Carlson, *A Mirror for Californians*, 54.

59. On the film industry's Depression-era preoccupations see Robert Sklar, *Movie-Made America: A Cultural History of American Movies* (New York, 1975), 175–214; Richard H. Pells, *Radical Visions and American Dreams: Culture and Social Thought in the Depression Years* (New York, 1973, reprinted Middletown, Conn., 1984), 263–91. Roger Dooley, *From Scarface to Scarlet: American Films in the 1930s* (New York, 1979), is a virtual encyclopedia of the period's films.

60. The manufacturing employment data are from Frank L. Kidner, *California Business Cycles* (Berkeley, 1946), 55. Kidner argues that California's business cycle closely paralleled the nation's, but he notes that the food product sector cushioned the initial collapse to some extent, while the new aircraft industry helped to give the state economy a somewhat stronger recovery than the national average (p.112–14). See also Emily H. Huntington, *Unemployment Relief and the Unemployed in the San Francisco Bay Region 1929–1934* (Berkeley, 1939), 5–9; Glen H. Elder, Jr., *Children of the Great Depression: Social Change in Life Experience* (Chicago, 1974), 18–20; Robert Edward Rapp, "Some Aspects of the Rural Relief Problem in California as Revealed in Ten Selected Counties" (unpublished Ph.D. diss., Stanford University, 1937), esp. 65–66.

61. Thompson, *Growth and Changes*, 143.

62. Cost of living differences ate up some of this. Stecker, *Intercity Differences in Cost of Living*, 5, reports that prices in Los Angeles exceeded Oklahoma City by approximately 7 percent.

63. U.S Bureau of the Census, *Sixteenth Census of the United States: 1940 Agriculture* (Wash., D.C., 1943), Vol. III, 47–48; Thompson, *Growth and Changes*, Appendix table 23, p. 373.

64. Another measure of the regional differential are the daily wage rates for general farm labor as reported for the Bureau of Agricultural Economics by E. D. Tetreau, "Profile of Farm Wage Rates in the Southwest," *Rural Sociology* IV (March 1939), 37.

State	Jan. 1, 1936	Jan. 1, 1937	Jan. 1, 1938
Arkansas	$ 0.90	$ 1.00	$ 1.05
Oklahoma	1.20	1.30	1.35
Texas	1.15	1.25	1.35
California	2.50	2.70	3.00

65. Tolan Committee, *Hearings*, 2210.

66. *Bakersfield Californian*, September 16, 1979. See also Tjensvold, "Migration from Oklahoma to Kern County," 20.

67. California State Relief Administration, M.H. Lewis, *State Welfare Survey*, Part I (n.p., 1935?) pagination omitted. For comparisons see Works Progress Administration, *Final Statistical Report of the Federal Emergency Relief Administration*, tables vii, viii, pp. 169–76.

68. Wilson, "Social Attitudes of Migratory Agricultural Workers," 124 (quoting Daniel Goddard*). Rapp, "Some Aspects of the Rural Relief Problem in California," 125, used 250 reports from farms and businesses in California to estimate the following average daily wage rates for June 1936:

	Skilled	Unskilled
Agriculture	$ 4.39	$ 2.98
Retail trades	4.15	3.60
Industry	5.08	3.78

69. Wilson, "Social Attitudes of Migratory Agricultural Workers," 289 (Martin Childs*).

70. *Ibid.*, 97 (Wiley Cuddard, Jr.*). Wilson noted that of the 60 Southwesterners he interviewed, 17 discussed letters from relatives about relief benefits as a "factor which influenced them or other migrants to come to California" (p. 104); Cheryl Beth Campbell, "A Study of the Federal Transient Program with Special Reference to Fifty Transient Families in Los Angeles" (unpublished MA thesis, University of Southern California, 1936), 92, also reported that many migrants were attracted by California's "liberal" relief policies. Other reports disagreed. See Tom Collins, Kern Migratory Labor Camp Report, Feb. 22, 1936, Box 22, and Bob Hardie letter to Tom Collins, Dec. 15, 1936, Box 19, in FSA Records, San Bruno. Tjensvold,

"Migration from Oklahoma to Kern County," 10, argues that those already receiving relief in the Southwest were probably less inclined to leave than others since it would mean giving up an income, however small, for the uncertainties of California, where they would have to wait at least a year before becoming eligible for most kinds of relief. See also Walter Stein, "The Okie as Farm Laborer," *Agricultural History*, 49 (Jan. 1975), 211–12.

71. U.S. Bureau of the Census, *1930 Population*, Vol. II, p. 158; *1940 State of Birth*, pp. 21, 26. See also Eldridge and Thomas, *Population Redistribution and Economic Growth*, Vol. III, pp. 115, 125; C. Horace Hamilton, "Continuity and Change in Southern Migration," in John C. McKinney and Edgar T. Thompson, eds., *The South in Continuity and Change* (Durham, 1965), 55–57.

72. On the importance of relatives in working-class migration decisions see Charles Tilly, *Migration to an American City*, (Wilmington, Del., 1965), 21–25; Fuller, *Rural Worker Adjustment to Urban Life*, 47–48; Jansen, "Migration: A Sociological Problem," 23–26.

73. Lange and Taylor, *An American Exodus*, 66.

74. Wilson, "Social Attitudes of Migratory Agricultural Workers," 102.

75. *Ibid.*, 104.

76. Mrs. L. G., Wasco field notes.

77. Melvin Shahan interview, by Jackie Malone, Oct. 29, 1976, California State University, Fullerton, Oral History Program, 31.

78. Tolan Committee, *Hearings*, part 7, p. 2905.

79. Hoadley, "170 Self-Resettled Agricultural Families," 55–57; Jamieson, "A Settlement of Migrant Families in the Sacramento Valley," 53–54; Goldschmidt, *As You Sow*, 151. The closest thing to a comparable study of Southwesterners who settled in the metropolitan areas was a 1935 survey of migrant families applying for help at the offices of the Federal Transient Service in Los Angeles, San Francisco, and San Bernardino. The sample included persons from all parts of the country, not just the Southwest. Moreover, those families most likely to need emergency assistance were precisely those without the kinds of kin connections under consideration here. Nevertheless, it is significant that 44 percent of the more than 400 families interviewed said they had come to California in part because of friends and relatives already there. See U.S. Works Progress Administration, Division of Social Research, John N. Webb and Malcolm Brown, *Migrant Families*, Research Monograph XVIII (Wash., D.C., 1938), 138.

80. John Blake interview, by author, Sept. 14, 1979, Bakersfield.

81. James Harvey Lackey interview, by Stacey Jagels, March 31 and April 2, 1981, Bakersfield, Odyssey Program; and by author, April 30, 1985. Other examples of young males on exploratory trips: Sherman Coleman interview, by author, June 12, 1985, Oakland; Davenport, "California, Here We Come," 10; Richard L. Neuberger, "The New Oregon Trail," *Collier's* (March 27, 1937), 15.

82. Hoadley, "170 Self-Resettled Agricultural Families," 58–59. On trans-Atlantic migration chains see Jon Gjerde, *From Peasants to Farmers: The Migration from Balestrand, Norway to the Upper Middle West* (Cambridge, 1985), 116–36; Joseph J. Barton, *Peasants and Strangers: Italians, Rumanians, and Slovaks in an American City, 1890–1950* (Cambridge, Mass., 1975), 48–63; Dino Cinel, *From Italy to San Francisco: The Immigrant Experience* (Stanford, 1982), 26–70.

83. James West (Carl Withers), *Plainville, U.S.A.* (New York, 1945), 25.

84. *The Voice of the Migrant* (Yuba City) (Nov. 19, 1940). Clara Davis interview, by author, Sept. 17, 1979, Bakersfield, and by Stacey Jagels, Jan. 29 and Feb. 12, 1981, Odyssey Program, 28, maintains that "if you're from Pauls Valley, Oklahoma you didn't have any problems out here because half the people out here were from Pauls Valley. I still know them."

85. Mr. L.R., Wasco field notes.

86. Lange and Taylor, *An American Exodus*, 61, 66.

87. Wilson, "Social Attitudes of Migratory Agricultural Workers," 101 (Henry Johnson*). McWilliams, *Ill Fares the Land*, 204, found evidence of the migration spirit in the big cities as well. The newspapers, he noted, were full of notices for rides to California. One issue of the *Oklahoma City Times* contained eight different notices.

88. U.S. Bureau of the Census, *1930 Census of Agriculture*, Vol. IV, pp. 412–27. These three states also ranked near the top in farm mobility in 1920 and 1925 census tabulations.

89. C.M. Evans testimony, Tolan Committee, *Hearings*, part 5,

90. Lange and Taylor, *An American Exodus*, 67.

91. Robert Turner McMillan, "The Interrelation of Migration and Socioeconomic Status of Open-Country Families in Oklahoma" (unpublished Ph.D. diss., Louisiana State University, 1943), 83–103. The comparative figures for other states are from C. E. Lively, "Spatial Mobility of the Rural Population with Respect to Local Areas," *American Journal of Sociology* 43 (July 1937), 93–94. McMillan also conducted a separate study of migration for the Bureau of Agricultural Economics, "Migration of Population in Five Oklahoma Townships" *Oklahoma Agricultural Experiment Station Bulletin* No. B-271 (Oct. 1943), which traced the movements of every member of selected rural communities during the 1930s. These data show that 59 percent of all initial residents had left these communities by the end of the decade, 34 percent had left the county, and 21 percent had left the state (my calculations from tables 3 and 17). This is a low rate of persistence even by urban standards. For comparative data on urban and rural frontier communities see Stephan Thernstrom, *The Other Bostonians: Poverty and Progress in the American Metropolis, 1880–1970* (Cambridge, Mass., 1973), 221–29. Two earlier studies confirm Oklahoma's high rates of rural mobility: Sanders, "The Economic and Social Aspects of Mobility of Oklahoma Farmers," 18–19; O.D. Duncan, "Some Social Aspects of Tenancy and Moving in Oklahoma," Oklahoma Agricultural Experiment Station *Current Farm Economics* (Dec. 1929).

92. McMillan, "The Interrelation of Migration and Socioeconomic Status," 56–57; Ruth Alice Allen, *The Labor of Women in the Production of Cotton* (Chicago, 1931), 37, 50–54; Agricultural State Policy Committee, *Agricultural Labor Problems in Arkansas*, paper No.1 (n.p., Oct. 31, 1936), 19–20; U.S. Resettlement Administration, Land Utilization Division, James G. Maddox, *The Farm Tenancy Situation* (Wash., D.C., 1936), 35–36. Douglas Hale, "The People of Oklahoma," 63, notes that the fluid habits of the tenant population had a disruptive impact on the educational opportunities for larger numbers of rural children.

93. Manes, "Pioneers and Survivors," 124–32; "Depression Pioneers," esp. 163–73.

94. Wilson, "Social Attitudes of Migratory Agricultural Workers," 75.

95. Confirming McMillan's findings on non-agricultural employment among farmers, John William Flucke, "The Influence of Economic Conditions of the Cultural Life of Farm Families in Kingfisher County" (unpublished MA thesis, University of Oklahoma, 1934), 48, reports that 38 percent of farmers in that county had nonfarm work experience.

96. See, for example, William Howarth, "The Okies: Beyond the Dust Bowl," *National Geographic* 166 (Sept. 1984), 323–49; Thomas W. Pew Jr., "Route 66: Ghost Road of the Okies," *American Heritage* 28 (Aug. 1977), 26–32; Stein, *California and the Dust Bowl Migration*, 26.

97. Of course migrants in other eras were not always committed to long stays. Recent studies have shown how frequently immigrants traveled to the United States intending to work for a time and then return home. Thomas J. Archdeacon, *Becoming American: An Ethnic History* (New York, 1983), 136–42, summarizes these findings. Another celebrated transcontinental trek, the gold rush of 1849, fit the same pattern. But modern transportation made this approach all the more feasible and also greatly facilitated the back and forth visiting pattern that has been the basis of the long-lasting commitments to old home areas often found among Southwesterners in California and Southern migrants in Northern cities. James J. Flink, *The Car Culture* (Cambridge, Mass., 1975), 140–90, describes the road-building programs of the 1920s and analyzes the automobile's impact on various features of modern life.

98. Tolan Committee, Hearings, Part 5, p. 2139.

99. Mrs. J.W., Wasco field notes.

100. Campbell, "A Study of the Federal Transient Program," 75, 108.

101. U.S. Department of Agriculture, Bureau of Agricultural Economics, *The Agricultural Labor Force in the San Joaquin Valley—1948* (Wash., D.C., 1950), 55–56; McWilliams, *Ill Fares the Land*, 196.

102. John Blake interview. Blake tells of a friend who made a good living for several years by shuttling people back and forth between Oklahoma and California. See also McWilliams, *Ill Fares the Land*, 204–5.

103. Morris family interview, by Margo McBane and Mary Winegarden, Richmond, July 12, 1978, Women Farmworkers Project.

104. Pew, "Route 66," 29.

105. Tolan Committee, *Hearings*, Part 7, 2904–5.

106. Buck Owens interview, by Jana Jae Greif, Bakersfield, Nov. 6, 1976, Oral History Collection, California State College Bakersfield Library. Arizona and New Mexico were not, however, simply way-stations. Significant numbers of Southwesterners settled there intentionally. Useful sources include: McWilliams, *Ill Fares the Land*, 70–90; U.S. Works Progress Administration, Malcolm Brown and Orin Cassmore, *Migratory Cotton Pickers in Arizona* (Wash., D.C., 1939); Edward C. Banfield, *Government Project* (Glencoe, Ill., 1951). In his marvelous retrospective photo essay, *Dust Bowl Descent* (Lincoln, Neb. 1984), 80–87, Bill Ganzel provides a glimpse of a New Mexico community of transplanted Oklahomans and Texans, as does Evon Vogt's 1955 anthropological study, *Modern Homesteaders: The Life of a Twentieth Century Frontier Community* (Cambridge, Mass., 1955).

Chapter 2. The Limits of Opportunity

1. Kevin Starr writes engagingly about the different sides of California in his two books, *Americans and the California Dream 1850–1915* (New York, 1973) and *Inventing the Dream: California Through the Progressive Era* (New York, 1985). So did Carey McWilliams, *California: The Great Exception* (New York, 1949) and *Southern California: An Island on the Land* (New York, 1946, reprinted Santa Barbara, 1979). The politics, architecture, and social life of San Francisco are treated in William Issel and Robert W. Cherny, *San Francisco 1865–1932: Politics, Power, and Urban Development* (Berkeley, 1986); Judd Kahn, *Imperial San Francisco: Politics and Planning in an American City, 1897–1906* (Lincoln, Neb., 1979); Michael Kazin, *Barons of Labor: The San Francisco Building Trades and Union Power in the Progressive Era* (Urbana, 1987); Charles Wollenberg, *Golden Gate Metropolis: Perspectives on Bay Area History* (Berkeley, 1985); Mel Scott, *The San Francisco Bay Area: A Metropolis in Perspective*, 2nd ed. (Berkeley, 1985).

2. The best descriptive source for the period is Federal Writers' Project, *California: A Guide to the Golden State* (New York, 1939). Useful too are Oliver Carlson, *A Mirror for Californians* (New York, 1941); Max Miller, *It Must Be the Climate* (New York, 1941). For an instructive present-day comparison see James D. Houston, *Californians: Searching for the Golden State* (New York, 1982).

3. Walter C. McKain, Jr., "The Western Specialty-Crop Areas," in Carl C. Taylor *et al.*, eds., *Rural Life in the United States* (New York, 1949), 434–45; Warren P. Tufts, "The Rich Pattern of California Crops," in Claude B. Hutchinson, ed., *California Agriculture* (Berkeley, 1946), 113–238.

4. U.S. Bureau of the Census, *Fifteenth Census of the United States: 1930 Population, Vol. III, Part 1: Reports by States: California* (Wash., D.C., 1933), 251; Warren S. Thompson, *Growth and Changes in California's Population* (Los Angeles, 1955), 67–88.

5. James Bryce, *The American Commonwealth*, Vol. 2, rev. ed. (New York, 1923), 426.

6. Wallace Stegner, "California Rising," in *Unknown California*, Jonathan Eisen, David Fine, and Kim Eisen, eds. (New York, 1985), 8. The classic restatements of the uniqueness thesis are McWilliams, *California: The Great Exception*, and James J. Parsons, "The Uniqueness of California," *American Quarterly* 7 (Spring 1955), 45–55.

7. Starr, *Americans and the California Dream* and *Inventing the Dream.*

8. Carey McWilliams describes California as a society of strangers in both *Southern California* and *California: The Great Exception*. Nathaniel West, *Day of the Locust* (New York, 1939), is one of many writers who have worried that fluidity makes for dangerous instability. Explorations of white California's mistreatment of racial minorities include Alexander Saxton, *The Indispensable Enemy: Labor and the Anti-Chinese Movement in California* (Berkeley, 1971); Roger Daniels and Spencer Olin, Jr., eds., *Racism in California: A Reader in the History of Oppression* (New York, 1972).

9. Earl Pomeroy called attention to urban origins of California in "The Urban Frontier of the Far West," in John G. Clark, ed., *Frontier Challenges: Responses to the Trans-Mississippi West* (Lawrence, 1971). San Francisco's exuberant begin-

nings are analyzed by Gunther Barth, *Instant Cities: Urbanization and the Rise of San Francisco and Denver* (New York, 1975); Roger W. Lotchin, *San Francisco: 1846–1856, From Hamlet to City* (New York, 1974); Peter R. Decker, *Fortunes and Failures: White-Collar Mobility in Nineteenth-Century San Francisco* (Cambridge, 1978). The role of New Englanders is mentioned by Louis B. Wright, *Culture on the Moving Frontier* (New York, 1955), 135–67, and Franklin Walker, *San Francisco's Literary Frontier* (New York, 1939), and highlighted by Starr, *Americans and the California Dream*. The modernism of small-town California needs more study, but a starting place is Elvin Hatch, *Biography of a Small Town* (New York, 1979). Evidence is available in the booster literature and local histories, some of which Stephen Stoll used in his undergraduate honors thesis, "The Valley Towns: Settlement and Boosterism in the San Joaquin Valley 1850–1890" (University of California, Berkeley History Department, 1988).

10. The destinations of migrants from the major cities of the Southwest were calculated from Donald J. Bogue, Henry S. Shryock, Jr., and Siegfried A. Hoermann, *Subregional Migration in the United States, 1935, Vol. I: Streams of Migration Between Subregions* (Oxford, Ohio, 1957), table 1, pp. lxi–cxxvii. Data on farm originators is from the 1940 Census Public Use Microdata Sample.

11. The 1940 Census Public Use Microdata Sample indicates that two-thirds of the San Joaquin Valley settlers, roughly 46,000 people, settled in the four cotton counties: Kern, Kings, Tulare, and Madera.

12. Calculated from Bogue, *et al.*, *Subregional Migration*, table 1, pp. ii–cci.

13. From the 1940 Census Public Use Microdata Sample: adult Southwestern newcomers to the metropolitan areas of California averaged 33.1 years old, 9.9 years of education, and 3.9 persons to a household. Comparable numbers for newcomers from other regions were 35.8, 10.9, and 3.5. The percentage of metropolitan originators was calculated from Bogue *et al.*, *Subregional Migration*, table 1, pp. ii–cli.

14. Leonard Joseph Leader, "Los Angeles and the Great Depression" (unpublished Ph.D. diss., University of California, Los Angeles, 1972), esp. 266; L. Bloch, *Report and Recommendations of the California State Unemployment Commission* (Sacramento, 1933), 190–92; U.S. Works Progress Administration, *Final Statistical Report of the Federal Emergency Relief Administration* (Wash., D.C., 1942), table 14, pp. 235–47; U.S. W.P.A., Katherine D. Wood, *Urban Workers on Relief: Part II: The Occupational Characteristics of Workers on Relief in 79 Cities, May 1934* (Wash., D.C., 1936); California State Relief Administration, M.H. Lewis, *State Welfare Survey*, Part I (n.d., 1935?), passim; Glen Elder, Jr., *Children of the Great Depression* (Chicago, 1974), 301–2; McWilliams, *Southern California*, 294–308.

15. Oliver Carlson, *A Mirror for Californians* (New York, 1941), 114.

16. Warren S. Thompson, *Growth and Changes in California's Population*, (Los Angeles, 1955), 39–40. For other descriptions of Los Angeles in this period see McWilliams, *Southern California*; Robert M. Fogelson, *The Fragmented Metropolis: Los Angeles, 1850–1930* (Cambridge, Mass., 1967).

17. Melvin Gerald Shahan interview, by Jackie Malone, Oct. 29, 1976, Oral History Program, California State University, Fullerton, 34.

18. Woody Guthrie, *Bound for Glory* (New York, 1943, 1970), 233. For similar stories see the Odyssey Program interviews with Talmage Lee Collins and Dorothy Rose.

19. Wofford and Ruth Clark interview, by author, La Mirada, Calif., June 8, 1981.

20. Melvin Shahan interview, 34.

21. California State Relief Administration, M.H. Lewis, *Transients in California* (San Francisco, 1936), 83; Sallye S. Masiello, "A Study of Fifty Young Married Couples Applying for Relief" (unpublished MSW thesis, University of Southern California, 1939), 155.

22. U.S. Works Progress Administration, *Juvenile Delinquency and Poor Housing in the Los Angeles Metropolitan Area* (Dec. 1937), cited in Jacqueline Rorabeck Kasun, *Some Social Aspects of Business Cycles in the Los Angeles Area, 1920–1950* (Los Angeles, 1954), 58; Clark interview.

23. Grace E. Dahle, "A Personnel Study of High School Pupils in an Industrial City" (unpublished MA thesis, University of Southern California, 1945), 27.

24. Frank Manies interview, by author, Lindsay, April 31, 1985.

25. Wanda Audrey Shahan Wall interview, by Jackie Malone, Oct. 6, 1976, Oral History Program, California State University, Fullerton, 14. See also Charles B. Spaulding, "The Development of Organization and Disorganization in the Social Life of a Rapidly Growing Working-Class Suburb Within a Metropolitan District" (unpublished Ph.D. diss., University of Southern California, 1939), 97–98.

26. The spread of urban styles is discussed in Donald Worster, *Dust Bowl: The Southern Plains in the 1930s* (New York, 1979), 165. He refers to a Kansas wheatbelt town, but James West (Carl Withers), *Plainville, U.S.A.* (New York, 1945), esp. 11–19, found the same urban influences in a tiny Missouri Ozark community. In keeping with the modernization biases of the period, most contemporary studies of Southwestern rural life focused on the need for still greater urban contacts, but their data on farmers' recreational, educational, and social activities indicate the important changes already under way. See Theodore Roosevelt Schaffler, "Factors Influencing the Standard of Living of Farm Families in Logan County [Oklahoma]" (unpublished MA thesis, University of Oklahoma, 1933), 53–89; T.C. McCormick, "Rural Social Organization in South-Central Arkansas," Arkansas Agricultural Experiment Station *Bulletin* No. 313 (Dec. 1934). An assessment that emphasizes the "narrowness of outlook" prevailing among Central Texas farm women is Ruth Allen, *The Labor of Women in the Production of Cotton* (Chicago, 1931), 35.

27. Quoted in McWilliams, *Southern California*, 160. Fogelson, *Fragmented Metropolis*, explores the implications of the city's suburban character.

28. Carlson, *A Mirror for Californians*, 116; Fogelson, *Fragmented Metropolis*, 63–84. U.S. Bureau of the Census, *Fifteenth Census: 1930 Population, Vol. III, Part 1*, table 13, p. 251, provides the following ethnic breakdown for Los Angeles County:

Native whites of native parentage	55%
Natives of foreign or mixed parents	20
Foreign-born whites	13
Hispanics and nonwhites	22

British and Canadians, the two leading immigrant groups, accounted for more than a third of the non-Hispanic foreign-born, followed by Germans, Eastern European Jews, Scandinavians, and Italians.

29. Robert Lewis Kessler, Jr., interview, by Michael Neely, May 26, 28, 1981, Auberry, Odyssey Program. Seymour J. Janow, "Volume and Characteristics of Recent Migration to the Far West," in Tolan Committee, *Hearings*, Part 6, tables 14, 18, pp. 2302, 2311, shows that former professionals and clerical workers were more likely than migrants of other occupations to regain employment at their former trade.

30. Travis Allen Williams interview, by author, Garden Grove, Aug. 21, 1980.

31. Wood, *Urban Workers on Relief*, Part II, appendix C, details unemployment rates for particular industries. See also Arthur G. Coons and Arjay R. Miller, *An Economic and Industrial Survey of the Los Angeles and San Diego Areas* (Sacramento, 1941), 84–174; Leader, "Los Angeles and the Great Depression," 10. The carpenter's story is from Cheryl Beth Campbell, "A Study of the Federal Transient Program with Special Reference to Fifty Transient Families in Los Angeles" (unpublished MA thesis, University of Southern California, 1936), 113.

32. Arthur M. Williams, *Way Yonder Pikee* (Napa, 1967), 48, an autobiographical typescript given to the author by Travis A. Williams. Other job-search stories can be found in Dorothea Mackenzie, "A Survey and Analysis of Fifty Selected American Families Receiving Aid in 1939 from the State Relief Administration" (unpublished MA thesis, University of Southern California, 1939), 22; Masiello, "A Study of Fifty Young Married Couples Applying for Relief," 157; Spaulding, "The Development of a Rapidly Growing Working-Class Suburb," 142.

33. Sherman Coleman interview, by author, Oakland, June 12, 1985.

34. Melvin Shahan interview, 43.

35. Frank Manies interview.

36. Morris family interview, by Margo McBane and Mary Winegarden, Richmond, July 1978, Women Farmworkers Project. Jewell Morris, her sister Gladys, and brother Chester are heard on this tape. But Chester's last name was not recorded. The influence of kin networks is also discussed in West, *Plainville*, 135. For thoughts on the relationship between job networks and occupational status in other settings see John Bodnar, Michael Weber, and Roger Simon, "Migration, Kinship, and Urban Adjustment: Blacks and Poles in Pittsburgh, 1900–1930," *Journal of American History* 66 (Dec. 1979), 548–65; Levi Varden Fuller, *Rural Worker Adjustment to Urban Life: An Assessment of the Research* (Ann Arbor, 1970), 52.

37. 1940 Census Public Use Microdata Sample. Changes in work opportunities for women generally during the thirties are discussed in Susan Ware, *Holding Their Own: American Women in the 1930s* (Boston, 1982), 21–50; Alice Kessler-Harris, *Out to Work: A History of Wage-earning Women in the United States* (New York, 1982), 250–72.

38. Lucinda Coffman interview, by Peggy Staggs, Fullerton, Nov. 1979. Also Peggy Staggs interview, by author, Huntington Beach, Aug. 18, 1980.

39. Robert S. Lynd and Helen Merrell Lynd, *Middletown in Transition: A Study in Cultural Conflicts* (New York, 1937), 178–79. Coffman was the only example of the Ma Joad syndrome to appear in the nearly 80 interviews that I conducted or consulted. On the other hand there are more frequent references to marriages broken by the strains of resettlement. For examples of women forced to make it on their own, sometimes with young children to care for, see the Odyssey Program

interviews with Lillie Dunn, Loye Holmes, and Vivian Kirschenmann. Also Campbell, "A Study of the Federal Transient Program," 118. Still, the Public Use Microdata Sample indicates that the number of divorces or separations was no different for this group than for other whites in California.

40. Quoted in Spaulding, "The Development of a Rapidly Growing Working-Class Suburb," 62.

41. Letter to President Roosevelt, March 15, 1936, Federal Emergency Relief Administration Records, RG 69, California Transient Complaints, National Archives. For other examples see Campbell, "A Study of the Federal Transient Program," 120; U.S. Works Progress Administration, John N. Webb and Malcolm Brown, *Migrant Families* (Wash., D.C., 1938), 25; James B. Reese, "Preliminary Report Transient Program of the State Relief Administration, Los Angeles County, February 1939," in Tolan Committee, *Hearings*, Part 7, p. 2895.

42. 1940 Census Public Use Microdata Sample. Two small serveys found Southwesterners over-represented among relief recipients. See Mackenzie, "A Survey of Fifty American Families Receiving Aid," 58–61; Masiello, "A Study of Fifty Young Married Couples Applying for Relief," 39.

43. The standard of living figures are from budgets prepared by the California State Relief Administration and the Heller Committee for Research in Social Economics, *Quantity and Cost Budgets for Four Income Levels* (Berkeley, 1939), both excerpted in the Minutes of Cotton Picking Wage Hearing, Sept. 28–29, 1939, Fresno, Calif., Exhibits A-D in McWilliams Collection.

44. U.S. Bureau of the Census, *1940 Population and Housing, Families—General Characteristics* (Wash., D.C., 1943), table 34, pp. 157–68, shows that median wage and salary income for families without other sources of income living in urban areas of the four Southwestern states was approximately $1,090, with 35 percent earning less than $725 (the cost-of-living-adjusted subsistence income). U.S. Works Progress Administration, Margaret Loomis Stecker, *Intercity Differences in Cost of Living in March 1935, 59 Cities*, Research Monograph XII (Wash., D.C., 1937), 5, reported a 7 percent cost of living difference between Los Angeles and Oklahoma City.

45. Sherman Coleman interview.

46. This is a modified version of the occupational hierarchy used by most analysts of social mobility. Stephan Thernstrom, *The Other Bostonians: Poverty and Progress in the American Metropolis* (Cambridge, Mass., 1973), 282–302, explains and justifies the scale. A few changes have been made. I have distinguished farm laborers from other unskilled laborers because of the special income and status disabilities of that occupation in California. I also deviate from Thernstrom's ranking of clerical and sales workers above craftsmen. His own examination of income data from the 1960 census shows that the skilled group earned slightly more than the lower white-collar group. This seems reason enough to combine the two into one strata. Finally, I divide service workers, considering the bulk of them equivalent to semi-skilled operatives, but putting police, fire, and other protection services in the skilled category.

47. Seymour J. Janow, "Volume and Characteristics of Recent Migration to the Far West," in Tolan Committee, *Hearings*, Part 6, p. 2307. The 1940 Census Public

Use Microdata Sample allows us to control farm background and education for the two groups of recent migrants to metropolitan areas. Doing so does not entirely dissolve the performance differences between Southwesterners and other white newcomers:

Southwesterners and other white newcomers:

Farm background	SWs	Others
Migrants who lived on farms in 1935	23%	13%
Occupational index of former farmers	2.6	2.9
Median personal income 1939	$685	$600
Education		
Migrants with 8th grade or less	40%	23%
Occupational index	2.8	3.3
Median personal income	$730	$875

48. Spaulding, "The Development of a Rapidly Growing Working-Class Suburb," 117–18. See also Cora Hendrick, "A Study of Home Buying by Works Progress Administration Clients" (unpublished MA thesis, University of Southern California, 1939). Dahle, "A Personnel Study of High School Pupils in an Industrial City," describes two similar communities located near Torrance. McWilliams, *Southern California*, 160, mentions one near El Monte.

49. Spaulding, "The Development of a Rapidly Growing Working-Class Suburb," 59–60, appendix A. As attention focused on the Dust Bowl migration late in the decade, journalists sometimes confused working-class subdivisions in the LA area with the Little Oklahomas developing in the valleys. Spaulding notes that Bell Gardens was incorrectly identified as an Okie community. For examples see George Gleason, *The Fifth Migration: A Report on the California Migratory Agricultural Worker Situation*, reprinted in Tolan Committee, *Hearings*, Part 7, p. 3006; "Private Households for the Okies," *Business Week* (March 9, 1940), 24.

50. Southwesterners were less occupationally limited in other valleys: in the south coast counties 36 percent were farm workers, 33 percent in San Bernadino, Riverside, Imperial counties, and 23 percent in the Sacramento Valley. In all non-metropolitan areas combined, 43 percent labeled themselves farm workers at the time of the census, with another 10 percent claiming temporary employment on work relief projects.

51. Ernesto Galarza, *Merchants of Labor: The Mexican Bracero Story* (Charlotte, N.C., 1964), 109; Carey McWilliams, *Factories in the Field* (Boston, 1939, reprint ed. Santa Barbara, 1971), 4.

52. Donald Worster, *Rivers of Empire: Water, Aridity and the Growth of the American West* (New York, 1985).

53. The story is told with more subtlety than we have space for in Donald J. Pisani, *From Family Farm to Agribusiness: The Irrigation Crusade in California and the West 1850–1931* (Berkeley, 1984); Worster, *Rivers of Empire*, 96–125; Lawrence J. Jelinek, *Harvest Empire: A History of California Agriculture*, 2nd ed. (San Francisco, 1982); Wallace Smith, *Garden of the Sun* (Fresno, 1939).

54. U.S. Bureau of the Census, *Fifteenth Census of the United States: 1930*

Agriculture, Vol. III, Part 3 (Wash., D.C., 1932), table 3, pp. 24–33; *Vol. II, Part 3*, table 12, p. 40.

55. McWilliams, *Factories in the Field*; Paul S. Taylor and Tom Vasey, "Contemporary Background of California Farm Labor," *Rural Sociology* I (Dec. 1936), 402–3. Other discussions of the development of large-scale farming include: Ellen Liebman, *California Farmland: A History of Large Agricultural Landholdings* (Totowa, N.J., 1983); Ernesto Galarza, *Farm Workers and Agri-Business in California, 1947–1960* (Notre Dame, Ind., 1977), 19–96; Pisani, *From Family Farm to Agribusiness*; Jelinek, *Harvest Empire*, 61–77.

56. U.S. Bureau of the Census, *1930 Census of Agriculture, Vol. III, Part 3*, table 6, pp. 54–57; California State Relief Administration, M.H. Lewis, *Migratory Labor in California* (San Francisco, 1936), 13; Jelinek, *Harvest Empire*, 67; Carlson, *A Mirror for Californians*, 66; M.R. Benedict, "The Economic and Social Structure of California Agriculture," in Claude B. Hutchinson, ed., *California Agriculture* (Berkeley, 1946), 415–18.

57. The centralization process is explored in Devra Anne Weber, "The Struggle for Stability and Control in the Cotton Fields of California: Class Relations in Agriculture, 1919–1942" (Ph.D. diss., University of California, Los Angeles, 1986), 33–82, 315. On Sunkist and other cooperatives see H.E. Erdman, "The Development and Significance of California Cooperatives, 1900–1915," *Agricultural History* 32 (July 1958), 179–84. For other aspects of the farmers' organization efforts see Cletis E. Daniels, *Bitter Harvest: A History of California Farmworkers 1870–1941* (Ithaca, 1981), 15–70; Clarke A. Chambers, *California Farm Organizations* (Berkeley, 1952).

58. U.S. Bureau of the Census, *Fifteenth Census: 1930 Population, Vol. III, Part 1*, table 20, pp. 273–76; U.S. Department of Agriculture, Bureau of Agricultural Economics, and the University of California, Institute of Industrial Relations, *The Agricultural Labor Force in the San Joaquin Valley, California—1948* (Wash., D.C., 1950), 13–15.

59. U.S. Bureau of the Census, *Fifteenth Census: 1930 Population, Vol. III, Part 1*, table 13, pp. 251–54. On the mixed economy of these areas see Walter Goldschmidt, *As You Sow* (Glencoe, 1947, reprinted Montclair, N.J., 1978), 6ff, who referred to the Central Valley as an urbanized rural society. Also his study for the Senate Committee to Study Problems of American Small Business, *Small Business and the Community: A Study in Central Valley of California on the Effects of Scale of Farm Operations*, 79th Congress, 2nd Session, S. Res. 26 (Wash., D.C., Dec. 23, 1946); McKain, "The Western Specialty-Crop Areas," 436; Paul Faulkner Tjensvold, "An Inquiry into the Reasons for the Post-Depression Migration from Oklahoma to Kern County in California" (unpublished MA thesis, University of Southern California, 1947), 28.

60. William Harland Boyd, John Ludeke, and Marjorie Rump, eds., *Inside Historic Kern* (Bakersfield, 1982), esp. 225–30; Smith, *Gardens of the Sun*.

61. George M. Peterson, *Composition and Characteristics of the Agricultural Population in California*, Giannini Foundation Bulletin No. 630 (Berkeley, 1939); U.S. Department of Labor, *Migration of Workers, 1938* (Wash., D.C., 1938), 85–90. Other helpful overviews of the agricultural labor system are Lloyd Fisher, *The Harvest Labor Market in California* (Cambridge, 1953); Levi Varden Fuller, "The

Development and Prospects of California's Agriculture," in Thompson, *Growth and Changes*, 273–93.

62. Sucheng Chan, *This Bitter-sweet Soil: The Chinese in California Agriculture, 1860–1910* (Berkeley, 1986); Levi Varden Fuller, "The Supply of Agricultural Labor as a Factor in the Evolution of Farm Organization in California" (unpublished Ph.D. diss., University of California, Berkeley, 1939); Daniel, *Bitter Harvest*, esp. 15–70; Paul S. Taylor and Tom Vasey, "Historical Background of California Farm Labor," *Rural Sociology* 1 (Sept. 1936), 281–95; Linda C. Majka and Theo J. Majka, *Farm Workers, Agribusiness, and the State* (Philadelphia, 1982).

63. Peterson, *Composition and Characteristics of the Agricultural Population*, 17.

64. Sheila Goldring Manes, "Depression Pioneers: The Conclusion of an American Odyssey. Oklahoma to California, 1930–1950" (unpublished Ph.D. diss., University of California, Los Angeles, 1982), 17; Goldschmidt, *As You Sow*, 152–53.

65. Goldschmidt, *As You Sow*, 34. The tenancy data is from U.S. Bureau of the Census, *1930 Census of Agriculture*, Vol. II, Part 3, tables 1, 12, pp. 518–22, 577–81; Vol. III, Part 3, table 7, p. 65. In 1930, the average Kern County farm was worth $31,079 compared to $3,000–$5,000 in the cotton areas of Oklahoma. See U.S. Bureau of the Census, *1930 Census of Agriculture, Vol. II, Part 3*, table 3, pp. 528–31; U.S. Department of Agriculture, Bureau of Agricultural Economics, "Summary of County Land-Use Planning Committees Estimates of Cost of Family-Type Farms in Oklahoma," RG83, General Correspondence 1941–46, National Archives.

66. Byrd Morgan interview, by Stacey Jagels, May 2, 1981, Oakhurst, Odyssey Program.

67. Velma May Cooper Davis interview, by Judith Gannon, May 25, 1981, Delano, Odyssey Program.

68. Charles M. Newsome interview, by Michael Neely, March 23, May 12, 1981, Visalia, Odyssey Program. Goldschmidt, *As You Sow*, 155–58, interviewed the handful of newcomers who had acquired land in the Wasco area and reported that nearly all had either had money when they arrived or got their start with substantial help from relatives already farming. See also the story of Bill Hammett (Clay Bennett*) who had rented farms in the 1920s but was forced into farm labor during the Depression, in California State Relief Administration, *Migratory Labor in California*, 142.

69. See Chapter 6, Table 6.2.

70. J.R. McClintock interview, by Judith Gannon, Bakersfield, March 4–5, 1981, Odyssey Program.

71. Tolan Committee, *Hearings*, Part 6, pp. 2203–4. Businesses operated by former farm laborers were advertised in some of the Farm Security Administration camp newspapers. See for example *The Hub* (Visalia) (Oct. 11, 1941); *The Migratory Worker* (Indio) (Nov. 26, 1938); *Shafter Press*, (April 16, 1936). For descriptions of enterprises in migrant residential areas see Lillian Creisler, " 'Little Oklahoma' or the Airport Community: A Study of the Social and Economic Adjustment of Self-settled Agricultural Drought and Depression Refugees" (unpublished MA thesis, University of California, Berkeley, 1940), 20; Stuart M. Jamieson, "A Settlement of Rural Migrant Families in the Sacramento Valley, California," *Rural Sociology* VII (March 1942), 58–59.

72. James Bright Wilson, "Social Attitudes of Certain Migratory Agricultural Workers in Kern County, California" (unpublished MA thesis, University of Southern California, 1942), 198.

73. Ethel Oleta Wever Belezzuoli interview, by Stacey Jagels, Tipton, March 18, April 10, 1981, Odyssey Program.

74. 1940 Census Public Use Microdata Sample. "Grapes of Joy—'Okies' Forge Ahead," *Current History*, 51 (March 1940), 49.

75.

Occupations Before and After Migration for Male Household Heads Settling in Kern, Tulare, Fresno, and Yuba Counties, 1930-1939*

	Before Moving to California					
	Farmers	Professionals/ proprietors	Sales/ clerical	Skilled workers	Semi-skilled	Labor (non-agr.)	Farm labor/ unemployed
1939 Occupation						
Farmers (owners and tenants)	17%	5%	3%	3%	4%	4%	2%
Professionals/ proprietors	2	53	10	3	4	2	2
Sales/clerical	2	10	52	2	4	2	2
Skilled workers	10	9	9	62	12	9	6
Semi-skilled	9	5	8	6	37	9	7
Labor (non-agr.)	14	9	8	8	13	39	12
Farm labor/ unemployed	46	10	10	15	26	33	69
Total	100%	100%	100%	99%	100%	98%	100%
N	(2,622)	(645)	(480)	(1,130)	(900)	(1,084)	(1,922)

Pre-migration occupational index = 3.4

1939 Occupational index = 3.0

*Sample includes migrants from all states, 60 percent of them from the Western South.

Source: Recalculated from table 5, Bureau of Agricultural Economics, Recent Migration to California, typescript preliminary report in McWilliams Collection.

76. 1940 Census Public Use Microdata Sample. Edward J. Rowell, *Summary Report on the Background and Problems Affecting Farm Labor in California* (n.p., March 1937), 32–34, mimeographed copy in McWilliams Collection; California State Department of Public Health, Anita E. Faverman, *A Report of the Migratory Demonstration July 1936–June 1937: A Study of the Health of 1,000 Children of Migratory Agricultural Laborers in California* (San Francisco, 1937), 12–14, mimeographed copy in the McWilliams Collection; California State Relief Administration, *Agricultural Migratory Workers in the San Joaquin Valley July and August 1937* (n.p., Dec. 1937), 11–14; Bureau of Agricultural Economics, *The Agricultural Labor Force in the San JoaquinValley, California—1948* (Wash., D.C., 1950), 21.

77. California State Chamber of Commerce, *The Migrants: A National Problem and Its Impact on California*, reprinted in the Tolan Committee, *Hearings*, Part 6, table 11, p. 2785.

78. John Steinbeck, *Their Blood Is Strong* (San Francisco, 1938), 33. This is a reprint of a series of articles which originally appeared in the *San Francisco News* (Oct. 5–11, 1936). Other journalistic accounts of migrant hardship include another *San Francisco News* series by Theodore Smith which appeared during February 1938; a series in the *Los Angeles Times*, July 21–25, 1937, by Ray Zemon; and Edith W. Lowry, *They Starve That We May Eat* (New York, 1938).

79. Reports by the California Division of Immigration and Housing and its energetic chief, Carey McWilliams, examine the conditions in private labor camps. See *Memorandum on Housing Conditions Among Migratory Workers in California* (Los Angeles, March 20, 1939), mimeographed copy in the McWilliams Collection, Migratory Labor-California file; also McWilliam's testimony before the La Follette Committee, *Hearings*, Part 59, pp. 21901–17 and Tolan Committee, *Hearings*, Part 6, pp. 2541–70. Useful too is housing expert Catherine Bauer's testimony and report, "The Housing of California's Agricultural Workers," Tolan Committee, *Hearings*, Part 6, pp. 2570–87.

80. Russell Fred Hurley, "The Migratory Worker:A Survey of Marysville Federal Migratory Camp and the 'Pear Orchard' Squatter Camp, Yuba City" (unpublished MA thesis, University of Southern California, 1939), 90. Kern County health officials estimated 3,881 families living in squatter camps during 1937. Kern County Health Department, *Survey of Kern County Migratory Labor Problem* (n.p., 1937), mimeographed copy in the Taylor Collection.

81. *Los Angeles Times*, July 21, 1937; California State Department of Public Health, Anita E. Faverman *et al.*, *Trailing Child and Maternal Health into California Migratory Agricultural Camps: Report of the Second Year of the Migratory Demonstration, July 1937–June 1938* (San Francisco, 1937), 2, mimeographed copy in the McWilliams Collection.

82. California State Department of Social Welfare, Bertha S. Underhill, *A Study of 132 Families in California Cotton Camps with Reference to Availability of Medical Care* (n.p., n.d.), 8, mimeographed copy in Taylor Collection.

83. Faverman, *Report of the Migratory Demonstration July 1936–June 1937*, 25.

84. Faverman, *Trailing Child and Maternal Health into Agricultural Camps*, 18. For more on the health problems of the migrants see Jacqueline Gordon Sherman, "The Oklahomans in California During the Depression Decade, 1931–1941" (unpublished Ph.D. diss., University of California, Los Angeles, 1970), 163–82; Omer Mills, "Health Problems Among Migratory Workers," talk given at the convention of the California League of Municipalities, Sept. 8, 1938, in the Federal Writers' Collection, carton 9, Bancroft Library, University of California, Berkeley (hereafter Federal Writers' Collection); W.M. Dickie, "Health Problems Among the Migrant Families," paper delivered to California Conference of Social Work, Oakland, May 18, 1939, in FSA Collection, carton 9, Bancroft; Edward J. Rowell, "The Child in the Migratory Camp—Health," *California Children* I (Sept. 15, 1938), 1–4.

85. Walter Stein, *California and the Dust Bowl Migration* (Westport, 1973), 75–77, 84–85; Lee Alexander Stone, "The Migrant Situation in Madera County, California," Tolan Committee, *Hearings*, Part 7, pp. 3054–55; Hurley, "The Migratory Worker," 90; Kern County Health Department, *Survey of Migratory Labor Problems, Supplementary Report as of July 1, 1938* (Bakersfield, 1938), 5, mimeographed

copy in McWilliams Collection. On the Farm Security Administration's health and food projects see Wilson, "Social Attitudes of Migratory Agricultural Workers," 263–69; U.S. Department of Agriculture, Farm Security Administration, "Material on Migrants" (n.p., 1940) typescript in FSA Collection, carton 10, Bancroft; U.S. Department of Agriculture, Farm Security Administration, John Beecher, "The Migratory Labor Program in California" (n.p., n.d.) typescript in same collection, carton 9.

86. Mr. J.W., Wasco field notes.

87. Hurley, "The Migratory Worker," 87.

88. Bureau of Agricultural Economics, *The Agricultural Labor Force, 1948*, 3–4. Lloyd Fellows, *Economic Aspects of the Mexican Population in California with Special Emphasis on the Need for Mexican Labor in Agriculture* (San Francisco, 1971, reprint of 1929 University of Southern California MA thesis), 19–21, reports the ethnic preferences expressed in a survey of 758 growers. For estimates of the ethnic breakdowns for particular crops see McWilliams, *Memorandum on Housing Conditions*, 5–6.

89. Paul S. Taylor and Edward J. Rowell, "Patterns of Agricultural Labor Migration Within California," *Monthly Labor Review* 47 (Nov. 1938), 980–90; Taylor and Vasey, "Contemporary Background of California Farm Labor," 401–19; California State Relief Administration, *Agricultural Migratory Laborers in the San Joaquin Valley, 1937*, passim; R.L. Adams, *Seasonal Labor Requirements for California Crops* (Berkeley, 1938); U.S. Department of Labor, *Migration of Workers*, 84–90.

90. California State Relief Administration, *Agricultural Migratory Laborers in the San Joaquin Valley, 1937*, 5–6. The $658 median was for families who had received nothing from relief agencies during the previous year. Full income data was not available on those who had accepted public assistance. Earlier studies using less careful samples reported much smaller average incomes. See California State Relief Administration, M.H. Lewis, *Migratory Labor in California* (San Francisco, 1936), 121; Rowell, *Summary Report on Problems Affecting Farm Labor*, 25–31. But the $658 median agrees with the Bureau of Agricultural Economics studies of 1938 earnings from agricultural labor as reported by Varden Fuller to the Tolan Committee, *Hearings*, Part 6, pp. 2259–60.

91. Roscoe Crawford interview, by Dixie Crawford Hicks, Oral History Program, California State University, Fullerton, 1976, 94. Also Doug Foster, "Dust Bowl Refugees Reminisce at Annual Fruit Tramp Picnic," *Salinas Californian* (Aug. 21, 1978).

92. U.S. Department of Agriculture, Bureau of Agricultural Economics, "Characteristics of Recent Migration to Far West and the Structure of Economic Opportunity for Migrants in Western Agriculture" (n.p., 1940), mimeographed copy in *Publications on Rural Sociology*, Vol. 2, pamphlet collection in Agricultural Library, University of California, Berkeley. A less complete reporting of these data can be found in Catherine Bauer's testimony to the Tolan Committee, *Hearings*, Part 6, p. 2572. The preferences of the newcomers were also made clear in the 1937 SRA survey of itinerant families, only 25 percent of whom indicated any interest in continuing to follow the crops. California State Relief Administration, *Agricultural Migratory Laborers in the San Joaquin Valley, 1937*, 13.

93. George O. Coalson, *The Development of the Migratory Farm Labor System in Texas: 1900–1950* (San Francisco, 1977), 12–18; Carey McWilliams, *Ill Fares the Land* (Boston, 1942), 230–40; Allen, *The Labor of Women in the Production of Cotton*, 113; U.S. Department of Labor, Children's Bureau, *The Welfare of Children in Cotton-Growing Areas of Texas* (Wash., D.C., 1924), 61–68.

94. Lucretia Penny, "Pea-Picker's Child," *Survey Graphic*, 24 (July 1935), 352.

95. *Marysville Camp News* (April 2, 1938), 131. The image of rootlessness clearly bothered many, as John Steinbeck learned when he published a series of newspaper articles under the headline "Harvest Gypsies." When Southwesterners wrote in complaining, he apologized in print, explaining, "I had no intention of insulting a people who are already insulted beyond endurance." *San Francisco News* (Oct. 20, 1936).

96. Charles Todd, "The Pea-Patch Press" (1946?), 9, unpublished typescript in Charles Todd Okie Studies Collection.

97. Wilson, "Social Attitudes of Migratory Agricultural Workers," 249. The difficulties of making a living as a migratory laborer are examined in California State Relief Administration, *Migratory Labor in California*; McWilliams, *Ill Fares the Land*; Marion Hathway, *The Migratory Worker and Family Life* (Chicago, 1934); Mauze, "A Study of Migratory Families in the San Joaquin Valley"; Helen Dunlap Packard, "The Social Welfare Problems of Migratory Workers in the Cotton Industry of the Southern San Joaquin Valley During 1937 and 1938" (unpublished MA thesis, University of Southern California, 1939).

98. Walter Evans Hoadley, Jr., "A Study of One Hundred Seventy Self-Resettled Agricultural Families, Monterey County, California, 1939" (unpublished MA thesis, University of California, Berkeley, 1940), 87–104, provides an excellent survey of the work patterns of resettled families in the Salinas Valley. See also Creisler, "Little Oklahoma," 27–41; 51–55; Jamieson, "A Settlement of Rural Migrant Families in the Sacramento Valley," 51–55. On the work of women and children see Wilson, "Social Attitudes of Agricultural Workers," 137–39; Goldschmidt, *As You Sow*, 89–92; DeVere A. Stephens, "An Analysis of the School and Home Problems of Migratory Children in the San Joaquin Valley" (unpublished MA thesis, University of Southern California, 1940), 57–63; National Child Labor Committee, James E. Sidel, *A Study of Child Labor Among Migrants on the Pacific Coast* (New York, 1939); Lillian B. Hill, "Adequacy of Education for Migratory Children in the State of California," La Follette Committee, *Hearings*, Part 62, pp. 22747–51; California Department of Public Health, *Report of the Migratory Demonstration July 1936–June 1937*, 38–39.

99. Dellar Ballard interview, by Margo McBane, Mary Winegarden, and Rick Topkins, Lindsay, July 19, 1978, Women Farmworkers Project. Also Morris family interview.

100. Kern County Health Department, C. F. Baughman, *Survey of Kern County Migratory Labor Problem, Supplementary Report as of July 1, 1939* (Bakersfield, 1939), 1, mimeographed copy in McWilliams Collection.

101. Fuller and Janow, "Jobs on Farms in California," 39; also Varden Fuller testimony, Tolan Committee, *Hearings*, Part 6, p. 2259. The sense that most felt "plenty sheepish" about accepting relief is found in Wilson's many interviews in "Social Attitudes of Migratory Agricultural Workers." See also Walter Stein, "The

'Okie' as Farm Laborer," *Agricultural History* 49 (Jan. 1975), 211–12; *Weed Patch Cultivator* (Jan. 27, 1939); FSA Region IX Monthly Narrative Reports, April 1941.

102. On conditions in these private facilities see McWilliams, *Memorandum on Housing Conditions Among Migratory Workers*; reports and testimony before the Tolan Committee, *Hearings*, Part 6, pp. 2541–70, and La Follette Committee, *Hearings*, Part 59, pp. 21887–919. See also California State Relief Administration, *A Social Survey of Housing Conditions Among Tulare County Relief Clients April– June 1939* (Tulare County, 1940).

103. Studies of the Farm Security Administration camps are numerous, but most of the early observers were too excited by the camps' liberal intentions to notice their limited impact. Many former migrants who have been interviewed in recent years claim to have avoided the camps, and the few contemporary surveys of migrant opinion appear to back them up, suggesting that many migrants saw them as charitable institutions. See Creisler, "Little Oklahoma," 36–37; Wilson, "Social Attitudes of Migratory Agricultural Workers," 171–99. Stein, *California and the Dust Bowl Migration*, 166–89, points out as well that those migrants who tried the camps often resented the paternalistic reform ethos of their idealistic young managers. See also his article, "A New Deal Experiment with Guided Democracy: The FSA Migrant Camps in California," in the Canadian Historical Association, *Historical Papers 1970*. Less critical earlier reports on the camps include: Sylvan Jacob Ginsburgh, "The Migrant Camp Program of the F.S.A. in California: A Critical Examination of Operations at the Yuba City and Thornton Camps" (unpublished MA thesis, University of California, Berkeley, 1943); Albert Croutch,"Housing Migratory Agricultural Workers in California, 1913–1948" (unpublished MA thesis, University of California, Berkeley, 1949); Hurley, "The Migratory Worker"; W.F. Baxter, "Migratory Labor Camps," *Quartermaster Review* (July–Aug. 1937), 1–16, reprint in the Federal Writers' Collection, carton 9; Lawrence I. Hewes, Jr., Report before the Special Committee Investigating the Interstate Migration of Destitute Citizens, (San Francisco, Sept. 25, 1940), mimeographed copy in the FSA Collection, carton 10, Bancroft; U.S. Department of Agriculture, Farm Security Administration, *Migrant Farm Labor: The Problem and Ways of Meeting It* (Wash., D.C., 1939). Also understandably positive are the camp manager's weekly narrative reports in the FSA Records, San Bruno.

104. Creisler, "Little Oklahoma," 26.

105. James Bright Wilson, "Religious Leaders, Institutions, and Organizations Among Certain Agricultural Workers in the Central Valley of California" (unpublished Ph.D diss., University of Southern California, 1944), 97–98.

106. Jamieson, "A Settlement of Rural Migrant Families in the Sacramento Valley," 59.

107. Dellar Ballard interview.

108. Descriptions of these and other Little Oklahomas can be found in the several housing reports by Carey McWilliams cited above. The Salinas subdivision is discussed in William Orville Jones, "The Salinas Valley: Its Agricultural Development, 1920–1940" (unpublished Ph.D. diss., Stanford University, 1947), 274.

109. Kern County Health Department, *Kern County Migratory Labor Problem, July 1, 1939*, 7.

110. Goldschmidt, *As You Sow*, 326. McWilliams Tolan Committee testimony,

Hearings, Part 6, pp. 2549–50. Carey McWilliams discussed the fears of the established communities in "Migration and Resettlement of the People," paper presented at the National Conference on Planning, July 8–11, 1940, San Francisco, mimeographed copy in FSA Collection, carton 9, Bancroft. See also Governor Culbert L. Olson, Address Before Banquet of Western Public Housing Officials, San Francisco, Dec. 20, 1939, copy in the FSA Collection, Bancroft; *San Francisco Examiner*, March 4, 1939; *Dinuba Sentinel*, July 11, 1940.

111. The literature on ethnic settlement patterns is summarized and evaluated in Kathleen Neils Conzen's important article, "Immigrants, Immigrant Neighborhoods, and Ethnic Identity: Historical Issues," *Journal of American History* 66 (Dec. 1979), 603–15. While acknowledging that cultural affinity provided the central motive for residential clustering, she agrees with David Ward, *Cities and Immigrants* (New York, 1971), esp. 105, and William L. Yancey, Eugene P. Ericksen, and Richard N. Juliani, "Emergent Ethnicity: A Review and Reformation," *American Sociological Review* 44 (June 1976), 384–85, that ecological factors such as housing supplies, transportation systems, and employment opportunities also shape settlement patterns. My point is that these conditions were primarily, perhaps exclusively, operative for Southwesterners, who showed few signs of caring about anything other than class and racial affinity when choosing neighborhoods. This is different also from Appalachians, who, according to Lewis M. Killian, "Southern White Laborers in Chicago's West Side" (unpublished Ph.D. diss., University of Chicago, 1949), 60–102, and Don Edward Merten, "Up Here and Down Home: Appalachian Migrants in Northtown" (unpublished Ph.D. diss., University of Chicago, 1974), 39–40, sought out their own kind in ethnically complex and unfamiliar Chicago.

112. Creisler, "Little Oklahoma," 27–29, 108.

113. Fuller and Janow, "Jobs on Farms in California," 43.

114. How many is not known. In their 1939 study of 1,000 resettled migrant families, most of whom engaged in agricultural work, Fuller and Janow found that 40 percent had become property owners ("Jobs on Farms," 37). This sample, however, seems to have been drawn primarily from just the sort of migrant subdivisions where property ownership was most common. On the other hand, the California State Relief Administration's *Social Survey of Housing Conditions Among Tulare County Relief Clients*, 26, found a 15 percent property ownership rate among the most disadvantaged segments of the population.

115. Creisler, "Little Oklahoma," 11. For similar statements see Wilson, "Religious Organizations Among Agricultural Workers," 95–100; Mrs. G.A. and Mrs. B.D., Wasco field notes.

116. Kern County Health Department, *Kern County Migratory Labor Problem, July 1, 1939*, 7; Byron Darnton, "Migrants' Dream of Owning Land Makes Them a Conservative Lot," *New York Times* (March 6, 1940).

117. Wilson, "Social Attitudes of Migratory Agricultural Workers," 132.

118. Mr. D.S., Wasco field notes. See also the comments in Theodore Smith, "Migrant Children Not Able to Do Well in Studies," *San Francisco News* (Feb. 16, 1938).

119. "Attention Chamber of Commerce," poem by Frank Kline, *Voice of the Migrant* (Marysville) (March 15, 1940).

120. Visalia, Aug. 30, 1941, Todd-Sonkin Recordings.

121. Testimony, Tolan Committee, *Hearings*, Part 7, p. 2907.

122. Dorothea Lange and Paul Schuster Taylor, *An American Exodus: A Record of Human Erosion* (New York, 1939), 109.

123. Wilson, "Social Attitudes of Migratory Agricultural Workers," 76.

Chapter 3. The Okie Problem

1. Walter Stein, *California and the Dust Bowl Migration* (Westport, 1973), examines the state and federal response to the migration in more detail than is called for here. My interpretation draws upon and agrees in most cases with his careful analysis.

2. For a good summary of the national outlook see Eric Beecroft and Seymour Janow, "Toward a National Policy of Migration," *Social Forces* XVII (May 1938), 475–92. California's early steps to curb interstate migration are outlined in "Statement of Gov. Culbert L. Olson of California," Tolan Committee, *Hearings*, Part 6, pp. 2234–36; also Part 26, pp. 10046–47.

3. On California's ethnocentric past see the several works by Roger Daniels, *The Politics of Prejudice: The Anti-Japanese Movement in California and the Struggle for Japanese Exclusion* (Berkeley, 1962); *Concentration Camps, U.S.A.: Japanese Americans and World War II* (New York, 1971); and with Spencer C. Olin, Jr., *Racism in California: A Reader in the History of Oppression* (New York, 1972). Also Alexander Saxton, *The Indispensable Enemy: Labor and the Anti-Chinese Movement in California* (Berkeley, 1971); Robert F. Heizer and Alan F. Almquist, *The Other Californians: Prejudice and Discrimination under Spain, Mexico, and the United States to 1920* (Berkeley, 1971); Ricardo Romo, *East Los Angeles: History of a Barrio* (Austin, 1983); Abraham Hoffman, "Stimulus to Repatriation: The 1931 Federal Deportation Drive and the Los Angeles Mexican Community," *Pacific Historical Review* 42 (May 1973), 205–19.

4. R. Hal Williams, *The Democratic Party and California Politics 1880–1896* (Palo Alto, 1973), 179–81; Donald L. McMurry, *Coxey's Army: A Study of the Industrial Army Movement of 1894* (Seattle, 1929, reprinted 1968), 15–17, 149–72; Carleton H. Parker, *The Casual Laborer and Other Essays* (New York, 1920). More generally see Alexander Keyssar, *Out of Work: The First Century of Unemployment in Massachusetts* (Cambridge, 1986), esp. 130–42; Joan M. Crouse, "Precedents from the Past: The Evolution of Laws and Attitudes Pertinent to the 'Welcome' Accorded to the Indigent Transient during the Great Depression," in Milton Plesor, ed., *An American Historian: Essays to Honor Selig Adler* (Buffalo, 1980), 191–203.

5. The escalating concern can be monitored in the local press, especially during and after the 1934 general election. See *Los Angeles Times* for Sept. 26, 27, Oct. 16, 19, 20; *Los Angeles Daily News*, Nov. 9, 15, 1934, June 18, 1935. The role of the Federal Transient Service and the impact of its closure are analyzed in California State Relief Administration, M.H. Lewis, *Transients in California* (San Francisco, 1936). Other sources on the initial migration problem include Nels Anderson, *Men on the Move* (Chicago, 1940), 63, passim; William T. Cross and Dorothy E. Cross, *Newcomers and Nomads in California* (Palo Alto, Calif., 1937); Cheryl Beth Campbell, "A Study of the Federal Transient Program with Special Reference to Fifty

Transient Families in Los Angeles" (unpublished MA thesis, University of Southern California, 1936); Walter Davenport, "California Here We Come," *Collier's* (Aug. 10, 1935), 10, 49.

6. *Los Angeles Times* (May 30, 1935, also Aug. 2, 3, Nov. 4).

7. *Los Angeles Times*, (May 18, 1935, Feb. 5, 1936); *Los Angeles Daily News* (Feb. 4, 1936); *Los Angeles Herald-Express* (Feb. 6, 1936); "Report of James E. Davis, Chief of Police, Los Angeles Police Department, March 11, 1936," Tolan Committee, *Hearings*, Part 7, p. 3035; California State Relief Administration, *Transients in California*, 245–66, appendix B; Stein, *California and the Dust Bowl Migration*, 73–74.

8. For a survey of nationwide press reaction see "California: No Hobo Utopia; Los Angeles Police Chief Sends Patrolmen to Guard Borders," *Literary Digest* (Feb. 15, 1936), 9; *Los Angeles Times* (Feb. 13, 1936), also reprinted some of the most caustic out-of-state comments.

9. Paul S. Taylor, "Again the Covered Wagon," *Survey Graphic* 24 (July 1935), 349; Paul Taylor and Clark Kerr, "Uprisings on the Farms," *Survey Graphic* 24 (Jan. 1935), 19. For an account of Taylor's pioneering efforts to study and publicize the plight of the migrants see Milton Meltzer, *Dorothea Lange: A Photographer's Life* (New York, 1978), 81–136.

10. "Squatter Army Wages Grim Battle for Life," *Los Angeles Times* (July 21, 1937). See also the series by John Steinbeck in the *San Francisco News* (Oct. 5–12, 1936); Katherine Glover, "California Farm Nomads," *New York Times* (Aug. 30, 1936); the series of articles by Robert Girvin in the *San Francisco Chronicle* (March 7–18, 1937); *Los Angeles Evening News* (March 30, 1937); and the series by Rex Miller in the *Christian Science Monitor* (Dec. 9–15, 1939).

11. "Our Unwanted Refugees," University of California Radio Service, Broadcast 2307, 9:45 p.m., Feb. 19, 1939, Station KGO San Francisco, and the California NBC Blue Network, transcript in McWilliams Collection.

12. Stein, *California and the Dust Bowl Migration*, 46–47; Commonwealth Club of California, *The Population of California* (San Francisco, 1946), 26–27, 56. An initial drop in population at the start of the decade, and, even more important, the seasonal flows of population due to agricultural employment, gave the impression of still greater increases.

13. Letter to the *Modesto Bee* (March 10, 1938). See also the letters to editor in the March 13, 1938, issue.

14. Lillian Creisler, " 'Little Oklahoma' or the Airport Community: A Study of the Social and Economic Adjustment of Self-settled Agricultural Drought and Depression Refugees" (unpublished MA thesis, University of California, Berkeley, 1940), 39, 68.

15. *Bakersfield Californian* (June 18, 1938).

16. See the *Farmer-Labor News*, published by the AFL affiliated Modesto Central Labor Council, esp. May 14 and Oct. 15, 1937; Devra Anne Weber, "The Struggle for Stability and Control in the Cotton Fields of California: Class Relations in Agriculture, 1919–1942" (Ph.D. diss., University of California, Los Angeles, 1986), 336.

17. California State Chamber of Commerce, *Migrants: A National Problem and Its Impact on California*, reprinted in Tolan Committee, *Hearings*, Part 6, pp. 2760,

2781, 2790. On school enrollment see Davis McEntire and N.L. Whetten, "The Migrants: Recent Migration to the Pacific Coast," *Land Policy Review* 2 (Sept.–Oct. 1939), 11, 17; F.W. Hart and L.H. Peterson, "A Report of a Survey of the Kern County Union High School District to the Governing Board of School Trustees and the Executive Staff" (Bakersfield, 1937), mimeographed copy in Bakersfield Public Library.

18. U.S. Department of Agriculture, Bureau of Agricultural Economics, Tyr V. Johnson and Frederick Arpke, "Interstate Migration and County Finance in California," *Migration and Settlement on the Pacific Coast* 10 (July 1942), 2.

19. Governor Culbert Olson Testimony, La Follette Committee, *Hearings*, Part 46, pp. 17259–60; California Chamber of Commerce, *Migrants*, 2762, 2782.

20. *Bakersfield Californian* (Dec. 22, 1939, Dec. 20, 1938); *Fresno Bee* (May 2, 1938); Stein, *California and the Dust Bowl Migration*, 83–86.

21. There were exceptions to this, of course. Walter Evans Hoadley, Jr., "A Study of One Hundred Seventy Self-resettled Agricultural Families, Monterey County, California, 1939" (unpublished MA thesis, University of California, Berkeley, 1940), 139–40, found that many merchants in the Salinas Valley recognized that the influx had helped the local economy, and that was no doubt true of some retailers in other areas too.

22. Kern County Health Department, C.F. Baughman, *Survey of Kern County Migratory Labor Problem, Supplementary Report as of July 1, 1939* (Bakersfield, 1939), 3, 8, 10, mimeographed copy in McWilliams Collection.

23. Karl L. Schaupp, M.D., "Development of Health Services to the Migrant Population in California and Arizona" (n.p., n.d.), 3, mimeographed copy in McWilliams Collection; Dr. Lee Alexander Stone, "The Migrant Situation in Madera County" (n.p., n.d.), 7, mimeographed copy in Haynes Collection, UCLA; California Department of Health, Anita E. Faverman, *A Report of the Migratory Demonstration July 1936–June 1937: A Study of the Health of 1,000 Children of Migratory Agricultural Laborers in California* (San Francisco, 1937), 9, 29; W.M. Dickie, "Health Problems Among the Migrant Families," 2–4, paper delivered at California Conference of Social Work, Oakland, May 18, 1939, mimeographed copy in FSA Collection, carton 9, Bancroft.

24. *Los Angeles Times* (July 24, 1937); *Bakersfield Californian* (Sept. 27, 1939). See also *Los Angeles Times* (July 22, 1937); *Sacramento Bee* (April 20, 1939).

25. "Agricultural Workers Health and Medical Association," Transcript of radio talk prepared by the Information Division of the Farm Security Administration and delivered over 25 California radio stations on the National Emergency Council May Schedule, 1938, copy in McWilliams Collection.

26. The best source on the political influence of the growers' organizations is Clarke A. Chambers, *California Farm Organizations* (Berkeley, 1952). For an excellent case study of the influence of agricultural interests at a community level see Goldschmidt, *As You Sow* (Glencoe, 1947, reprint ed. Montclair, N.J., 1978); See also Carey McWilliams, *Factories in the Field* (Santa Barbara, 1971).

27. Stein, *California and the Dust Bowl Migration*, 76; Warren S. Thompson, *Growth and Changes in California's Population* (Los Angeles, 1955), 373.

28. California Chamber of Commerce, *Migrants: A National Problem*, table 11, p. 2785.

29. These efforts will be examined in more detail in Chapter 5.

30. Cletis E. Daniel, *Bitter Harvest: A History of California Farmworkers, 1870–1941* (Ithaca, 1981) examines the strike wave in much detail, especially the role of Communist leaders. Weber, "The Struggle for Stability and Control in the Cotton Fields of California," 95–200, emphasizes the self-organization of Mexican workers. Other sources include Linda C. Majka and Theo J. Majka, *Farm Workers, Agribusiness, and the State* (Philadelphia, 1982); Stuart M. Jamieson, "Labor Unionism in Agriculture" (Ph.D. diss., University of California, Berkeley, 1943), 208–93; Paul S. Taylor and Clark Kerr, "Uprisings on the Farms," *Survey Graphic* (Jan. 1935), 19–22. On the Associated Farmers see Chambers, *California Farm Organizations*, esp. 39–52; McWilliams, *Factories in the Field*, 230–63; and the extensive documentation compiled by the La Follette Committee in its *Hearings* and Part VIII of its *Reports*.

31. Tolan Committee, *Interstate Migration*, 376, 379.

32. John Steinbeck, *Their Blood Is Strong* (San Francisco, 1938), 28. See also McWilliams, *Factories in the Field*, 306.

33. Melvyn Dubofsky, "Not So 'Turbulent Years': Another Look at the American 1930s," *Amerikastudien* 24 (1979), 5–20. The article is primarily concerned with working-class mobilization rather than electoral politics, but related assessments can be found in the numerous accounts that credit Roosevelt with calming the forces of conflict, e.g., William E. Leuchtenburg, *Franklin D. Roosevelt and the New Deal* (New York, 1963); Paul K. Conkin, *The New Deal* (Arlington Heights, Ill., 1975).

34. On Sinclair's dramatic bid for the governorship see Clarence F. McIntosh, "Upton Sinclair and the EPIC Movement, 1933–1936" (unpublished Ph.D. diss., Stanford University, 1955); Charles E. Larsen, "The Epic Campaign of 1934," *Pacific Historical Review* 27 (May 1958), 127–48; Upton Sinclair, *I, Candidate for Governor and How I Got Licked* (Pasadena, 1935); Greg Mitchell, "Summer of '34," *Working Papers Magazine* 9–10 (Nov./Dec. 1982 and Jan./Feb. 1983); Leonard Leader, "Upton Sinclair's EPIC Switch: A Dilemma for American Socialists," *Southern California Quarterly* 62 (Winter 1980), 361–81.

35. There is no adequate general study of California politics during the Depression decade, but some sense of the state's turbulent mood can be gleaned from Royce D. Delmatier, Clarence F. McIntosh, Earl G. Waters, eds., *The Rumble of California Politics 1848–1970* (New York, 1970), 230–99; Delmatier, "The Rebirth of the Democratic Party in California, 1928–1938" (Ph.D. diss., University of California Berkeley, 1955); Ronald Chinn, "Democratic Party Politics in California, 1920–1956" (Ph.D. diss., University of California, Berkeley, 1958); Luther Whiteman and Samuel L. Lewis, *Glory Roads: The Psychological State of California* (New York, 1936).

36. Robert E. Burke, *Olson's New Deal for California* (Berkeley, 1953), 6–22.

37. *Los Angeles Times* (Sept. 26, 1934); Stein, *California and the Dust Bowl Migration*, 80–81.

38. *Los Angeles Times*. (Oct. 16, 20, 1934).

39. California State Relief Administration, *Agricultural Migratory Laborers in the San Joaquin Valley, July and August 1937* (n.p., Dec. 1937), 39.

40. *Los Angeles Times* (July 26, 1937).

41. Catherine Bauer, "The Housing of California's Agricultural Workers," Tolan Committee *Hearings*, Part 6, p. 2578; U.S. Department of Agriculture, Farm Security Administration, F.N. Mortenson, "A Progress Study of 347 Families Occupying the Labor Homes and Cooperative Farms on 16 Projects of the Farm Security Administration in Region IX, 1940," typed MS (n.p., 1941), 24, in FSA Collection, carton 2, Bancroft.

42. "Dustbowlers Worry California," *Business Week* (Sept. 24, 1938), 33; "Migrant Workers Pack Political Punch This Year," United Press report, July 26, 1938, clipping in McWilliams Collection.

43. Valley electoral patterns can be traced in Michael P. Rogin and John L. Shover, *Political Change in California: Critical Elections and Social Movements, 1890–1966* (Westport, 1970), 42; Delmatier, *Rumble of California Politics*, 203, 234, 245. On Johnson's farm policy and support: Spencer C. Olin, Jr., *California's Prodigal Sons: Hiram Johnson and the Progressives, 1911–1917* (Berkeley, 1968), 26–29, 105–10; Donald J. Pisani, *From Family Farm to Agribusiness: The Irrigation Crusade in California and the West* (New York, 1985), 355–80. On Johnson's later years see Fred Greenbaum, "Hiram Johnson and the New Deal," *Pacific Historian* 18 (1974), 20–35; Otis Graham, *Encore for Reform: The Progressives and the New Deal* (New York, 1967), 115, 147.

44. Chambers, *California Farm Organizations*, surveys the political commitments of agriculture during the 1930s. Carey McWilliams's *Factories in the Field* is the classic statement of the left position, which can also be seen in the activities of Robert La Follette's Senate subcommittee. In the course of its nationwide investigation of anti-labor activities, the committee focused extensively on California agriculture. In hearings which yielded nearly 10 volumes of testimony and reports, the senators exposed both the union-busting activities of the growers' organizations and the economic plight of the Dust Bowl migrants.

45. The abrupt change in attitude is well illustrated in the editorial pronouncements of the conservative press. After editorializing on July 22, 1937, in favor of federal aid to help the migrants because "these people are human beings and American citizens, not loafers or tramps," the *Los Angeles Times* changed its position and a year later was calling for "measures to protect California from criminal activities from the swarm of indigents foisted on the State by the Federal government's bungling relief policies" (Sept. 6, 1938). Similar flip-flops can be seen in the views of *Business Week* (July 3, 1937, Sept. 24, 1938), and the *Bakersfield Californian*. See Stein, *California and the Dust Bowl Migration*, 77–79.

46. *Pacific Rural Press* (Sept. 17, 1938), 260; *Los Angeles Times* (June 10, 13, 1938); Stein, *California and the Dust Bowl Migration*, 97–99, analyzes the membership lists and supporters of the California Citizens Association and suggests that the group represented a Who's Who of "the most important conservative, anti-New Deal blocs in the state," including large growers, oil companies, banks, and real estate interests. Another careful presentation of the conservative position is California Chamber of Commerce, *Migrants: A National Problem*.

47. Stein, *California and the Dust Bowl Migration*, 99; "And Still They Come," *California* 58 (Sept. 1938), 29; *Fresno Bee* (June 19, 1938); *Riverside Daily Press* (July 28, 1938).

48. *Los Angeles Times* (June 10, 1938).

49. *Pacific Rural Press* (Sept. 17, 1938).

50. Loring A. Schuler, "The Dust Bowl Moves to California," *California* 58 (Aug. 1938), 5.

51. *Ibid.*

52. "Flee the Dust Bowl for California," *Business Week* (July 3, 1937), 36–37.

53. "Dustbowlers Worry California," 33–34.

54. "And Still They Come," 14. See also Mr. R.P., Wasco field notes; "Migrants are Becoming Voters," *California* 58 (Oct. 1938), 21.

55. Burke, *Olson's New Deal for California*, 33; Voter Registration and Election Results Arvin Area, Goldschmidt, Records, San Bruno; Stein, *California and the Dust Bowl Migration*, 93.

56. McWilliams, *Factories in the Field*, 7. The best source on McWilliams is his colorful autobiography, *The Education of Carey McWilliams* (New York, 1978).

57. *Sacramento Bee* (March 9, April 23, 1940); Stein, *California and the Dust Bowl Migration*, 190–215.

58. *San Francisco Examiner* (March 6, 1939). On the Houser bill see the Tolan Committee, *Hearings*, Part 7, pp. 3035–37; Stein, *California and the Dust Bowl Migration*, 122.

59. Olson's struggles with the economy bloc over relief and migration have been expertly recounted by his biographer, Robert E. Burke, in *Olson's New Deal for California* (Berkeley, 1953), 88–95, 126–38, 162–68. Also important are Chambers, *California Farm Organizations*, 82–97; Stein, *California and the Dust Bowl Migration*, 109–36. SRA policies are explained in California State Relief Adminstration, *Unemployment Relief in Labor Disputes: A Study of the Policies and Actions of the California State Relief Administration from 1936 to 1939, Regarding Aid to Persons Engaged in Labor Disputes* (Los Angeles, 1939), copy in McWilliams Collection. The data on the reduced caseload is from James Bright Wilson, "Social Attitudes of Migratory Agricultural Workers in Kern County, California" (unpublished MA thesis, University of Southern California, 1942), 256.

60. *San Francisco Examiner* (March 3, 1939); *Los Angeles Times* (Jan. 29, Feb. 27, 1939); *Los Angeles Daily News* (March 1, 1939).

61. Letter from R.W. Henderson to the Regional Director of FSA, Nov. 6, 1939, in the FSA Records, Box 22, San Bruno; Stein, *California and the Dust Bowl Migration*, 95–96.

62. Stein, *California and the Dust Bowl Migration*, 130. Tolan Committee, *Hearings*, Part 26, provides a massive report on the case, including important legal documents relating to this historic decision.

63. James Bright Wilson, "Religious Leaders, Institutions and Organizations Among Certain Agricultural Workers in the Central Valley of California" (unpublished Ph.D. diss., University of Southern California, 1944), 161–62. See also "Okies Welcomed," *Business Week* (Nov. 8, 1941), 29; *Fresno Bee* (July 17, 1942); Joel Warkentin, "A Decade of Migratory Labor in the San Joaquin Valley 1940–1950," (unpublished MA thesis, University of California, Berkeley, 1952), 21–22.

64. John Steinbeck, *The Grapes of Wrath* (New York, 1963), 280. See also W. Richard Fossey, "Talkin' Dust Bowl Blues: A Study of Oklahoma's Cultural Identity During the Great Depression," *The Chronicles of Oklahoma* 55 (Spring 1977), 12–33.

65. Goldschmidt, *As You Sow*, 61. Similar observations can be found in Wilson, "Social Attitudes of Migratory Agricultural Workers," 247; Stuart M. Jamieson, "A Settlement of Rural Migrant Families in the Sacramento Valley, California," *Rural Sociology* VII (March 1942), 50; Judith Wright, "A Study of the Community Organization of Hemet, California with Special Reference to Problems and Resources" (unpublished MSW thesis, University of Southern California, 1939), 27; George Gleason, *The Fifth Migration: A Report of the California Migratory Agricultural Worker Situation*, reprinted in Tolan Committee, *Hearings*, Part 7, 2998.

66. Lawrence Hewes, *Boxcar in the Sand* (New York, 1957), 115.

67. *Ibid.*, 116.

68. Ben Hibbs, "Footloose Army," *Country Gentleman* (Feb. 1940), reprint in Migrant Labor Collection, Bakersfield Public Library; Wasco field notes.

69. Wasco field notes.

70. J.H. Currie, "Labor Camps in the San Joaquin," *Pacific Rural Press* 83 (June 19, 1937).

71. Alice Reichard, "California's Adult Children," *Country Gentleman* (Feb. 1940), reprint in Fresno Public Library, migrant labor file. Similar descriptions can be found in Frank J. Taylor, "Labor on Wheels," *Country Gentleman* (July 1938), 12.

72. Interview by author, Oakland, June 12, 1985.

73. Melvin Gerald Shahan interview, by Jackie Malone, Oct. 29, 1976. Oral History Program, California State University, Fullerton, 44.

74. Wanda Audrey Shahan Wall interview, by Jackie Malone, Oct. 6, 1976. Oral History Program, California State University, Fullerton, 17. Like Coleman, adults generally deny any significant problems: Ruby Barnes interview by author, Long Beach, June 3, 1981; Audie Moffitt interview by author, Long Beach, June 5, 1981. In his study of Bell Gardens, Charles B. Spaulding indicated that Okies were held in modest disdain. "The Development of Organization and Disorganization in the Social Life of a Rapidly Growing Working-Class Suburb Within a Metropolitan District" (unpublished Ph.D. diss., University of Southern California, 1939), 54–55, 99–101.

75. Creisler, "Little Oklahoma," 63–75, 90–94. For an earlier survey of the opinions of nearly 300 influential farmers and health officials representing each of the state's 33 agricultural counties, see California State Relief Administration, *Agricultural Migratory Laborers in the San Joaquin Valley*, 27–43. The report's authors concluded that the typical view of the Dust Bowl migrant was that they are "of a low mentality and are not particularly good workers. They are for the most part restive, non-dependable, and do not make good use of the little [intelligence] they have."

76. Jamieson, "A Settlement of Rural Migrant Families in the Sacramento Valley," 50; Stein, *California and the Dust Bowl Migration*, 59–60. Goldschmidt, *As You Sow*, 72–73, puts it somewhat differently but agrees that the newcomer's "outsider" status was a product of the social structure of California's agricultural communities.

77. Richard C. Bailey, *Bakersfield, Heart of the Golden Empire* (Woodland Hills, Calif., 1984), 36–37; Wallace Smith, *Garden of the Sun* (Fresno, 1939), 265–67. Devra Weber emphasizes the role of Southerners in "The Struggle for Stability

and Control in the Cotton Fields of California," 47–48. See also John Turner, *White Gold Comes to California* (Bakersfield, 1981), 36–44; William J. Briggs and Henry Cauthen, *The Cotton Man: Notes on the Life and Times of Wofford B. "Bill" Camp* (Columbia, S.C., 1983).

78. Wilson and Peterson, *Who's Who in Kern County* (Bakersfield, 1941).

79. Creisler, "Little Oklahoma," 28, 108. See the letter from Mrs. James Dunn in *Voice of the Migrant* (Marysville) (Feb. 23, 1940), in which she complains of being considered "one of those Oakies" even though she was born and raised in California. Goldschmidt, *As You Sow*, 72–73, makes the same point.

80. Interview by Michael Neely, May 1, 1981, Fresno, Odyssey Project. For a similar report by a North Dakotan see John Otto, "Okies, Arkies and Texans: One Man's Recollections of Migrant Workers in Depression California," *California Historical Courier* 40 (Dec. 1978), 5–6. Elizabeth Day, a Nebraskan, tells of her efforts to distinguish herself from Okies in her Odyssey Program interview.

81. Mr. C.S., Wasco field notes.

82. Wasco field notes. Former President Hoover made the same distinctions in an interview with the *Los Angeles Times* (April 5, 1940).

83. Shields McIlwaine, *The Southern Poor White from Lubberland to Tobacco Road* (Norman, 1939); Sylvia Jenkins Cook, *From Tobacco Road to Route 66: The Southern Poor White in Fiction* (Chapel Hill, 1976); Rubert B. Vance, *Human Geography of the South* (Chapel Hill, 1935), 463–65; Merrill Maguire Skaggs, *The Folk of Southern Fiction* (Athens, Ga., 1972), 16–22.

84. Kevin Starr, *Americans and the California Dream* (New York, 1973), 192–93. Piker also had an Old English meaning as robber or thief (*Oxford English Dictionary*). Eric Foner, *Free Soil, Free Labor, Free Men* (New York, 1970), 47, discusses antebellum northern images of Southern poor whites.

85. William King, "El Monte 1851–1941" (MA thesis, Claremont Graduate School, 1966), 14.

86. Letter to John P. McLaughlin from George ?, Assistant Deputy Commissioner of Labor, Dec. 20, 1920, McWilliams Collection; Emma Duke, "California the Golden," *The American Child* 2 (Nov. 1920), 236.

87. Harry B. Ansted, "The Auto-Camp Community: A New Type of Social Institution," *Journal of Applied Sociology* 9 (Nov.–Dec. 1924), 138, 140.

88. Ronnie Dugger, *The Politician: The Life and Times of Lyndon Johnson: The Drive for Power, from the Frontier to Master of the Senate* (New York, 1982), 100–103. Roger Daniels was kind enough to tell me about this.

89. Interview by Stacey Jagels, Oildale, Feb. 24, 26, 1981, Odyssey Program. Also the several interviews with earlier migrants in Wasco field notes; Elbert Garretson and Clarence Graham Odyssey Program interviews. On the other hand Hazel Mitchell, in her interview in the same series, tells of hearing cruel comments in her first school years in Kern County in 1928–29.

90. George B. Tindall, "The Benighted South: Origins of a Modern Image," *Virginia Quarterly Review* 40 (Spring 1964), 281–94; George B. Tindall, *The Emergence of the New South, 1913–1945* (Baton Rouge, 1967), 184–218.

91. Jerry Tompkins, ed., *D-Days at Dayton: Reflections on the Scopes Trial* (Baton Rouge, 1965), 36; Tindall, *Emergence of the New South*, 210.

92. The genre included novels like Caldwell's *Tobacco Road* (New York, 1932)

and *God's Little Acre* (New York, 1933), Faulkner's *Light in August* (New York, 1932), and Steinbeck's *The Grapes of Wrath* (New York, 1939). Nonfictional studies included James Agee and Walker Evans, *Let Us Now Praise Famous Men* (New York, 1939); Erskine Caldwell and Margaret Bourke-White, *You Have Seen Their Faces* (New York, 1937); Arthur F. Raper, *Preface to Peasantry* (Chapel Hill, 1936); Arthur F. Raper and Ira De A. Reid, *Sharecroppers All* (Chapel Hill, 1941); Margaret Jarman Hagood, *Mothers of the South: Portraiture of the White Tenant Farm Women* (Chapel Hill, 1939). The federal government funded a great deal of research on the problems of tenant farmers and Southern poor whites. See especially Federal Writers' Project, *These Are Our Lives* (Chapel Hill, 1939); T.J. Woofter Jr., *Landlord and Tenant on the Cotton Plantation*, WPA Research Monograph V (Wash., D.C., 1936).

The image of the sharecropper was related to that of the "hillbilly," another segment of the South's poor white population. "Hillbillies" had become a focus of public attention early in the twentieth century, and throughout the 1920s and 1930s they remained a favorite cultural curiosity for urban Americans. Thought of as quaint relics of an earlier stage of frontier civilization, the mountaineers were the subject of both serious study and endless ridicule. Hillbilly humorists and hillbilly comic strips like "Li'l Abner" and "Barney Google" helped spread the notion of a ludicrous "race" of people cut off from the modern world. The stereotype of the hillbilly inevitably became intertwined with images of other Southern poor whites, adding to the primitive backwoods public conception of the entire group. Henry Shapiro, *Appalachia on Our Mind: The Southern Mountains and Mountaineers in American Consciousness, 1890–1920* (Chapel Hill, 1978) is a fascinating study of the changing public conception of the "hillbilly."

93. Quoted in C.L. Sonnichsen, "The Sharecropper Novel in the Southwest," *Agricultural History*, 43 (April 1969), 249.

94. Erskine Caldwell, *Tobacco Road*. Caldwell's perception of Southern tenant farmers can also be seen in the follow-up nonfiction book he wrote in collaboration with photographer Margaret Bourke-White, *You Have Seen Their Faces*. Accompanying photographs of what must have been the most diseased and forlorn-looking sharecroppers the authors could find, Caldwell wrote: "Ten million persons on Southern tenant farms are living in degradation and defeat. They have been beaten and subjected. They are depleted and sterile. All has been taken from them and they have nothing. . . . But they are still people, they are human beings. They have life. The older ones . . . are wasted human beings whose blood made the cotton leaves green and the blossoms red. . . . The young people still have strong bodies and the will to succeed. . . . With hope and a dream before them, they can change a hell into a living paradise" (p. 48).

95. Mildred Rutherford Mell, "Poor Whites of the South," *Social Forces* 17 (Dec. 1938), 153; McIlwaine, *The Southern Poor White*, 242.

96. Schuler, "Dust Bowl Moves to California," 5.

97. 1940 Census Public Use Microdata Sample.

98. Arthur Lundin, "Observations Made During Stay at Arvin Migratory Labor Camp, July 10 to July 17, 1936," in the FSA Collection, Box 21, San Bruno.

99. Jackson J. Benson, 'To Tom, Who Lived It': John Steinbeck and the Man from Weedpatch," *Journal of Modern Literature* V (April 1976), 188.

100. Tom Collins, Kern Migratory Camp Report, March 7, 1936, FSA Records, Box 23, San Bruno.

101. On Collin's literary efforts see Benson, " 'To Tom, Who Lived It,' " 151–210. William Stott, *Documentary Expression and Thirties America* (Chicago, 1973), is the essential guide to the broader effort. The Library of Congress Archive of Folk Culture houses part of the WPA collection, but most of it is scattered in libraries across the country. Portions of the invaluable ex-slave narratives have been published, as have three volumes of narratives by whites, mostly Southerners: Federal Writers' Collection, *These Are Our Lives* (Chapel Hill, 1939); Tom E. Terrill and Jerrold Hirsch, eds., *Such as Us: Southern Voices of the Thirties* (Chapel Hill, 1978); Ann Banks, *First Person America* (New York, 1980).

102. Wanda D. Mann, "Migrant Nursing," *Pacific Coast Journal of Nursing* 37 (Nov. 1941), 659; California Department of Public Health, Anita E. Faverman, *Trailing Child and Maternal Health into Migratory Agricultural Camps: Report of the Second Year of the Migratory Demonstration, July 1937–June 1938* (San Francisco, 1937), 45, mimeographed copy in McWilliams Collection; Esther A. Canter, "California 'Renovates' the DustBowler," *Hygeia* (May 1940), 421–23, 454–55; Mary Sears, R.N., "The Nurse and the Migrant," *Pacific Coast Journal of Nursing* 37 (March 1941), 144–46. Kern County Health Department, "Survey of Kern County Migratory Labor Problem" (n.p., 1937), mimeographed copy in McWilliams Collection.

103. Florence McGehee, *Please Excuse Johnny* (New York, 1952), 9–18; Statement of W. Max Smith, District Superintendent of Merced City elementary schools, Tolan Committee, *Hearings*, Part 6, p. 2436; *Fresno County Schools Bulletin* I (April 1945), 11. To get an idea of the lengths to which some well-meaning observers had to go to reconcile their presumptions about the newcomers' background with the reality they actually observed, witness the following discussion by a Kern County High School teacher of the literary aptitudes of her "Okie" pupils. Complaining that they do not appreciate the classic adventure novels like *Ivanhoe*, she noted disparagingly that instead "like most primitives, my subjects *like* poetry, provided they can recognize it as such. They come of a ballad-loving race, of English and Scotch-Irish stock. In the tests for appreciation of poetry they show surprising soundness of judgement and feeling for rhythm" (Evelyn Rudd, "Reading List—Design for Living," typed MS (n.p., 1941?) in Wasco field notes.

104. Charles Todd and Robert Sonkin, "Ballads of the Okies," *New York Times Magazine* (Nov. 17, 1940).

105. A.E. Anderson, "The Children in Fruit-Pickers Camps," *Oakland Post Enquirer* (Aug. 23, 1937).

106. Letter to Professor Gerald Haslam, Jan. 1975, in Charles Todd Collection.

107. Interview with Wofford and Ruth Clark, by author, La Mirada, Calif., June 8, 1981. Tod Moquist analyzed the opinions of the former migrants interviewed by the Odyssey Program and reports a mixture of favorable and unfavorable opinions: "Migrant Response to *The Grapes of Wrath*: Evidence from Oral History in the San Joaquin Valley," paper delivered at the Third John Steinbeck Festival, Salinas, Aug. 8, 1982. See also Guy Logsdon, "The Dust Bowl and the Migrant," *The American Scene* 12:1 (1971); Sue Sanders, *The Real Causes of Our Migrant Problem* (n.p., 1940), 7.

108. Reichard, "Adult Children."

109. Sears, "The Nurse and the Migrant," 145.

Chapter 4. The Dilemma of Outsiders

1. *Voice of the Migrant* (Jan. 26, 1940).

2. Letter to editor, *Modesto Bee* (March 2, 1938).

3. Letter to editor, *Modesto Bee* (March 24, 1938).

4. Letter to editor, *Modesto Bee* (March 23, 1938).

5. Letter to editor, *Fresno Bee* (March 19, 1938).

6. Lillian Creisler, " 'Little Oklahoma' or the Airport Community: A Study of the Social and Economic Adjustment of Self-settled Agricultural Drought and Depression Refugees" (unpublished MA thesis, University of California, Berkeley, 1940), 103.

7. Letter from Mrs. Carl Austin, Los Angeles, March 25, 1936, to President Roosevelt, California Transient Complaints, FERA Records, National Archives. See also the statements of E.R. Hughes in *Voice of the Migrant* (Marysville) (Feb. 16, 1940) and Arthur Brown* in James Bright Wilson, "Social Attitudes of Certain Migratory Agricultural Workers in Kern County, California" (unpublished MA thesis, University of Southern California, 1942), 77.

8. *Tow-Sack Tattler* (Arvin) (Nov. 11, 1939).

9. Seymour J. Janow and William Gilmartin, "Labor and Agricultural Migration to California, 1935–1940," *Monthly Labor Review* 53 (July 1941), 31. See also the testimony of S.G. Rubinow, Administrator SRA, Tolan Committee, *Hearings*, Part 7, p. 2877. Tolan Committee, *Interstate Migration*, 490A–496C, counted 5,350 unemployment insurance claimants and their families returning to the Southwest from California during 1939. Most agricultural workers, however, would not have been counted in this study.

10. Robert T. McMillan, *Migration of Population in Five Oklahoma Townships*, Oklahoma Agricultural Experimental Station Bulletin No. B-271 (Stillwater, Oct. 1943), 35.

11. Clara Davis tells this story in her Odyssey Program interview, 27.

12. Thomas W. Pew, Jr., "Route 66, Ghost Road of the Okies," *American Heritage* 28 (Aug. 1977), 32.

13. Todd-Sonkin Recordings, Arvin, Aug. 1, 1940.

14. Todd-Sonkin Recordings, Arvin, Aug. 24, 1941.

15. Mr. J.J., Wasco field notes. See also Lucretia Penny, "Pea-Picker's Child," *Survey Graphic* 24 (July 1935), 352.

16. Janet Sutter, "The Way West," *San Diego Union* (Sept. 9, 1985). Lissa Churchill Gray, "Population Growth, Pope County, Arkansas, with Emphasis upon Migration, 1920–1976" (unpublished MA thesis, University of Arkansas, 1977), 51ff, interviewed 40 people who had returned to that county from California between 1969 and 1975. For other reports of the retirement exodus see George Baker, "66, Road Back in Time," *Sacramento Bee* (Jan. 1, 1978); "The Okies," unattributed undated Associated Press clipping in Charles Todd Collection.

17. Jan. 1975 letter to Prof. Gerald Haslam in Charles Todd Collection.

18. Letter to Prof. Gerald Haslam, dated Feb. 1979, in Charles Todd Collection.

19. Interview by Stacey Jagels, Tulare, March 19, 21, 1981, Odyssey Program, 45–46.

20. Interview by Tod Moquist, Shafter, March 18, April 7, 27, 1982, Odyssey Program. For other examples see Michael Fessier, Jr., "Grapes of Wrath, 1977," *New West* (July 18, 1977), 24–31.

21. There is a strong parallel in the experience of Appalachian migrants to northern cities. See Don Edward Merten's perceptive study, "Up Here and Down Home: Appalachian Migrants in Northtown" (unpublished Ph.D. diss., University of Chicago, 1974), 289–93; Harry K. Schwarzweller, J.S. Brown, and J.J. Mangalam, *Mountain Families in Transition* (University Park, Pa. 1971); and by the same authors, "Kentucky Mountain Migration and the Stem-Family: An American Variation on a Theme by Le Play," in Clifford J. Jansen, ed., *Readings in the Sociology of Migration* (New York, 1970), 93–120.

22. We have only limited information about ecological factors. We know from the Public Use Microdata Samples that Southwesterners accounted for 21 percent of the adult San Joaquin Valley population in 1940 and 27 percent in 1950, with the concentration heavier in Kern County and probably weaker in Stanislaus. And the representation should have been higher still in the prime marriage ages. The number of Southwestern brides and grooms in the marriage samples, however, exceeds these estimates, accounting for 48 percent and 54 percent of the 1939 and 1949 Kern samples, 24 percent and 36 percent of the Stanislaus samples.

The class factor can be seen in the table. Occupational data is available only for grooms and the sample sizes are tiny, but the results suggest that endogamous behavior was much more common among the laboring class than at higher occupational levels.

Endogamous Marriage Rate for Southwestern* Grooms by Occupational Class

	Kern 1939	Kern 1949	Stan. 1939	Stan. 1949
White collar	47%	46%	45%	35%
N =	(38)	(37)	(22)	(26)
Blue collar	52%	58%	48%	56%
N =	(65)	(69)	(27)	(59)
Laborer	80%	86%	58%	75%
N =	(64)	(43)	(53)	(63)

*Includes California-born with two Southwestern parents.
Source: See Appendix D.

23. Interview by Stacey Jagels, Fresno, March 10, 1981, 21. Also Terry Clipper and Elizabeth Day interviews in same collection.

24. *Antioch Ledger* (Dec. 9, 1938).

25. John Maynard, untitled senior thesis (an oral history of the Dust Bowl migration in Kern County), University of California, Santa Cruz, Winter 1968, 16. See also Mr. and Mrs. Claude Botkin interview notes, Arvin, April 14, 1944, Goldschmidt Records, Box 66, San Bruno.

26. Hoadley, "A Study of 170 Self-Resettled Agricultural Families," 126.

27. Charles Todd, untitled MS (n.p., 1941?) in Charles Todd Collection. See

also comments of two other Oklahomans in Todd-Sonkin field notes, 10; Carey McWilliams, "California Pastoral," *Antioch Review* 2 (March 1946), 114–16.

28. Goldschmidt, *As You Sow*, 73. For other examples of this approach see Reverend Brown interview notes, Arvin, April 1944, Goldschmidt Records, Box 66, San Bruno; Camille Gavin, "All They Brought with Them Was Their Pride ...," *Bakersfield Californian* (Aug. 26, 1979); Wilson, "Social Attitudes of Agricultural Workers," 197; Clara Davis Odyssey interview, 37.

29. Interview by author, Santa Monica, June 3, 1981.

30. Interview by Michael Neely, Auberry, May 26, 28, 1981, Odyssey Program, 16.

31. Interview by author, Huntington Beach, Aug. 18, 1980.

32. Interview by author, Long Beach, June 3, 1981.

33. David Lyon, "Campfires Dotted the Still Nights," *Bakersfield Californian* (May 27, 1979). Other examples of this sort of dissociation can be found in the letter by C.A. Tilghman, *Los Angeles Times* (July 18, 1937); and Charles B. Spaulding, "The Development of Organization and Disorganization in the Social Life of a Rapidly Growing Working-Class Suburb Within a Metropolitan District" (unpublished Ph.D. diss., University of Southern California, 1939), 71.

34. The sources for all of these stories must remain anonymous. The "closet Okie" confession is in a letter dated Nov. 8, 1977 to Prof. Gerald Haslam, Charles Todd Collection.

35. See Beatrice W. Griffith, *American Me* (Boston, 1948), 236–37; Gordon W. Allport, *The Nature of Prejudice* (New York, 1958), abridged ed., 142–43; Andrew M. Greeley, *Why Can't They Be Like Us?* (New York, 1971), 54–56.

36. Bruce Ray Berryhill, "The Relationship Between Regional and Social Dialects and Linguistic Adaptation" (unpublished MA thesis, California State University, Fresno, 1976). For examples of accent changing see Odyssey Program interviews with Jewell Egbert, Martha Jackson, Byrd Morgan, Dorothy Rose, and Vernon Seabolt.

37. Mr. E.C., Mr. D.C., and Mr. W.B.B., Wasco field notes. On the other hand, Mr. H.S., a Texan who had obtained a farm near Wasco, had joined the Associated Farmers and talked disparagingly about the migrant population. Also Goldschmidt, *As You Sow*, 155–59; Clarence Graham interview, Odyssey Program.

38. Wilson, "Social Attitudes of Agricultural Workers," 149. See also the comments of Dale Morrison in Oliver Carlson, "Up from the Dust," *U.S.A.* (Aug. 1952), 100; Katherine Archibald, *Wartime Shipyard: A Study in Social Disunity* (Berkeley, 1947), 52.

39. Camille Gavin, "Depression Wasn't All Tragedy, but It Was Tough," *Bakersfield Californian* (Sept. 9, 1979); also Shirley Cox interview by author, Bakersfield, Sept. 14, 1979. Other incidents are recorded in the Odyssey Program interviews and *Voice of the Migrant* (Marysville) (Feb. 23, 1940).

40. Creisler, "Little Oklahoma," 55. Also the interview with an American Legion post commander, Wasco field notes; and Mr. Ernest interview notes, Arvin, April 13, 1944, Goldschmidt Records, Box 66, San Bruno.

41. Goldschmidt, *As You Sow*, 138. For other examples of religious and social organizations that remained off-limits to poor Southwesterners see George Gleason, *The Fifth Migration: A Report on the California Migratory Agricultural Situ-*

ation, reprinted in Tolan Committee, *Hearings*, Part 7, p. 3000; Wilson, "Religious Organizations Among Agricultural Workers," 171–75. Lawrence Hewes, *Boxcar in the Sand* (New York, 1957), 115.

42. Mr. C.S., Wasco field notes.

43. Wilson, "Social Attitudes of Agricultural Workers," 248 (Clyde Storey*).

44. *Ibid.*, 316 (John Bailey*). For similar comments see Mrs. D.L., Wasco field notes; Creisler, "Little Oklahoma," 64; Dorothea Lange and Paul Schuster Taylor, *An American Exodus: A Record of Human Erosion* (New York, 1939), 60.

45. Wilson, "Social Attitudes of Agricultural Workers," 149.

46. *Ibid.*, 281. Other reports include Archibald, *Wartime Shipyard*, 54; Viola Mitchell interview, Odyssey Program, 9. See also the discussion in chapter 5.

47. Wilson, "Social Attitudes of Agricultural Workers," 272–73.

48. Herbert H. Mansing, Resettlement Administration, Investigation Division, Confidential Report, 1936, in the FSA Collection, Box 18, San Bruno. See also Frank Stockton interview notes, Arvin, April 3, 1944, Goldschmidt Records, Box 66, San Bruno.

49. A.E. Anderson, "Gaunt Women," *Oakland Post Enquirer* (Aug. 31, 1937); Hewes, *Boxcar in the Sand*, 112; California Department of Public Health, Anita Faverman, *Report of the Migratory Demonstration July 1936–June 1937: A Study of the Health of 1,000 Children of Migratory Agricultural Laborers in California* (San Francisco, 1937), 6, mimeographed copy in McWilliams Collection.

50. *Bakersfield Californian* (Sept. 16, 1979).

51. Clara Davis interview, by author; also Odyssey Program interview, 37.

52. Mrs. J.R., Wasco field notes; also the comments of Mrs. I.G.: "The people here are awful friendly—but most of them are from back there it seems like." For similar recollections see Morris family interview by Margo McBane and Mary Winegarden, Richmond, July 1978, Women Farmworkers Project. Also John Blake interview by author, Bakersfield, Sept. 14, 1979; Ed Crane, Hadley Yocum, and J.R. McClintock interviews, Odyssey Program.

53. Creisler, "Little Oklahoma," p. 64.

54. See Chapter 5. The quote is from Althes Robbins letter to the *Modesto Bee* (March 2, 1938).

55. *Voice of the Migrant* (Marysville) (Dec. 8, 1939, Feb. 23, 1940); Shirley Cox interview.

56. This is from two separate letters to Professor Gerald Haslam dated Nov. 8, 1977, and July 8, 1978, in Charles Todd Collection. See also Creisler, "Little Oklahoma," 52–53.

57. William Law, "Problems of the Migratory Student," *California Journal of Secondary Education*, 14 (March 1939), 172. There is a substantial literature on the educational problems of migrant children. See Edward J. Rowell, "The Children of the Migratory Camp—Education," copy in the Haynes Collection; Emmett Berry, "A Report on the Education of Children of Migrant Families, Porterville Elementary School System, February 19, 1940," Tolan Committee, *Hearings*, Part 6, pp. 2435–37; Lester A. Kirkendall, "Education and the Recent Western Migration," *The Journal of Educational Sociology* 14 (April 1941), 488–501; "A Study of the Migratory Children in Kern County for the School Year 1936–1937," typescript (n.p., n.d.) in Federal Writers' Collection, carton 37; Rita M. Hansen,

"Educating Elementary School Children of Seasonal-Migrant Agricultural Workers in the San Joaquin Valley" (unpublished Ed.D. diss., Stanford University, 1949); Clarence E. Spencer, "A Study of Pupil Age-Grade-Progress in the Schools of the Southern District of Kern County," Tolan Committee, *Hearings*, Part 6, pp. 2438–55; Jettye Fern Grant, "A Comparison of the Educational Achievement of Migratory Children and Children of Permanent California Residents" (unpublished MA thesis, University of Southern California, 1941).

58. Shirley Cox interview.

59. Ronald B. Taylor, "California's Okies Look Back on Pain of the '30s," *Los Angeles Times* (Oct. 5, 1980).

60. Creisler, "Little Oklahoma," 52. For other incidents see Shafter Camp Manager's Report, Oct. 1939, FSA Collection, Box 46, San Bruno; Vera Criswell interview, Odyssey Program, 35.

61. The quote is from Leo B. Hart interview by Gerald Stanley (n.p., n.d.) in Oral History Collection, California State College, Bakersfield, Library. Hart was Superintendent of Schools in Kern County and worked hard to improve educational facilities for migrant children. See his account *Our Conquest: A Report on the Development of Kern County Rural Schools 1939–1946* (Bakersfield, 1946). See also Gerald Stanley, "Educating the Children of the Grapes of Wrath: The Strange Story of Arvin Federal Emergency School, 1940–44," *California History* 59 (Summer 1980); educational strategies can also be seen in: Report of Mary K. Davies, headteacher Yuba City Camp nursery school, May 1941, FSA Collection, carton 2, Bancroft; Gladys L. Potter, "Specific Suggestions for the Organization of Instruction in Elementary Schools," *California Journal of Education* (Feb. 2, 1939), typed copy in Federal Writers' Collection, carton 10; and in the same collection Mildred Krohn, "Migratory Home," *Sierra Educational News* (Nov. 1938); Irma Weill, "We've Been Rollin'," *The Family* 16 (Feb. 1936), 319.

62. Rita M. Hansen, "Educating the Children of Seasonal Migrant Agricultural Workers in the San Joaquin Valley," *Journal of Elementary Education* 18 (May 1950), 248. See also the statement of W. Max Smith, district superintendent of Merced City elementary schools, Tolan Committee, *Hearings*, Part 6, p. 2436.

63. Yuba County Superintendent of Schools, *A Survey of the Eduational Needs of Exceptional Children and Youth in Yuba County* (n.p., 1948–49), 23; Evelyn Rudd, "Reading List—Design for Living," typed MS (n.p., 1941?) in Walter Goldschmidt's personal files.

64. Law, "Problems of the Migratory Student," 172.

65. Rowell, "The Child of the Migratory Camp—Education," 5.

66. *Voice of the Migrant* (Marysville) (Feb. 23, 1940). Some parents apparently did not know what was going on in the schools. One woman explained that only much later did her children tell her that they felt looked down upon. "They knew, I guess, that they had to go to school there, and they didn't say too much about it. But after they got out of the school they talked about it. . . . They felt bad. They felt that them kids up there thought that they were better than they." (Bertha Leuwellan interview, by Margo McBane and Jim Stein, Visalia, July 20, 1978, Women Farmworkers Project.

67. Kern County Mental Hygiene Society, "A Study of the Effect of Mobility on the Adjustment of School Children Made by a Preparatory Commission for the

International Congress of Mental Health, London, August 11–21, 1948," typed MS (n.p., n.d.), 7, 30, in Bakersfield Public Library. See also Helen Hefferman, "Children of Seasonal Workers," *California Journal of Elementary Education* (1938?), 16, typed copy in Federal Writers' Collection, carton 9; DeVere A. Stephens, "An Analysis of the School and Home Problems of Migratory Children" (unpublished MA thesis, University of Southern California, 1940), 52; Hansen, "Educating the Children of Agricultural Workers" (article), 247.

68. Wilson, "Religious Organizations Among Agricultural Workers," 122.

69. *Ibid.*

70. Goldschmidt, *As You Sow*, 100, 161.

71. Carlson, "Up from the Dust," *U.S.A.* (Aug. 1952), 100.

72. Mark Jones, "Dust Bowl Clan Marks 44 Years in West," *Los Angeles Times* (Aug. 2, 1981).

73. Interview by Barbara Loomis, Portland, Oregon, Dec. 1978.

74. Gleason, *The Fifth Migration*, 2999. See also Wilson, "Religious Organizations Among Agricultural Workers," 108–9.

75. Letter to Prof. Gerald Haslam, Oct. 16, 1978, in Charles Todd Collection.

76. Todd-Sonkin field notes, 14, 66.

77. Stephens, "An Analysis of the School Problems of Migratory Children," 31–32, 52.

78. Wilson, "Social Attitudes of Agricultural Workers," 239.

79. Robert E. Lantz testimony, Governor's Committee to Survey the Agricultural Labor Resources of the San Joaquin Valley, *Transcript of Public Hearing, August 3, 1950, Corcoran, California* (n.p., n.d.), 74.

80. Vernon Pruit testimony, Governor's Committee to Survey the Agricultural Labor Resources of the San Joaquin Valley, *Corcoran Hearing*, 127. See also Gould, "A Report of the Poplar Project," 576.

81. Gleason, *The Fifth Migration*, 2999.

82. Kern County Mental Hygiene Society, "A Study of the Effect of Mobility on School Children," 12, reported that 462 of Kern County's juvenile offenders during 1945 and 1946 had been born in the Southwest while 337 were California-born. *San Francisco Independent* (Dec. 20, 1939) reported that 18 percent of the inmates of San Quentin prison came from the "Dust Bowl states." The 1950 Public Use Microdata Sample also contains a suggestive bit of data. The sample size was too tiny for any solid conclusions but 8 out of 31 state prison inmates enumerated were whites born in the Southwest, more than twice the expected representation. See also Anne Roller Issler, "California and Its Migrants," *Survey* 85 (Oct. 1949), 547; Testimony of B.C. Hawkins, Juvenile Judge of Stanislaus County, in California State Legislature, Assembly, Interim Committee on Juvenile Delinquency, H.R.268, *Preliminary Report* (Sacramento, 1944), 10; Judge Floyd and Mayor George Eaton interview notes, April and May 1944, Goldschmidt Records, Box 66, San Bruno. My thanks to Neil Basen for the *Independent* reference.

83. *Kern County Union High School District Bulletin* I (Jan. 1946); Creisler, "Little Oklahoma," 51–52, 110; Don Townsend interview by author, Modesto, Jan. 18, 1978. Townsend, an attendance officer with the Modesto schools, grew up in the city's Little Oklahoma and observed the high drop-out rate among his contemporaries.

84. U.S. Department of Agriculture, Bureau of Agricultural Economics and Farm Security Administration, *Population in Farm Security Administration Camps*, No. 1 (Berkeley, 1940), 17. On the very high drop-out rate in the camps see also the School Site Report, Arvin-Lamont Area, Jan. 10, 1941, in Goldschmidt Records, Box 66, San Bruno.

85. Willodine Winningham interview.

Chapter 5. Plain-Folk Americanism

1. My definition of subculture follows Milton M. Gordon, *Assimilation in American Life* (New York, 1964), 39. For a rich discussion of the uses and possible definitions see Edward Merten, "Up Here and Down Home: Appalachian Migrants in Northtown" (unpublished Ph.D. diss., 1974, University of Chicago), 180–99; J. Milton Yinger, "Contraculture and Subculture," *American Sociological Review* 25 (1960), 625–35.

2. Walter Goldschmidt, *As You Sow* (Glencoe, 1947, reprint ed. Montclair, N.J., 1978), 60–61, 70. Few other scholars even raised the question of Okies as a separate cultural group. Most concerned themselves strictly with the parameters of economic adjustment, as in the work of Paul Taylor, his students Lillian Creisler and Walter Hoadley, Carey McWilliams, and the Bureau of Agricultural Economics investigators. James Wilson collected wonderful material on the social attitudes and religious outlooks of the migrants in his two studies, but offered little interpretation of its significance.

3. Stuart M. Jamieson, "A Settlement of Rural Migrant Families in the Sacramento Valley, California," *Rural Sociology* VII (March 1942), 50–51, 57. Writing in 1947, Paul Faulkner Tjensvold also commented on the Southern cultural characteristics of the migrants and noted that some of these were being maintained in California. "An Inquiry into the Reasons for the Post-Depression Migration from Oklahoma to Kern County in California" (unpublished MA thesis, University of Southern California, 1947), 45.

4. The ethnic formulation was sharply criticized at the 1947 meeting of the American Sociological Association. In a panel on the state of ethnic research, UCLA sociologist Leonard Bloom suggested that Okies had the characteristics of an ethnic group. Other panelists dismissed the idea, one suggesting that Bloom might as well include "Townsendites [or] the Aimee McPhersonites" under the ethnic heading. "Concerning Ethnic Research," *American Sociological Review* 13 (April 1948), 171–82. The standard understanding of ethnicity in that period is found in W. Lloyd Warner and Leo Srole, *The Social Systems of American Ethnicity* (New Haven, 1945), 28.

In contrast, recent ethnic studies tend to employ a more elastic definition that accepts the possibility of new or "emergent" ethnic groups. See for instance William L. Yancy, Eugene P. Ericksen, and Richard N. Juliani, "Emergent Ethnicity: A Review and Reformulation," *American Sociological Review* 41 (June 1976), 391–403; Abner Cohen in *Urban Ethnicity* (New York, 1974), ix–xxiv; Donald L. Horowitz, "Ethnic Identity," in Nathan Glazer and Daniel P. Moynihan, eds., *Ethnicity: Theory and Experience* (Cambridge, 1975), 111–40; Jonathan D. Sarna, "From Immigrants to Ethnic: Toward a New Theory of 'Ethnicization,' " *Ethnicity* 5 (Dec. 1978), 370–77; Kathleen Neils Conzen, "Immigrants, Immigrant Neighborhoods, and Ethnic Identity: Historical Issues," *Journal of American History* 66 (Dec. 1979), 603–15.

5. John Shelton Reed, *The Enduring South: Subcultural Persistence in Mass Society* (Chapel Hill, 1972); *Southerners: The Social Psychology of Sectionalism* (Chapel Hill, 1983); *Southern Folk, Plain and Fancy: Native White Social Types* (Athens, Ga., 1986); Lewis M. Killian, *White Southerners* (New York, 1970), 143–44; also Merten, "Up Here and Down Home," 311–13. Their ideas have been seconded by George Brown Tindall, *The Ethnic Southerners* (Baton Rouge, 1976), 1–21; and, most important, by the *Harvard Encyclopedia of American Ethnic Groups*, Stephan Thernstrom, Ann Orlov, and Oscar Handlin, eds. (Cambridge, 1980), 944–48.

6. This definition follows the one proposed by R.A. Schermerhorn, *Comparative Ethnic Relations: A Framework for Theory and Research* (Chicago, 1970), 12, and employed by Werner Sollars in his review of "Theory of American Ethnicity . . . ," *American Quarterly* 33 (1981 Bibliography issue), 257–83. Other uses of the term are surveyed Wsevolod W. Isajiw, "Definitions of Ethnicity," *Ethnicity* 1 (July 1974), 111–24.

7. We cannot pretend to any unanimity on the issue of social structure in either the Southwest or the greater South. The lumpers and the splitters have been going at it continuously since the days of Frederick Law Olmstead. Here I am following John Reed's sensible suggestion of a two-race, two-class model in *Southern Folk, Plain and Fancy*, 23.

8. Dewey Grantham, *Southern Progressivism: The Reconciliation of Progress and Tradition* (Knoxville, 1983), 87–107; Lawrence Goodwyn, *Democratic Promise: The Populist Moment in America* (New York, 1976); Raymond Arsenault, *The Wild Ass of the Ozarks: Jeff Davis and the Social Bases of Southern Politics* (Philadelphia, 1984); Alan Brinkley, *Voices of Protest: Huey Long, Father Coughlin and the Great Depression* (New York, 1982), esp. 47–53; V.O. Key, *Southern Politics in State and Nation* (New York, 1950), 261–68; James R. Green, *Grassroots Socialism: Radical Movements in the Southwest 1895–1943* (Baton Rouge, 1978), 396–437; Worth Robert Miller, "Oklahoma Populism: A History of the People's Party of Oklahoma Territory" (unpublished Ph.D. diss., University of Oklahoma, 1984); John Thompson, *Closing the Frontier: Radical Response in Oklahoma, 1889–1923* (Norman, 1986).

9. Charles Todd, "The Pea-Patch Press," typescript in Charles Todd Collection. The best collection of the FSA newspapers resides in the Documents Library, University of California, Berkeley, but the Farm Security Administration Collections at San Bruno and at Bancroft Library contain additional issues. Sheldon S. Kagan, "Goin' Down the Road Feelin' Bad: John Steinbeck's *The Grapes of Wrath* and Migrant Folklore" (unpublished Ph.D. diss., University of Pennsylvania, 1971) makes some interesting comments on the literary quality, the humor, and the political values revealed in the camp newspapers.

10. *Westley Worldbeater* (May 22, 1942). For other versions of this poem see *Covered Wagon News* (Shafter) (July 13, 1940); *Thornton's Camp Paper* (Fall 1940).

11. *Camp Echo* (Brawley) (Jan. 13, 1939). Also recorded by Margaret Valiant in her Migrant Camp Recordings, Archive of Folk Culture, Library of Congress. "Root Hog or Die" by Bill Jackson in Todd-Sonkin Recordings is another example of the same theme.

12. Two recent works explore the toughness theme in American culture: Elliot J. Gorn, *The Manly Art: Bare-Knuckle Prize Fighting in America* (Ithaca, 1986); Rupert Wilkinson, *American Tough: The Tough-Guy Tradition and American Character* (New York, 1986). Roland Marchand, *Advertising the American Dream* (Berkeley, 1985), 285–333, shows that many of these images were appearing in the advertising of the 1930s.

13. "A Grumbler," *Weed Patch Cultivator* (Arvin) (Nov. 11, 1938).

14. *Thornton's Camp Paper* (Fall 1940).

15. *Migratory Clipper* (Indio) (March 9, 1940). See also "The Optimist" in *Voice of the Migrant* (Marysville) (Dec. 15, 1939); "Depression" in *Covered Wagon News* (Shafter) (July 27, 1940); "Old Mrs. So and So," *Tow-Sack Tattler* (Arvin) (Sept. 8, 1939).

16. *Tow-Sack Tattler* (Arvin) (Nov. 11, 1939).

17. *Covered Wagon News* (Shafter) (Aug. 24, 1940).

18. Bertram Wyatt-Brown, *Southern Honor: Ethics and Behavior in the Old South* (New York, 1982). I would also strongly recommend Merten's chapter on honor in "Up Here and Down Home," 142–79.

19. *Agri-News* (Shafter) (Aug. 11, 1939). Also *Tow-Sack Tattler* (Arvin) (Oct. 25, 1940).

20. *Voice of the Agricultural Worker* (Yuba City) (May 28, 1940).

21. *Tow-Sack Tattler* (Arvin) (Oct. 28, 1939). See also Oct. 20 and Nov. 11, 1939, issues. For an example of the stoic attitude expected of children, see Todd-Sonkin field notes, 6.

22. Sept. 8, 1939. The popularity of the matches and the social pressure to fight is recalled by Oscar "Scotty" Kludt in his interview by Michael Neely, Fresno, May 1, 1981, Odyssey Program, 22. See also Lawrence I. Hewes, Jr., Report Before the Special Committee Investigating the Interstate Migration of Destitute Citizens, San Francisco, Sept. 25, 1940, mimeographed copy in FSA Collection, Box 10, Bancroft. If the coverage in the *Bakersfield Californian* (Kern County's major daily) is any indication, professional wrestling was also extremely popular. And it was hardly accidental that some of the featured wrestlers sported names like "Bob Montgomery, the Arkansas blond caveman" and "Otis Clingman, the popular Texas cowboy."

23. *Agri-News* (July 21, 1939).

24. In his discussion of honor and fighting among Chicago's Southern whites, Merten, "Up Here and Down Home," 289, also observes that these values became exaggerated in the new setting. There is a rich literature on the Southern use of violence as an expression of masculine honor. In addition to the studies already cited, see John Shelton Reed, *One South: An Ethnic Approach to Regional Culture* (Baton Rouge, 1982), 139–53; Sheldon Hackney, "Southern Violence," *American Historical Review* 74 (Feb. 1969), 906–25; Raymond D. Gastil, *Culture Regions of the United States* (Seattle, 1975), 97–116; H.C. Brearley, "The Pattern of Violence," in William T. Couch, ed., *Culture in the South* (Chapel Hill), 678–92; Evon Z. Vogt, *Modern Homesteaders: The Life of a Twentieth Century Frontier Community* (Cambridge, Mass., 1955), 158–59; Elliot J. Gorn, " 'Gouge and Bite, Pull Hair and Scratch': The Social Significance of Fighting in the Southern Backcountry," *American Historical Review* 90 (Feb. 1985), 18–43.

25. Gerald Haslam, *Okies: Selected Stories* (Santa Barbara, 1975), 60.

26. Interview by Stacey Jagels, Oakhurst, May 2, 1981, Odyssey Program, 23.

27. Interview by Michael Neely, Visalia, March 23, May 12, 1981, Odyssey Program, 38.

28. Interview by Stacey Jagels, Bakersfield, March 31, April 2, 1981, Odyssey Program, 43.

29. Interview by Stacey Jagels, Hanford, June 2, 1981, Odyssey Program, 24.

30. My thoughts on group myths have been informed by Michaela di Leonardo's recent exploration of Italian-American ethnic identity in *The Varieties of Ethnic Experience: Kinship, Class, and Gender Among California Italian Americans* (Ithaca, 1984). She notes that Italians hold a number of assumptions about group characterological and behavioral traits, some of which are clearly not unique to the group. Regardless, the assumptions themselves have significance. It is the belief in distinctiveness that constitutes one of the essentials of the group relationship. Related points about the content of ethnic identity are made by Talcott Parsons, "Some Theoretical Considerations on the Nature and Trends of Change of Ethnicity," in Glazer and Moynihan, *Ethnicity: Theory and Experience*, 64–66; Fredrik Barth, introduction to *Ethnic Groups and Boundaries: The Social Organization of Culture Difference* (Oslo, 1969), 11–16.

31. Gerald Haslam, "The Okies: Forty Years Later," *The Nation* 220 (March 15, 1975), 302. See also her Jan. 1975 letter to Haslam in Charles Todd Collection.

32. Mark Jones, "Dust Bowl Clan Marks 44 Years in West," *Los Angeles Times* (Aug. 2, 1981).

33. Interview, 38.

34. Interview by author, Reedley, April 31, 1985.

35. George Baker, "66, The Road Back in Time," *Sacramento Bee* (Jan. 1, 1978) (emphasis added).

36. Redneck Populism might be another term for what I am describing. Several recent studies have guided my thinking about plain folks' political values, most importantly Robert Emil Botsch's excellent *We Shall Not Overcome: Populism and Southern Blue-Collar Workers* (Chapel Hill, 1980). Arsenault, *The Wild Ass of the Ozarks*; J. Wayne Flynt, *Dixie's Forgotten People: The South's Poor Whites* (Bloomington, 1979). Useful but marred by its condescending tone is Julian B. Roebuck and Mark Hickson III, *The Southern Redneck: A Phenomenological Class Study* (New York, 1982).

37. *The Hub* (Visalia) (Sept. 13, 1940); *Covered Wagon News* (Shafter) (March 12, 1940); *Tow-Sack Tattler* (Sept. 8, 1939). See also Eric H. Thomsen, "Maverick Universities or How the Migrant Gets an Education" (speech before the San Francisco Public School Forum, Jan. 29, 1937), in FSA Collection, carton 2, Bancroft; James West (Carl Withers), *Plainville U.S.A.* (New York, 1945), 135–36, 212–13; Vogt, *Modern Homesteaders*, 143–45. These occupational valuations were basically similar to those described by Bruce Palmer, *Man Over Money: The Southern Populist Critique of American Capitalism* (Chapel Hill, 1980), 9–19.

38. *Agri-News* (Aug. 25, 1939).

39. *Covered Wagon News*, quoted in Todd, "Pea-Patch Press," page numbers omitted.

40. James Bright Wilson, "Social Attitudes of Migratory Agricultural Workers in Kern County, California" (unpublished MA thesis, University of Southern Cal-

ifornia, 1942), 178–79, also Norris* (181). Walter Stein discusses the problem of relations between the migrants and camp managers in "A New Deal Experiment with Guided Democracy: The FSA Migrant Camps in California," Canadian Historical Association, *Historical Papers 1970*, 132–46.

41. *Camp Echo* (Brawley) (Dec. 9, 1939).

42. *Voice of the Agricultural Worker* (Yuba City) (May 28, 1940).

43. *Weed Patch Cultivator* (Arvin) (Nov. 11, 1938); *Voice of the Migrant* (Marysville) (Feb. 23, 1940). "The Future" in *Tow-Sack Tattler* (Arvin) (Nov. 17, 1939), is a little less cautious, counseling neither ambition nor passivity, but suggesting the importance of "choosing the right tools for life's work."

44. Brinkley, *Voices of Protest*, 165–68; Keith L. Bryant, Jr., *Alfalfa Bill Murray* (Norman, 1968), 177–213, and "Oklahoma and the New Deal" in John Braeman, Robert H. Bremner, and David Brody, eds., *The New Deal: The State and Local Levels* (Columbus, 1975), 172–73, 183; Harry S. Ashmore, *Arkansas: A Bicentennial History* (New York, 1978), 137–46; David Ellery Rison, "Arkansas During the Great Depression" (unpublished Ph.D. diss., University of California, Los Angeles, 1974), 57–62; Key, *Southern Politics in State and Nation*, 261–68; Green, *Grass-roots Socialism*, 396–437; Norman D. Brown, *Hood, Bonnet, and Little Brown Jug: Texas Politics, 1921–1928* (College Station, Texas, 1984); Lionel V. Patenaude, *Texans, Politics and the New Deal* (New York, 1983), 86–120; Donald W. Whisenhunt, *The Depression in Texas: The Hoover Years* (New York, 1983), 197–229; George Norris Green, *The Establishment in Texas Politics: The Primitive Years 1938–1957* (Westport, 1979), 13–14. For Missouri's different political habits, see John H. Fenton, *Politics in the Border States* (New Orleans, 1957), 126–70.

45. Lillian Creisler, " 'Little Oklahoma' or the Airport Community: A Study of the Social and Economic Adjustment of Self-settled Agricultural Drought and Depression Refugees" (unpublished MA thesis, University of California, Berkeley, 1940), 60; Walter Evans Hoadley, "A Study of One Hundred Seventy Self-resettled Agricultural Families Monterey County, California, 1939" (unpublished MA thesis, University of California, Berkeley, 1940), 138. The Ham 'n' Eggs movement is described in Jackson K. Putnam, *Old-Age Politics in California: From Richardson to Reagan* (Palo Alto, 1970), 89–114; Robert E. Burke, *Olson's New Deal for California* (Berkeley, 1953); Carey McWilliams, *Southern California: An Island on the Land* (New York, 1946), 303–8.

46. *Tow-Sack Tattler* (Arvin) (Oct. 28, 1939). Also *Tent City News* (Gridley) (Sept. 23, 1939); *Bakersfield Californian* (Oct. 9, 1939); Lloyd Stalcup and Mr. Becker interviews, Todd-Sonkin Recordings.

47. California State Relief Administration, M.H. Lewis, *Migratory Labor in California* (San Francisco, 1936), 140. Hammett is given the pseudonym Clay Bennett in this source.

48. Wilson, "Social Attitudes of Migratory Agricultural Workers," 343. See also the comments of activist Jesse Carter* (341–42).

49. Stuart M. Jamieson, "The Origins and Present Structure of Labor Unions in Agriculture and Allied Industries in California," Exhibit 9576, La Follette *Hearings*, Part 62, p. 22540; Jamieson, "A Settlement of Rural Migrant Families in the Sacramento Valley," 57–59; Jamieson, *Labor Unionism in American Agriculture* (Wash., D.C., 1945), 119; Fred Snyder, "Jobless Hordes in California Offer an

Opportunity for Adroit Campaign of Skillful Radical Propaganda," *San Francisco Examiner* (Feb. 28, 1939, also March 1, 2, 5, 1939); Norman Lowenstein, "Strikes and Strike Tactics in California Agriculture: A History" (unpublished MA thesis, University of California, Berkeley, 1940), 113; *Tow-Sack Tattler* (Arvin) (Oct. 16, 1939); *Farmer-Labor News* (Feb. 19, 1937); *The Rural Worker* (Nov. 1936).

50. On the formation of UCAPAWA and the beginnings of its California campaign see 1936 and 1937 issues of *The Rural Worker* and the *CIO News—Cannery Workers Edition*. Accounts of the campaign can be found in Walter J. Stein, *California and the Dust Bowl Migration* (Westport, 1973), 220–82; Devra Anne Weber, "The Struggle for Stability and Control in the Cotton Fields of California: Class Relations in Agriculture, 1919–1942" (unpublished Ph.D. diss., University of California, Los Angeles, 1986), 312–402; Cletis E. Daniel, *Bitter Harvest: A History of California Farmworkers, 1870–1941* (Ithaca, 1981), 276–85; Linda C. Majka and Theo J. Majka, *Farm Workers, Agribusiness, and the State* (Philadelphia, 1982), 113–35. And for an insider's view see the Dorothy Healey interview, by Margo McBane, March 7, 1978, Women Farmworkers Project.

51. *CIO News—Cannery Workers Edition* (Oct. 22, Dec. 5, 1938); Weber, "The Struggle for Stability and Control in the Cotton Fields of California," 354–58; Clarke A. Chambers, *Farm Organizations: A Historical Study of the Grange, the Farm Bureau and the Associated Farmers 1929–1941* (Berkeley, 1952), 72–73.

52. La Follette Committee, *Report*, 78th Congress, Part 8, pp. 1476–80; Lowenstein, "Strikes and Strike Tactics," 107–9.

53. The strike can be followed in the *Bakersfield Californian* (Sept. 22–Oct. 28, 1939). Weber, "The Struggle for Stability and Control in the Cotton Fields of California," 368–402, provides the newest and richest account. Others include Bryan Theodore Johns, "Field Workers in California Cotton" (unpublished MA thesis, University of California, Berkeley, 1948), 117–46; La Follette Committee, *Report*, 78th Congress, Part 8, pp. 1492–1527; and *Hearings*, Part 51, pp. 18633–773; Chambers, *Farm Organizations*, 72–81.

54. Todd-Sonkin Recordings, Visalia, Aug. 13, 1941. See the union's report of the difficulty of recruiting "half starved workers" in *UCAPAWA News* (April 1940).

55. Charles L. Todd, "California, Here We Stay!," typescript (New York, 1946?) in Charles Todd Collection; Ben Hibbs, "Footloose Army," *Country Gentleman* (Feb. 1940), 5, reprint in Migrant Labor Collection, Bakersfield Public Library; *New York Times*, (March 6, 1940); Wilson, "Social Attitudes of Agricultural Workers," 358; California Governor's Committee to Survey the Agricultural Labor Resources of the San Joaquin Valley, *Agricultural Labor in the San Joaquin Valley: Final Report and Recommendations* (Sacramento, 1951), 289. It is interesting to follow organized labor's evaluation of Okies as potential unionists in *Farmer-Labor News* and *UCAPAWA News*. Through 1939 the journals were blindly optimistic, bending over backwards to deny stories that "you can't organize the Oklahomans into the union" (*Farmer-Labor News* (April 23, 1937)). The tune changed after the cotton strike. In early 1941, Clyde Champion, chief UCAPAWA organizer, told Goldschmidt that the Okies were hopeless: "These people from Oklahoma aren't very class-conscious. It isn't in their background" (*As You Sow*, 71). See also *UCAPAWA News* (April 1940).

56. Stein, *California and the Dust Bowl Migration*, 264–65. He elaborated on

this theme in his paper, "Cultural Gap: Organizing California's Okies in the 1930's," presented at the Southwest Labor History Conference, Stockton, Calif., April 25, 1975. Cautioning that some Okies were strong unionists, Sheila Goldring Manes, on the basis of interviews with former organizers, essentially agrees with Stein's assessment. See "Depression Pioneers: The Conclusion of an American Odyssey, Oklahoma to California, 1930–1950, A Reinterpretation" (unpublished Ph.D. diss., University of California, Los Angeles, 1982), 388–94. The most thorough study to date of the UCAPAWA cotton campaign is Devra Weber's "The Struggle for Stability and Control in the Cotton Fields of California." She prefers not to engage directly the question of Okie sympathy, correctly emphasizing the systemic obstacles to union success and stressing in particular the strategic importance of an integrated cotton industry response. UCAPAWA's more successful campaign among Hispanic cannery workers is the subject of Vicki L. Ruiz, *Cannery Women, Cannery Lives: Mexican Women, Unionization, and the California Food Processing Industry, 1930–1950* (Albuquerque, 1987).

57. Goodwyn, *Democratic Promise*. On the Socialist campaigns see Oscar Ameringer, *If You Don't Weaken: The Autobiography of Oscar Ameringer* (New York, 1940); Green, *Grass-roots Socialism*; Garin Burbank, *When Farmers Voted Red: The Gospel of Socialism in the Oklahoma Countryside, 1910–24* (Westport, 1976); Manes, "Depression Pioneers," 186–222; Thompson, *Closing the Frontier*.

58. Creisler, "Little Oklahoma," 40; Hoadley, "A Study of 170 Self-resettled Agricultural Families," 112; Wilson, "Social Attitudes of Migratory Agricultural Workers," 324–59.

59. Wilson, "Social Attitudes of Migratory Agricultural Workers," 347; *UCAPAWA News* (Feb. 1940); Mr. P.N., Wasco field notes; Creisler, "Little Oklahoma," 40

60. Dellar Ballard interview by Margo McBane, Mary Winegarden, and Rick Topkins, Lindsay, July 19, 1978, Women Farmworkers Project; *Hub* spring 1940 issues. See also the anonymous interview with a former UCAPAWA organizer in the Women Farmworker's Project series; Mr. C.C., Wasco field notes.

61. Charles C. Alexander, *The Ku Klux Klan in the Southwest* (Lexington, 1965); Green, *Grass-roots Socialism*, 345–408; Burbank, *When Farmers Voted Red*, 160–89.

62. Green, *Grass-roots Socialism*, 397, calls the 1930s the "Indian Summer" of Southwestern radicalism. The only significant rural stirrings occurred in the Arkansas Delta where the Southern Tenant Farmers Union built a short-lived biracial organization. See Donald Grubbs, *Cry from the Cotton: The Southern Tenant Farmer's Union and the New Deal* (Chapel Hill, 1971); Jamieson, *Labor Unionism in American Agriculture*, 264–71; Manes, "Depression Pioneers," 239–44; James R. Scales and Danney Goble, *Oklahoma Politics: A History* (Norman, 1982), 214–17; Jacqueline Gordon Sherman, "The Oklahomans in California During the Depression Decade 1931–1941" (unpublished Ph.D. diss., University of California, Los Angeles, 1970), 45–47.

63. Wilson, "Social Attitudes of Migratory Agricultural Workers," 333.

64. Robert Girvin, "Migrant Workers Thinkers," *San Francisco Chronicle* (March 10, 1937).

65. Wilson, "Social Attitudes of Migratory Agricultural Workers," 339 (Free-

man*). For examples of anti-Communism in the FSA camps see *Covered Wagon* (Indio) (March 4, 1939); letter from J.H. Ward to Earl R. Becker in FSA Collection, box 22, San Bruno; Stein, *California and the Dust Bowl Migration*, 268–69.

66. Peter Friedlander, *The Emergence of a UAW Local 1936–1939: A Study in Class and Culture* (Pittsburgh, 1975), 97–110, found differences in the response of Catholic and Protestant workers (some Southerners) in a Detroit auto parts plant. More generally on the response to Communists see Bert Cochran, *Labor and Communism: The Conflict That Shaped American Unions* (Princeton, 1977), 82–102; Harvey Klehr, *The Heyday of American Communism: The Depression Decade* (New York, 1984), 223–51.

67. Wilson, "Social Attitudes of Agricultural Workers," 331–32.

68. James Bright Wilson, "Religious Leaders, Institutions and Organizations Among Certain Agricultural Workers in the Central Valley of California" (unpublished Ph.D. diss., University of Southern California, 1944), 316. The political direction of the evangelicals is examined further in Chapter 7.

69. Burbank, *When Farmers Voted Red*. Also on the relationship between Protestantism and radicalism see Herbert Gutman, "Protestantism and the American Labor Movement: The Christian Spirit in the Gilded Age," in Gutman, *Work, Culture, and Society in Industrializing America* (New York, 1976), 79–117.

70. Jamieson, "A Settlement of Migrant Families in the Sacramento Valley," 57; medical case history No. 33, FSA Collection, Bancroft, carton 2; Interview with Lillie Ruth Ann Counts Dunn, by Judith Gannon, Feb. 14, 16, 1981, Bakersfield, Odyssey Program.

71. See Wilson, "Social Attitudes of Agricultural Workers." Of the eight informants involved with the union, only one was a church member. Nevertheless, all believed in God and considered themselves Christians.

72. Wasco field notes; Stein, *California and the Dust Bowl Migration*, 270. Cletis Daniel, *Bitter Harvest: A History of California Farmworkers 1870–1941* (Ithaca, 1981), 185, discusses racial tensions between Okies, blacks, and Mexicans in the 1933 CAWIU campaign.

73. *New York Times* (March 6, 1940); Paul S. Taylor, "Again the Covered Wagon," *Survey Graphic* 24 (July 1935), 349; Katherine Douglas, "Uncle Sam's Co-op for Individualists," *Coast Magazine* (June 1939).

74. The argument that rural Southwesterners were committed individualists who operated best within minimal community structures gains some support from anthropologist Evon Vogt's *Modern Homesteaders*, study of an Okie community in New Mexico.

75. See the discussion of manhood in Nick Salvatore, *Eugene V. Debs: Citizen and Socialist* (Urbana, 1982), 25–26.

76. Mr. D.H., Wasco field notes.

77. Edgar Crane interview by Judith Gannon, Shafter, April 7, 1981, Odyssey Program, 10–11.

78. Wilson, "Social Attitudes of Migratory Agricultural Workers," 319.

79. *Ibid.*, 320. Also, Tom Higgenbothan interview, Aug. 18, 1940, Todd-Sonkin Recordings; Goldschmidt, *As You Sow*, 167.

80. Interview by Stacey Jagels, March 31, April 2, 1981, Bakersfield, Odyssey Program, 33. A revealing interview with a grower who realized the importance of

treating his workers with respect can be found in Goldschmidt Records, Box 66, San Bruno. Several former migrants interviewed by the Odyssey Program tell of remaining loyal to employers in the face of union pressure. See interviews with Grover C. Holliday, 48–49; Velma May Cooper Davis, 14–15; James Harrison Ward, 35; Alvin Laird, 21–22; and Clara Davis interview by author, Bakersfield, Sept. 17, 1979.

81. California's system of racial relations is surveyed in Roger Daniels and Harry H.L. Kitano, *American Racism: Exploration of the Nature of Prejudice* (Englewood Cliffs, N.J. 1970), esp. 35–72. Useful too are Roger Daniels and Spencer C. Olin, Jr., eds., *Racism in California* (New York, 1972); Charles M. Wollenberg, *All Deliberate Speed* (Berkeley, 1976); Lawrence de Graaf, *Negro Migration to Los Angeles, 1930–1950* (San Francisco, 1974).

82. Martha Lee Martin Jackson interview by Stacey Jagels, Clovis, March 10, 1981, Odyssey Program, 22.

83. *Fresno Bee* (March 22, 1938). Also printed in *Modesto Bee* (March 23, 1938).

84. *Modesto Bee* (March 9, 1938).

85. Wilson, "Social Attitudes of Migratory Agricultural Workers," 149–50, 310.

86. *Ibid.*, 150, 316. See also *The Hub* (Visalia) (May 24, 31, June 12, 1940); Tom Collins, Reports of the Marysville Migrant Camp, 1935, in Taylor Collection.

87. Wilson, "Social Attitudes of Agricultural Workers," 143.

88. On the FSA camps' unofficial policy of racial exclusion see Tom Collins letter to Eric Thompson, Oct. 12, 1936 in FSA Records, Box 20, San Bruno. Examples of racist humor in the camp newspapers include: *Covered Wagon* (Indio) (Dec. 10, 1938); *Tow-Sack Tattler* (Arvin) (Sept. 28, 1939, Nov. 22, 1940); *Tent City News* (Nov. 25, 1939). Todd-Sonkin Recordings provide other examples.

89. Interview by Stacey Jagels, Oildale, Feb. 24, 26, 1981, Odyssey Program, 12.

90. Mrs. L.R., Wasco field notes.

91. Interview by Judith Gannon, Porterville, Jan. 24, 1981, Odyssey Program, 11, 18.

92. Interview, 35–36.

93. Evelyn Rudd, "Reading List—Design for Living," typescript in Goldschmidt's Wasco field notes.

94. Interview by Stacey Jagels, Bakersfield, Jan. 26, 29, 1981, pp. 25–27.

95. Wilson, "Social Attitudes of Migratory Agricultural Workers," 143. Goldschmidt, *As You Sow*, 68, records a similar vignette about a popular black labor contractor. Evidence of amicable relations between Okies and Hispanics is more readily found. Margaret Valiant's Migrant Camp Recordings, Library of Congress, contains examples of these two groups interacting at FSA camps in the Imperial Valley. See also Bill Jackson's interview in Todd-Sonkin Recordings.

96. Gerald Haslam writes sensitively about the continuing pattern of racial hostility in "Oildale" and "Workin' Man's Blues" in *Voices of a Place* (Walnut Creek, Calif., 1987), 56–64, 78–97.

97. Katherine Archibald, *Wartime Shipyard: A Study of Social Disunity* (Berkeley, 1947), 70–71.

98. *Ibid.*, 75.

99. James Richard Wilburn, "Social and Economic Aspects of the Aircraft In-

dustry in Metropolitan Los Angeles During World War II" (Ph.D. diss., University of California, Los Angeles, 1971), 185; Lawrence Hewes, *Boxcar in the Sand* (New York, 1957), 213.

100. Interview, 36.

101. *The Covered Wagon* (Indio) (April 22, 1939). Other examples: the poem "Sooner's Luck" in Todd-Sonkin Recordings; *Marysville Camp News* (July 16, 1938). Alvin Laird and Charles Newsome tell "prune-picker" stories in their Odyssey Program interviews.

102. Todd-Sonkin field notes. See also *Voice of the Agricultural Worker* (Yuba City) (Dec. 3, 1940).

103. Archibald, *Wartime Shipyard*, 55.

104. *Modesto Bee* (March 29, 1938). Also *Camp Echo* (Brawley) (Dec. 2, 1939).

105. Interview by Judith Gannon, South Pasadena, April 5, 1981, Odyssey Program, 34.

Chapter 6. Up from the Dust

1. Oliver Carlson, "Up from the Dust," *U.S.A.* (Aug. 1952), 97–104. For similar descriptions see Dan Fowler, "What's Become of the Okies," *Look* (Jan. 13, 1953), 19–21.

2. Gerald D. Nash, *The American West Transformed: The Impact of the Second World War* (Bloomington, 1985), esp. 62; James J. Parsons, "California Manufacturing," *Geographic Review* 39 (April 1949), 229–41; Warren A. Beck and Ynez D. Haase, *Historical Atlas of California* (Norman, 1974), 87–88; James Richard Wilburn, "Social and Economic Aspects of the Aircraft Industry in Metropolitan Los Angeles During World War II" (unpublished Ph.D. diss., University of California, Los Angeles, 1971), 44; Margaret S. Gordon, *Employment Expansion and Population Growth: The California Experience: 1900–1950*, (Berkeley, 1954) 60–62, 106–9.

3. Nash, *The American West Transformed*, 19; Warren S. Thompson, *Growth and Changes in California's Population* (Los Angeles, 1955), 25; Richard R. Lingeman, *Don't You Know There's a War On? The American Home Front 1941–45* (New York, 1970), 69.

4. *Vital Speeches of the Day* 10 (May 1, 1944), 432; Nash, *The American West Transformed*, 203–4.

5. Calculated from U.S. Bureau of the Census, *United States Census of Population: 1950, Special Reports: State of Birth*, vol. IV, Part 4, Chapter A (Wash., D.C., 1953), table 13, pp. 19–23; *Sixteenth Census of the United States: 1940, Population State of Birth of Native Population* (Wash., D.C., 1944), table 20, pp. 17–28. Commonwealth Club of California, *The Population of California* (San Francisco, 1946), 126–29; Lawrence B. de Graaf, *Negro Migration to Los Angeles, 1930–1950* (San Francisco, 1974).

6. Interview by Margo McBane, Visalia, April 19, 1978, Women Farmworkers Project, 17; Ronald W. Jones, "Underemployed Workers in Rural Oklahoma— With Particular Reference to Wartime Needs" (Little Rock, Oct. 1942), 47–51, typescript in Bureau of Agricultural Economics, RG83, General Correspondence 1941–46, National Archives; Gerald Schultz, "Some Effects of the War on Rural Life in Missouri, 1939–1945," Missouri Agricultural Experimental Station, *Research*

Bulletin No. 401 (Columbia, 1946), 19; Sheila Goldring Manes, "Depression Pioneers: The Conclusion of an American Odyssey, Oklahoma to California, 1930–1950, a Reinterpretation" (unpublished Ph.D. diss., University of California, Los Angeles, 1982), 368–69.

7. Grace D. Dahle, "A Personnel Study of High School Pupils in an Industrial City" (unpublished MA thesis, University of Southern California, 1945), 119–26.

8. A good account of recruiting techniques is found in Kenneth Tuttle Darling, "Controlled Manpower: Experiences of World War II—A Study of the Activities of the War Manpower Commission in the Los Angeles-Harbor Shipyard Industry" (unpublished MA thesis, University of Redlands, 1951), 88–89. See also Richard Finnie, *Marinship: The History of a Wartime Shipyard* (San Francisco, 1947), 44; Anne Roller Issler, "Shipyards and the Boys," *Survey Graphic* 33 (March 1944), 174; Wilburn, "Aircraft Industry in Los Angeles," 90–96, 132; Robert B. Robertson testimony, Tolan Committee, *Hearings*, Part 7, pp. 2805–6.

9. Charles N. Reynolds, Population Committee for the Central Valley Project Studies, *The Distribution of California Population, Statistical Memorandum*, 2 (Berkeley, 1943), 36, mimeographed copy in RG83, Central Valley Project Studies, Box 54, San Bruno; Commonwealth Club, *The Population of California*, 23–25.

10. Morris family interview by Margo McBane and Mary Winegarden, Richmond, July 12, 1978, Women Farmworkers Project. Chester's last name was not recorded.

11. Interview by Stacey Jagels, Bakersfield, March 31, April 2, 1982, Odyssey Program, and by author, April 30, 1985; Paul Faulkner Tjensvold, "An Inquiry into the Reasons for the Post-Depression Migration from Oklahoma to Kern County in California" (unpublished MA thesis, University of Southern California, 1947), 47.

12. U.S. Bureau of the Census, *Wartime Changes in Population and Family Characteristics—San Diego Congested Area: March 1944* Series CA-2, No. 2, (n.p., July 13, 1944); also reports for *San Francisco* (no. 3) and *Los Angeles* (no. 5).

13. Darling, "Controlled Manpower," 92; Kaiser Company, Inc., *A Booklet of Illustrated Facts About the Shipyards at Richmond California* (Richmond, June 30, 1944), 31; Louise Lillian Haun, "The Attitude of Workers Toward Their Jobs in the California Shipbuilding Industry During World War II" (unpublished MA thesis, University of Southern California, 1945), 21, 114–15.

14. "Traveling," *San Francisco News* (May 13, 1941); U.S. Works Projects Administration, *Recent Migration into Los Angeles, Long Beach, and Nine Other Cities in Los Angeles County, California*, mimeograph copy (n.p., Jan. 8, 1942), 5.

15. Audie Moffitt interview by author, Long Beach, June 5, 1981; Ruby Barnes interview by author, Long Beach, June 3, 1981.

16. Dahle, "A Personnel Study of High School Students in an Industrial City," 40–41.

17. The quote belongs to Nash, *The American West Transformed*, 69–70; James A. McVittie, *An Avalanche Hits Richmond: A Report* (Richmond, 1944); Hubert Owen Brown, "The Impact of War Worker Migration on the Public School System of Richmond, California from 1940 to 1945" (unpublished Ph.D. diss., Stanford, 1973); "Richmond Took a Beating," *Fortune* 31 (Feb. 1945), 262–69.

18. The best source on boomtown conditions is House Subcommittee of Com-

mittee on Naval Affairs. 78th Congress, 1st session, *Hearings on Congested Areas* (Wash., D.C., 1943–44). Nash, *The American West Transformed*, 56–74, is a well-balanced survey that avoids some of the breathless hyperbole of contemporary reports. Useful among the latter are "Boom Town: San Diego," *Life* (July 28, 1941), 64–69; Zelma Parker, "Strangers in Town," *Survey* 79 (June 1943), 170–71. See also the photo essay, "Home Is Where You Hang Your Hat," in the Richmond Kaiser shipyards magazine *Fore 'n' Aft* (Feb. 4, 1944).

19. *Fore 'n' Aft* 3 (Jan. 22, 1943), 8. On women in war industries see Katherine Archibald, *Wartime Shipyard: A Study of Social Disunity*, 15–39; William Henry Chafe, *The American Woman: Her Changing Social, Economic, and Political Roles, 1920–1970* (New York, 1972), 135–95; Karen Anderson, *Wartime Women: Sex Roles, Family Relations, and the Status of Women During World War II* (Westport, 1981).

20. Interview by author, June 12, 1985, Oakland. See also Elton Mayo and George F.F. Lombard, *Teamwork and Labor Turnover in the Aircraft Industry of Southern California*, Harvard School of Business Administration, Business Research Series 32 (Oct. 1944); Issler, "Shipyards and the Boys," 174–77.

21. Interview.

22. Interview by author, Lindsay, April 31, 1985.

23. Interview by author, Santa Monica, June 3, 1981.

24. Interview by author, Camarillo, April 1, 1985.

25. Archibald, *Wartime Shipyard*, 45, 47.

26. Zelma Parker, "Strangers in Town," *Survey* 79 (June 1943), 170; Brown, "The Impact of War Worker Migration," 169–72.

27. *Fore 'n' Aft* 3 (July 2, 1943), 10.

28. Archibald, *Wartime Shipyard*, 55.

29. Quoted in Matt Weinstock, *My L.A.* (Los Angeles, 1947), 150.

30. *Fore 'n' Aft* 3 (June 11, 1943), 8; also (Sept. 27), 7.

31. *Fore 'n' Aft*, 3 (Dec. 3, 1943), 4.

32. The Delano Record, *Souvenir War Album* (Delano, 1945); U.S. Department of Agriculture, Bureau of Agricultural Economics, *Acreage Limitation and Excess Land Problems: Central Valley Project* (n.p., March 1944), 92.

33. *Fresno Bee* (Sept. 25, 1946); James Bright Wilson, "Religious Leaders, Institutions and Organizations Among Certain Agricultural Workers in the Central Valley of California" (unpublished Ph.D. diss., University of Southern California, 1944), 109.

34. From the 1950 Census Public Use Microdata Sample:

Percent of Male California Residents Aged 24 to 46 in 1950 Who Served in Military During World War II, by Group

	Percent	*(N)*
Southwesterners	49%	(791)
Other American-born whites	45	(3832)
Foreign-born whites	63	(337)
Hispanics/nonwhites	56	(754)

Note: Men between 18 and 38 were draft eligible. Counting those who were 38 in 1942 as well as those turning 18 in 1944 yields the 24–46 age span for 1950.

35. Central Valley Project Studies, *Report of the Committee on Problem No. 6 Wartime Shifts in the Industrial Economy of the Central Valley and Their Implications for the Use of Project Resources After the War* (Berkeley, 1946), 89–105, mimeographed copy in Central Valley Project Studies, Box 41, San Bruno; Thompson, *Growth and Changes in California's Population*, 131–35.

36. "Wartime Wages, Income, and Manpower in Farming," *Monthly Labor Review* 58 (Jan. 1944), 16; Joel Warkentin, "A Decade of Migratory Labor in the San Joaquin Valley, 1940–1950" (MA thesis, University of California, Berkeley, 1952), 71–98; Paul S. Taylor, "The Effect of War on the Social and Economic Status of Farm Laborers," *Rural Sociology* 8 (June 1943), 141. The quote is from Wilson, "Religious Organizations Among Agricultural Workers," 113.

37. Wilson, "Religious Organizations Among Agricultural Workers," 159.

38. *Ibid.*, 126. See also Lloyd H. Fisher, *The Harvest Labor Market* (Cambridge, Mass., 1953), 18; Roscoe Crawford interview by Dixie Crawford Hicks, 1976, Oral History Program, California State University, Fullerton.

39. Interview by Michael Neely, Visalia, March 4, 16, 1981, pp. 30–32.

40. Hazel Oleta Thompson Smalling interview by Judith Gannon, Tulare, March 23, 26, 1981, pp. 20–23; Talmage Lee Collins interview by Michael Neely, Bakersfield, Jan. 21, 28, 1981, p. 23; Edgar Crane interview by Gannon, Shafter, April 7, 1981, p. 7 (all Odyssey Program); Dan Fowler, "What's Become of the Okies," *Look* 17 (Jan. 13, 1953), 20; *The Hub* (Visalia) (Oct. 11, 1941).

41. Fowler, "What's Become of the Okies," 21; Roberta Huntsman, "The Third Migration," Social Science 185 paper in Special Collections, California State University, Fresno. See also Ceres Camp Manager's Report, Feb. 1943 in FSA Records, box 30, San Bruno; Hadley Leon Yocum interview by Stacey Jagels, Hanford, June 2, 1981, Odyssey Program, 21–22.

42. Viola Lillian Maxwell Mitchell interview by Stacey Jagels, Oildale, Jan. 12, 1981, Odyssey Program, 11; Crane interview, 7.

43. Interview by Stacey Jagels, Bakersfield, March 31, April 2, 1981, Odyssey Program, 44.

44. Terry Bennett Clipper interview by Judith Gannon, May 8, 9, 1981, Bakersfield, Odyssey Program. For other examples of men returning to opportunities in the Valley see Frank Manies Odyssey interview; Report to Dr. Carl C. Taylor, Head of Division of Farm Population and Rural Welfare from Walter C. McKain, Jr., March 7, 1944, in RG83, BAE Regional Files 1907–46, Western, National Archives; Weinstock, *My L.A.*, 76.

45. Lester Velie, "The Americans Nobody Wants," *Collier's* (April 1, 1950), 15; and his "Home Is a Dream," *Collier's* (April 8, 1950), 27, 54–55. Also "Grapes of Wrath 1950," *Newsweek* (March 27, 1950), 23; "Farm Housing: End of an Era," *Fortnight* (Jan. 2, 1948), 11. The best source on the state of the agricultural labor market in the late 1940s and on the renewed difficulties of some Southwesterners are the hearings of the California Governor's Committee to Survey the Agricultural Labor Resources of the San Joaquin Valley (1950) and the Committee's *Agricultural Labor in the San Joaquin Valley: Final Report and Recommendations* (Sacramento, 1951), esp. 81–101. Also important, U.S. Department of Agriculture, Bureau of Agricultural Economics, *The Agricultural Labor Force in the San Joaquin Valley, California—1948* (Wash., D.C., 1950).

46. William C. Beatty, Jr., Patricia Pickford, Thomas M. Brigham, *A Prelimi-*

nary Report on a Study of Farm Laborers in Fresno County from January 1, 1959 to July 1, 1959 (n.p., n.d.) mimeographed copy in Special Collections, University of California, Los Angeles; William H. Metzler, *Cotton Mechanization and Labor Stabilization, Kern County, California*, mimeographed review draft (n.p., Dec. 6, 1962) in Bakersfield Public Library.

47. Consumer price data is from U.S. Bureau of the Census, *Historical Statistics of the United States: Colonial Times to 1957* (Wash., D.C., 1957), 125. Median family income data for urban wage and salary workers for the West South Central Division comes from U.S. Bureau of the Census, *Sixteenth Census: Population and Housing, Families—General Characteristics* (Wash., D.C., 1943), table 34, pp. 157–68. The press made much of the improved incomes of "defense Okies," featuring stories of families heading back to Oklahoma at the end of the war with pockets full of money. See "Grapes of Joy," *Newsweek* (Sept. 3, 1945), 31; " 'Okies,' 'Arkies' in Well Fixed So. Cal. Exodus," *Los Angeles Evening Herald Express* (Aug. 27, 1945).

48. Southwesterners were disproportionately represented in certain valley industries. As before, construction remained a major source of employment, occupying 13 percent of Southwestern-born male workers, second only to agriculture. Automotive-related occupations, including truck driving, car mechanics, and gas station work, employed another 8 percent, followed by the oil and gas industry with 5 percent. In each of these sectors Southwesterners comprised close to a third of the labor force. Employing more women than men, seasonal cannery work had become still more of an Okie occupational enclave. Some 48 percent of valley cannery workers were Oklahomans, Arkansans, Texans, and Missourians.

49. On changing occupational structure see Cecil L. Dunn and Philip Neff, *The Arvin Area of Kern County: An Economic Survey of the Southeastern San Joaquin Valley in Relation to Land Use and the Size and Distribution of Income* (n.p., 1947).

50. The percentage of married women with husbands present who considered themselves in the labor force rose from 14 percent in 1940 to 25 percent in 1950, an increase similar to that experienced by other groups of white women. 1940 and 1950 Census Public Use Microdata Samples.

51. Letter to Carl C. Taylor from W.C. Holley, May 6, 1946, Bureau of Agricultural Economics, RG83, Project Files, Farm Practices and Rural Life 1938–53, National Archives; *Fresno Bee* (Sept. 1, 5, 13, 18, 20, 25, 1946).

52. Interview by author; also Odyssey interview, 19, 34.

53. Oliver Carlson, "Up from the Dust," *U.S.A.* (Aug. 1952), 101.

Chapter 7. Special to God

1. Samuel S. Hill, Jr., *Southern Churches in Crisis* (Boston, 1966), 17–18; Wilbur Zelinsky, "An Approach to the Religious Geography of the United States: Patterns of Church Membership in 1952," *Annals of the Association of American Geographers* 51 (June 1961), 139–93.

2. U.S. Bureau of the Census, *Census of Religious Bodies: 1936*, Vol. I (Wash., D.C., 1941), table 22, pp. 270–72. Samuel S. Hill, ed., *Religion in the Southern States* (Macon, 1983) contains chapters on the growth patterns of religious groups and institutions in each of the four Southwestern states.

3. Kenneth K. Bailey, *Southern White Protestantism in the Twentieth Century* (New York, 1964), 78–86; Charles C. Alexander, *The Ku Klux Klan in the Southwest* (Lexington, 1965), 84–88; Orville W. Taylor, "Arkansas," in Hill, *Religion in the Southern States*, 54–55. On the influence of religion generally in the South see Hill, *Southern Churches in Crisis*, and his anthology, *Religion and the Solid South* (Nashville, 1972); Charles Reagan Wilson, ed., *Religion in the South* (Jackson, Miss., 1985); Tod A. Baker, Robert P. Steed, and Lawrence W. Moreland, eds., *Religion and Politics in the South: Mass and Elite Perspectives* (New York, 1983).

4. United States Brewers Association, Inc., *Brewers Almanac* (n.p., 1974), 112–26; Jimmie Lewis Franklin, *Born Sober: Prohibition in Oklahoma, 1907–1959* (Norman, 1971).

5. James West (Withers), *Plainville, U.S.A.* (New York, 1945), esp. 142–64; Robin Room, "Drinking in the Rural South: Some Comparisons in a National Sample," paper presented at the Symposium on Law and Drinking Behavior, Center for Alcohol Studies, University of North Carolina, Chapel Hill, Nov. 17–19, 1970, p.14

6. Interview by Tom Norris, May 23, 1983, Sacramento, Sacramento History Center. Wilbur J. Cash has some delightful thoughts on the South's "social schizophrenia" in *The Mind of the South* (New York, 1941), 56–60.

7. James Bright Wilson, "Social Attitudes of Certain Migratory Agricultural Workers in Kern County, California" (unpublished MA thesis, University of Southern California, 1942), 365 (Frank Hart*). See also the Odyssey Program interviews with James Lackey and Joyce Vernon Seabolt.

8. Wilson, "Social Attitudes of Migratory Agricultural Workers," 368 (Henry Rollin*).

9. James Bright Wilson, "Religious Leaders, Institutions and Organizations Among Certain Agricultural Workers in the Central Valley of California (unpublished Ph.D. diss., University of Southern California, 1944), 175.

10. *Ibid.*, 176. For other examples of the same kind of attitudes, see: George Gleason, *The Fifth Migration*, reprinted in Tolan Committee, *Hearings*, Part 7, p. 3000; Lawrence Hewes, *Boxcar in the Sand* (New York, 1957), 115.

11. Wilson, "Social Attitudes of Agricultural Workers," 367–68. On the work of the Home Missions Council see Edith W. Lowry, *They Starve That We May Eat* (New York, 1938); Wilson, "Religious Organizations Among Agricultural Workers," 450–55.

12. Walter Goldschmidt, *As You Sow* (Glencoe, 1947, reprinted 1978), 145.

13. *Ibid.*

14. Charles B. Spaulding, "The Development of Organization and Disorganization in the Social Life of a Rapidly Growing Working-Class Suburb Within a Metropolitan District" (unpublished Ph.D. diss., University of Southern California, 1939), 196–207, 211–25; Peggy Staggs interview by author, Aug. 18, 1980, Huntington Beach.

15. Grover C. Holliday interview, by Michael Neely, March 9, 1981, Arvin, California Odyssey Oral History Program, California State College, Bakersfield. The composition of the congregation is shown in the 1944 Arvin Congregational Church membership list in Goldschmidt Records, Box 66, San Bruno. Also Hazel Mitchell Odyssey Program interview.

16. On the differences between Northern and Southern religion see Bailey, *Southern White Protestantism in the Twentieth Century*, 163–65, passim; Hill, *Southern Churches in Crisis*; John Lee Eighmy, *Churches in Cultural Captivity: A History of the Social Attitudes of Southern Baptists* (Knoxville, 1972); George M. Marsden, *Fundamentalism and American Culture: The Shaping of Twentieth-Century Evangelicalism 1830–1925* (New York, 1980), 103, 165, 178.

17. Wofford and Ruth Clark interview, by author, La Mirada, June 8, 1981.

18. Maggie Averill Steel Mouser interview, by Tod Moquist, March 18, April 7, 27, 1982, Shafter, Odyssey Program, 22.

19. Wilson, "Religious Organizations Among Agricultural Workers," 359; Gleason, *The Fifth Migration*, 3000.

20. Maggie Mouser interview, 23.

21. Vera Ruth Woodall Criswell interview, by Stacey Jagels, Feb. 24, 26, 1981, Oildale, Odyssey Program, 45.

22. Eldon G. Ernst, "Religion in California," *Pacific Theological Review* 19 (Winter 1986), 48. An excellent introductory survey of the field is Douglas Firth Anderson's unpublished paper, "California Protestantism, 1848–1935: Historiographic Explorations and Regional Method for a Nascent Field" (Aug. 31, 1983) in the Graduate Theological Union Library, Berkeley. On early Protestant efforts see Kevin Starr, *Americans and the California Dream, 1850–1915* (New York, 1973), 69–109. Also important, Gregory H. Singleton, *Religion in the City of Angels: American Protestant Culture and Urbanization, Los Angeles, 1850–1930* (Ann Arbor, 1979).

23. For examples of some early Southern Baptist efforts to set up churches in California, see Floyd Looney, *History of California Southern Baptists* (Fresno, 1954), 14; Elmer L. Gray, *Heirs of Promise: A Chronicle of California Southern Baptists, 1940–1978* (Fresno, 1978), 15–18; Sam A. Harvey, "The Roots of California Southern Baptists 1880–1940" (unpublished Th.D. diss., Golden Gate Seminary, 1973).

24. Growth patterns and property values can be followed in the *Journal of the Annual Session of the Pacific Conference of the Methodist Episcopal Church, South* (Los Angeles); and they are discussed in Richard Drewry Jervey, *The History of Methodism in Southern California and Arizona* (Nashville, 1960). A useful general study with some California references is Robert Watson Sledge, *Hands on the Ark: The Struggle for Change in the Methodist Episcopal Church South, 1914–1939* (Lake Junaluska, N.C., 1975). For a snappy portrait of Rev. Robert Shuler, the one energetic voice in California Southern Methodism, see David Clark, "Miracles for a Dime: From Chautauqua Tent to Radio Station with Sister Aimee," *California Historical Quarterly* 57 (Winter 1978/79), 357–58. The property value ranking is from Census Bureau, *Census of Religious Bodies: 1936*, table 3, pp. 33–35.

25. Calculated from Bureau of the Census, *Census of Religious Bodies, 1936*, Vol. 1, table 29, pp. 374–413.

26. Timothy L. Smith, "Religion and Ethnicity in America," *American Historical Review* 83 (Dec. 1978), 1174–75.

27. General works on the subject include Vinson Synan, *The Holiness-Pentecostal Movement in the United States* (Grand Rapids, 1971); Robert Mapes Anderson, *Vision of the Disinherited: The Making of American Pentecostalism* (New York, 1979); Nils Bloch-Hoell, *The Pentecostal Movement: Its Origin, Develop-*

ment, and Distinctive Character (London, 1964); John Thomas Nichol, *Pentecostalism* (New York, 1966). Important earlier studies include Anton T. Boisen, "Economic Distress and Religious Experience: A Study of the Holy Rollers," *Psychiatry* II (May 1939), 185–94; John B. Holt, "Holiness Religion: Culture Shock and Social Reorganization," *American Sociological Review* V (Oct. 1940), 740–47; Liston Pope, *Millhands and Preachers: A Study of Gastonia* (New Haven, 1942), 126–40.

28. William D. Edmondson, "Fundamentalist Sects of Los Angeles, 1900–1930" (unpublished Ph.D. diss., Claremont Graduate School, 1969); Anderson, *Vision of the Disinherited*, 124–25, 165; William D. Blomgren, "Aimee Semple McPherson and the Foursquare Gospel, 1921–1944" (unpublished MA thesis, Stanford University, 1952). McPherson was a bit too flamboyant for the rest of the Pentecostal movement. For a comparison of her Foursquare Gospel sect with others, see Gertrude Beckett Keene, "Distinctive Social Values of the Pentecostal Churches: A Sociological Field Study" (unpublished MA thesis, University of Southern California, 1938). Spaulding, "Development of a Working-Class Suburb," 196–207, 211–25, describes the activities of several Holiness churches in the Bell Gardens area. Singleton, *Religion in the City of Angels* is an intriguing general study of the city's religious institutions.

29. The role of "farmer-preachers" is emphasized in Goldschmidt, *As You Sow*, 139–41. For a look at the operating procedures of a particular denomination, see George Harold Paul, "The Religious Frontier in Oklahoma: Dan T.Muse and the Pentecostal Holiness Church" (unpublished Ph.D. diss., University of Oklahoma, 1965).

30. Wilson, "Religious Organization Among Agricultural Workers," 337. Also *Shafter Press*, May 20, 1949, for histories of various Holiness churches in Shafter.

31. Mrs. J.R., Wasco field notes. See also Goldschmidt, *As You Sow*, 145.

32. Gleason, *The Fifth Migration*, 3000. Similar reports are found in Tom Collins, Reports of Marysville Migrant Camp (n.p., 1935), 5, mimeographed copy in Taylor Collection; Spaulding, "Development of a Working-Class Suburb," 196–97. For a intriguing discussion of Holiness musical practices see Stephen R. Tucker, "Pentecostalism and Popular Culture in the South: A Study of Four Musicians," *Journal of Popular Culture* 16 (Winter 1982), 68–80.

33. Wilson, "Religious Organizations Among Agricultural Workers," 273.

34. Goldschmidt, *As You Sow*, 133.

35. Melvin Shahan interview, 29. In their interviews with the author, Peggy Staggs and Frank Manies give accounts of church members helping to locate jobs or providing other help. For other examples of church charity see Wilson, "Social Attitudes of Agricultural Workers," 364; Irma Weill, "We've Been Rollin'," *The Family* 16 (Feb. 1936), 319; Mrs. I.G., Wasco field notes. As late as 1952 the average Assemblies of God or Nazarene congregation in the San Joaquin Valley claimed only 90 members. National Council of Churches, *Churches and Church Membership in the United States*, series C, numbers 58, 59, table 128.

36. Anderson, *Vision of the Disinherited*; Goldschmidt, *As You Sow*, 126–33; Pope, *Millhands and Preachers*, 133–40. A recent examination of that argument is Harry G. Lefever, "The Religion of the Poor: Escape or Creative Force?," *Journal for the Scientific Study of Religion* 16 (Sept. 1977), 225–36.

37. On the recent history and social composition see David Edwin Harrell, Jr.,

All Things Are Possible: The Healing and Charismatic Revivals in Modern America (Bloomington, 1975); James Davison Hunter, *American Evangelicalism: Conservative Religion and the Quandary of Modernity* (New Brunswick, 1983), 23–72.

38. Wilson, "Religious Organizations Among Agricultural Workers," 261, 284.

39. Lucretia Penny, "Pea-Picker's Child," *Survey Graphic* (July 1935), 353; Gleason, *The Fifth Migration*, 3000; Spaulding, "Development of a Working-Class Suburb," 198.

40. Goldschmidt, *As You Sow*, 130.

41. *Ibid.*, 133; Keene, "Social Values of Pentecostal Churches," 44.

42. Wilson, "Religious Organizations Among Agricultural Workers," 268.

43. Orvill Sanders, *The Fruit Hangs Ripe* (N. Hollywood, 1951), 6. The date of this letter is not specified and it may have been written in the 1940s, after the denomination had begun founding churches in California.

44. Looney, *History of California Southern Baptists*, 13–19; Gray, *A Chronicle of California Southern Baptists*, 16–27. Many of these early churches affiliated with the Landmark Baptists, a small Arkansas-based denomination.

45. *Ibid.*

46. Sanders, *The Fruit Hangs Ripe*, 22.

47. National Council of Churches of Christ in the United States of America, *Churches and Church Membership in the United States—An Enumeration and Analysis by Counties, States and Regions* (New York, 1957), Series B, no. 1, table 11. For accounts of the founding of individual churches, see Looney, *History of California Southern Baptists*, passim; "Church with a Vision: A History of Centinela Southern Baptist Church" (n.p., n.d.), mimeographed copy in Golden Gate Seminary Library vertical file; Harold Wayne Swindall, "Isam Bradley Hodges: Founder and First President of Golden Gate Seminary" (unpublished MA thesis, Golden Gate Seminary, 1972).

48. Sanders, *The Fruit Hangs Ripe*, 17.

49. Looney, *History of California Southern Baptists*, 282; interview with Rev. Louis Hendricks, by author, June 2, 1981, Whittier. See also Spaulding, "The Development of a Working-Class Suburb," 203–4.

50. Dexter C. Ogan, "A Brief History of the First Southern Baptist Church of Calwa" (Calwa, 1955), typescript in Golden Gate Seminary Library vertical file. See also Sanders, *The Fruit Hangs Ripe*, 22; Wilson, "Religious Organizations Among Agricultural Workers," 291.

51. Charles Y. Stark and Rodney Glock, *American Piety: The Nature of Religious Commitment* (Berkeley, 1968), 43, 60–62.

52. G. Thomas Halbrooks, "Growing Pains: The Impact of Expansion on Southern Baptists Since 1942," *Baptist History and Heritage* 17 (July 1982), 50–51; and in the same issue, Leon McBeth, "Expansion of the Southern Baptist Convention to 1951," 42–43; Gray, *Heirs of Promise*, 34; Robert Andrew Baker, *Relations Between Northern and Southern Baptists* (Fort Worth, 1948), 217–22; Max Eugene Willcockson, "The Northern and Southern Baptist Conventions: A Comparison of Structure and Function" (unpublished Bachelor of Divinity thesis, University of Chicago, 1944), 112–16; Tom J. Nettlers, "Southern Baptists: Regional to National Transition," *Baptist History and Heritage* 16 (Jan. 1981), 13–23; Al Fasol, "A History of Representative Southern Baptist Preaching, 1930–1945" (unpublished Th.D. diss., Southwestern Baptist Theological Seminary, 1975), 26–27.

53. Interview by author.

54. Kern Camp Manager's Report, April 4, 1936, in Taylor Collection.

55. Wilson, "Religious Organizations Among Agricultural Workers," 291, 310.

56. J.A. Pauly interview notes, Goldschmidt Records, San Bruno, Box 66; Rita M. Hanson, "Educating Elementary School Children of Seasonal-Migrant Agricultural Workers in San Joaquin Valley" (unpublished Ed.D. diss., Stanford University, 1949), 248; testimony of W. Max Smith, District Superintendent, Merced City Elementary Schools, Tolan Committee, *Hearings*, Part 6, p. 2436.

57. John Beecher, "The Migratory Labor Program in California" (n.p., n.d.), typescript in FSA Collection, Bancroft, carton 9. In same collection, carton 7, see Robert S. Hardie and Norman I. Course, "A Brief Presentation of the Problem Presented by California's Migratory Agricultural Workers" (n.p., n.d.), typescript. Also Eric H. Thompsen, "Our Migrant Brother," Bulletin of Council of Women for Home Missions (n.p., n.d.), 6, mimeographed copy in Federal Writers' Collection, carton 35.

58. *Richmond Independent* (June 17, 1943), quoted in Hubert Owen Brown, "The Impact of War Worker Migration on the Public School System of Richmond, California from 1940–1945" (unpublished Ph.D. diss., Stanford University, 1973), 170.

59. Interview by Judith Gannon, April 5, 1981, South Pasadena, Odyssey Program, 35.

60. George M. Marsden, "From Fundamentalism to Evangelicalism: A Historical Analysis," in David F. Wells and John D. Woodbridge, eds., *The Evangelicals*, rev. ed. (Grand Rapids, 1975), 142–62; Joel A. Carpenter, "From Fundamentalism to the New Evangelical Coalition," in George Marsden, ed., *Evangelicalism and Modern America* (Grand Rapids, 1984), 3–16.

61. Wilson, "Religious Organizations Among Agricultural Workers," 347. For other examples of discord see Kern Camp Manager's Reports, Dec. 18, 1935, Jan. 25, Feb. 15, 1936, in Taylor Collection; Spaulding, "Development of a Working-Class Suburb," 225; Lillian Creisler, " 'Little Oklahoma' or the Airport Community" (unpublished MA thesis, University of California, Berkeley, 1940), 60; Gleason, *The Fifth Migration*, 3000–3001.

62. Wilson, "Religious Organizations Among Agricultural Workers," 262; Rev. N.D., Wasco field notes.

63. Anderson, *Vision of the Disinherited*, 208.

64. Sanders, *The Fruit Hangs Ripe*, 18.

65. Rev. Buren Higdon interview by author, Oakland, June 5, 1979. His first assignment was in Oregon, working with Southwesterners who settled there.

66. For example, weekly radio schedules in the *Bakersfield Californian* always listed the denomination's broadcasts as "Southern Missionary." See also Halbrooks, "Growing Pains: The Impact of Expansion on Southern Baptists Since 1942," 50–51.

67. Higdon, who was head of the Southern Baptist Convention's East Bay district, estimated 75 percent. Others at his office suggested the 50 percent figure.

68. Vera Criswell interview, 49; Sanders, *The Fruit Hangs Ripe*, 32. It is significant that the only use of the self-label "Southerner" in the more than forty Odyssey program interviews are by Maggie Mouser and Elbert Garretson, both active Southern Baptists.

69. Rev. Buren Higdon interview.

70. Interview by author, June 8, 1981, La Mirada. Maggie Mouser's continued ties to her hometown provide another Southern Baptist example. See Chapter 4, *supra.*

71. These are the estimates of several ministers and staff members at the Northern District headquarters of the Assemblies of God and at Bethel College, both located in Santa Cruz, California.

72. Phone interview by author, Nov. 16, 1986.

73. George H. Williams and Rodney L. Petersen, "Evangelicals: Society, the State, the Nation (1925–75)," in Wells and Woodbridge, *The Evangelicals*, 231–68; Hunter, *American Evangelicalism*, 41–48.

74. Harrell, *All Things Are Possible*, esp. 41–52; Marshall Frady, *Billy Graham: A Parable of American Righteousness* (Boston, 1979); Joe E. Barnhardt, *The Billy Graham Religion* (Philadelphia, 1972).

75. Hunter, *American Evangelicalism*, 42, 48.

76. Calculated from National Council of Churches *Churches and Church Membership in the United States*, Series B, No. 5, table 12.

77. *Ibid.*, Series C, No. 58, 59, table 128. Many independent churches and tiny sects did not cooperate with the survey with the result that the evangelical camp is underestimated.

78. The new respect for Okie churches comes through clearly in the series of articles on the 24 churches in the town of Shafter in the *Shafter Press* (May 20, 1949). Walter Goldschmidt's 1944 interviews with the clergy of Dinuba reveal the beginnings of the new spirit. See especially the interview with the minister of the Presbyterian church.

79. Oliver Carlson, "Up from the Dust," *U.S.A* (Aug. 1952), 102.

80. National Council of Churches, *Churches and Church Membership in the United States*, Series C, Nos. 58–59, table 128; Douglas W. Johnson, Paul R. Picard, Bernard Quinn, *Churches and Church Membership in the United States, 1971* (Wash., D.C., 1974), table 2, p. 13; Bernard Quinn, Herman Anderson, Martin Bradley, Paul Goetting, Peggy Shriver, *Churches and Church Membership in the United States 1980* (Atlanta, 1982), table 3, p. 11.

81. Professor Eldon Ernst of the Graduate Theological Union (Berkeley) and Douglas Anderson, who is completing a doctoral dissertation on California Protestantism, were kind enough to share their observations with me.

82. Phone interview by author, Nov. 25, 1986.

83. Phone interview by author, Nov. 16, 1986. On the usual commitments of Congregationalists see Sydney E. Ahlstrom, *A Religious History of the American People*, Vol. 2 (New York, 1975), 238.

84. Ruth Wadel phone interview by author, Feb. 2, 1987.

85. On the diversity see the essays in Marsden, *Evangelicalism and Modern America*, especially the introduction; also Richard John Neuhaus and Michael Cromatie, eds., *Piety and Politics: Evangelicals and Fundamentalists Confront the World* (Wash., D.C., 1987). The location of the Fuller Theological Seminary (Presbyterian) in Pasadena has given California an important role in progressive evangelicalism.

Chapter 8. The Language of a Subculture

1. Business Establishments-Arvin file and Deputy Sheriff Joe Kelly interview, Goldschmidt Records, San Bruno, Box 66. For descriptions of the bar scene see California Odyssey interviews with Loye Lucille Martin Holmes and Charles Newsome; Paul Westmoreland interview, by Tom Norris, May 23, 1983, Sacramento, Sacramento History Center; and author's interview with Pat and Lester Hair, April 31, 1985, Reedley. E.R. Huston testimony, California Governor's Committee to Survey the Agricultural Labor Resources of the San Joaquin Valley, Transcript of Corcoran Hearing, 67. For a fictional treatment of the honky-tonk scene by a second-generation Okie, see the stories in Gerald Haslam, *Okies* (Santa Barbara, 1975).

2. Interview by Judith Gannon, April 5, 1981, South Pasadena, Odyssey Program, 34. Quite a few country-music performers began their careers playing gospel music in church. See, for example, the interviews with Buck Owens and Bill Woods, by Jana Jae Greif, Nov. 6 and May 12, 1976, Oral History Collection, California State Bakersfield, Library.

3. Anne and Norm Cohen, "Folk and Hillbilly Music: Further Thoughts on Their Relation," *John Edwards Memorial Foundation Quarterly* (hereafter *JEMF Quarterly*) 13 (1977), 50–55. The seminal exploration of country music origins is Archie Green, "Hillbilly Music: Source and Symbol," *Journal of American Folklore* 78 (July–Sept. 1965), 204–28. The standard full-length treatment is Bill C. Malone, *Country Music USA: A Fifty-Year History* (Austin, 1968). Other essential works include D.K. Wilgus, "Country-Western Music and the Urban Hillbilly," *Journal of American Folklore* 83 (April–June 1970), 157–79, and Patricia Averill, "Can the Circle Be Unbroken: A Study of the Modernization of Rural Born Southern Whites Since World War I Using Country Music" (Ph.D. diss., 1975, University of Pennsylvania). Two journals devote themselves to the study of country music: *John Edwards Memorial Foundation Quarterly* and *Journal of Country Music*.

4. Malone, *Country Music USA*, 79–102; Nolan Porterfield, *Jimmie Rodgers: The Life and Times of America's Blue Yodeler* (Urbana, 1979).

5. Norm Cohen, "Transcripts: Interview with Johnny Crockett," *JEMF Quarterly* 1 (1965), 18–26; "Materials Toward a Study of Early Country Music on Radio. III: Fresno, California," *JEMF Quarterly* 5 (1969), 7–9.

6. Henry Young, *Haywire Mac and the Big Rock Candy Mountain* (Oakland, 1981), esp. 53. My thanks to Archie Green for this reference and much other help.

7. Ken Griffis, "The Beverly Hill Billies," *JEMF Quarterly*, 16 (1980), 3–17. For an example of the yokel promotion tactics of the group's manager see "Hillbilly Trainer Talks," Los Angeles *Daily News* (Dec. 1, 1934).

8. *Modesto Bee* (March 14, l938). See also Lillian Creisler, " 'Little Oklahoma' or the Airport Community: A Study of the Social and Economic Adjustment of Self-settled Agricultural Drought and Depression Refugees" (unpublished MA thesis, University of California, Berkeley, 1940), 55; Green, "Hillbilly Music: Source and Symbol."

9. Norm Cohen, "America's Music: Written and Recorded," *JEMF Quarterly* 16 (1980), 128

10. Richard A. Peterson and Russell Davis, Jr., "The Fertile Crescent of Country

Music," *Journal of Country Music* 6 (Spring 1975), 19-27. The *Billboard* column carried the caption "What the Records Are Doing for Me." Southwestern musical tastes and contributions are examined in William W. Savage, Jr., *Singing Cowboys and All That Jazz* (Norman, 1983); Guy Logsdon, "Early Radio in Oklahoma," unpublished typescript.

11. Norman D. Brown, *Hood, Bonnet, and Little Brown Jug: Texas Politics, 1921-1928* (College Station, Texas, 1984), 433-44; Malone, *Country Music USA*, 109.

12. Todd-Sonkin field notes. See also Ray Zeman, "Squatter Army," *Los Angeles Times* (July 21, 1937); Robert S. Hardie and Norman I. Course, "A Brief Presentation of the Problem Presented by California's Migratory Agricultural Workers" (n.p., n.d.), typescript in FSA Collection, Bancroft, carton 7; Mae Saunders, "Migrants Regard Sue Sanders as True Friend," *Bakersfield Californian* (Oct. 21, 1939).

13. Interview by author, Bakersfield, Sept. 18, 1979.

14. Woody Guthrie, *Bound for Glory* (New York, 1943; reprinted 1970), 253.

15. Clarence J. Glacken, Report of a Visit to the Resettlement Camp at Arvin, San Francisco, Aug. 14, 1936, FSA Records, San Bruno, box 21; Arvin Camp Report, May 8, 1937, same collection, box 19; Todd-Sonkin field notes. The dances are remembered fondly by Clara Davis, interview by author, Bakersfield, Sept. 17, 1979, and Morris family interview by Margo McBane and Mary Weingarden, Richmond, July 12, 1978, History of Women Farmworkers Project.

16. Creisler, " 'Little Oklahoma,' " 55.

17. Joe Klein, *Woody Guthrie: A Life* (New York, 1980), 91-92. Radio station talent contests also came under fan pressure. See Region IX Monthly Narrative Reports, Oct. 1941, in FSA Collection, Bancroft, carton 2; Todd-Sonkin field notes, 32; Keith Olesen, liner notes for *Maddox Brothers and Rose: 1946-1951, Volume 1* (Arhoolie Records 5016, 1976).

18. Douglas B. Green, "The Singing Cowboy: An American Dream," *Journal of Country Music* 7 (May 1978), 10-20; Gene Autry with Mickey Herskowitz, *Back in the Saddle Again* (New York, 1978). Stephen Ray Tucker, "The Western Image of Country Music" (MA thesis, Southern Methodist University, 1976); Malone, *Country Music USA*, 145-53.

19. Background information on these and other country musicians can be found in Averill's encyclopedic study, "Can the Circle Be Unbroken." See also Tucker, "The Western Image of Country Music," 60-68; "Music from the Lone Star State," in Country Music Magazine, *Illustrated History of Country Music*, 102-37.

20. Klein, *Woody Guthrie*, 87-89, 92, 102.

21. Todd-Sonkin field notes and recordings. For other examples of professional music ambitions see Esther A. Canter, "California 'Renovates' the Dust Bowler," *Hygeia* (May 1940), 455; Saunders, "Migrant's True Friend," *Bakersfield Californian* (Oct. 21, 1939); Letter from Mrs. J.A.S. to Prof. Gerald Haslam in Charles Todd Collection. Describing her marriage at age 17, she says of her husband, "like most 'Okies' he was a musician."

22. Malone, *Country Music USA*, 210-11. Also see the Spade Cooley file in the John Edwards Memorial Foundation Collection, University of North Carolina Library.

23. Olesen, liner notes for *Maddox Brothers and Rose*. Arhoolie Records has

also issued recordings of two of the group's radio broadcasts, *The Maddox Brothers and Rose—On the Air: 1940 and 1945* (Arhoolie 5028, 1983).

24. Interview by Tom Norris. For other career stories see Bill Woods interview; and the following articles in *JEMF Quarterly*: Ken Griffis, "I Remember Johnny Bond," 14 (Aug. 1978), 110; Gene Bear and Ken Griffis, "The Porky Freeman Story," 11 (Spring 1975), 33–34; Merle Travis, "Recollections of Merle Travis, 1944–1955," 15 (Summer 1979), 107–14.

25. Merle Haggard with Peggy Russell, *Sing Me Back Home: My Story* (New York, 1981), 108.

26. Interview by author, March 27, April 1, 1985. On Wills's career see Charles R. Townsend, *San Antonio Rose: The Life and Music of Bob Wills* (Urbana, 1976).

27. Gerald F. Vaughn, "Foreman Phillips: Western Swing's Kingmaker," and Ken Griffis, "The Tex Williams Story," both in *JEMF Quarterly* 15 (Spring 1979), 5–6, 28. Westmoreland explains his use of the "Okie" moniker in his interview with Tom Norris.

28. "Do Re Mi," words and music by Woody Guthrie. TRO—© Copyright 1961 and 1963 Ludlow Music, Inc., New York, N.Y. Used by permission.

29. These Dust Bowl ballads were first recorded by Alan Lomax for the Library of Congress, Archive of Folksong, in 1940, then recorded again and released commercially by Victor. They have been re-issued several times since, most recently in 1977 as "Woody Guthrie: A Legendary Performer" (RCA-CPL 1-20099(c)). *The Maddox Brothers and Rose—On the Air: 1940 and 1945* features a 1945 radio transcription of "Do Re Mi." The details of Guthrie's life are found in Klein, *Woody Guthrie,* as well Guthrie's own *Bound for Glory.* The best analysis of his artistry is Richard A. Reuss, "Woody Guthrie and His Folk Tradition," *Journal of American Folklore* 83 (July–Sept. 1970), 273–303.

30. On his departure from country music idiom see Malone, *Country Music USA*, 139; Gerald Haslam, "The Okies: Forty Years Later," *The Nation* (March 15, 1975).

31. Sherry B. Ortner, "On Key Symbols," *American Anthropologist* 75 (1973), 1338–46. The attempt to analyze music as a cultural system has generated instructive work in other musical genres: Manuel Pena, *The Texas-Mexican Conjunto: History of a Working-Class Music* (Austin, 1985); Simon Frith, *Sound Effects: Youth, Leisure, and the Politics of Rock 'n' Roll* (New York, 1981); Roger C. Owen, Nancy E. Walstrom, and Ralph C. Michelsen, "Musical Culture and Ethnic Solidarity: A Baja California Case Study," *Journal of American Folklore* 82 (1969), 99–111; Lawrence W. Levine, *Black Culture and Black Consciousness* (New York, 1977).

32. Paul Di Maggio, Richard A. Peterson, and Jack Esco, Jr., "Country Music: Ballad of the Silent Majority," in R. Serge Denisoff and Richard A. Peterson, eds., *The Sounds of Social Change* (Chicago, 1972), 41; Averill, "Can the Circle Be Unbroken," 30–34. Alex S. Freedman, "The Sociology of Country Music," *Southern Humanities Review*, 3 (Fall 1969), 358–62.

33. I am following here the techniques of cultural system analysis pioneered by symbolic anthropologists, especially Clifford Geertz, *The Interpretion of Cultures* (New York, 1973); Averill, "Can the Circle Be Unbroken," attempts something similar, arguing that country music conveys Southern culture.

34. Norm Cohen, liner notes to *Going Down the Valley: Vocal and Instrumental*

Styles in Folk Music from the South (New World 236); Averill, "Can the Circle Be Unbroken," 303–4, 337–48; Edmonds, "Myths and Migrants," 67–72.

35. By Jimmie Rodgers and Elsie McWilliams. Copyright 1929 by Peer International Corporation. Copyright renewed by Peer International Corporation. International copyright secured. All rights reserved. Used by permission.

36. Sung my Willard Duke, Todd-Sonkin Recordings.

37. James Bright Wilson, "Social Attitudes of Certain Migratory Agricultural Workers in Kern County, California" (unpublished MA thesis, University of Southern California, 1942), 247.

38. "Texas Plains," words and music by Stuart Hamblen. © Copyright 1933, 1942 by Music Corporation of America, Inc. Copyright renewed. Rights administered by MCA Music Publishing, a division of MCA, Inc., New York, NY, 10019. Used by permission. All rights reserved.

39. Listening to it is the only way to begin to appreciate the themes of country music. But I have also learned much from Patricia Averill's mammoth compilation and analysis of song lyrics in "Can the Circle Be Unbroken." More than 1,500 pages in length and studded with intriguing ideas, her study also lists more than 2,000 songs from the 1930s, 1950s, and 1960s, and excerpts lyrics from many of them.

40. "Behind These Stone Walls" is the Carter Family song. The anti-urban thrust of country music is detailed in Ivan M. Tribe, "The Hillbilly Versus the City: Urban Images in Country Music," *JEMF Quarterly* 10 (1974), 41–51; Wilgus, "Country-Western Music and the Urban Hillbilly"; Anthony O. Edmonds, "Myths and Migrants: Images of Rural and Urban Life in Country Music" *Indiana Social Studies Quarterly* 28 (Winter 1975–76), 67–72.

41. Quoted in Averill, "Can the Circle Be Unbroken," 730.

42. "Back in the Saddle" by Ray Whitley and Gene Autry. Copyright Western Music Publishing Co., 1939, renewed 1964. All rights reserved. Used by permission.

43. Thoughts on the cowboy and popular culture are found in John Tuska, *The Filming of the West* (Garden City, 1976). On the origins of cowboy music see Thomas F. Johnson, "That Ain't Country: The Distinctiveness of Commercial Western Music," *JEMF Quarterly* 17 (1981), 75–84; Tucker, "The Western Image of Country Music"; James White, *Get Along Little Dogies* (Urbana, 1975).

44. Sympathetic observers like Paul Taylor encouraged the association between Okies and pioneers as is obvious from the title of his seminal report on the migration: "Again the Covered Wagon," *Survey Graphic* 24 (July 1935), 348–68. But the migrants needed no coaxing. For a sampling see *Tow-Sack Tattler* (Arvin) (Oct. 6, 28, 1939, Nov. 1, 1940); *Voice of the Agricultural Worker* (Yuba City) (May 21, 1940). Evelyn Ruud, "Reading List—Design for Living" (n.p., 1941?) typescript in Wasco field notes, Walter Goldschmidt's personal files; Todd-Sonkin field notes, 5.

45. Katherine Archibald, *Wartime Shipyard: A Study in Social Disunity* (Berkeley, 1947), 44–45. See also Zelma Parker, "Strangers in Town," *Survey* 79 (June 1943), 171; *Campers' Tribune* (Thornton) (Nov. 22, 1940).

46. Interview with Lois Smith Barnes, by Michael Needly, Fresno, June 15, 18, 1982, Odyssey Program, 4, 12–13.

47. K. Vincent, liner notes to *Merle Haggard: Okie from Muskogee* (Capitol Records ST-384); Paul Hemphill, "Okie from Muskogee," in *The Good Old Boys* (New York, 1975).

48. Hemphill, "Okie from Muskogee," 140.

49. There is no census data on the children of interstate migrants. The 1970 Public Use Microdata Sample shows that the average age of Southwesterners had reached 45 compared with 32 for the general population. Appendix A gives the geographic distribution of Southwesterners in California as of 1970.

50. "Mama Tried" by Merle Haggard. Copyright © 1968 Tree Publishing Co., Inc. All rights reserved. International copyright secured. Used by permission of the publisher.

51. From "Sing Me Back Home," which is also the title of his autobiography, *Sing Me Back Home: My Story* (New York, 1981), from which I take the details of his early life.

52. Haggard, *Sing Me Back Home*, 104–15, 190–222; "Merle Haggard Discography," *JEMF Quarterly* 7 (1971), 18–22; Glenn Hunter, "The Bakersfield Sound," *Westways* 7 (July 1979), 28–32; Jana Jae Greif, "Nashville West: The Musical Heritage of Bakersfield," History 373 paper, Spring 1976, in California State College, Bakersfield library. See also her interviews with Buck Owens and Bill Woods at the same location.

53. Peterson and Di Maggio, "From Region to Class, the Changing Locus of Country Music," 497–506; Bill C. Malone, *Southern Music American Music* (Lexington, 1979), 88–97, 125–31; George O. Carney, "Country Music and the Radio: A Historical Geographic Assessment" *Rocky Mountain Social Science Journal* 11 (Jan. 1974), 19–32. James C. Cobb takes the story further in "From Muskogee to Luckenbach: Country Music and the 'Southernization' of America," *Journal of Popular Culture* 16 (Winter 1982), 81–91.

54. Arthur B. Shostak, *Blue-Collar Life* (New York, 1969), 211–27; Samuel Lubell, *The Hidden Crisis in American Politics* (New York, 1970), 69–88; Richard Krickus, *Pursuing the American Dream: White Ethnics and the New Populism* (Bloomington, 1976); Seymour Martin Lipset and Earl Raab, *The Politics of Unreason: Right-Wing Extremism in America, 1790–1970* (New York, 1970), 378–424; Jody Carlson, *George Wallace and the Politics of Powerlessness* (New Brunswick, N.J., 1981).

55. Di Maggio, Peterson, and Esco, "Country Music: Ballad of the Silent Majority," 38–55; Jens Lund, "Fundamentalism, Racism, and Political Reaction in Country Music," in Denisoff and Peterson, *The Sounds of Social Change*, 79–91. See also Averill's compilation of political references in "Can the Circle Be Unbroken," 665–83, 1197–1206.

56. James R. Mills, *A Disorderly House: The Brown-Unruh Years in Sacramento* (Berkeley, 1987)

57. Michael Barone, Grant Ujifusa, Douglas Matthews, *The Almanac of American Politics, 1972* (New York, 1972), 71–73; *1978* (New York, 1977), 77–79.

58. Hunter, "The Bakersfield Sound," 28. For Kern County's voting record see Michael W. Donley, Stuart Allan, Patricia Caro, Clyde P. Patton, *Atlas of California* (Portland, 1979), 55–56.

59. "Hungry Eyes" by Merle Haggard. Copyright © 1969, 1971 Tree Publishing

Co., Inc. All rights reserved. International copyright secured. Used by permission of the publisher.

60. "Roots of My Raising" by Tommy Collins. Copyright © 1970, 1976 Tree Publishing Co., Inc. All rights reserved. International copyright secured. Used by permission of the publisher.

61. Buck Owens recorded "California Okie" in 1975. Larry Hosgood and Tommy Collins contributed other songs. Samples of the literary production can be found in Gerald W. Haslam and James D. Houston, eds., *California Heartland: Writings from the Great Central Valley* (Santa Barbara, 1978); Jane Watts. ed., *Valley Light: Writers of the San Joaquin* (Bakersfield, 1978); California Odyssey Project, *Guide to "Roots of My Raising"* (Bakersfield, 1982). On Okie studies projects see Lyon, "Campfires Dotted the Still Night," *Bakersfield Californian* (May 27, 1979); Don Wegars, "The Okies Take a Place in American History," *San Francisco Chronicle* (Oct. 16, 1978).

62. Letter to Prof. Gerald Haslam, Nov. 8, 1977, in Charles Todd Collection; Frank Manies interview by author, Lindsay, April 31, 1985; Peggy Staggs interview by author, Huntington Beach, Aug. 18, 1980; Ernest Martin Odyssey Program interview, 36; Lyons, "Campfires Dotted the Still Night"; Don Wegars, "How Okies Made Their Way," *San Francisco Chronicle* (Oct. 17, 1978).

63. Michael Novak, *The Rise of the Unmeltable Ethnics* (New York, 1971) is the manifesto of the new ethnicity. Stephen Steinberg debunks it as a fad in *The Ethnic Myth* (Boston, 1981), 3–74, as does Herbert Gans, "Symbolic Ethnicity: The Future of Ethnic Groups and Cultures in America," *Ethnic And Racial Studies* 2 (Jan. 1979), 1–18.

64. "The B/tr Wrap Up" in Charles Todd Collection.

Index

Lightning Source UK Ltd.
Milton Keynes UK
UKOW02f0447091216
289477UK00001B/15/P